BASIC DOCUMENTS
ON HUMAN RIGHTS

BASIC DOCUMENTS ON HUMAN RIGHTS

Edited by

IAN BROWNLIE

*Fellow of Wadham College
Oxford*

CLARENDON PRESS · OXFORD

1971

Oxford University Press, Ely House, London W.1

GLASGOW   NEW YORK   TORONTO   MELBOURNE   WELLINGTON
CAPE TOWN   SALISBURY   IBADAN   NAIROBI   DAR ES SALAAM   LUSAKA   ADDIS ABABA
BOMBAY   CALCUTTA   MADRAS   KARACHI   LAHORE   DACCA
KUALA LUMPUR   SINGAPORE   HONG KONG   TOKYO

PRINTED IN GREAT BRITAIN
BY WILLIAM CLOWES AND SONS, LIMITED
LONDON, BECCLES AND COLCHESTER

PREFACE

THE object of this work is to provide a useful collection of sources on human rights in the form of a handbook. It is hoped that the collection will be of help to a variety of readers and not merely to those with specialist interests in political science, international relations, or law.

The author believes that the service provided by the present collection of materials is not equally well provided by existing publications. Naturally it cannot be claimed that there is any originality in the idea of collecting documents on human rights. The preface is the appropriate place for drawing attention to a forerunner: *Human Rights: A Compilation of International Instruments of the United Nations*, 94 pp., published by the United Nations in 1967 (A/CONF 32/4; Sales No. E.68.XIV.6). This contains conventions, declarations, and certain recommendations adopted by organs of the United Nations and by the Specialized Agencies up to 31 December 1966. The collection which follows is not, of course, confined to instruments of the United Nations.

The introductory notes to the treaties and conventions reprinted in this volume give only a general indication of the number of States which have signed the various agreements or which have become parties by ratification or accession. Signature does not normally make the signatory State a party but indicates a provisional intention to become a party.

Readers who are concerned to discover significant and detailed pieces of treaty information should use up-to-date official publications or other sources. A State which appears to have become a party to a treaty by ratification may have subsequently denounced the agreement. States may subject their adherence to a treaty to various reservations. It has not been possible in the present publication to record reservations and related information—for example, the acceptance of reservations by other States.

A matter of importance in examining the precise effect of a treaty is the extent to which the treaty has become incorporated in the domestic law of the State. For example, in the United Kingdom most treaties have no binding effect on the courts unless given internal application by Act of Parliament. Thus the United Kingdom has ratified the I.L.O. Conventions on Freedom of Association, and on the Right to Organize and Collective Bargaining, but there is no corresponding Act of Parliament: see Wedderburn, *The Worker and the Law* (Penguin Books, 1965), pp. 16–17.

Subject to what has been said above about the need for keeping treaty information up to date, the United Kingdom is a party to the treaties and conventions open to its participation and contained in the present volume except for: the International Covenant on Economic, Social and Cultural Rights, 1966 (p. 199); the International Covenant on Civil and Political Rights, 1966 (p. 211); The Optional Protocol to the last item (p. 232); the Equal Remuneration Convention, 1951 (p. 291); the Discrimination (Employment and Occupation) Convention, 1958 (p. 296); the Social Policy (Basic Aims and Standards) Convention, 1962 (p. 313); and apart from Protocol 1, the Protocols to the European Convention on Human Rights (pp. 357 *seq.*).

I am grateful to Éprime Eshag, Fellow of Wadham College, Oxford, and Senior Research Officer, Oxford University Institute of Economics and Statistics, for his assistance in preparing the contents of Part Ten and, in particular, in writing the text for the third item in that Part; and to Dr. C. Wilfred Jenks, presently Director-General of the International Labour Office, and to members of his staff, for their co-operation.

IAN BROWNLIE

Wadham College
Oxford

24 November 1970

CONTENTS

PART THREE

IMPLEMENTATION AND STANDARD-SETTING IN CONVENTIONS SPONSORED BY THE UNITED NATIONS

PART FOUR

CONTRIBUTION OF THE INTERNATIONAL LABOUR ORGANIZATION

PART FIVE

CONTRIBUTION OF THE UNITED NATIONS EDUCATIONAL, SCIENTIFIC, AND CULTURAL ORGANIZATION

PART SIX

EUROPEAN INSTITUTIONS AND CONVENTIONS

PART SEVEN

LATIN AMERICAN DEVELOPMENTS

PART EIGHT

DEVELOPMENTS IN AFRICA AND ASIA

1*

PART NINE

THE CONCEPT OF EQUALITY

PART TEN

TRADE AND DEVELOPMENT

PART ONE

FUNDAMENTAL RIGHTS IN NATIONAL LEGAL SYSTEMS

INTRODUCTION

LONG before international agreements and institutions were concerned with problems of human rights, national political systems were giving legal recognition to 'the rights and liberties of the subject', the 'rights of man and the citizen', and the like. The more modern concept of human rights is essentially the familiar territory, often described as the 'rule of law', 'constitutionalism', 'civil liberties', 'constitutional rights', and 'fundamental rights'.

In this Part a selection of provisions from national constitutions is presented. The provisions are for the most part concerned with setting standards. It is well known that implementation is the chief difficulty, and many constitutions bear but an obscure relation to the actual state of affairs in political and legal life. Moreover, even the rules themselves contain serious exceptions and qualifications; for example, that a right is protected 'except as provided by law'. All systems provide for derogation from constitutional guarantees in time of war or other emergency. In systems in which the rule of law exists, in that government is according to law and rights are guaranteed under the constitution, the enjoyment of rights may be severely curtailed by economic and social inequality. In a country which suffers from poverty and illiteracy the courts of law may seem remote from the peasant, and legal services are still expensive in many parts of the world. In short, the human-rights situation in a given country is composed of many elements, some of these are not matters of law, and the constitution can only be one of the elements in the situation.

I. UNITED KINGDOM:
BILL OF RIGHTS, 1688

PART only of this document is reproduced, and modern spelling is used. For a full text see Halsbury, *Statutes*, 3rd edn., Vol. 6, p. 489. The Bill of Rights is in form a statute like any other, and it is known by its short rather than its original cumbersome title. Because it is a statute it is a part of the law of the land and may be applied by the courts. It is a good example of the way in which particular incidents may generate generally acceptable models. The Bill of Rights was a part of the major settlement between the Crown and Parliament consequent on the struggles of the Stuart period. Like Magna Carta it is a demarcation of powers primarily, but it also contains general principles of State policy and law. Some of these have come to have universal significance. Thus the prohibition of illegal and cruel punishments was to appear in many other contexts, including the Universal Declaration of Human Rights (below, p. 106). The English Bill of Rights as a whole has inspired more sophisticated developments in other countries. In recent years some British lawyers and public figures have advocated the adoption of a modern Bill of Rights: see *New Law Journal*, 16 April 1970, p. 372; 23 April 1970, p. 395. There is, of course, the difficulty of adopting such a Bill if it is intended to be fundamental law, i.e. cannot be changed by subsequent parliaments, either at all or except by resort to a special procedure. The British Constitution rests on parliamentary supremacy and, with the possible exception of the Act of Union with Scotland, has no room for fundamental or entrenched provisions.

TEXT

AN ACT DECLARING THE RIGHTS AND LIBERTIES OF THE SUBJECT AND SETTLING THE SUCCESSION OF THE CROWN

Whereas the lords spiritual and temporal and commons assembled at Westminster fully and freely representing all the estates of the people of this realm did upon the thirteenth day of February in the year of our Lord one thousand six hundred and eighty-eight present unto their Majesties then called and known by the names and style of William and Mary, Prince and Princess of Orange, being present in their proper persons, a certain declaration in writing made by the said lords and commons in the words following, viz.

Whereas the late King James the Second by the assistance of diverse evil councillors, judges, and ministers employed by him did endeavour to subvert and extirpate the Protestant religion and the laws and liberties of this kingdom.

By assuming and exercising a power of dispensing with and suspending of laws and the execution of laws without consent of Parliament.

By committing and prosecuting diverse worthy prelates for humbly petitioning to be excused from concurring to the said assumed power.

By issuing and causing to be executed a commission under the great seal for erecting a court called the court of commissioners for ecclesiastical causes.

By levying money for and to the use of the Crown, by pretence of prerogative, for other time and in other manner than the same was granted by Parliament.

By raising and keeping a standing army within this kingdom in time of peace without consent of Parliament and quartering soldiers contrary to law.

By causing several good subjects being protestants to be disarmed at the same time when papists were both armed and employed contrary to the law.

By violating the freedom of election of members to serve in Parliament.

By prosecutions in the Court of Kings Bench for matters and causes cognizable only in Parliament and by diverse other arbitrary and illegal courses.

And whereas of late years partial, corrupt and unqualified persons have been returned and served on juries in trials and particularly diverse jurors in trials for high treason which were not freeholders.

And excessive bail hath been required of persons committed in criminal cases to elude the benefit of the laws made for the liberty of subjects.

And excessive fines have been imposed.

And illegal and cruel punishments inflicted.

And several grants and promises made of fines and forfeitures before any conviction or judgment against the persons upon whom the same were to be levied.

All which are utterly and directly contrary to the known laws and statutes and freedoms of this realm.

And whereas the said late King James the Second having abdicated the government and the throne being thereby vacant, his highness, the Prince of Orange (whom it hath pleased Almighty God to make the glorious instrument of delivering this kingdom from popery and arbitrary power) did (by the advice of the lords spiritual and temporal and diverse principal persons of the commons) cause letters to be written to the lords spiritual and temporal being protestants and other letters to the several counties, cities, universities, boroughs, and cinque ports for the choosing of such persons to represent them as were of right to be sent to Parliament to meet and sit at Westminster upon the two and twentieth day of January of this year one thousand six hundred and eighty-eight in order to ordain such an establishment that their religion, laws and liberties might not again be in danger of being subverted, upon which letters elections having been accordingly made.

And thereupon the said lords spiritual and temporal and commons, pursuant to their respective letters and elections, being now assembled in a full and free representative of this nation taking into their most serious consideration the best means for attaining the ends aforesaid do in the first place (as their ancestors in like cases have usually done) for the vindicating and asserting of their ancient rights and liberties, declare.

Suspending power.—That the pretended power of suspending of laws and the execution of laws by regal authority without the consent of Parliament is illegal.

Late dispending power.—That the pretended power of dispending with laws or the execution of laws by regal authority as it hath been assumed and exercised of late is illegal.

Ecclesiastical Courts illegal.—That the commission for erecting the late court of commissioners for ecclesiastical causes and all other commissions and courts of like nature are illegal and pernicious.

Levying money.—That levying money for or to the use of the crown by pretence of prerogative without grant of Parliament for longer time or in other manner than the same is or shall be granted is illegal.

Right to Petition.—That it is the right of subjects to petition the king and all commitments and prosecutions for such petitioning are illegal.

Standing Army.—That the raising or keeping a standing army within the kingdom in time of peace unless it be with the consent of Parliament is against the law.

Subjects' arms.—That the subjects which are protestants may have arms for their defence suitable to their conditions and as allowed by law.

Freedom of election.—That the election of members of Parliament ought to be free.

Freedom of speech.—That the freedom of speech and debate or proceedings in Parliament ought not to be impeached or questioned in any court or place out of Parliament.

Excessive bail.—That excessive bail ought not to be required nor excessive fines imposed nor cruel and unusual punishment inflicted.

Juries.—That jurors ought to be duly impanelled and returned.

Grants of forfeiture.—That all grants and promises of fines and forfeitures of particular persons before conviction are illegal and void.

Frequent Parliaments.—And that for redress of all grievances and for the amending, strengthening and preserving of the laws Parliament ought to be held frequently.

And they do claim, demand and insist upon all and singular the premises as their undoubted rights and liberties and that no declarations, judgments, doings or proceedings to the prejudice of the people in any of the said premises ought in any wise to be drawn hereafter into consequence or example. To which demand of their rights they are particularly encouraged by the declaration of His Highness the Prince of Orange as being the only means for obtaining a full redress and remedy therein. Having therefore an entire confidence that his said Highness, the Prince of Orange, will perfect the deliverance so far advanced by him and will still preserve them from the violation of their rights which they have here asserted and from all other attempts upon their religion, rights and liberties. The said lords spiritual and temporal and commons assembled at Westminster do resolve that William and Mary, Prince and Princess of Orange, be and be declared King and Queen of England, France, and Ireland and the dominions thereunto belonging to hold the crown and royal dignity of the said kingdoms and dominions to them, the said Prince and Princess, during their lives and the life of the survivor of them. And the sole and full exercise of the regal power be only in and executed by the said Prince of Orange in the names of the said prince and princess during their joint lives and after their deceases the said Crown and royal dignity of the said kingdoms and dominions to be to the heirs of the body of the said princess and for default of such issue to the Princess Anne of Denmark and the heirs of her body and for default of such issue to the heirs of the body of the said Prince of Orange. And the lords spiritual and temporal and commons do pray the said prince and princess to accept the same accordingly. And that the oaths hereafter mentioned be taken by all persons of whom the oaths of allegiance and supremacy might be required by law instead of them and that the said oaths of allegiance and supremacy be abrogated.

I, A.B., do sincerely promise and swear that I will be faithful and bear true allegiance to their Majesties, King William and Queen Mary. So help me God.

I, A.B., do swear that I do from my heart abhor, detest and abjure as impious and heretical this damnable doctrine and position that princes excommunicated or deprived by the Pope or any authority of the See of Rome may be deposed or murdered by their subjects or any other whatsoever.

II. FRANCE: DECLARATION OF THE RIGHTS OF MAN AND OF THE CITIZEN, 1789

THIS Declaration is an obvious reflection of the ideals which lay behind the French Revolution. It is a fairly complete code of the principles of constitutional government and the rule of law, and is the first of its kind. Its inspiration is a liberalism, like that of Locke in England, which leaves a good place for 'property' alongside 'liberty'. Thus, in spite of the end of revolution in France, the Declaration was to influence many constitutions of the parliamentary type of the nineteenth century and later in Europe and Latin America. The Declaration was affirmed in the preambles to the French Constitutions of 1946 and 1958.

TEXT

Article 1

Men are born and remain free and equal in respect of rights. Social distinctions shall be based solely upon public utility.

Article 2

The purpose of all civil associations is the preservation of the natural and imprescriptible rights of man. These rights are liberty, property and resistance to oppression.

Article 3

The nation is essentially the source of all sovereignty, nor shall any body of men or any individual exercise authority which is not expressly derived from it.

Article 4

Liberty consists in the power of doing whatever does not injure another. Accordingly the exercise of the natural rights of every man has not other limits than those which are necessary to secure to every other man the free exercise of the same rights; and these limits are determinable only by the law.

Article 5

The law ought to prohibit only actions hurtful to society. What is not prohibited by the law should not be hindered; nor should any one be compelled to do that which the law does not require.

Article 6

The law is an expression of the common will. All citizens have a right to concur, either personally or by their representation in its formation. It should be the same for all, whether it protects or punishes; and all being equal in its sight, are equally eligible to all honours, places and employments, according to their different abilities, without any other distinction than that of their virtues and talents.

Article 7

No one shall be accused, arrested or imprisoned, save in the cases determined by law, and according to the forms which it has prescribed. All who solicit, promote, execute, or cause to be executed, arbitrary orders, ought to be punished, and every citizen summoned or apprehended by virtue of the law, ought immediately to obey, and becomes culpable if he resists.

Article 8

The law should impose only such penalties as are absolutely and evidently necessary; and no one ought to be punished but by virtue of a law promulgated before the offence, and legally applied.

Article 9

Every man being counted innocent until he has been convicted, whenever his arrest becomes indispensable, all vigour more than is necessary to secure his person ought to be provided against by law.

Article 10

No man is to be interfered with because of his opinions, not even because of religious opinions, provided his avowal of them does not disturb public order as established by law.

Article 11

The unrestrained communication of thoughts or opinions being one of the most precious rights of man, every citizen may speak, write and publish freely, provided he be responsible for the abuse of this liberty, in the cases determined by law.

Article 12

A public force being necessary to give security to the rights of men and of citizens, that force is instituted for the benefit of the community, and not for the particular benefit of the person to whom it is entrusted.

Article 13

A common contribution being necessary for the support of the public force, and for defraying the other expenses of government, it should be divided equally among the members of the community, according to their abilities.

Article 14

Every citizen has a right, either of himself or his representative, to a free voice in determining the necessity of public contributions, the appropriation of them, and their amount, mode of assessment, and duration.

Article 15

The community has the right to demand of all its agents an account of their conducts.

Article 16

Every community in which a security of rights and a separation of powers is not provided for needs a constitution.

Article 17

The right to property being inviolable and secured, no one shall be deprived of it, except in cases of evident public necessity; legally ascertained, and on condition of a previous just indemnity.

III. UNITED STATES:
BILL OF RIGHTS, 1791

VIRGINIA and other States which were to join together in the United States had their own bills of rights on the model of the English Bill of Rights (above, p. 3). Like the French Declaration of the Rights of Man, the American Constitution, together with the first ten amendments (which comprise the Bill of Rights of 1791), is an early and influential example of constitutionalism and legally recognized rights. Articles XIII of 1865, XIV of 1868, and XV of 1870 represent the amendments consequent upon the Civil War. The effect of the Bill of Rights was limited in the Federal Constitution because it bound the Federal Government and not the States. However, the three Civil War amendments are far-reaching, and the Supreme Court has used the 'due process of law' clause in the Fourteenth Amendment in order to incorporate the substance of other amendments, and thus enforce the Bill of Rights against the States. In the United States much depends upon the interpretation of the Constitution by the Supreme Court: witness the decision in *Brown* v. *Board of Education*, 347 U.S. 483 (1954), which changed a judicial conception of racial equality in relation to the Fourteenth Amendment which had been established in a previous decision of 1896.

For further reference see: Corwin, *The Constitution and What It Means To-day*, 1958; Emerson, Haber, and Dorsen, *Political and Civil Rights in the United States*, 3rd edn., 1967; Barrett, Bruton, and Honnold, *Constitutional Law Cases and Materials*, 3rd edn., 1968; Chafee, *How Human Rights Got into the Constitution*, 1952; Schwartz, *A Commentary on the Constitution of the United States*, 1963–68; Schwartz, *American Constitutional Law*, 1955; Konvitz, *Bill of Rights Reader*, 4th edn., 1968; Kauper, *Constitutional Law Cases and Materials*, 2nd edn., 1960.

TEXT

Article I
Congress shall make no law respecting an establishment of religion, or prohibiting the free exercise thereof; or abridging the freedom of speech, or of the press; or the right of the people peaceably to assemble, and to petition the Government for a redress of grievances.

Article II

A well regulated Militia, being necessary to the security of a free State, the right of the people to keep and bear Arms, shall not be infringed.

Article III

No Soldier shall, in time of peace be quartered in any house, without the consent of the Owner, nor in time of war, but in a manner to be prescribed by law.

Article IV

The rights of the people to be secure in their persons, houses, papers, and effects, against unreasonable searches and seizures, shall not be violated, and no Warrants shall issue, but upon probable cause, supported by Oath or affirmation, and particularly describing the place to be searched, and the persons or things to be seized.

Article V

No person shall be held to answer for a capital, or otherwise infamous crime, unless on a presentment or indictment of a Grand Jury, except in cases arising in the land or naval forces, or in the Militia, when in actual service in time of War or public danger; nor shall any person be subject for the same offence to be twice put in jeopardy of life or limb; nor shall be compelled in any Criminal Case to be a witness against himself, nor be deprived of life, liberty, or property, without due process of law; nor shall private property be taken for public use, without just compensation.

Article VI

In all criminal prosecutions, the accused shall enjoy the right to a speedy and public trial, by an impartial jury of the State and district wherein the crime shall have been committed, which district shall have been previously ascertained by law, and to be informed of the nature and cause of the accusation; to be confronted with the witnesses against him; to have compulsory process for obtaining witnesses in his favor, and to have the Assistance of Counsel for his defence.

Article VII

In Suits at common law, where the value in controversy shall exceed twenty dollars, the right of trial by jury shall be preserved, and no fact tried by a jury, shall be otherwise re-examined in any Court of the United States than according to the rules of the common law.

Article VIII

Excessive bail shall not be required, nor excessive fines imposed, nor cruel and unusual punishments inflicted.

Article IX

The enumeration in the Constitution, of certain rights, shall not be construed to deny or disparage others retained by the people.

Article X

The powers not delegated to the United States by the Constitution, nor prohibited by it to the States, are reserved to the States respectively, or to the people.

Article XIII

Section 1.—Neither slavery nor involuntary servitude, except as a punishment for crime whereof the party shall have been duly convicted, shall exist within the United States, or any place subject to their jurisdiction.

Section 2.—Congress shall have power to enforce this article by appropriate legislation.

Article XIV

Section 1.—All persons born or naturalized in the United States, and subject to the jurisdiction thereof, are citizens of the United States and of the State wherein they reside. No State shall make or enforce any law which shall abridge the privileges or immunities of citizens of the United States; nor shall any State deprive any person of life, liberty, or property, without due process of law; nor deny to any person within its jurisdiction the equal protection of the laws.

Article XV

Section 1.—The right of citizens of the United States to vote shall not be denied or abridged by the United States or by any State on account of race, color, or previous condition of servitude.

Section 2.—The Congress shall have power to enforce this article by appropriate legislation.

[Later amendments omitted.]

IV. CANADA: BILL OF RIGHTS, 1960

CANADA has adopted a modern Bill of Rights as a Federal statute and the Provinces have adopted similar laws (for example, the Human Rights Code of Ontario and the Human Rights Act of Alberta). The Federal Bill of Rights seems to have had most effect in protecting fundamental rights at the legislative stage. Otherwise, it has had very limited effect, since the courts have been unwilling to treat the Bill as providing much more than rules of construction for Federal statutes. Its effect on Provincial legislation remains uncertain.

For reference see Laskin, *Canadian Constitutional Law*, 3rd edn., 1966, pp. 970–6; Tarnopolsky, *The Canadian Bill of Rights*, 1966; Schmeiser, *Civil Liberties in Canada*, 1964; *Robertson and Rosetanni* v. *The Queen* [1963] S.C.R. 651; *Batary* v. *A.-G. for Saskatchewan* [1965] S.C.R. 465; *Walter et al* v. *A.-G. for Alberta* (1966) 54 W.W.R. 385; *Regina* v. *Drybones* (1967), 64 D.L.R. (2d) 260; *R.* v. *Steinberg* [1967] 1 O.R. 733; *Re Vinarao* (1968), 66 D.L.R. (2d) 736; *Whitfield* v. *Canadian Marconi Co.* (1968) D.L.R. (2d) 251. See also Hucker and McDonald, *McGill Law Journal*, 15 (1969), p. 220.

TEXT

AN ACT FOR THE RECOGNITION AND PROTECTION OF HUMAN RIGHTS AND FUNDAMENTAL FREEDOMS

The Parliament of Canada, affirming that the Canadian Nation is founded upon principles that acknowledge the supremacy of God, the dignity and worth of the human person and the position of the family in a society of free men and free institutions;

Affirming also that men and institutions remain free only when freedom is founded upon respect for moral and spiritual values and the rule of law;

And being desirous of enshrining these principles and the human rights and fundamental freedoms derived from them, in a Bill of Rights which shall reflect the respect of Parliament for its constitutional authority and which shall ensure the protection of these rights and freedoms in Canada:

Therefore Her Majesty, by and with the advice and consent of the Senate and House of Commons of Canada, enacts as follows:

PART I

BILL OF RIGHTS

1. It is hereby recognized and declared that in Canada there have existed and shall continue to exist without discrimination by reason of race, national origin, colour, religion or sex, the following human rights and fundamental freedoms, namely,

(a) the right of the individual to life, liberty, security of the person and enjoyment of property, and the right not to be deprived thereof except by due process of law;

(b) the right of the individual to equality before the law and the protection of the law;

(c) freedom of religion;

(d) freedom of speech;

(e) freedom of assembly and association; and

(f) freedom of the press.

2. Every law of Canada shall, unless it is expressly declared by an Act of the Parliament of Canada that it shall operate notwithstanding the *Canadian Bill of Rights*, be so construed and applied as not to abrogate, abridge or infringe or to authorize the abrogation, abridgment or infringement of any of the rights or freedoms herein recognized and declared, and in particular, no law of Canada shall be construed or applied so as to

(a) authorize or effect the arbitrary detention, imprisonment or exile of any person;

(b) impose or authorize the imposition of cruel and unusual treatment or punishment;

(c) deprive a person who has been arrested or detained
   (i) of the right to be informed promptly of the reason for his arrest or detention,
   (ii) of the right to retain and instruct counsel without delay, or
   (iii) of the remedy by way of *habeas corpus* for the determination of the validity of his detention and for his release if the detention is not lawful;

(d) authorize a court, tribunal, commission, board or other authority to compel a person to give evidence if he is denied counsel, protection against self crimination or other constitutional safeguards;

(e) deprive a person of the right to a fair hearing in accordance with the principles of fundamental justice for the determination of his rights and obligations;

(f) deprive a person charged with a criminal offence of the right to be presumed innocent until proved guilty according to law in a fair and public hearing by an independent and impartial tribunal, or of the right to reasonable bail without just cause; or

(g) deprive a person of the right to the assistance of an interpreter in any proceedings in which he is involved or in which he is a party or a witness, before a court, commission, board or other tribunal, if he does not understand or speak the language in which such proceedings are conducted.

3. The Minister of Justice shall, in accordance with such regulations as may be prescribed by the Governor in Council, examine every proposed regulation submitted in draft form to the Clerk of the Privy Council pursuant to the *Regulations Act* and every Bill introduced in or presented to the House of Commons, in order to ascertain whether any of the provisions thereof are inconsistent with the purposes and provisions of this Part and he shall report any such inconsistency to the House of Commons at the first convenient opportunity.

4. The provisions of this Part shall be known as the *Canadian Bill of Rights*.

PART II

5. (1) Nothing in Part I shall be construed to abrogate or abridge any human right or fundamental freedom not enumerated therein that may have existed in Canada at the commencement of this Act.

(2) The expression 'law of Canada' in Part I means an Act of the Parliament of Canada enacted before or after the coming into force of this Act, any order, rule or regulation thereunder, and any law in force in Canada or in any part of Canada at the commencement of this Act that is subject to be repealed, abolished or altered by the Parliament of Canada.

(3) The provisions of Part I shall be construed as extending only to matters coming within the legislative authority of the Parliament of Canada.

6. Section 6 of the *War Measures Act* is repealed and the following substituted therefor:

'6. (1) Sections 3, 4 and 5 shall come into force only upon the issue of a proclamation of the Governor in Council declaring that war, invasion or insurrection, real or apprehended, exists.

(2) A proclamation declaring that war, invasion or insurrection, real or apprehended, exists shall be laid before Parliament forthwith after its issue, or, if Parliament is then not sitting, within the first fifteen days next thereafter that Parliament is sitting.

(3) Where a proclamation has been laid before Parliament pursuant to subsection (2), a notice of motion in either House signed by ten members thereof and made in accordance with the rules of that House within ten days of the day the proclamation was laid before Parliament, praying that the proclamation be revoked, shall be debated in that House at the first convenient opportunity within the four sitting days next after the day the motion in that House was made.

(4) If both Houses of Parliament resolve that the proclamation be revoked, it shall cease to have effect, and sections 3, 4 and 5 shall cease to be in force until those sections are again brought into force by a further proclamation but without prejudice to the previous operation of those sections or anything duly done or suffered thereunder or any offence committed or any penalty or forfeiture or punishment incurred.

(5) Any act or thing done or authorized or any order or regulation made under the authority of this Act, shall be deemed not to be an abrogation, abridgment or infringement of any right or freedom recognized by the *Canadian Bill of Rights*.'

V. GERMAN FEDERAL REPUBLIC: BASIC LAW, 1949

THE Basic Law of the German Federal Republic (West Germany) is fairly representative as the modern written constitution of a parliamentary democracy. The application of the Constitution involves judicial review, and thus the provisions must be construed in the light of the relevant judicial decisions. The preamble and Chapter I of the Basic Law are reproduced from an English version of the Basic Law contained in *The Bulletin*, special issue, published by the Press and Information Office of the German Federal Government, Bonn, 1966.

See for reference: McWhinney, *Constitutionalism in Germany and the Federal Supreme Court*, 1962; Kauper, *Michigan Law Review*, 58 (1960), p. 1091.

TEXT

PREAMBLE

THE German People in the Laender Baden, Bavaria, Bremen, Hamburg, Hesse, Lower Saxony, Northrhine-Westphalia, Rhineland-Palatinate, Schleswig-Holstein, Wuerttemberg-Baden and Wuerttemberg-Hohenzollern, conscious of its responsibility before God and Men, animated by the resolve to preserve its national and political unity and to serve the peace of the World as an equal partner in a united Europe, desiring to give a new order to political life for a transitional period, has enacted, by virtue of its constituent power, this Basic Law of the Federal Republic of Germany.

It has also acted on behalf of those Germans to whom participation was denied.

The entire German people is called on to achieve in free self-determination the unity and freedom of Germany.

I. BASIC RIGHTS

Article 1

1. The dignity of man is inviolable. To respect and protect it shall be the duty of all state authority.

2. The German people therefore acknowledges inviolable and inalienable human rights as the basis of every community, of peace and of justice in the world.

3. The following basic rights shall bind the legislature, the executive and the judiciary as directly enforceable law.

Article 2

1. Everyone shall have the right to the free development of his personality insofar as he does not violate the rights of others or offend against the constitutional order or the moral code.

2. Everyone shall have the right to life and to inviolability of his person. The freedom of the individual shall be inviolable. These rights may only be encroached upon pursuant to a law.

Article 3

1. All persons shall be equal before the law.

2. Men and women shall have equal rights.

3. No one may be prejudiced or favoured because of his sex, his parentage, his race, his language, his homeland and origin, his faith or his religious or political opinions.

Article 4

1. Freedom of faith and of conscience, and freedom of creed, religious or ideological (*weltanschaulich*), shall be inviolable.

2. The undisturbed practice of religion is guaranteed.

3. No one may be compelled against his conscience to render war service involving the use of arms. Details shall be regulated by a federal law.

Article 5

1. Everyone shall have the right freely to express and disseminate his opinion by speech, writing and pictures and freely to inform himself from generally accessible sources. Freedom of the press and freedom of reporting by radio and motion pictures are guaranteed. There shall be no censorship.

2. These rights are limited by the provisions of the general laws, the provisions of law for the protection of youth, and by the right to inviolability of personal honour.

3. Art and science, research and teaching shall be free. Freedom of teaching shall not absolve from loyalty to the constitution.

Article 6

1. Marriage and family enjoy the special protection of the state.

2. The care and upbringing of children are the natural right of the parents and a duty primarily incumbent on them. The national community shall watch over the performance of this duty.

3. Separation of children from the family against the will of the persons entitled to bring them up may take place only pursuant to a law, if those so entitled fail in their duty or if the children are otherwise threatened with neglect.

4. Every mother shall be entitled to the protection and care of the community.

5. Illegitimate children shall be provided by legislation with the same opportunities for their physical and spiritual development and their position in society as are enjoyed by legitimate children.

Article 7

1. The entire educational system shall be under the supervision of the state.

2. The persons entitled to bring up a child shall have the right to decide whether it shall receive religious instruction.

3. Religious instruction shall form part of the ordinary curriculum in state and municipal schools, except in secular (*bekenntnisfrei*) schools. Without prejudice to the state's right of supervision, religious instruction shall be given in accordance with the tenets of the religious communities. No teacher may be obliged against his will to give religious instruction.

4. The right to establish private schools is guaranteed. Private schools, as a substitute for state or municipal schools, shall require the approval of the state and shall be subject to the laws of the Laender. This approval must be given if private schools are not inferior to the state or municipal schools in their educational aims, their facilities and the professional training of their teaching staff, and if a segregation of pupils according to the means of the parents is not promoted. This approval must be withheld if the economic and legal position of the teaching staff is not sufficiently assured.

5. A private elementary school shall be admitted only if the educational authority finds that it serves a special pedagogic interest, or if, on the application of persons entitled to bring up children, it is to be established as an inter-denominational or denominational or ideological school and a

state or municipal elementary school of this type does not exist in the commune (*Gemeinde*).

6. Preparatory schools (*Vorschulen*) shall remain abolished.

Article 8

1. All Germans shall have the right to assemble peacefully and unarmed without prior notification or permission.

2. With regard to open-air meetings this right may be restricted by or pursuant to a law.

Article 9

1. All Germans shall have the right to form associations and societies.

2. Associations, the objects or activities of which conflict with the criminal laws or which are directed against the constitutional order or the concept of international understanding, are prohibited.

3. The right to form associations to safeguard and improve working and economic conditions is guaranteed to everyone and to all trades and professions. Agreements which restrict or seek to hinder this right shall be null and void; measures directed to this end shall be illegal.

Article 10

Secrecy of the mail and secrecy of posts and telecommunications shall be inviolable. Restrictions may be ordered only pursuant to a law.

Article 11

1. All Germans shall enjoy freedom of movement throughout the federal territory.

2. This right may be restricted only by a law and only in cases in which an adequate basis of existence is lacking and special burdens would arise to the community as a result thereof or in which the restriction is necessary for the protection of youth against neglect, for combating the danger of epidemics or for the prevention of crime.

Article 12

1. All Germans shall have the right freely to choose their trade or profession, their place of work and their place of training. The practice of trades and professions may be regulated by law.

2. No one may be compelled to perform a particular work except within the framework of a traditional compulsory public service which applies

generally and equally to all. Anyone who refuses on conscientious grounds to render war service involving the use of arms, may be required to render an alternative service. The duration of this alternative service shall not exceed the duration of military service. Details shall be regulated by a law which shall not prejudice freedom of conscience and shall provide also for the possibility of an alternative service having no connection with any unit of the armed forces.

3. Women shall not be required by law to render service in any unit of the armed forces. On no account shall they be employed in any service involving the use of arms.

4. Forced labour may be imposed only in the event that a person is deprived of his freedom by the sentence of a court.

Article 13

1. The home shall be inviolable.

2. Searches may be ordered only by a judge or, in the event of danger in delay, by other organs as provided by law and may be carried out only in the form prescribed by law.

3. Otherwise, this inviolability may be encroached upon or restricted only to avert a common danger or a mortal danger to individuals, or, pursuant to a law, to prevent imminent danger to public security and order, especially to alleviate the housing shortage, to combat the danger of epidemics or to protect endangered juveniles.

Article 14

1. The rights of ownership and of inheritance are guaranteed. Their content and limits shall be determined by the laws.

2. Property imposes duties. Its use should also serve the public weal.

3. Expropriation shall be permitted only in the public weal. It may take place only by or pursuant to a law which provides for the nature and extent of the compensation. The compensation shall be determined upon just consideration of the public interest and of the interests of the persons affected. In case of dispute regarding the amount of compensation, recourse may be had to the ordinary courts.

Article 15

Land, natural resources and means of production may for the purpose of socialization be transferred into public ownership or other forms of publicly controlled economy by a law which provides for the nature and extent of the compensation. In respect of such compensation Article 14, paragraph 3, sentences 3 and 4, shall apply *mutatis mutandis*.

Article 16

1. No one may be deprived of his German citizenship. Loss of citizenship may arise only pursuant to a law, and against the will of the person affected it may arise only if such person does not thereby become stateless.

2. No German may be extradited to a foreign country. Persons persecuted for political reasons shall enjoy the right of asylum.

Article 17

Everyone shall have the right individually or jointly with others to address . written requests or complaints to the competent authorities and to the representative assemblies.

Article 17a

1. Laws concerning military service and alternative service may, by provisions applying to members of the Armed Forces and of alternative services during their period of military or alternative service, restrict the basic right freely to express and to disseminate opinions by speech, writing and pictures (Article 5, paragraph 1, first half-sentence), the basic right of assembly (Article 8), and the right of petition (Article 17) insofar as it permits to address requests or complaints jointly with others.

2. Laws for defence purposes, including the protection of the civilian population, may provide for the restriction of the basic rights of freedom of movement (Article 11) and inviolability of the home (Article 13).

Article 18

Whoever abuses freedom of expression of opinion, in particular freedom of the press (Article 5, paragraph 1), freedom of teaching (Article 5, paragraph 3), freedom of assembly (Article 8), freedom of association (Article 9), the secrecy of mail, posts and telecommunications (Article 10), ownership (Article 14), or the right of asylum (Article 16, paragraph 2) in order to combat the free democratic basic order, shall forfeit these basic rights. The forfeiture and its extent shall be pronounced by the Federal Constitutional Court.

Article 19

1. Insofar as under this Basic Law a basic right may be restricted by or pursuant to a law, such law must apply generally and not solely to an

individual case. Furthermore, the law must name the basic right, indicating the Article.

2. In no case may a basic right be infringed upon in its essential content.

3. The basic rights shall apply also to domestic juristic persons to the extent that the nature of such rights permits.

4. Should any person's right be violated by public authority, recourse to the court shall be open to him. If no other court has jurisdiction, recourse shall be to the ordinary courts.

VI. U.S.S.R.: CONSTITUTION, 1936

THE U.S.S.R. is a federal union and what follows is a chapter from the Federal Constitution of 1936, which, with amendments, is still in force. It is reproduced from an English version published by the Foreign Languages Publishing House, Moscow. In principle the Constitution of 1936 was much more liberal than the first Constitution of 1923: the new model was a reflection of the consolidation of Soviet power, and was intended to provide a foundation for the confident and substantial development of Soviet life after the difficult early years. In practice the new Constitution, like the American Constitution, has been to a great extent a hostage of the political system in which it operated. In any case, its first twenty years of life overlapped with the criminal acts of the Stalin era (the years 1934–53) and the crisis of the war years (1941–5).

For further reference see the following works published in English: Denisov and Kirichenko, *Soviet State Law*, 1960; Romashkin (ed.), *Fundamentals of Soviet Law*, 1962; Hazard, Shapiro and Maggs, *The Soviet Legal System*, 2nd edn., 1969; Johnson, *An Introduction to the Soviet Legal System*, 1969; Berman, *Justice in the U.S.S.R.*, 1963; Hazard, *The Soviet System of Government*, 4th edn., 1968.

The Soviet provisions have influenced constitutions in other Socialist States: see, for example, the Constitutions of Mongolia (1960), Poland (1952), and Rumania (1965).

TEXT

CHAPTER X. FUNDAMENTAL RIGHTS AND DUTIES OF CITIZENS

Article 118

Citizens of the U.S.S.R. have the right to work, that is, the right to guaranteed employment and payment for their work in accordance with its quantity and quality.

The right to work is ensured by the socialist organization of the national economy, the steady growth of the productive forces of Soviet society, the elimination of the possibility of economic crises, and the abolition of unemployment.

Article 119

Citizens of the U.S.S.R. have the right to rest and leisure.

The right to rest and leisure is ensured by the establishment of an eight-hour day for industrial, office, and professional workers, the reduction of the working day to seven or six hours for arduous trades and to four hours in shops where conditions of work are particularly arduous; by the institution of annual vacations with full pay for industrial, office, and professional workers, and by the provision of a wide network of sanatoriums, holiday homes and clubs for the accommodation of the working people.

Article 120

Citizens of the U.S.S.R. have the right to maintenance in old age and also in case of sickness or disability.

This right is ensured by the extensive development of social insurance of industrial, office and professional workers at state expense, free medical service for the working people, and the provision of a wide network of health resorts for the use of the working people.

Article 121

Citizens of the U.S.S.R. have the right to education.

This right is ensured by universal compulsory eight-year education; by extensive development of secondary general polytechnical education, vocational-technical education, and secondary specialized and higher education based on close links between school, and life and production; by utmost development of evening and extra-mural education; by free education in all schools; by a system of state grants; by instruction in schools being conducted in the native language, and by the organization in the factories, state farms and collective farms of free vocational, technical and agronomic training for the working people.

Article 122

Women in the U.S.S.R. are accorded equal rights with men in all spheres of economic, government, cultural, political and other public activity.

The possibility of exercising these rights is ensured by women being accorded an equal right with men to work, payment for work, rest and leisure, social insurance and education, and by state protection of the interests of mother and child, state aid to mothers of large families and unmarried mothers, maternity leave with full pay, and the provision of a wide network of maternity homes, nurseries and kindergartens.

Article 123

Equality of rights of citizens of the U.S.S.R., irrespective of their nationality or race, in all spheres of economic, government, cultural, political and other public activity, is an indefeasible law.

Any direct or indirect restriction of the rights of, or, conversely, the establishment of any direct or indirect privileges for, citizens on account of their race or nationality, as well as any advocacy of racial or national exclusiveness or hatred and contempt, are punishable by law.

Article 124

In order to ensure to citizens freedom of conscience, the church in the U.S.S.R. is separated from the state, and the school from the church. Freedom of religious worship and freedom of antireligious propaganda is recognized for all citizens.

Article 125

In conformity with the interests of the working people, and in order to strengthen the socialist system, the citizens of the U.S.S.R. are guaranteed by law:

(*a*) freedom of speech;
(*b*) freedom of the press;
(*c*) freedom of assembly, including the holding of mass meetings;
(*d*) freedom of street processions and demonstrations.

These civil rights are ensured by placing at the disposal of the working people and their organizations printing presses, stocks of paper, public buildings, the streets, communications facilities and other material requisites for the exercise of these rights.

Article 126

In conformity with the interests of the working people, and in order to develop the organizational initiative and political activity of the masses of the people, citizens of the U.S.S.R. are guaranteed the right to unite in public organizations: trade unions, co-operative societies, youth organizations, sport and defence organizations, cultural, technical and scientific societies; and the most active and politically-conscious citizens in the ranks of the working class, working peasants and working intelligentsia voluntarily unite in the Communist Party of the Soviet Union, which is the vanguard of the working people in their struggle to build communist society and is the leading core of all organizations of the working people, both public and state.

Article 127

Citizens of the U.S.S.R. are guaranteed inviolability of the person. No person may be placed under arrest except by decision of a court or with the sanction of a procurator.

Article 128

The inviolability of the homes of citizens and privacy of correspondence are protected by law.

Article 129

The U.S.S.R. affords the right of asylum to foreign citizens persecuted for defending the interests of the working people, or for scientific activities, or for struggling for national liberation.

Article 130

It is the duty of every citizen of the U.S.S.R. to abide by the Constitution of the Union of Soviet Socialist Republics, to observe the laws, to maintain labour discipline, honestly to perform public duties, and to respect the rules of socialist intercourse.

Article 131

It is the duty of every citizen of the U.S.S.R. to safeguard and fortify public, socialist property as the sacred and inviolable foundation of the Soviet system, as the source of the wealth and might of the country, as the source of the prosperity and culture of all the working people.

Persons committing offences against public, socialist property are enemies of the people.

Article 132

Universal military service is law.

Military service in the Armed Forces of the U.S.S.R. is an honourable duty of the citizens of the U.S.S.R.

Article 133

To defend the country is the sacred duty of every citizen of the U.S.S.R. Treason to the Motherland—violation of the oath of allegiance, desertion to the enemy, impairing the military power of the state, espionage—is punishable with all the severity of the law as the most heinous of crimes.

VII. REPUBLIC OF INDIA:
CONSTITUTION, 1949

THE Indian Constitution is based upon experience in other federal systems modified to suit the requirements of Indian political conditions. It contains a carefully drafted Part concerning Fundamental Rights, followed by a definition of 'directive principles of State policy'. The fundamental rights are justiciable: in other words they are law and may be protected by the courts. The directive principles are not justiciable. The Constitution can only be fully understood by reference to the decisions of the Supreme Court, interpreting its provisions.

For further reference see: Basu, *Commentary on the Constitution of India*, 5th edn., 8 vols, 1965–8; Basu, *Shorter Constitution of India*, 3rd edn., 1960; Gledhill, *The Republic of India: The Development of its Laws and Constitution*, 2nd edn., 1964; Sri Ram Sharma, *Public Law*, 1958, p. 119; Jain, *Indian Constitutional Law*, 1962; Banerjee, *Our Fundamental Rights—their nature and extent (as judicially determined)*, 1960.

The parts of the Constitutions adopted by Pakistan in 1956 and 1962, which correspond to Parts III and IV of the Indian Constitution, have a broadly similar content, except that certain provisions reflect the fact that Pakistan is an Islamic Republic. The Indian Constitution is secular.

TEXT

PART III

FUNDAMENTAL RIGHTS

GENERAL

Article 12

In this Part, unless the context otherwise requires, 'the State' includes the Government and Parliament of India and the Government and the Legislature of each of the States and all local or other authorities within the territory of India or under the control of the Government of India.

Article 13 [1]

1. All laws in force in the territory of India immediately before the commencement of this Constitution, in so far as they are inconsistent with the provisions of this Part, shall, to the extent of such inconsistency, be void.

2. The State shall not make any law which takes away or abridges the rights conferred by this Part and any law made in contravention of this clause shall, to the extent of the contravention, be void.

3. In this article, unless the context otherwise requires,

   (*a*) 'law' includes any Ordinance, order, bye-law, rule, regulation, notification, custom or usage having in the territory of India the force of law;

   (*b*) 'laws in force' includes laws passed or made by a Legislature or other competent authority in the territory of India before the commencement of this Constitution and not previously repealed, notwithstanding that any such law or any part thereof may not be then in operation either at all or in particular areas.

Right to Equality

Article 14

The State shall not deny to any person equality before the law or the equal protection of the laws within the territory of India.

Article 15

1. The State shall not discriminate against any citizen on grounds only of religion, race, caste, sex, place of birth or any of them.

2. No citizen shall, on grounds only of religion, race, caste, sex, place of birth or any of them, be subject to any disability, liability, restriction or condition with regard to:

   (*a*) access to shops, public restaurants, hotels and places of public entertainment; or

   (*b*) the use of wells, tanks, bathing *ghats*, roads and places of public resort maintained wholly or partly out of State funds or dedicated to the use of the general public.

---

[1] In its application to the State of Jammu and Kashmir, in Article 13, references to the commencement of the Constitution shall be construed as references to the commencement of the Constitution (Application to Jammu and Kashmir) Order, 1954, *i.e.*, the 14th day of May, 1954.

3. Nothing in this article shall prevent the State from making any special provision for women and children.

4. Nothing in this article or in clause 2 of Article 29 shall prevent the State from making any special provision for the advancement of any socially and educationally backward classes of citizens or for the Scheduled Castes and the Scheduled Tribes.[1]

Article 16

1. There shall be equality of opportunity for all citizens in matters relating to employment or appointment to any office under the State.

2. No citizen shall, on grounds only of religion, race, caste, sex, descent, place of birth, residence or any of them, be ineligible for, or discriminated against in respect of, any employment or office under the State.

3.[2] Nothing in this article shall prevent Parliament from making any law prescribing, in regard to a class or classes of employment or appointment to an office under the Government of, or any local or other authority within, a State or Union territory, any requirement as to residence within that State or Union territory prior to such employment or appointment.

4. Nothing in this article shall prevent the State from making any provision for the reservation of appointments or posts in favour of any backward class of citizens which, in the opinion of the State, is not adequately represented in the services under the State.

5. Nothing in this article shall affect the operation of any law which provides that the incumbent of an office in connection with the affairs of any religious or denominational institution or any member of the government body thereof shall be a person professing a particular religion or belonging to a particular denomination.

Article 17

'Untouchability' is abolished and its practice in any form is forbidden. The enforcement of any disability arising out of 'Untouchability' shall be an offence punishable in accordance with law.

Article 18

1. No title, not being a military or academic distinction, shall be conferred by the State.

---

[1] In its application to the State of Jammu and Kashmir, reference to Scheduled Tribes in cl. 4 of Article 15 shall be omitted.

[2] In cl 3 of Article 16, the reference to the State shall be construed as not including a reference to the State of Jammu and Kashmir.

2*

2. No citizen of India shall accept any title from any foreign State.

3. No person who is not a citizen of India shall, while he holds any office of profit or trust under the State, accept without the consent of the President any title from any foreign State.

4. No person holding any office of profit or trust under the State shall, without the consent of the President, accept any present, emolument, or office of any kind from or under any foreign State.

RIGHT TO FREEDOM

Article 19[1]

1. All citizens shall have the right:

    (*a*) to freedom of speech and expression;
    (*b*) to assemble peaceably and without arms;
    (*c*) to form associations or unions;
    (*d*) to move freely throughout the territory of India;
    (*e*) to reside and settle in any part of the territory of India;
    (*f*) to acquire, hold and dispose of property; and
    (*g*) to practise any profession, or to carry on any occupation, trade or business.

2. Nothing in sub-clause (*a*) of clause 1 shall affect the operation of any existing law, or prevent the State from making any law, in so far as such law imposes reasonable restrictions on the exercise of the right conferred by the said sub-clause in the interests of the sovereignty and integrity of India, the security of the State, friendly relations with foreign States, public order, decency or morality, or in relation to contempt of court, defamation or incitement to an offence.

3. Nothing in sub-clause (*b*) of the said clause shall affect the operation of any existing law in so far as it imposes, or prevent the State from

---

[1] In its application to the State of Jammu and Kashmir, for a period of ten years from the 14th May, 1954, Article 19 shall be subject to the following modifications:

    (i) in cls. 3 and 4, after the words 'in the interests of', the words 'the security of the State or' shall be inserted;

    (ii) in cl. 5, for the words 'or for the protection of the interests of any Scheduled Tribe', the words 'or in the interests of the security of the State' shall be substituted;

    (iii) the following new clause shall be added, namely:

        '7. The words 'reasonable restrictions' occurring in clauses 2, 3, 4 and 5 shall be construed as meaning such restrictions as the appropriate Legislature deems reasonable.'

making any law imposing, in the interests the sovereignty and integrity of India, or of public order, reasonable restrictions on the exercise of the right conferred by the said sub-clause.

4. Nothing in sub-clause (c) of the said clause shall affect the operation of any existing law in so far as it imposes, or prevent the State from making any law imposing, in the interests the sovereignty and integrity of India or, of public order or morality, reasonable restrictions on the exercise of the right conferred by the said sub-clause.

5. Nothing in sub-clauses (d), (e) and (f) of the said clause shall affect the operation of any existing law in so far as it imposes, or prevent the State from making any law imposing, reasonable restrictions on the exercise of any of the rights conferred by the said sub-clauses either in the interests of the general public or for the protection of the interests of any Scheduled Tribe.

6. Nothing in sub-clause (g) of the said clause shall affect the operation of any existing law in so far as it imposes, or prevent the State from making any law imposing, in the interests of the general public, reasonable restrictions on the exercise of the right conferred by the said sub-clause, and, in particular, nothing in the said sub-clause shall affect the operation of any existing law in so far as it relates to, or prevent the State from making any law relating to,

(i) the professional or technical qualifications necessary for practising any profession or carrying on any occupation, trade or business, or

(ii) the carrying on by the State, or by a corporation owned or controlled by the State, of any trade, business, industry or service, whether to the exclusion, complete or partial, of citizens or otherwise.

Article 20

1. No person shall be convicted of any offence except for violation of a law in force at the time of the commission of the act charged as an offence, nor be subjected to a penalty greater than that which might have been inflicted under the law in force at the time of the commission of the offence.

2. No person shall be prosecuted and punished for the same offence more than once.

3. No person accused of any offence shall be compelled to be a witness against himself.

Article 21

No person shall be deprived of his life or personal liberty except according to procedure established by law.

Article 22

1. No person who is arrested, shall be detained in custody without being informed, as soon as may be, of the grounds for such arrest nor shall he be denied the right to consult, and to be defended by, a legal practitioner of his choice.

2. Every person who is arrested and detained in custody shall be produced before the nearest magistrate within a period of twenty-four hours of such arrest excluding the time necessary for the journey from the place of arrest to the court of the magistrate and no such person shall be detained in custody beyond the said period without the authority of a magistrate.

3. Nothing in clauses 1 and 2 shall apply:

   (*a*) to any person who for the time being is an enemy alien; or
   (*b*) to any person who is arrested or detained under any law providing for preventive detention.

4.[1] No law providing for preventive detention shall authorise the detention of a person for a longer period than three months unless:

   (*a*) an Advisory Board consisting of persons who are, or have been, or are qualified to be appointed as, Judges of a High Court has reported before the expiration of the said period of three months that there is in its opinion sufficient cause for such detention:
   Provided that nothing in this sub-clause shall authorise the detention of any person beyond the maximum period prescribed by any law made by Parliament under sub-clause (*b*) of clause 7; or
   (*b*) such person is detained in accordance with the provisions of any law made by Parliament under sub-clauses (*a*) and (*b*) of clause 7.

5. When any person is detained in pursuance of an order made under any law providing for preventive detention, the authority making the order shall, as soon as may be, communicate to such person the grounds on which the order has been made and shall afford him the earliest opportunity of making a representation against the order.

---

[1] In its application to the State of Jammu and Kashmir, in cl. 4 and cl. 7 of Article 22, for the word 'Parliament', the words 'the Legislature of the State' shall be substituted.

6. Nothing in clause 5 shall require the authority making any such order as is referred to in that clause to disclose facts which such authority considers to be against the public interest to disclose.

7.[1] Parliament may by law prescribe:

(a) the circumstances under which, and the class or classes of cases in which, a person may be detained for a period longer than three months under any law providing for preventive detention without obtaining the opinion of an Advisory Board in accordance with the provisions of sub-clause (a) of clause 4;

(b) the maximum period for which any person may in any class or classes of cases be detained under any law providing for preventive detention; and

(c) the procedure to be followed by an Advisory Board in an inquiry under sub-clause (a) of clause 4.

RIGHT AGAINST EXPLOITATION

Article 23

1. Traffic in human beings and *begar* and other similar forms of forced labour are prohibited and any contravention of this provision shall be an offence punishable in accordance with law.

2. Nothing in this article shall prevent the State from imposing compulsory service for public purposes, and in imposing such service the State shall not make any discrimination on grounds only of religion, race, caste or class or any of them.

Article 24

No child below the age of fourteen years shall be employed to work in any factory or mine or engaged in any other hazardous employment.

RIGHT TO FREEDOM OF RELIGION

Article 25

1. Subject to public order, morality and health and to the other provisions of this Part, all persons are equally entitled to freedom of conscience and the right freely to profess, practise and propagate religion.

2. Nothing in this article shall affect the operation of any existing law or prevent the State from making any law:

[1] See p. 34, n. 1.

(a) regulating or restricting any economic, financial, political or other secular activity which may be associated with religious practice;

(b) providing for social welfare and reform or the throwing open of Hindu religious institutions of a public character to all classes and sections of Hindus.

Explanation I.—The wearing and carrying of *kirpans* shall be deemed to be included in the profession of the Sikh religion.

Explanation II.—In sub-clause (b) of clause 2, the reference to Hindus shall be construed as including a reference to persons professing the Sikh, Jaina or Buddhist religion, and the reference to Hindu religious institutions shall be construed accordingly.

Article 26

Subject to public order, morality and health, every religious denomination or any section thereof shall have the right:

(a) to establish and maintain institutions for religious and charitable purposes;

(b) to manage its own affairs in matters of religion;

(c) to own and acquire movable and immovable property; and

(d) to administer such property in accordance with law.

Article 27

No person shall be compelled to pay any taxes, the proceeds of which are specifically appropriated in payment of expenses for the promotion or maintenance of any particular religion or religious denomination.

Article 28

1. No religious instruction shall be provided in any educational institution wholly maintained out of State funds.

2. Nothing in clause 1 shall apply to an educational institution which is administered by the State but has been established under any endowment or trust which requires that religious instruction shall be imparted in such institution.

3. No person attending any educational institution recognized by the State or receiving aid out of State funds shall be required to take part in any religious instruction that may be imparted in such institution or to attend any religious worship that may be conducted in such institution or in any premises attached thereto unless such person or, if such person is a minor, his guardian has given his consent thereto.

CULTURAL AND EDUCATIONAL RIGHTS

Article 29

1. Any section of the citizens residing in the territory of India or any part thereof having a distinct language, script or culture of its own shall have the right to conserve the same.

2. No citizen shall be denied admission into any educational institution maintained by the State or receiving aid out of State funds on grounds only of religion, race, caste, language or any of them.

Article 30

1. All minorities, whether based on religion or language, shall have the right to establish and administer educational institutions of their choice.

2. The State shall not, in granting aid to educational institutions, discriminate against any educational institution on the ground that it is under the management of a minority, whether based on religion or language.

RIGHT TO PROPERTY

Article 31[1]

1. No person shall be deprived of his property save by authority of law.

2. No property shall be compulsorily acquired or requisitioned save for a public purpose and save by authority of a law which provides for compensation for the property so acquired or requisitioned and either fixes the amount of the compensation or specifies the principles on which, and the manner in which, the compensation is to be determined and given; and no such law shall be called in question in any court on the ground that the compensation provided by that law is not adequate.

2A. Where a law does not provide for the transfer of the ownership or right to possession of any property to the State or to a corporation

---

[1] In its application to the State of Jammu and Kashmir, in Article 31, cls. 3, 4 and 6 shall be omitted and for cl. 5, the following clause shall be substituted, namely with

'5. Nothing in clause 2 shall affect:

(*a*) the provisions of any existing law; or

(*b*) the provisions of any law which the State may hereafter make:

    (i) for the purpose of imposing or levying any tax or penalty; or

    (ii) for the promotion of public health or the prevention of danger to life or property; or

    (iii) with respect to property declared by law to be evacuee property'.

owned or controlled by the State, it shall not be deemed to provide for the compulsory acquisition or requisitioning of property, notwithstanding that it deprives any person of his property.

3. No such law as is referred to in clause (2) made by the Legislature of a State shall have effect unless such law, having been reserved for the consideration of the President, has received his assent.

4. If any Bill pending at the commencement of this Constitution in the Legislature of a State has, after it has been passed by such Legislature, been reserved for the consideration of the President and has received his assent, then, notwithstanding anything in this Constitution, the law so assented to shall not be called in question in any court on the ground that it contravenes the provisions of clause 2.

5. Nothing in clause 2 shall affect:

   (a) the provisions of any existing law other than a law to which the provisions of clause 6 apply, or

   (b) the provisions of any law which the State may hereafter make:

      (i) for the purpose of imposing or levying any tax or penalty, or
      (ii) for the promotion of public health or the prevention of danger to life or property, or
      (iii) in pursuance of any agreement entered into between the Government of the Dominion of India or the Government of India and the Government of any other country, or otherwise, with respect to property declared by law to be evacuee property.

6. Any law of the State enacted not more than eighteen months before the commencement of this Constitution may within three months from such commencement be submitted to the President for his certification; and thereupon, if the President by public notification so certifies, it shall not be called in question in any court on the ground that it contravenes the provisions of clause 2 of this article or has contravened the provisions of sub-section (2) of section 299 of the Government of India Act, 1935.

Article 31A

1. Notwithstanding anything contained in Article 13, no law providing for:

   (a)   acquisition by the State of any estate or of any rights therein or the extinguishment or modification of any such rights, or

   (b) the taking over of the management of any property by the State for a limited period either in the public interest or in order to secure the proper management of the property, or

(*c*) the amalgamation of two or more corporations either in the public interest or in order to secure the proper management of any of the corporations, or

(*d*) the extinguishment or modification of any rights of managing agents, secretaries and treasurers, managing directors, directors or managers of corporations, or of any voting rights of shareholders thereof, or

(*e*) the extinguishment or modification of any rights accruing by virtue of any agreement, lease or licence for the purpose of searching for, or winning, any mineral or mineral oil, or the premature termination or cancellation of any such agreement, lease or licence,

shall be deemed to be void on the ground that it is inconsistent with, or takes away or abridges any of the rights conferred by Article 14, Article 19 or Article 31:

Provided[1] that where such law is a law made by the Legislature of a State, the provisions of this article shall not apply thereto unless such law, having been reserved for the consideration of the President, has received his assent.

2. In this article,

(*a*)[2] the expression 'estate' shall, in relation to any local area, have the same meaning as that expression or its local equivalent has in the existing law relating to land tenures in force in that area, and

[1] In its application to the State of Jammu and Kashmir, the proviso to cl. 1 of Article 31A shall be omitted.

[2] In its application to the State of Jammu and Kashmir, for sub-clause (*a*) of cl. 2 of Article 31A, the following sub-clause shall be substituted, namely:

'(*a*) "estate" shall mean land which is occupied or has been let for agricultural purposes or for purposes subservient to agriculture, or for pasture, and includes:

   (i) sites of buildings and other structures on such land;

   (ii) trees standing on such land;

   (iii) forest land and wooded waste;

   (iv) area covered by or fields floating over water;

   (v) sites of *jandars* and *gharats*;

   (vi) any *jagir*, *inam*, *muafi* or *mukarrari* or other similar grant, but does not include:

     (i) the site of any building in any town, or town area or village *abadi* or any land appurtenant to any such building or site;

     (ii) any land which is occupied as the site of a town or village; or

     (iii) any land reserved for building purposes in a municipality or notified area or cantonment or town area or any area for which a town planning scheme is sanctioned'.

shall also include any *jagir*, *inam* or *muafi* or other similar grant and in the States of Madras and Kerala, any *janmam* right;

(*b*) the expression 'rights', in relation to an estate, shall include any rights vesting in a proprietor, sub-proprietor, under-proprietor, tenure-holder (*raiyat*, *under-raiyat*) or other intermediary and any rights or privileges in respect of land revenue.

Article 31B

Without prejudice to the generality of the provisions contained in Article 31A, none of the Acts and Regulations specified in the Ninth Schedule nor any of the provisions thereof shall be deemed to be void, or ever to have become void, on the ground that such Act, Regulation or provision is inconsistent with, or takes away or abridges any of the rights conferred by, any provisions of this Part, and notwithstanding any judgment, decree or order of any court or tribunal to the contrary, each of the said Acts and Regulations shall, subject to the power of any competent Legislature to repeal or amend it, continue in force.

RIGHT TO CONSTITUTIONAL REMEDIES

Article 32

1. The right to move the Supreme Court by appropriate proceedings for the enforcement of the rights conferred by this Part is guaranteed.

2. The Supreme Court shall have power to issue directions or orders or writs, including writs in the nature of *habeas corpus*, *mandamus*, prohibition, *quo warranto* and *certiorari*, whichever may be appropriate, for the enforcement of any of the rights conferred by this Part.

3.[1] Without prejudice to the powers conferred on the Supreme Court by clauses 1 and 2, Parliament may by law empower any other court to exercise within the local limits of its jurisdiction all or any of the powers exercisable by the Supreme Court under clause 2.

---

[1] In its application to the State of Jammu and Kashmir, cl. 3 of Article 32 shall be omitted; and after cl. 2, the following new clause shall be inserted, namely:

'2a. Without prejudice to the powers conferred by clauses 1 and 2, the High Court shall have power throughout the territories in relation to which it exercises jurisdiction to issue to any person or authority, including in appropriate cases any Government within those territories, directions or orders or writs, including writs in the nature of *habeas corpus*, *mandamus*, prohibition, *quo warranto* and *certiorari*, or any of them, for the enforcement of any of the rights conferred by this Part.'

4. The right guaranteed by this article shall not be suspended except as otherwise provided for by this Constitution.

Article 33

Parliament may by law determine to what extent any of the rights conferred by this Part shall, in their application to the members of the Armed Forces or the Forces charged with the maintenance of public order, be restricted or abrogated so as to ensure the proper discharge of their duties and the maintenance of discipline among them.

Article 34

Notwithstanding anything in the foregoing provisions of this Part, Parliament may by law indemnify any person in the service of the Union or of a State or any other person in respect of any act done by him in connection with the maintenance or restoration of order in any area within the territory of India where martial law was in force or validate any sentence passed, punishment inflicted, forfeiture ordered or other act done under martial law in such area.

Article 35[1]

Notwithstanding anything in this Constitution,

(a) Parliament shall have, and the Legislature of a State shall not have, power to make laws:

(i) with respect to any of the matters which under clause 3 of Article 16, clause 3 of Article 32, Article 33 and Article 34 may be provided for by law made by Parliament; and

[1] In its applications to the State of Jammu and Kashmir, in Article 35,
(i) references to the commencement of the Constitution shall be construed as references to the commencement of the Constitution (Application to Jammu and Kashmir) Order, 1954 (14th May, 1954);
(ii) in cl. (a) (i), the words, figures and brackets 'clause 3 of Article 16, clause 3 of Article 32' shall be omitted; and
(iii) after cl. (b), the following clause shall be added, namely:
'(c) no law with respect to preventive detention made by the Legislature of the State of Jammu and Kashmir, whether before or after the commencement of the Constitution (Application to Jammu and Kashmir) Order, 1954, shall be void on the ground that it is inconsistent with any of the provisions of this Part, but any such law shall, to the extent of such inconsistency, cease to have effect on the expiration of ten years from the commencement of the said Order, except as respects things done or omitted to be done before the expiration thereof.'

(ii) for prescribing punishment for those acts which are declared to be offences under this Part;

and Parliament shall, as soon as may be after the commencement of this Constitution, make laws for prescribing punishment for the acts referred to in sub-clause (ii);

(b) any law in force immediately before the commencement of this Constitution in the territory of India with respect to any of the matters referred to in sub-clause (i) of clause (a) or providing for punishment for any act referred to in sub-clause (ii) of that clause shall, subject to the terms thereof and to any adaptations and modifications that may be made therein under Article 372, continue in force until altered or repealed or amended by Parliament.

Explanation.—In this article, the expression 'law in force' has the same meaning as in Article 372.[1]

PART IV[2]

DIRECTIVE PRINCIPLES OF STATE POLICY

Article 36

In this Part, unless the context otherwise requires, 'the State' has the same meaning as in Part III.

Article 37

The provisions contained in this Part shall not be enforceable by any

---

[1] In its application to the State of Jammu and Kashmir, after Article 35, the following new article shall be added, namely:

'35A. *Saving of laws with respect to permanent residents and their rights.* Notwithstanding anything contained in this Constitution, no existing law in force in the State of Jammu and Kashmir, and no law hereafter enacted by the Legislature of the State,
   (a) defining the classes of persons who are, or shall be, permanent residents of the State of Jammu and Kashmir; or
   (b) conferring on such permanent residents any special rights and privileges or imposing upon other persons any restrictions as respects:
      (i) employment under the State Government;
      (ii) acquisition of immovable property in the State;
      (iii) settlement in the State; or
      (iv) right to scholarships and such other forms of aid as the State Government may provide,
shall be void on the ground that it is inconsistent with or takes away or abridges any rights conferred on the other citizens of India by any provisions of this Part.'

[2] Not applicable to the State of Jammu and Kashmir.

court, but the principles therein laid down are nevertheless fundamental in the governance of the country and it shall be the duty of the State to apply these principles in making laws.

Article 38

The State shall strive to promote the welfare of the people by securing and protecting as effectively as it may a social order in which justice, social, economic and political, shall inform all the institutions of the national life.

Article 39

The State shall, in particular, direct its policy towards securing:

(a) that the citizens, men and women equally, have the right to an adequate means of livelihood;

(b) that the ownership and control of the material resources of the community are so distributed as best to subserve the common good;

(c) that the operation of the economic system does not result in the concentration of wealth and means of production to the common detriment;

(d) that there is equal pay for equal work for both men and women;

(e) that the health and strength of workers, men and women, and the tender age of children are not abused and that citizens are not forced by economic necessity to enter avocations unsuited to their age or strength;

(f) that childhood and youth are protected against exploitation and against moral and material abandonment.

Article 40

The State shall take steps to organize village *panchayats* and endow them with such powers and authority as may be necessary to enable them to function as units of self-government.

Article 41

The State shall, within the limits of its economic capacity and development, make effective provision for securing the right to work, to education and to public assistance in cases of unemployment, old age, sickness and disablement, and in other cases of undeserved want.

Article 42

The State shall make provision for securing just and humane conditions of work and for maternity relief.

Article 43

The State shall endeavour to secure, by suitable legislation or economic organization or in any other way, to all workers, agricultural, industrial or otherwise, work, a living wage, conditions of work ensuring a decent standard of life and full enjoyment of leisure and social and cultural opportunities and, in particular, the State shall endeavour to promote cottage industries on an individual or co-operative basis in rural areas.

Article 44

The State shall endeavour to secure for the citizens a uniform civil code throughout the territory of India.

Article 45

The State shall endeavour to provide, within a period of ten years from the commencement of this Constitution, for free and compulsory education for all children until they complete the age of fourteen years.

Article 46

The State shall promote with special care the educational and economic interests of the weaker sections of the people, and, in particular, of the Scheduled Castes and the Scheduled Tribes, and shall protect them from social injustice and all forms of exploitation.

Article 47

The State shall regard the raising of the level of nutrition and the standard of living of its people and the improvement of public health as among its primary duties and, in particular, the State shall endeavour to bring about prohibition of the consumption except for medicinal purposes of intoxicating drinks and of drugs which are injurious to health.

Article 48

The State shall endeavour to organise agriculture and animal husbandry on modern and scientific lines and shall, in particular, take steps for preserving and improving the breeds, and prohibiting the slaughter, of cows and calves and other milch and draught cattle.

Article 49

It shall be the obligation of the State to protect every monument or place or object of artistic or historic interest, declared by or under law made by Parliament to be of national importance, from spoliation, disfigurement, destruction, removal, disposal or export, as the case may be.

Article 50

The State shall take steps to separate the judiciary from the executive in the public services of the State.

Article 51

The State shall endeavour to:

- (a) promote international peace and security;
- (b) maintain just and honourable relations between nations;
- (c) foster respect for international law and treaty obligations in the dealings of organized peoples with one another; and
- (d) encourage settlement of international disputes by arbitration.

VIII. PEOPLE'S REPUBLIC OF CHINA: CONSTITUTION, 1954

THE first Constitution of China after the taking of power on the mainland by Communist forces in 1949 is necessarily conditioned by the circumstances of recent revolutionary struggle and foreign hostility. Thus political rights may be denied to those hostile to the political system. Moreover, since 1954 no further attempt has been made to renovate the Constitution to accord with political changes. This is hardly surprising in view of the existence of a self-generated process of political struggle in recent years. The state of the rule of law in China may be difficult to assess in orthodox Western terms. However, hostile commentators have been too ready to see political ferment and clashes as evidence of general anarchy. Communist China needs to be evaluated in relation to pre-1949 conditions, and also in comparison with the situation of the rule of law in Western-sponsored Formosa or South Korea. More especially, the actual state of the peasant in China, compared with his counterpart in India, may provide the ultimate test for the progress of protection of human rights in Asia.

For further reference see: Liu Shao-Chi, *Report on the Draft Constitution of the People's Republic of China; Constitution of the People's Republic of China*, Peking, 1962; Larson and others, *Sovereignty Within the Law*, 1965, pp. 255–9; Luke T. Lee, *China and International Agreements*, 1969, pp. 140–63.

The corresponding Parts of the Constitutions of the Democratic People's Republic of Korea (North Korea), of 1948, and the Democratic Republic of Vietnam (North Vietnam), of 1959, contain similar provisions.

TEXT

CHAPTER III. FUNDAMENTAL RIGHTS AND DUTIES OF CITIZENS

Article 85

Citizens of the People's Republic of China are equal before the law.

Article 86

Citizens of the People's Republic of China who have reached the age of eighteen have the right to vote and stand for election whatever their nationality, race, sex, occupation, social origin, religious belief, education, property status, or length of residence, except insane persons and persons deprived by law of the right to vote and stand for election.

Women have equal rights with men to vote and stand for election.

Article 87

Citizens of the People's Republic of China have freedom of speech, freedom of the press, freedom of assembly, freedom of association, freedom of procession and freedom of demonstration. By providing the necessary material facilities, the state guarantees to citizens enjoyment of these freedoms.

Article 88

Citizens of the People's Republic of China have freedom of religious belief.

Article 89

Freedom of the person of citizens of the People's Republic of China is inviolable. No citizen may be arrested except by decision of a people's court or with the sanction of a people's procuratorate.

Article 90

The homes of citizens of the People's Republic of China are inviolable, and privacy of correspondence is protected by law.

Citizens of the People's Republic of China have freedom of residence and freedom to change their residence.

Article 91

Citizens of the People's Republic of China have the right to work. To guarantee enjoyment of this right, the state, by planned development of the national economy, gradually creates more employment, and better working conditions and wages.

Article 92

Working people in the People's Republic of China have the right to rest and leisure. To guarantee enjoyment of this right, the state prescribes working hours and holidays for workers and office employees; at the same time it gradually expands material facilities to enable working people to rest and build up their health.

Article 93

Working people in the People's Republic of China have the right to material assistance in old age, illness or disability. To guarantee enjoyment of this right, the state provides social insurance, social assistance and public health services and gradually expands these facilities.

Article 94

Citizens of the People's Republic of China have the right to education. To guarantee enjoyment of this right, the state establishes and gradually extends the various types of schools and other cultural and educational institutions.

The state pays special attention to the physical and mental development of young people.

Article 95

The People's Republic of China safeguards the freedom of citizens to engage in scientific research, literary and artistic creation and other cultural activity. The state encourages and assists citizens engaged in science, education, literature, art and other fields of culture to pursue their creative work.

Article 96

In the People's Republic of China women enjoy equal rights with men in all spheres—political, economic, cultural, social and domestic.

The state protects marriage, the family, and the mother and child.

Article 97

Citizens of the People's Republic of China have the right to bring complaints against any person working in organs of state for transgression of law or neglect of duty by making a written or verbal statement to any organ of state at any level. People suffering loss by reason of infringement by persons working in organs of state of their rights as citizens have the right to compensation.

Article 98

The People's Republic of China protects the proper rights and interests of Chinese resident abroad.

Article 99

The People's Republic of China grants the right of asylum to any foreign national persecuted for supporting a just cause, taking part in the peace movement or engaging in scientific activity.

Article 100

Citizens of the People's Republic of China must abide by the Constitution and the law, uphold discipline at work, keep public order and respect social ethics.

Article 101

The public property of the People's Republic of China is sacred and inviolable. It is the duty of every citizen to respect and protect public property.

Article 102

It is the duty of citizens of the People's Republic of China to pay taxes according to law.

Article 103

It is the sacred duty of every citizen of the People's Republic of China to defend the homeland.

It is the honourable duty of citizens of the People's Republic of China to perform military service according to law.

IX. UNITED ARAB REPUBLIC: CONSTITUTION, 1964

EGYPT has continued to bear the name United Arab Republic although the union with Syria was terminated in 1961. The Constitution of the U.A.R. is presented as representative of the more socially responsible and modern type of Arab State. Foreign commentators all too commonly judge the quality of government in the Middle East and North Africa on the basis of the attitude of the State concerned toward Western commercial and political interests. Progressive governments thus get a bad press whilst feudal regimes are passed over in silence.

The text below is taken from A. J. Peaslee, *Constitutions of the Nations*, revised 3rd edn., Vol. I, *Africa*, p. 45 (reprinted by permission of the publishers, Martinus Nijhoff, The Hague).

TEXT

PART I

THE STATE

Article 1

The United Arab Republic is a democratic, socialist State based on the alliance of the working powers of the people.

The Egyptian people are part of the Arab nation.

Article 2

Sovereignty is for the people, and its practice in the manner specified in the Constitution.

Article 3

National unity, formed by the alliance of the people's powers, representing the working people, being the farmers, workers, soldiers, intellectuals and national capital, make up the Arab Socialist Union, as the power representative of the people, driver of the Revolution's potentialities, and protector of sound democratic values.

Article 4

The United Arab Republic nationality is defined by the law.

Article 5

Islam is the religion of the State and Arabic its official language.

PART II

BASIC CONSTITUENTS OF THE SOCIETY

Article 6

Social solidarity is the basis of the Egyptian society.

Article 7

The family is the basis of the society founded on religion, morality and patriotism.

Article 8

The State guarantees equality of opportunity to all Egyptians.

Article 9

The economic foundation of the State is the socialist system which prohibits any form of exploitation in a way which ensures the building of the socialist society with its twin foundations: sufficiency and justice.

Article 10

The entire national economy is directed in accordance with the development plan laid down by the State.

Article 11

Natural wealth, whether subterranean or within territorial waters, as well as all its resources and energy are the property of the State which guarantees their proper exploitation.

Article 12

The people control all the means of production, and direct their surplus in accordance with the development plan laid down by the State to increase the wealth and to continuously raise the standard of living.

Article 13

Ownership assumes the following forms:

(a) *State Ownership*
Or, the ownership of the people through the creation of an able and strong public sector which leads progress in all spheres and assumes the main responsibility in the development plan.
(b) *Co-operative Ownership*
Or, the ownership of all the members of the co-operative society.
(c) *Private Ownership*
A private sector which takes part in the development, within the framework of its overall plan, without any exploitation.
The people's supervision covers the three sectors and controls them all.

Article 14

Capital is to be used in the service of the national economy and must not, in the ways of its use, be in conflict with the general good of the people.

Article 15

Public funds have their sanctity and their protection is the duty of every citizen.

Citizens must safeguard and consolidate the ownership of the people, as the basis of the socialist system, and a source of the prosperity of the working people, and strength of the motherland.

Article 16

Private ownership is safeguarded and the law organizes its social function, and ownership is not expropriated except for the general good and against a fair compensation in accordance with the law.

Article 17

The law fixes the maximum limit of land ownership and defines the measures of protecting small land ownerships.

Article 18

The State encourages co-operation and looks after co-operative establishments in all their forms.

Article 19

The State guarantees, in accordance with the law, the consolidation of the family, and the protection of motherhood and childhood.

Article 20

The State guarantees social insurance service and Egyptians have the right to aid in cases of old-age, sickness, incapacity to work and unemployment.

Article 21

Work in the United Arab Republic is a right, a duty and an honour for every able citizen.

Public offices are an assignment for their occupants. The aim of State officials, in the performance of their functions, is to serve the people.

Article 22

The institution of civil titles is prohibited.

Article 23

The Armed Forces of the United Arab Republic belong to the people and their function is the protection of the socialist gains of the popular struggle, the safeguarding of the country and the security and integrity of its territory.

PART III

PUBLIC RIGHTS AND DUTIES

Article 24

Egyptians are equal before the law. They have equal public rights and duties without discrimination between them due to race, origin, language, religion or creed.

Article 25

There is no crime or penalty except by virtue of the law. Penalty is inflicted only for acts committed subsequent to the promulgation of the law prescribing them.

Article 26

Penalty is personal.

Article 27

No person may be arrested or detained except in conformity with the provisions of the law.

Article 28

The right of defence in person or by mandate is guaranteed by the law.

Article 29

Every person accused of a crime must be provided with counsel for his defence.

Article 30

No Egyptian may be deported from the country or prevented from returning to it.

Article 31

No Egyptian may be prohibited from residing in any place and no Egyptian may be forced to reside in a particular place, except in the cases defined by the law.

Article 32

The extradition of political refugees is prohibited.

Article 33

Homes have their sanctity and they may not be entered, except in the cases, and in the manner, prescribed by the law.

Article 34

Freedom of belief is absolute. The State protects the freedom of the practice of religion and creeds in accordance with custom provided this does not infringe upon public order or conflict with morality.

Article 35

Freedom of opinion and scientific research is guaranteed. Every individual has the right to express his opinion and to publicize it verbally or in writing or by photography or by other means within the limits of the law.

Article 36

Freedom of the press, printing and publication is guaranteed within the limits of the law.

Article 37

Egyptians have the right to peaceable assembly, without carrying arms and without the need for prior notice.

Public meetings, processions and gatherings are allowed within the limits of the law.

Article 38

All Egyptians are entitled to education which is guaranteed by the State through the establishment of various kinds of schools, universities, educational and cultural institutions and the expansion thereof. The State gives special care to the physical, mental and moral growth of youth.

Article 39

The State supervises public education which is regulated by law. Education, in its various stages, in State schools and universities is free of charge.

Article 40

Just treatment of Egyptians is guaranteed by the State according to the work performed by them and through the fixing of working hours, assessment of wages, social insurance, health insurance, insurance against unemployment, and the organization of the right to rest and vacations.

Article 41

The creation of syndicates is a guaranteed right. Syndicates have a moral person in the manner determined by the law.

Article 42

Health care is a right to all Egyptians, guaranteed by the State through the establishment of various kinds of hospitals and health institutions, and the expansion thereof.

Article 43

The defence of the motherland is a sacred duty, military service is an honour for Egyptians and conscription is obligatory in accordance with the law.

Article 44

Payment of taxes and public imposts is a duty, in accordance with the law.

Article 45

Egyptians have the right to vote in the manner specified by the law. Their participation in public life is their national duty.

X. NIGERIA: CONSTITUTION, 1963

SINCE the military coup in 1966 the status of the Nigerian Constitution has been problematical. Nevertheless, it is thought to be usefully typical of the constitutions adopted by the recently independent States of English-speaking Africa. Several of these constitutions contain justiciable guarantees of the kind provided in the Nigerian Constitution. The Nigerian provisions bear many similarities to the European Convention on Human Rights (below, p. 339). They may be compared with the constitutions of Kenya, Malawi, Sierra Leone, Uganda, and Zambia.

For further reference see: De Smith, *The New Commonwealth and its Constitutions*, 1964, especially Chapter 5; Holland, *Current Legal Problems*, 1962, p. 145; Elias, *Nigeria: The Development of its Laws and Constitution*, 1967; Ezera, *Constitutional Development in Nigeria*, 2nd edn., 1964; Odumosu, *The Nigerian Constitution: Its History and Development*, 1963; Nwabueze, *Constitutional Law of the Nigerian Republic*, 1964; Davies, *International and Comparative Law Quarterly*, 11 (1962), p. 919.

On the constitutional life of Kenya since independence see Ghai and McAuslan, *Public Law and Political Change in Kenya*, 1970; and Ghai, *Constitutions and the Political Order in East Africa*, University College, Dar es Salaam, Inaugural Lecture Series No. 10, February 1970.

TEXT

CHAPTER III. FUNDAMENTAL RIGHTS

Article 18

1. No person shall be deprived intentionally of his life, save in execution of the sentence of a court in respect of a criminal offence of which he has been found guilty.

2. A person shall not be regarded as having been deprived of his life in contravention of this section if he dies as the result of the use, to such extent and in such circumstances as are permitted by law, of such force as is reasonably justifiable:

(*a*) for the defence of any person from violence or for the defence of property;

(*b*) in order to effect an arrest or to prevent the escape of a person detained;

(*c*) for the purpose of suppressing a riot, insurrection or mutiny; or

(*d*) in order to prevent the commission by that person of a criminal offence.

3. The use of force in any part of Nigeria in circumstances in which and to the extent to which it would have been authorized in that part on the first day of November 1959, by the Code of Criminal Law established by the Criminal Code Ordinance, as amended, shall be regarded as reasonably justifiable for the purpose of this section.

Article 19

1. No person shall be subjected to torture or to inhuman or degrading punishment or other treatment.

2. Nothing in this section shall invalidate any law by reason only that it authorizes the infliction in any part of Nigeria of any punishment that was lawful and customary in that part on the first day of November, 1959.

Article 20

1. No person shall be held in slavery or servitude.

2. No person shall be required to perform forced labour.

3. For the purposes of this section 'forced labour' does not include:

(*a*) any labour required in consequence of the sentence or order of a court;

(*b*) any labour required of members of the armed forces of the Federation in pursuance of their duties as such or, in the case of persons who have conscientious objections to service in the armed forces, any labour required instead of such service;

(*c*) any labour required in the event of any emergency or calamity threatening the life or well-being of the community; or

(*d*) any labour that forms part of normal communal or other civil obligations.

Article 21

1. No person shall be deprived of his personal liberty save in the following cases and in accordance with a procedure permitted by law:

(*a*) in consequence of his unfitness to plead to a criminal charge, in execution of the sentence or order of a court in respect of a criminal offence of which he has been found guilty or in the execution of the order of a court of record punishing him for contempt of itself;

(b) by reason of his failure to comply with the order of a court or in order to secure the fulfilment of any obligation imposed upon him by law;

(c) for the purpose of bringing him before a court in execution of the order of a court or upon reasonable suspicion of his having committed a criminal offence or to such extent as may be reasonably necessary to prevent his committing a criminal offence;

(d) in the case of a person who has not attained the age of twenty-one years, for the purpose of his education or welfare;

(e) in the case of persons suffering from infectious or contagious disease, persons of unsound mind, persons addicted to drugs or alcohol or vagrants for the purpose of their care or treatment or the protection of the community; or

(f) for the purpose of preventing the unlawful entry of any person into Nigeria or for the purpose of effecting the expulsion, extradition or other lawful removal from Nigeria of any person or the taking of proceedings relating thereto.

2. Any person who is arrested or detained shall be promptly informed, in language that he understands, of the reasons for his arrest or detention.

3. Any person who is arrested or detained in accordance with paragraph (c) of subsection 1 of this section shall be brought before a court without undue delay and if he is not tried within a reasonable time he shall (without prejudice to any further proceedings that may be brought against him) be released either unconditionally or upon such conditions as are reasonably necessary to ensure that he appears for trial at a later date.

4. Any person who is unlawfully arrested or detained shall be entitled to compensation.

5. Nothing in this section shall invalidate any law by reason only that it authorizes the detention for a period not exceeding three months of a member of the armed forces of the Federation or a member of a police force in execution of a sentence imposed by an officer of the armed forces of the Federation or a police force, as the case may be, in respect of an offence punishable by such detention of which he has been found guilty.

Article 22

1. In the determination of his civil rights and obligations a person shall

be entitled to a fair hearing within a reasonable time by a court or other tribunal established by law and constituted in such manner as to secure its independence and impartiality:

Provided that nothing in this subsection shall invalidate any law by reason only that it confers on any person or authority power to determine:

   (*a*) questions arising in the administration of a law that affect or may affect the civil rights and obligations of any person; or

   (*b*) chieftaincy questions.

2. Whenever any person is charged with a criminal offence, he shall, unless the charge is withdrawn, be entitled to a fair hearing within a reasonable time by a court.

3. The proceedings of a court or the proceedings of any tribunal relating to the matters mentioned in subsection 1 of this section (including the announcement of the decisions of the court or tribunal) shall be held in public:

Provided that:

   (*a*) a court or such a tribunal may exclude from its proceedings persons other than the parties thereto in the interests of defence, public safety, public order, public morality, the welfare of persons who have not attained the age of twenty-one years, the protection of the private lives of the parties or to such extent as it may consider necessary by reason of special circumstances in which publicity would be contrary to the interests of justice; and

   (*b*) if in any proceedings before a court or such a tribunal a Minister of the Government of the Federation or a Minister of the Government of a Region certifies that it would not be in the public interest for any matter to be publicly disclosed, the court or tribunal shall make arrangements for evidence relating to that matter to be heard in private and shall take such other action as may be necessary or expedient to prevent the disclosure of the matter.

4. Every person who is charged with a criminal offence shall be presumed to be innocent until he is proved guilty:

Provided that nothing in this section shall invalidate any law by reason only that the law imposes upon any such person the burden of proving particular facts.

5. Every person who is charged with a criminal offence shall be entitled:

   (*a*) to be informed promptly, in language that he understands and in detail, of the nature of the offence;

(b) to be given adequate time and facilities for the preparation of his defence;

(c) to defend himself in person or by persons of his own choice who are legal practitioners;

(d) to examine in person or by his legal representatives the witnesses called by the prosecution before any court and to obtain the attendance and carry out the examination of witnesses to testify on his behalf before the court on the same conditions as those applying to the witnesses called by the prosecution; and

(e) to have without payment the assistance of an interpreter if he cannot understand the language used at the trial of the offence:

Provided that nothing in this subsection shall invalidate any law by reason only that the law prohibits legal representation in a court established by or under the Native Courts Law, 1956, the Sharia Court of Appeal Law, 1960, or the Court of Resolution Law, 1960, of Northern Nigeria, the Customary Courts Law, 1956, of Eastern Nigeria, or the Customary Courts Law of Western Nigeria, as amended, or any law replacing any of those laws.

6. When any person is tried for any criminal offence, the court shall keep a record of the proceedings and the accused person or any person authorized by him in that behalf shall be entitled to obtain copies of the record within a reasonable time upon payment of such fee as may be prescribed by law.

7. No person shall be held to be guilty of a criminal offence on account of any act or omission that did not, at the time it took place, constitute such an offence and no penalty shall be imposed for any criminal offence heavier than the penalty in force at the time the offence was committed.

8. No person who shows that he has been tried by any competent court for a criminal offence and either convicted or acquitted shall again be tried for that offence or for a crimnal offence having the same ingredients as that offence save upon the order of a superior court; and no person who shows that he has been pardoned for a criminal offence shall again be tried for that offence.

9. No person who is tried for a criminal offence shall be compelled to give evidence at the trial.

10. No person shall be convicted of a criminal offence unless that offence is defined and the penalty therefor is prescribed in a written law: Provided that nothing in this subsection shall prevent a court of record from punishing any person for contempt of itself notwithstanding

that the act or omission constituting the contempt is not defined in a written law and the penalty therefor is not so prescribed.

Article 23

1. Every person shall be entitled to respect for his private and family life, his home and his correspondence.

2. Nothing in this section shall invalidate any law that is reasonably justifiable in a democratic society:

(a) in the interest of defence, public safety, public order, public morality, public health or the economic well-being of the community; or

(b) for the purpose of protecting the rights and freedom of other persons.

Article 24

1. Every person shall be entitled to freedom of thought, conscience and religion, including freedom to change his religion or belief and freedom, either alone or in community with others and in public or in private, to manifest and propagate his religion or belief in worship, teaching, practice and observance.

2. No person attending any place of education shall be required to receive religious instruction or to take part in or attend any religious ceremony or observances if such instruction, ceremony or observances relate to a religion other than his own.

3. No religious community or denomination shall be prevented from providing religious instruction for pupils of that community or denomination in any place of education maintained wholly by that community or denomination.

4. Nothing in this section shall invalidate any law that is reasonably justifiable in a democratic society:

(a) in the interest of defence, public safety, public order, public morality or public health; or

(b) for the purpose of protecting the rights and freedom of other persons, including their rights and freedom to observe and practise their religions without the unsolicited intervention of members of other religions.

Article 25

1. Every person shall be entitled to freedom of expression, including

freedom to hold opinions and to receive and impart ideas and information without interference.

2. Nothing in this section shall invalidate any law that is reasonably justifiable in a democratic society:

(a) in the interest of defence, public safety, public order, public morality or public health;

(b) for the purpose of protecting the rights, reputations and freedom of other persons, preventing the disclosure of information received in confidence, maintaining the authority and independence of the courts or regulating telephony, wireless broadcasting, television, or the exhibition of cinematograph films; or

(c) imposing restrictions upon persons holding office under the state, members of the armed forces of the Federation or members of a police force.

Article 26

1. Every person shall be entitled to assemble freely and associate with other persons, and in particular he may form or belong to trade unions and other associations for the protection of his interests.

2. Nothing in this section shall invalidate any law that is reasonably justifiable in a democratic society:

(a) in the interest of defence, public safety, public order, public morality or public health;

(b) for the purpose of protecting the rights and freedoms of other persons; or

(c) imposing restrictions upon persons holding office under the state, members of the armed forces of the Federation or members of a police force.

Article 27

1. Every citizen of Nigeria is entitled to move freely throughout Nigeria and to reside in any part thereof; and no citizen of Nigeria shall be expelled from Nigeria or refused entry thereto.

2. Nothing in this section shall invalidate any law that is reasonably justifiable in a democratic society:

(a) restricting the movement or residence of any person within Nigeria in the interest of defence, public safety, public order, public morality or public health;

(b) for the removal of persons from Nigeria to be tried outside Nigeria for criminal offences or to undergo imprisonment outside Nigeria in execution of the sentences of courts in respect of criminal offences of which they have been found guilty;

(c) imposing restrictions upon the movement or residence within Nigeria of members of the public service of the Federation or the public service of a Region, members of the armed forces of the Federation or members of a police force.

3. Nothing in this section shall invalidate any law by reason only that the law imposes restrictions with respect to the acquisition or use by any person of land or other property in Nigeria or any part thereof.

4. Nothing in this section shall invalidate any law by reason only that the law provides for the removal or exclusion of a person who is or was a chief by reference to a territory or a part of a territory from a particular area within that territory.

Article 28

1. A citizen of Nigeria of a particular community, tribe, place of origin, religion or political opinion shall not, by reason only that he is such a person:

(a) be subjected either expressly by, or in the practical application of, any law in force in Nigeria or any executive or administrative action of the Government of the Federation or the Government of a Region to disabilities or restrictions to which citizens of Nigeria of other communities, tribes, places of origin, religions or political opinions are not made subject; or

(b) be accorded either expressly by, or in the practical application of, any law in force in Nigeria or any such executive or administrative action any privilege or advantage that is not conferred on citizens of Nigeria of other communities, tribes, places of origin, religions or political opinions.

2. Nothing in this section shall invalidate any law by reason only that the law:

(a) prescribes qualifications for service in an office under the state or as a member of the armed forces of the Federation or a member of a police force or for the service of a body corporate established directly by any law in force in Nigeria;

(b) imposes restrictions with respect to the appointment of any person to an office under the state or as a member of the armed forces of the

Federation or a member of a police force or to an office in the service of a body corporate established directly by any law in force in Nigeria;

(c) imposes restrictions with respect to the acquisition or use by any person of land or other property; or

(d) imposes any disability or restriction or accords any privilege or advantage that, having regard to its nature and to special circumstances pertaining to the persons to whom it applies, is reasonably justifiable in a democratic society.

Article 29

1. An Act of Parliament shall not be invalid by reason only that it provides for the taking, during periods of emergency, of measures that derogate from the provisions of section 18, 21, 22 or 28 of this Constitution, but no such measures shall be taken in pursuance of any such Act during any period of emergency save to the extent that those measures are reasonably justifiable for the purpose of dealing with the situation that exists during that period of emergency:

Provided that nothing in this section shall authorize any derogation from the provisions of section 18 of this Constitution except in respect of deaths resulting from acts of war or any derogation from the provisions of subsection 7 of section 22 of this Constitution.

2. In this section 'period of emergency' means a period of emergency for the purposes of section 70 of this Constitution.

Article 30

1. Where:

(a) any person is detained in pursuance of an Act of Parliament derogating from the provisions of section 21 of this Constitution; or

(b) the movement or residence of any person within Nigeria who is a citizen of Nigeria is lawfully restricted (otherwise than by order of a court) in the interest of defence, public safety, public order, public morality or public health,

that person shall be entitled to require that his case should be referred within one month of the beginning of the period of detention or restriction and thereafter during that period at intervals of not more than six months to a tribunal established by law and that tribunal may make recommendations concerning the necessity or expediency of continuing the detention or restriction to the authority that has ordered it:

Provided that such authority, unless it is otherwise provided by law, shall not be obliged to act in accordance with any such recommendation.

2. A tribunal established for the purposes of this section shall be constituted in such manner as to ensure its independence and impartiality and its chairman shall be a legal practitioner appointed by the Chief Justice of Nigeria.

Article 31

1. No property, movable or immovable, shall be taken possession of compulsorily and no right over or interest in any such property shall be acquired compulsorily in any part of Nigeria except by or under the provisions of a law that:

(a) requires the payment of adequate compensation therefor; and
(b) gives to any person claiming such compensation a right of access, for the determination of his interest in the property and the amount of compensation, to the High Court having jurisdiction in that part of Nigeria.

2. Nothing in this section shall affect the operation of any law in force on the thirty-first day of March, 1958, or any law made after that date that amends or replaces any such law and does not:

(a) add to the kinds of property that may be taken possession of or the rights over and interests in property that may be acquired;
(b) add to the purposes for which or circumstances in which such property may be taken possession of or acquired;
(c) make the conditions governing entitlement to any compensation or the amount thereof less favourable to any person owning or interested in the property; or
(d) deprive any person of any such right as is mentioned in paragraph (b) of subsection 1 of this section.

3. Nothing in this section shall be construed as affecting any general law:

(a) for the imposition or enforcement of any tax, rate or due;
(b) for the imposition of penalties or forfeitures for breach of the law, whether under civil process or after conviction of an offence;
(c) relating to leases, tenancies, mortgages, charges, bills of sale or any other rights or obligations arising out of contracts;
(d) relating to the vesting and administration of the property of persons adjudged or otherwise declared bankrupt or insolvent, of persons of unsound mind, of deceased persons and of companies,

other bodies corporate and unincorporate societies in the course of being wound up;

(e) relating to the execution of judgments or orders of courts;

(f) providing for the taking of possession of property that is in a dangerous state or is injurious to the health of human beings, plants or animals;

(g) relating to enemy property;

(h) relating to trusts and trustees;

(i) relating to the limitation of actions;

(j) relating to property vested in bodies corporate directly established by any law in force in Nigeria;

(k) relating to the temporary taking of possession of property for the purposes of any examination, investigation or enquiry; or

(l) providing for the carrying out of work on land for the purpose of soil-conservation.

4. The provisions of this section shall apply in relation to the compulsory taking of possession of property, movable or immovable, and the compulsory acquisition of rights over and interests in such property by or on behalf of the State.

Article 32

1. Any person who alleges that any of the provisions of this Chapter has been contravened in any territory in relation to him may apply to the High Court of that territory for redress.

2. Subject to the provisions of section 115 of this Constitution, the High Court of a territory shall have original jurisdiction to hear and determine any application made to it in pursuance of this section and may make such orders, issue such writs and give such directions as it may consider appropriate for the purpose of enforcing, or securing the enforcement, within that territory of any rights to which the person who makes the application may be entitled under this Chapter.

3. Parliament may make provision with respect to the practice and procedure of the High Courts of the territories for the purposes of this section and may confer upon those courts such powers in addition to those conferred by this section as may appear to be necessary or desirable for the purpose of enabling those courts more effectively to exercise the jurisdiction conferred upon them by this section.

Article 33

Without prejudice to the generality of section 165 of this Constitution, in this Chapter, unless it is otherwise expressly provided or required by the context:

'court' means any court of law in Nigeria but, except in relation to a member of the armed forces of the Federation, does not include a court-martial;

'law' includes an unwritten rule of law;

'member of the armed forces of the Federation' includes any person who is subject to naval, military or air-force law; and

'member of a police force' includes a person who is subject to any law relating to the discipline of a police force.

XI. DAHOMEY: CONSTITUTION, 1964

THE Constitution of Dahomey is offered as representative of French-speaking independent African States south of the Sahara. The English version of the provisions supplied below is taken from A. J. Peaslee, *Constitutions of the Nations*, revised 3rd edn., Vol. I: *Africa* (1965), p. 151 (reprinted by permission of the publishers, Martinus Nijhoff, The Hague).

For further reference see Mangin, *Revue des droits de l'homme*, Vol. i (1968), p. 543, 'Les droits de l'homme dans les pays de l'Afrique francophone'.

TEXT

PREAMBLE

The people of Dahomey, on the morrow of the Revolution of October 28, 1963, reaffirm their fundamental opposition to any regime based on arbitrary and personal power.

They solemnly proclaim their attachment to the principles of democracy and the rights of man as defined in the Declaration of the Rights of Man and the Citizen of 1789, in the Universal Declaration of 1948, and as they are guaranteed by this Constitution.

They affirm their desire to co-operate in peace and friendship with all of the peoples who share their ideal of liberty, justice, human solidarity, on the basis of the principles of equality, of mutual interest and mutual respect for national sovereignty and territorial integrity.

They proclaim their attachment to the cause of African unity and undertake to do everything in their power to achieve this.

TITLE I

THE STATE AND SOVEREIGNTY

Article 1

The State of Dahomey is an independent and sovereign republic.

The national emblem is the tricolour flag: starting from the staff, one green stripe across the top of the flag and covering two fifths of its height, two equal horizontal stripes, the upper one yellow and lower one red.

The seal and armorial bearings of the State shall be determined by law.

The national anthem of the Republic is '*L'Aube Nouvelle*.'

The motto of the Republic is 'fraternity, justice, work.'

The official language is French.

Article 2

The Republic of Dahomey is one and indivisible, secular, democratic and social.

Its principle is government of the people, by the people and for the people.

Article 3

National sovereignty belongs to the people.

No section of the people, no community, nor any individual may usurp this right.

Article 4

The people shall exercise its sovereignty through its elected representatives and by means of referendum. The conditions for recourse to referendum shall be established by law.

The Supreme Court shall supervise the regularity of referendum operations and shall proclaim their results.

Article 5

Suffrage shall be universal, equal and secret.

All Dahomean nationals of both sexes who have reached their majority and who enjoy civil and political rights may vote under the conditions to be determined by law.

Article 6

Political parties and groups shall be instrumental in the expression of the suffrage. They shall be formed freely and they shall carry on their activities freely on condition that they respect the laws of the Republic, the principles of democracy, of national sovereignty and of territorial integrity.

TITLE II

THE RIGHTS AND DUTIES OF THE CITIZEN

Article 7

The Republic of Dahomey guarantees the fundamental liberties. It guarantees freedom of speech, press, assembly, association, procession and manifestation under conditions determined by law.

Article 8

The Republic of Dahomey recognizes that all citizens have the right to work and shall attempt to create the conditions to make this right effective.

Article 9

The freedom of the worker to form unions and to strike is recognized. This right shall be exercised under conditions stipulated by law.

Article 10

No one may be arbitrarily detained.

All accused persons shall be presumed innocent until their guilt has been proved as the result of a procedure providing the guarantees indispensable to their defence. The judicial authority, guardian of individual liberty, shall ensure respect for this principle under the conditions stipulated by law.

Article 11

The domicile is inviolable.

Article 12

The law guarantees secrecy of correspondence.

Article 13

The Republic ensures equality before the law to everyone without distinction of origin, race, sex, religion or political affiliation. It respects all beliefs.

All particularist propaganda of a racial, regional or ethnic character, as well as any manifestation of racial discrimination shall be punished by law.

Article 14

The defence of the nation and of the territorial integrity is a sacred duty for every Dahomean citizen.

XII. VENEZUELA: CONSTITUTION, 1961

CHOOSING a constitution to 'represent' Latin America is not an easy task. The Venezuelan provisions are fairly typical of the elaborate constitutionalism of Latin America, not the less because of the provisions for suspension and restriction of guarantees and the concern with the political status of the armed forces. Latin America has for long presented the paradox of a sophisticated legal order existing side by side with backward social structures, and ruling elites who tolerate constitutionalism as long as it does not provide a path towards social justice. See, further, Part Seven below.

The text of the Constitution is taken from A. J. Peaslee, *Constitutions of the Nations*, revised 3rd. edn., Vol. IV, p. 466 (reprinted by permission of the publishers, Martinus Nijhoff, The Hague).

TEXT

TITLE III

OF INDIVIDUAL AND SOCIAL RIGHTS AND DUTIES

CHAPTER I. GENERAL PROVISIONS

Article 20

All Venezuelans have the duty to defend their country, to fulfill and obey the Constitution and the laws of the Republic, as well as the decrees, orders, and resolutions which, in accordance with their powers, the public authorities may dictate. They shall not serve against Venezuela in any event, or against her allies in case of armed international conflict, and, should they do so, they shall be considered as traitors to the Nation.

All foreigners are obliged to obey the laws in the same manner required of Venezuelans while they reside in the territory of the Republic.

Article 21

Without prejudice to the provisions of international agreements, all foreigners in Venezuela shall have the duties and the rights which this

Constitution and the laws grant them; however, neither their rights nor their duties can be greater than those of Venezuelans.

The laws can establish restrictions regarding the exercise of the rights corresponding to all foreigners, or to a determinate class of them, when this is required as the result of grave motives of internal or external security or for reasons of public health.

Confiscation can be imposed only upon foreigners, and only in the event of conflict with their country.

Article 22

All naturalized Venezuelans shall enjoy the same political rights as Venezuelans by birth, except for such restrictions as may be fixed by law.

Article 23

All persons shall have the right to do that which does not prejudice others, and no one shall be obliged to do that which the law does not require, nor shall anyone be prevented from carrying out what the law does not prohibit.

Article 24

In no case may nationals or foreigners claim that the Nation, the states, or the municipalities should compensate them for direct or indirect damages or expropriations which have not been executed by proper authorities acting in their public capacity.

Article 25

The enunciation of the rights and duties made in this Title shall not be understood to be a denial of any other rights and duties which belong to the inhabitants of the Republic and which do not appear expressly in this Title.

Article 26

No law, decree, ordinance, resolution, or regulation can diminish the rights granted by this Constitution to Venezuelans and to foreigners. All dispositions contrary to this principle shall be null, and the Supreme Court of Justice shall so declare them.

Article 27

Whoever shall issue, sign, execute, or order the execution of decrees, resolutions, or ordinances which violate any of the rights guaranteed by this Constitution shall be culpable and shall be punished in accordance with the law, except in the cases of measures directed to the defence of the Republic or to the conservation or re-establishment of peace, dictated by competent public officials in their official capacity, in the cases foreseen by Articles 76 and 77 of this Constitution.

Article 28
The period for the prescription of criminal actions corresponding to the crimes of violation of any of the individual guarantees shall be six years, and this period shall not begin to run, with respect to public officials, until the day following the date on which the person to whom the criminal act is attributed has ceased to exercise his public functions.

CHAPTER II. INDIVIDUAL GUARANTEES

Article 29
The Nation guarantees to all its inhabitants the inviolability of life. No law shall establish the death penalty, nor shall any authority apply the said penalty.

Article 30
The Nation guarantees personal liberty and security to all its inhabitants and, as a consequence:

(1) No one shall be subjected to forcible recruitment. Military service is compulsory and shall be rendered in conformity with the law.

(2) No one shall be arrested or detained, unless he has been caught in the act, without there first being issued a summary information setting forth the commission of a punishable offence calling for corporal punishment and the written order of the official authorized by the law to decree said detention, it being necessary always to set forth in the said order the reason therefor. The summary proceedings shall not in any case be prolonged for more than thirty days after judicial detention. In the crimes of injury, defamation, disrespect, or offence against persons or judicial, political, or administrative bodies invested with public authority, the accused shall be granted a trial, and he shall not be permitted to leave the place of the proceedings until the matter has been decided. Detention shall only follow by virtue of a final sentence.

(3) No one shall continue under detention if, by means of final judicial

sentence, there shall have been destroyed the basis for such detention, nor shall anyone continue under detention after he has been granted freedom under bond in those cases when the law permits this benefit. The granting and the forwarding of the bond shall not occasion any payment.

(4) No one shall be held incomunicado, or be obliged to take an oath, or be submitted to questioning in criminal cases against himself, or against his relatives within the fourth grade of consanguinity and the second grade of affinity, or against his spouse, or the person with whom he is living in marital status.

(5) No one shall be judged by specially created tribunals or commissions, except by his regular judges and by virtue of pre-existing law.

(6) No one shall be condemned in a criminal case without first having been personally notified of the charges and heard in the form provided by law.

(7) No one shall be deprived of his liberty for failure to perform civil obligations not defined as crimes by the law.

(8) No one shall be condemned to corporal punishment for more than twenty years.

(9) No one shall be condemned to opprobrious or perpetual punishment, nor shall anyone be submitted to tortures or other measures which cause physical suffering.

(10) No one shall continue to be deprived of his liberty after he has fulfilled the penalty imposed upon him.

(11) No one shall be tried for the same offence which was the basis of a previous trial.

Article 31

The detentions which administrative authorities may make in conformity with the law shall not be subject to the provisions of section 2 of the preceding Article; however, the arrests which the said authorities may make shall not exceed a period of fifteen days and shall be granted pursuant to written resolution setting forth the reason therefor whenever such arrests are to exceed a forty-eight hour period.

The law shall determine the procedures to which repeated offenders shall be submitted.

Article 32

All persons detained or taken in violation of the guarantees established in this Constitution regarding individual liberty may have recourse to habeas corpus. This recourse may be exercised by the person himself, or by any other person in his name, and it shall be admissible when the law does not provide for any ordinary judicial recourse against the order, act, or procedure which motivates it.

The law shall specify the tribunals which shall have jurisdiction and which shall decide in short and summary form the charges involved, as well as all the other conditions necessary for the exercise of this remedy.

Article 33

The Nation recognizes asylum for political motives, subject only to the limitations established by the laws, the principles of international law, and public treaties.

Article 34

All persons may travel freely throughout the national territory, change their domicile, absent themselves from the Republic and return thereto, bring their property into the country or remove it therefrom, without any limitations other than those established by the laws.

In no case may the entrance of nationals into the country be impeded arbitrarily.

Article 35

The Nation guarantees the inviolability of the home, which cannot be entered by force except in order to prevent the commission of a crime or in order to execute the decisions which the tribunals of justice may dictate pursuant to law. The home shall be subject, in accordance with the law, to the visits of health and fiscal authorities, due notice having first been given by the authorities or functionaries which order or make the inspection.

Article 36

Oral, written, or any other form of correspondence shall be inviolable. No letters, telegrams, private papers, or any other means of correspondence shall be seized except upon fulfilment of the legal formalities by the judicial authority and preserving always all secrets relative to domestic and private life which have no bearing on the proceedings at issue. All books, vouchers, and accounting documents shall be subject to inspection or check by the competent authorities, in conformity with the laws.

Article 37

The Nation guarantees the liberty of thought, manifested by word, by writing, by means of print, by radio, or other systems of publicity, as to which previous censorship cannot be established; however, there shall remain subject to punishment, in accordance with legal prescriptions, all expressions which constitute offences against the public morals, contumely, defamation, disrespect, and instigation to transgress the law.

There shall be forbidden anonymous articles and war propaganda or propaganda which has as its object the provocation of disobedience to the laws, but this prohibition shall not limit the analysis or criticism of legal precepts.

Article 38

The Nation guarantees the liberty of conscience and of worship, the latter liberty, however, being subjected to the supreme inspection of the national executive in accordance with the law.

Article 39

No one shall be required to declare his religious belief or his political ideology, except when the law so requires it.

Article 40

No one shall invoke religious beliefs or disciplines in order to avoid obedience to the laws of the Republic or to impede others in the exercise of their rights.

Article 41

There is guaranteed the right to public or private assembly, for legal purposes and without weapons. The law shall regulate the right of public assembly and the right of manifestation.

Article 42

There are guaranteed the rights of association and of syndicalization for lawful purposes; these rights shall be exercised in accordance with the laws.

Article 43

There is guaranteed the freedom of petition before any public functionary or official entity, with the right to obtain an opportune reply.

Article 44

The Nation guarantees the right of both active and passive suffrage in the terms set forth in this Constitution.

Article 45

There is guaranteed to every citizen the right to accuse before the competent tribunals those officials who may be liable to punishment for the violation of their duties.

Article 46

The Nation guarantees equality to all its inhabitants, by virtue of which:

(*a*) All persons shall be judged by the same laws and shall enjoy equally their protection.

(*b*) No titles of hereditary nobility or distinction shall be granted, nor shall racial discrimination be permitted.

(*c*) The identification of a person in documents relating to his civil status shall not contain any mention of the nature of his filiation, establish any difference in births, or indicate the civil status of his parents.

(*d*) No other official style of address shall be given except that of 'Citizen' and 'You', except for diplomatic protocol.

CHAPTER III. OF THE FAMILY

Article 47

The State shall protect the family no matter what its origin, as well as motherhood, regardless of the civil status of the mother, who shall, further, be assisted in case of abandonment.

Article 48

The law shall determine all matters relative to the organization of the family patrimony which shall not be subject to attachment.

Article 49

The State guarantees the full protection of the child from its conception until its full growth, in order that such growth might be realized in an environment of material and moral security.

As a consequence, there shall be established, among others, the conditions necessary:

(*a*) In order that the children might enjoy the right to know their parents;

(*b*) In order that the parents might fulfil their duty to aid, educate, and feed their children, regardless of what the filiation of the same might be;

(*c*) In order that minors might be protected and judged by special laws;

(*d*) In order to prevent the exploitation of minors in work.

The State shall share with the parents, in a subsidiary manner and within the economic possibilities of the parents, the responsibility incumbent on them for the rearing of their children.

A special code shall govern this protection and shall establish an organization charged with the administration of the same.

Article 50

The State shall adopt measures for the elimination of the social causes of prostitution and shall watch over the recovery of those affected by it.

CHAPTER IV. OF HEALTH AND SOCIAL SECURITY

Article 51

The State shall watch over the maintenance of the public health.

All inhabitants of the Republic have the right to the protection of their health. The State shall establish the services necessary for the prevention and treatment of sicknesses.

Article 52

The inhabitants of the Republic have the right to live protected against the risks of a social nature which might affect them and against the want which results from them.

The State shall establish, in progressive form, an ample and efficient system of social security and shall stimulate the construction of low-cost housing destined for the economically needy class.

CHAPTER V. OF EDUCATION

Article 53

There is guaranteed to all the inhabitants of the Republic the right to an education.

Education is an essential function of the State, which shall have the obligation to create and maintain institutions and services sufficient to attend to the educational needs of the country and to furnish to the

Venezuelan people the indispensable means for improving their cultural level.

Article 54

National education shall be organized as an integral process, correlated in its various terms, and it shall be aimed to achieve the harmonious development of the human personality, in order to create citizens fit for life and for the exercise of democracy, to stimulate the culture of the Nation and to develop the spirit of human solidarity.

Article 55

There is guaranteed the liberty of instruction. All natural or juridical persons may dedicate themselves freely to the sciences and arts, and found chairs and establishments for the teaching of the same, under the supreme inspection and vigilance of the State, with the limitations and within the conditions of orientation and organization which the law may fix.

The State may establish, as its exclusive function, all matters relating to national professorships and teaching.

Article 56

Private initiative in educational matters shall deserve the encouragement of the State, provided that it is in accordance with the principles contained in this Constitution and in the laws.

Article 57

Education must be in charge of persons qualified to teach, verified in accordance with the law.

The State guarantees to professional teachers working conditions and a level of life consonant with their high mission.

Article 58

Primary education is obligatory. Education granted in official establishments is free for all. In accordance with the law, the State shall grant to those individuals who lack the resources the means necessary to permit them to complete their educational obligation and to pursue their studies without any limitations other than those derived from their vocation and their aptitude.

Article 59

The artistic and historic wealth of the country shall be under the control and protection of the State, in accordance with the law.

Article 60

The professions which require a diploma cannot be exercised without first possessing the same and without first fulfilling the formalities required by law. The law shall determine those professions which must be exercised by means of the granting of a diploma by the State.

Special Paragraph: The State reserves the right to require that professional men lend their services to the Nation and in conformity with the provisions of law.

CHAPTER VI. OF WORK

Article 61

Work is a duty and a right. Every individual must contribute to the progress of society by means of work. The State shall see to it that every competent person can obtain the means of subsistence through work and because of this it shall prevent the establishment of any conditions which in any form might diminish the dignity or the liberty of persons.

Article 62

The law shall provide for all that which may be necessary for the greater efficiency, responsibility, and encouragement of work, adequately regulating and establishing the protection which must be granted to workers in order to guarantee their stability in their work and the betterment of their material, moral, and intellectual conditions. The Nation shall encourage the technical instruction of workers.

Article 63

Labour legislation shall consecrate the following rights and precepts, applicable to manual labour as well as intellectual or technical labour, in addition to other rights which may contribute to the betterment of the conditions of the workers:

(1) Maximum normal work day of eight hours for day work and seven hours for night work, except for specified work, with weekly remunerated rest day, in accordance with the law. The law may establish a progressively smaller maximum work day, in general, or for determinate industries in particular;

(2) Equal salary for equal work, without distinction for sex, nationality, or race;

(3) Minimum subsistence salary, sufficient to satisfy the needs of the worker;

(4) Annual paid vacations, without distinction between labourers and employees;

(5) Liability for occupational risks;

(6) Prior notice payment and indemnity in case of termination or rupture of the work contract, length of service payment and pension after a fixed period of service, subject to such conditions as the law may fix;

(7) Stability of work for the members of the board of directors of workers' syndicates, except in cases of withdrawals that are fully justified;

(8) Collective labour contract, in which a closed shop clause can be included;

(9) Conciliation in order to settle the conflicts between employers and workers;

(10) The right to strike, except in the public services that may be fixed by law;

(11) Special protection in the work of minors and women with the right, in the case of minors, to apprenticeships and the setting of a minimum age for admission into the various types of work, and, in the case of women, remunerated rest both before and after childbirth;

(12) A system of participation in the profits of companies in favour of employees and labourers, and the encouragement of savings among the same;

(13) The responsibility for complying with social laws, on the part of the natural or juridical person for whose benefit the work is being done, even when the labour contract shall be entered into by an intermediary or contractor, without affecting the responsibility of the latter;

(14) Non-attachability of salary to the extent and in those cases fixed by law;

(15) Immunity of the money of workers, when such money comes from benefits or rights granted by the law;

(16) Non-renounceability of the provisions of law which favour the workers.

Article 64

The State shall see to the establishment of the salary for workers with families through adequate institutions in conformity with the law.

CHAPTER VII. OF THE NATIONAL ECONOMY

Article 65

The Nation guarantees the right of property. By virtue of its social function, property shall be subjected to the contributions, restrictions, and obligations established by law for purposes of public utility or of the general welfare.

Every author or inventor has an exclusive property right in his work or invention, and he who invents a trade mark has the right to exploit it; all of this to be in conformity with the provisions established by the laws and by treaties.

The law may establish special prohibitions covering the acquisition, transfer, use, and enjoyment of specified classes of property, be it because of the nature of said property, its quality, or its location in the national territory.

Article 66

The State shall look to the defence and conservation of the natural resources of the Venezuelan territory and shall regulate the use, enjoyment, and exploitation of the same, in accordance with the objects previously cited.

Article 67

In conformity with the law, the expropriation of any type of property shall be declared only for reasons of public utility or social welfare, by means of final sentence and upon payment of the price of the same.

In those cases where there is involved the expropriation of lands destined for the realization of the agricultural reform and of the expropriation of real property for the purposes of extension and improvement of population centres, the payment for the same may be deferred for a determinate period of time, a sufficient guarantee first having been given, in conformity with the provisions of law.

No confiscation of property of any kind shall be decreed or carried out, except as provided in the third paragraph of Article 21 of this Constitution.

Article 68

The right of private territorial property shall be conditioned on the preceding provisions and on the obligation to keep the lands and woods which are its object in production that is socially useful. The law shall determine the operation of this provision and the conditions for its application.

Article 69

The State shall carry out a planned and systematic action aimed to transform the national agrarian structure, to rationalize agricultural and cattle raising exploitation, to organize and distribute credit, to better living conditions of rural areas, and to promote the progressive economic and social emancipation of the rural population.

A special law shall determine the technical conditions and other conditions consonant with the national welfare by means of which it shall make effective and workable the exercise of the right which the Nation recognizes in farm associations and in individuals, qualified for farm or cattle-raising work but who lack tillable lands or who do not possess the same in sufficient quantity, to be granted the said lands and the means necessary to make them produce.

Article 70

All the lands acquired by nationals or foreigners in the Venezuelan territory and destined for the exploitation of mineral concessions, including petroleum and other combustible minerals, shall pass in full title to the patrimony of the Nation, without any compensation, upon the extinguishment for any reason of the respective concession.

Article 71

The State shall support and encourage the organization of all types of co-operatives and institutions designed for the betterment of the economy of the people. The law shall assure the timely supplying of the necessary technical, administrative, and economic means.

Article 72

It is the duty of the State to obtain the incorporation of the Indians into the national life.

A special legislation shall resolve all matters related to this subject, having due regard for the cultural characteristics and the economic conditions of the Indian population.

Article 73

All persons may dedicate themselves freely to commerce, industry, or the exercise of any other lucrative activity, without any limitations other than those established by this Constitution and the laws for reasons of health or public safety. The State shall protect private initiative; however, it can reserve for itself the exercise of determinate industries, exploitations, or services of public welfare in order to assure their normal functioning or the defence or the credit of the Nation, and the State shall also reserve the right to dictate measures of an economic nature in order to plan, rationalize, and stimulate production, and to regulate the distribution and the consumption of wealth for the purpose of achieving the development of the national economy.

No monopolies shall be granted; nevertheless, concessions may be granted, of an exclusive nature and for a limited period of time, in order to stimulate the establishment and the development of works or services involving public welfare, provided that there shall not be involved, directly or indirectly, the obligation to guarantee income or profits to invested capital.

Article 74

Exportation cannot be prohibited or limited except when the general welfare of the Nation requires the same.

Article 75

The Republic shall have a council of national economy composed of representatives of capital, labour, the liberal professions, and the State, in the form and with the attributes determined by law.

CHAPTER VIII. OF THE SUSPENSION AND RESTRICTION OF GUARANTEES

Article 76

In cases of civil or international war, or when there is an imminent danger that one or the other might occur, or in cases of grave circumstances which affect the economic or social life of the Nation, the President of the Republic, in session with the council of ministers, may restrict or suspend in all or in part of the national territory the exercise of constitutional guarantees, except for those consecrated in Article 29 and in section 9 of Article 30 of this Constitution.

The decree of restriction or suspension of guarantees shall set forth the following:

(1) The motives which justify it;
(2) The specification of the guarantees which are to be restricted or suspended;
(3) The territory to be affected by the restriction or suspension.

Guarantees shall be restricted or suspended only to the extent required for the security of the country and the restoration of normality, and the decree which orders the restriction or suspension shall be submitted to the National Congress, or to the permanent commission of the same, within ten days following its promulgation, and it shall be annulled upon termination of the causes which motivated it.

Article 77

If the circumstances do not require the restriction or suspension of guarantees, but there are well-founded indications of the existence of plans or activities which have as their object the destruction of constituted powers, by means of a coup d'état or other violent means, the President of the Republic, in session with the council of ministers, may order the preventive detention of those persons whom there is strong reason to consider as implicated in said plans or activities. These measures shall be submitted, within ten days following their execution, to the consideration of the National Congress or, during the recess of that body, to the permanent commission, for approval or rejection; and they shall be suspended upon termination of the causes which motivated them. If they shall be approved by the National Congress or by the permanent commission and shall not have been suspended within sixty days following the said approval, the President of the Republic, upon termination of that period of time, shall submit the said measures to the cognizance of the Supreme Court of Justice which shall decide concerning their continuation or suspension, taking into consideration, in addition to the dispositions of law, the security of the State and the preservation of public order.

Article 78

The restriction of guarantees shall in no case affect the functioning of the public powers of the Nation, whose members shall always enjoy the prerogatives recognized by law.

TITLE IV

OF SOVEREIGNTY AND THE PUBLIC POWER

CHAPTER I. OF SUFFRAGE

Article 79

Sovereignty resides in the people, who may exercise it by means of suffrage and through the agency of the public power.

Article 80

Suffrage is the special right and public function of all Venezuelans; nevertheless, it may be extended for municipal elections and in accordance with the law to foreigners who have more than ten years of uninterrupted residence in the country.

Article 81

There shall be considered as electors all Venezuelans, male and female, over eighteen years of age, not subject by definitely final sentence to civil interdiction or to criminal punishment which carries with it political disqualification.

Article 82

There shall be eligible and competent for the fulfilment of any public office all electors who know how to read and write and are over twenty-one years of age, without any restrictions other than those established in this Constitution and those derived from the conditions of fitness which, in order to carry out the determinate offices, the law might require.

Article 83

The law shall regulate concerning the principle of proportionate representation of minorities, and shall see to it that no political party or group shall predominate in the electoral agencies.

CHAPTER II. OF THE PUBLIC POWER AND ITS EXERCISE

Article 84

The public power shall be exercised in conformity with this Constitution and the laws which define its attributes and faculties. Every act which goes beyond the said definition shall constitute a usurpation of attributes.

Article 85

Since the Republic has possession of the right of ecclesiastical patronage, it shall exercise the same in conformity with the law. Nevertheless, there may be celebrated agreements or treaties to regulate relations between the Church and the State.

Article 86

The public power shall be distributed among the municipal, state, and national powers; and its organization and functioning shall be governed in all cases by the principles of republican, federal, popular, representative, alternative, and responsible government.

Article 87

All usurped authority shall be ineffective and acts done under it shall be null. All decisions taken through direct or indirect use of force or through assembly of the people in subversive attitude shall be equally null.

Article 88

The exercise of the public power occasions the responsibility of the individual for exceeding the authority which this Constitution fixes or for violation of the law which determines its functions, in the terms established in the Constitution itself.

All public officials shall also be subject to punishment, in accordance with the law, for the offences committed by them.

Article 89

Every public official shall be obligated to take an oath before taking office, to make a sworn statement of his property in those cases fixed by law, and to submit to all the requisites and consequences determined by law for the exercise of offices which involve the administration of public funds.

Article 90

The State shall dictate a statute which shall govern its relations with public officials and employees in which the rules for entering into office, leaving office, removal, suspension, and retirement shall be established.

All public employees shall be at the service of the Nation and not of any political party.

Article 91

No one shall fulfill more than one remunerated public office at any one time. The acceptance of a second office of this kind shall imply the renunciation of the first. There are excepted from this disposition all casual, academic, electoral, professorial, public-medical, and municipal-council offices.

Article 92

No public employee shall accept any offices, honours or compensations from foreign governments without obtaining the proper authorization from the Senate chamber. All violators shall be punished in conformity with the law.

CHAPTER III. OF THE NATIONAL ARMED FORCES

Article 93

The national armed forces constitute a non-political institution, essentially professional, obedient, and not deliberative; and shall be organized in order to guarantee the national defence, maintain internal stability, and support the fulfilment of the Constitution and the laws.

In time of peace it shall not be permitted to requisition or demand assistance of any kind except from the civil authorities and in the form and manner determined by the law.

Article 94

The national armed forces shall be classified and organized in conformity with the law and they shall have the special duties fixed by the law.

Article 95

The State shall see to it that the organization and functions which are assigned to the national armed forces correspond always to the standard of dignity of their members and to the concept of an impersonal institution at the exclusive service of the Nation.

The military armed forces shall have as their special mission that of guaranteeing the national defence, and only in those circumstances set forth by the law may they be assigned other incidental functions which, in all cases, shall refer to the maintenance of public order.

Article 96

The military armed forces shall be composed of that contingent which, in proportion to its population, may be called to the service in each one of the states, in the federal district, and in the federal territories and dependencies, in accordance with the law.

Article 97

The states and municipalities shall not maintain other forces except those of the municipal police.

Article 98

All weapons of war which may be found in the country, or which may be brought in from the exterior, belong to the Nation and they shall be under the control of the executive office fixed by law.

Article 99

As long as they remain in active service, the members of the national armed forces shall not exercise the right of suffrage, belong to any political parties, or take part in their activities.

Article 100

On election days the national armed forces shall have permanent service assignment and they may leave their barracks only for the purpose of guaranteeing public order and the normal and free prosecution of the elections.

Article 101

Military ranks shall be obtained only in conformity with the law, and those who possess them cannot be deprived of them or of the honours and pensions pertaining thereto, except in those cases and in the manner determined by law.

Article 102

The President of the United States of Venezuela is the commander-in-chief of the national armed forces, and he shall command them through the executive offices and by means of those officials fixed by law.

Article 103

The supreme council of national defence is the chief agency of direction and co-ordination of the national armed forces, and it shall be composed of the President of the Republic, who shall preside over the same, and of the members of the executive cabinet and of those functionaries of said armed forces which the law may determine.

PART TWO

STANDARD-SETTING BY THE
UNITED NATIONS ORGANIZATION

INTRODUCTION

A MAJOR achievement of the draftsmen of the Charter of the United Nations was the emphasis of the provisions on the importance of social justice and human rights as the foundation for a stable international order. The Organization, and especially the General Assembly and the Economic and Social Council, has given impetus to the development of standards concerning human rights. The United Nations has undertaken both general propaganda work and the burden of drafting legal instruments containing detailed provisions.

The bodies most closely concerned with consideration of questions of human rights have been the Commission on Human Rights created by the Economic and Social Council, and the Division of Human Rights of the United Nations Secretariat. In addition there is a Commission on the Status of Women, and the Human Rights Commission has created two Sub-Commissions: on Freedom of Information and of the Press, and on the Prevention of Discrimination and the Protection of Minorities.

For further reference see *The United Nations and Human Rights*, U.N. Office of Public Information, 1968; the *Yearbook of the United Nations*; and Humphrey, *American Journal of International Law*, 62 (1968), p. 869.

Certain of the Specialized Agencies associated with the United Nations are also concerned with human rights, the International Labour Organization being the most prominent in this respect. On the I.L.O. and UNESCO see, further, below. The Specialized Agencies make periodic reports on human rights, which are forwarded to the Commission on Human Rights and other bodies by the Secretary-General of the United Nations.

The instruments reproduced in this section belong to the period of the United Nations, with the exception of the Slavery Convention of 1926. This has been included as a part of the existing controls on slavery.

I. RELEVANT PROVISIONS OF THE UNITED NATIONS CHARTER

TEXT

WE THE PEOPLES OF THE UNITED NATIONS DETERMINED

to save succeeding generations from the scourge of war, which twice in our lifetime has brought untold sorrow to mankind, and

to reaffirm faith in fundamental human rights, in the dignity and worth of the human person, in the equal rights of men and women and of nations large and small, and

to establish conditions under which justice and respect for the obligations arising from treaties and other sources of international law can be maintained, and

to promote social progress and better standards of life in larger freedom,

AND FOR THESE ENDS

to practise tolerance and live together in peace with one another as good neighbours, and

to unite our strength to maintain international peace and security, and

to ensure, by the acceptance of principles and the institution of methods, that armed force shall not be used, save in the common interest, and

to employ international machinery for the promotion of the economic and social advancement of all peoples,

HAVE RESOLVED TO COMBINE OUR EFFORTS TO ACCOMPLISH THESE AIMS

Accordingly, our respective Governments, through representatives assembled in the City of San Francisco, who have exhibited their full powers found to be in good and due form, have agreed to the present Charter of the United Nations and do hereby establish an international organization to be known as the United Nations.

Chapter I. Purposes and Principles

Article 1

The Purposes of the United Nations are:

1. To maintain international peace and security, and to that end: to take effective collective measures for the prevention and removal of threats to the peace, and for the suppression of acts of aggression or other breaches of the peace, and to bring about by peaceful means, and in conformity with the principles of justice and international law, adjustment or settlement of international disputes or situations which might lead to a breach of the peace;

2. To develop friendly relations among nations based on respect for the principle of equal rights and self-determination of peoples, and to take other appropriate measures to strengthen universal peace;

3. To achieve international co-operation in solving international problems of an economic, social, cultural, or humanitarian character, and in promoting and encouraging respect for human rights and for fundamental freedoms for all without distinction as to race, sex, language, or religion; and

4. To be a centre for harmonizing the actions of nations in the attainment of these common ends.

Article 2

The Organization and its Members, in pursuit of the Purposes stated in Article 1, shall act in accordance with the following Principles:

1. The Organization is based on the principle of the sovereign equality of all its Members.

2. All Members, in order to ensure to all of them the rights and benefits resulting from membership, shall fulfil in good faith the obligations assumed by them in accordance with the present Charter.

3. All Members shall settle their international disputes by peaceful means in such a manner that international peace and security, and justice, are not endangered.

4. All Members shall refrain in their international relations from the threat or use of force against the territorial integrity or political independence of any State, or in any other manner inconsistent with the Purposes of the United Nations.

5. All Members shall give the United Nations every assistance in any

action it takes in accordance with the present Charter, and shall refrain from giving assistance to any State against which the United Nations is taking preventive or enforcement action.

6. The Organization shall ensure that States which are not Members of the United Nations act in accordance with these Principles so far as may be necessary for the maintenance of international peace and security.

7. Nothing contained in the present Charter shall authorize the United Nations to intervene in matters which are essentially within the domestic jurisdiction of any State or shall require the Members to submit such matters to settlement under the present Charter; but this principle shall not prejudice the application of enforcement measures under Chapter VII.

Article 10

The General Assembly may discuss any questions or any matters within the scope of the present Charter or relating to the powers and functions of any organs provided for in the present Charter, and, except as provided in Article 12, may make recommendations to the Members of the United Nations or to the Security Council or to both on any such questions or matters.

Article 13

1. The General Assembly shall initiate studies and make recommendations for the purpose of:

(a) promoting international co-operation in the political field and encouraging the progressive development of international law and its codification;

(b) promoting international co-operation in the economic, social, cultural, educational, and health fields, and assisting in the realization of human rights and fundamental freedoms for all without distinction as to race, sex, language, or religion.

2. The further responsibilities, functions, and powers of the General Assembly with respect to matters mentioned in paragraph 1 (b) above are set forth in Chapters IX and X.

Article 16

The General Assembly shall perform such functions with respect to the international trusteeship system as are assigned to it under Chapters XII

4*

and XIII, including the approval of the trusteeship agreements for areas not designated as strategic.

CHAPTER IX. INTERNATIONAL ECONOMIC AND SOCIAL CO-OPERATION

Article 55

With a view to the creation of conditions of stability and well-being which are necessary for peaceful and friendly relations among nations based on respect for the principle of equal rights and self-determination of peoples, the United Nations shall promote:

(*a*) higher standards of living, full employment, and conditions of economic and social progress and development;

(*b*) solutions of international economic, social, health, and related problems; and international cultural and educational co-operation; and

(*c*) universal respect for, and observance of, human rights and fundamental freedoms for all without distinction as to race, sex, language, or religion.

Article 56

All Members pledge themselves to take joint and separate action in co-operation with the Organization for the achievement of the purposes set forth in Article 55.

Article 57

1. The various specialized agencies, established by inter-governmental agreement and having wide international responsibilities, as defined in their basic instruments, in economic, social, cultural, educational, health, and related fields, shall be brought into relationship with the United Nations in accordance with the provisions of Article 63.

2. Such agencies thus brought into relationship with the United Nations are hereinafter referred to as specialized agencies.

Article 58

The Organization shall make recommendations for the co-ordination of the policies and activities of the specialized agencies.

Article 59

The Organization shall, where appropriate, initiate negotiations among the States concerned for the creation of any new specialized agencies required for the accomplishment of the purposes set forth in Article 55.

Article 60

Responsibility for the discharge of the functions of the Organization set forth in this Chapter shall be vested in the General Assembly and, under the authority of the General Assembly, in the Economic and Social Council, which shall have for this purpose the powers set forth in Chapter X.

CHAPTER X. THE ECONOMIC AND SOCIAL COUNCIL

Composition

Article 61

1. The Economic and Social Council shall consist of twenty-seven Members of the United Nations elected by the General Assembly.

2. Subject to the provisions of paragraph 3, nine members of the Economic and Social Council shall be elected each year for a term of three years.[1] A retiring member shall be eligible for immediate re-election.

3. At the first election after the increase in the membership of the Economic and Social Council from eighteen to twenty-seven members, in addition to the members elected in place of the six members whose term of office expires at the end of that year, nine additional members shall be elected. Of these nine additional members, the term of office of three members so elected shall expire at the end of one year, and of three other members at the end of two years, in accordance with arrangements made by the General Assembly.

4. Each member of the Economic and Social Council shall have one representative.

Functions and Powers

Article 62

1. The Economic and Social Council may make or initiate studies and

[1] General Assembly Resol. 1991 (XVIII), B, para. 3, '*Further decides* that, without prejudice to the present distribution of seats in the Economic and Social Council the nine additional members shall be elected according to the following pattern:
(*a*) Seven from African and Asian states;
(*b*) One from Latin American states;
(*c*) One from Western European and other states.'

reports with respect to international economic, social, cultural, educational, health, and related matters and may make recommendations with respect to any such matters to the General Assembly, to the Members of the United Nations, and to the specialized agencies concerned.

2. It may make recommendations for the purpose of promoting respect for, and observance of, human rights and fundamental freedoms for all.

3. It may prepare draft conventions for submission to the General Assembly, with respect to matters falling within its competence.

4. It may call, in accordance with the rules prescribed by the United Nations, international conferences on matters falling within its competence.

Article 63

1. The Economic and Social Council may enter into agreements with any of the agencies referred to in Article 57, defining the terms on which the agency concerned shall be brought into relationship with the United Nations. Such agreements shall be subject to approval by the General Assembly.

2. It may co-ordinate the activities of the specialized agencies through consultation with and recommendations to such agencies and through recommendations to the General Assembly and to the Members of the United Nations.

Article 64

1. The Economic and Social Council may take appropriate steps to obtain regular reports from the specialized agencies. It may make arrangements with the Members of the United Nations and with the specialized agencies to obtain reports on the steps taken to give effect to its own recommendations and to recommendations on matters falling within its competence made by the General Assembly.

2. It may communicate its observations on these reports to the General Assembly.

Article 65

The Economic and Social Council may furnish information to the Security Council and shall assist the Security Council upon its request.

Article 66

1. The Economic and Social Council shall perform such functions as

fall within its competence in connexion with the carrying out of the recommendations of the General Assembly.

2. It may, with the approval of the General Assembly, perform services at the request of Members of the United Nations and at the request of specialized agencies.

3. It shall perform such other functions as are specified elsewhere in the present Charter or as may be assigned to it by the General Assembly.

Voting

Article 67

1. Each member of the Economic and Social Council shall have one vote.
2. Decisions of the Economic and Social Council shall be made by a majority of the members present and voting.

Procedure

Article 68

The Economic and Social Council shall set up commissions in economic and social fields and for the promotion of human rights, and such other commissions as may be required for the performance of its functions.

Article 69

The Economic and Social Council shall invite any Member of the United Nations to participate, without vote, in its deliberations on any matter of particular concern to that Member.

Article 70

The Economic and Social Council may make arrangements for representatives of the specialized agencies to participate, without vote, in its deliberations and in those of the commissions established by it and for its representatives to participate in the deliberations of the specialized agencies.

Article 71

The Economic and Social Council may make suitable arrangements for consultation with non-governmental organizations which are concerned with matters within its competence.

Such arrangements may be made with international organizations and, where appropriate, with national organizations after consultation with the Members of the United Nations concerned.

Article 72

1. The Economic and Social Council shall adopt its own rules of procedure, including the method of selecting its President.

2. The Economic and Social Council shall meet as required in accordance with its rules, which shall include provisions for the convening of meetings on the request of a majority of its members.

CHAPTER XI. DECLARATION REGARDING NON-SELF-GOVERNING TERRITORIES

Article 73

Members of the United Nations which have or assume responsibilities for the administration of territories whose peoples have not yet attained a full measure of self-government recognize the principle that the interests of the inhabitants of these territories are paramount, and accept as a sacred trust the obligation to promote to the utmost, within the system of international peace and security established by the present Charter, the well-being of the inhabitants of these territories, and to this end:

(*a*) to ensure, with due respect for the culture of the peoples concerned, their political, economic, social, and educational advancement, their just treatment, and their protection against abuses;

(*b*) to develop self-government, to take due account of the political aspirations of the peoples, and to assist them in the progressive development of their free political institutions, according to the particular circumstances of each territory and its peoples and their varying stages of advancement;

(*c*) to further international peace and security;

(*d*) to promote constructive measures of development, to encourage research, and to co-operate with one another and, when and where appropriate, with specialized international bodies with a view to the practical achievement of the social, economic, and scientific purposes set forth in this Article; and

(*e*) to transmit regularly to the Secretary-General for information purposes, subject to such limitation as security and constitutional considerations may require, statistical and other information of a technical nature, relating to economic, social, and educational conditions in the territories for which they are respectively responsible other than those territories to which Chapters XII and XIII apply.

Article 74

Members of the United Nations also agree that their policy in respect of the territories to which this Chapter applies, no less than in respect of their metropolitan areas, must be based on the general principle of good neighbourliness, due account being taken of the interests and well-being of the rest of the world, in social, economic, and commercial matters.

CHAPTER XII. INTERNATIONAL TRUSTEESHIP SYSTEM

Article 75

The United Nations shall establish under its authority an international trusteeship system for the administration and supervision of such territories as may be placed thereunder by subsequent individual agreements. These territories are hereinafter referred to as trust territories.

Article 76

The basic objectives of the trusteeship system, in accordance with the Purposes of the United Nations laid down in Article 1 of the present Charter, shall be:

(*a*) to further international peace and security;

(*b*) to promote the political, economic, social, and educational advancement of the inhabitants of the trust territories, and their progressive development towards self-government or independence as may be appropriate to the particular circumstances of each territory and its peoples and the freely expressed wishes of the people concerned, and as may be provided by the terms of each trusteeship agreement;

(*c*) to encourage respect for human rights and for fundamental freedoms for all without distinction as to race, sex, language, or religion, and to encourage recognition of the interdependence of the peoples of the world; and

(*d*) to ensure equal treatment in social, economic and commercial matters for all Members of the United Nations and their nationals, and also equal treatment for the latter in the administration of justice, without prejudice to the attainment of the foregoing objectives and subject to the provisions of Article 80.

Article 77

1. The trusteeship system shall apply to such territories in the following

categories as may be placed thereunder by means of trusteeship agreements:

(*a*) territories now held under mandate;
(*b*) territories which may be detached from enemy States as a result of the Second World War; and
(*c*) territories voluntarily placed under the system by States responsible for their administration.

2. It will be a matter for subsequent agreement as to which territories in the foregoing categories will be brought under the trusteeship system and upon what terms.

Article 78

The trusteeship system shall not apply to territories which have become Members of the United Nations, relationship among which shall be based on respect for the principle of sovereign equality.

Article 79

The terms of trusteeship for each territory to be placed under the trusteeship system, including any alteration or amendment, shall be agreed upon by the States directly concerned, including the mandatory power in the case of territories held under mandate by a Member of the United Nations, and shall be approved as provided for in Articles 83 and 85.

Article 80

1. Except as may be agreed upon in individual trusteeship agreements, made under Articles 77, 79, and 81, placing each territory under the trusteeship system, and until such agreements have been concluded, nothing in this Chapter shall be construed in or of itself to alter in any manner the rights whatsoever of any States or any peoples or the terms of existing international instruments to which Members of the United Nations may respectively be parties.

2. Paragraph 1 of this Article shall not be interpreted as giving grounds for delay or postponement of the negotiation and conclusion of agreements for placing mandated and other territories under the trusteeship system as provided for in Article 77.

Article 81

The trusteeship agreement shall in each case include the terms under which the trust territory will be administered and designate the authority which will exercise the administration of the trust territory. Such authority, hereinafter called the administering authority, may be one or more States or the Organization itself.

Article 82

There may be designated, in any trusteeship agreement, a strategic area or areas which may include part or all of the trust territory to which the agreement applies, without prejudice to any special agreement or agreements made under Article 43.

Article 83

1. All functions of the United Nations relating to strategic areas, including the approval of the terms of the trusteeship agreements and of their alteration or amendment, shall be exercised by the Security Council.

2. The basic objectives set forth in Article 76 shall be applicable to the people of each strategic area.

3. The Security Council shall, subject to the provisions of the trusteeship agreements and without prejudice to security considerations, avail itself of the assistance of the Trusteeship Council to perform those functions of the United Nations under the trusteeship system relating to political, economic, social, and educational matters in the strategic areas.

Article 84

It shall be the duty of the administering authority to ensure that the trust territory shall play its part in the maintenance of international peace and security. To this end the administering authority may make use of volunteer forces, facilities, and assistance from the trust territory in carrying out the obligations towards the Security Council undertaken in this regard by the administering authority, as well as for local defence and the maintenance of law and order within the trust territory.

Article 85

1. The functions of the United Nations with regard to trusteeship agreements for all areas not designated as strategic, including the approval of the terms of the trusteeship agreements and of their alteration or amendment, shall be exercised by the General Assembly.

2. The Trusteeship Council, operating under the authority of the General Assembly, shall assist the General Assembly in carrying out these functions.

CHAPTER XIII. THE TRUSTEESHIP COUNCIL

Composition

Article 86

1. The Trusteeship Council shall consist of the following Members of the United Nations:

(*a*) those Members administering trust territories;

(*b*) such of those Members mentioned by name in Article 23 as are not administering trust territories; and

(*c*) as many other Members elected for three-year terms by the General Assembly as may be necessary to ensure that the total number of members of the Trusteeship Council is equally divided between those Members of the United Nations which administer trust territories and those which do not.

2. Each member of the Trusteeship Council shall designate one specially qualified person to represent it therein.

Functions and Powers

Article 87

The General Assembly and, under its authority, the Trusteeship Council, in carrying out their functions, may:

(*a*) consider reports submitted by the administering authority;

(*b*) accept petitions and examine them in consultation with the administering authority;

(*c*) provide for periodic visits to the respective trust territories at times agreed upon with the administering authority; and

(*d*) take these and other actions in conformity with the terms of the trusteeship agreements.

Article 88

The Trusteeship Council shall formulate a questionnaire on the political, economic, social, and educational advancement of the inhabitants of each trust territory, and the administering authority for each trust territory within the competence of the General Assembly shall make an annual report to the General Assembly upon the basis of such questionnaire.

Voting

Article 89

1. Each member of the Trusteeship Council shall have one vote.

2. Decisions of the Trusteeship Council shall be made by a majority of the members present and voting.

Procedure

Article 90

1. The Trusteeship Council shall adopt its own rules of procedure, including the method of selecting its President.

2. The Trusteeship Council shall meet as required in accordance with its rules, which shall include provision for the convening of meetings on the request of a majority of its members.

Article 91

The Trusteeship Council shall, when appropriate, avail itself of the assistance of the Economic and Social Council and of the specialized agencies in regard to matters with which they are respectively concerned.

II. UNIVERSAL DECLARATION OF HUMAN RIGHTS

THE references to human rights in the Charter of the United Nations (see pre-amble, Articles, 1, 55, 56, 62, 68, and 76) have provided the basis for elaboration of the content of standards and of the machinery for implementing protection of human rights. On 10 December 1948 the General Assembly of the United Nations adopted a Universal Declaration of Human Rights (U.N. Doc. A/811). The voting was forty-eight for and none against. The following eight states abstained: Byelorussian S.S.R., Czechoslovakia, Poland, Saudi Arabia, Ukrainian S.S.R., U.S.S.R., Union of South Africa, and Yugoslavia. (The reasons for the abstentions are referred to in Ganji, *ubi infra*, p. 149.) The Declaration is not a legally binding instrument *as such*, and some of its provisions depart from exist-ing and generally accepted rules. Nevertheless some of its provisions either con-stitute general principles of law (see the Statute of the International Court of Justice, art. 38 (1) (c)), or represent elementary considerations of humanity. More important is its status as an authoritative guide, produced by the General Assembly, to the interpretation of the Charter. In this capacity the Declaration has considerable indirect legal effect, and it is regarded by the Assembly and by some jurists as a part of the 'law of the United Nations'. On the Declaration, see Oppenheim, *International Law*, 8th ed., i, pp. 744–6; Waldock, 106 *Recueil des cours de l'académie de droit international* (1962, II), pp. 198–9; Verdoodt, *Naissance et signification de la Déclaration Universelle des Droits de l'Homme*, 1964. Generally on human rights see Lauterpacht, *International Law and Human Rights*, 1950; Ganji, *International Protection of Human Rights*, 1962; Ezejiofor, *Protection of Human Rights under the Law*, 1964; Robinson, *The Universal Declaration of Human Rights*, 1958; McDougal and Bebr, 58 *American Journal of International Law* (1964), pp. 603–41; and 11 *Howard Law Journal*, Spring 1965.

The Declaration has an importance of its own, and, until the status of the Covenants (below) is better known, the Declaration cannot be regarded as having merely an historical significance.

TEXT

PREAMBLE

Whereas recognition of the inherent dignity and of the equal and inalien-able rights of all members of the human family is the foundation of free-dom, justice and peace in the world,

Whereas disregard and contempt for human rights have resulted in barbarous acts which have outraged the conscience of mankind, and the advent of a world in which human beings shall enjoy freedom of speech and belief and freedom from fear and want has been proclaimed as the highest aspiration of the common people,

Whereas it is essential, if man is not to be compelled to have recourse, as a last resort, to rebellion against tyranny and oppression, that human rights should be protected by the rule of law,

Whereas it is essential to promote the development of friendly relations between nations,

Whereas the peoples of the United Nations have in the Charter re-affirmed their faith in fundamental human rights, in the dignity and worth of the human person and in the equal rights of men and women and have determined to promote social progress and better standards of life in larger freedom,

Whereas Member States have pledged themselves to achieve, in co-operation with the United Nations, the promotion of universal respect for and observance of human rights and fundamental freedoms.

Whereas a common understanding of these rights and freedoms is of the greatest importance for the full realization of this pledge.

Now, Therefore,

THE GENERAL ASSEMBLY

proclaims

This universal declaration of human rights as a common standard of achievement for all peoples and all nations, to the end that every individual and every organ of society, keeping this Declaration constantly in mind, shall strive by teaching and education to promote respect for these rights and freedoms and by progressive measures, national and international, to secure their universal and effective recognition and observance, both among the peoples of Member States themselves and among the peoples of territories under their jurisdiction.

Article 1

All human beings are born free and equal in dignity and rights. They are endowed with reason and conscience and should act towards one another in a spirit of brotherhood.

Article 2

Everyone is entitled to all the rights and freedoms set forth in this Declaration, without distinction of any kind, such as race, colour, sex, language, religion, political or other opinion, national or social origin, property, birth or other status.

Furthermore, no distinction shall be made on the basis of the political, jurisdictional or international status of the country or territory to which a person belongs, whether it be independent, trust, non-self-governing or under any other limitation of sovereignty.

Article 3

Everyone has the right to life, liberty and security of person.

Article 4

No one shall be held in slavery or servitude; slavery and the slave trade shall be prohibited in all their forms.

Article 5

No one shall be subjected to torture or to cruel, inhuman or degrading treatment or punishment.

Article 6

Everyone has the right to recognition everywhere as a person before the law.

Article 7

All are equal before the law and are entitled without any discrimination to equal protection of the law. All are entitled to equal protection against any discrimination in violation of this Declaration and against any incitement to such discrimination.

Article 8

Everyone has the right to an effective remedy by the competent national tribunals for acts violating the fundamental rights granted him by the constitution or by law.

Article 9

No one shall be subjected to arbitrary arrest, detention or exile.

Article 10

Everyone is entitled in full equality to a fair and public hearing by an independent and impartial tribunal, in the determination of his rights and obligations and of any criminal charge against him.

Article 11

1. Everyone charged with a penal offence has the right to be presumed innocent until proved guilty according to law in a public trial at which he has had all the guarantees necessary for his defence.

2. No one shall be held guilty of any penal offence on account of any act or omission which did not constitute a penal offence, under national or international law, at the time when it was committed. Nor shall a heavier penalty be imposed than the one that was applicable at the time the penal offence was committed.

Article 12

No one shall be subjected to arbitrary interference with his privacy, family, home or correspondence, nor to attacks upon his honour and reputation. Everyone has the right to the protection of the law against such interference or attacks.

Article 13

1. Everyone has the right to freedom of movement and residence within the borders of each state.

2. Everyone has the right to leave any country, including his own, and to return to his country.

Article 14

1. Everyone has the right to seek and to enjoy in other countries asylum from persecution.

2. This right may not be invoked in the case of prosecutions genuinely arising from non-political crimes or from acts contrary to the purposes and principles of the United Nations.

Article 15

1. Everyone has the right to a nationality.

2. No one shall be arbitrarily deprived of his nationality nor denied the right to change his nationality.

Article 16

1 Men and women of full age, without any limitation due to race, nationality or religion, have the right to marry and to found a family.

They are entitled to equal rights as to marriage, during marriage and at its dissolution.

2. Marriage shall be entered into only with the free and full consent of the intending spouses.

3. The family is the natural and fundamental group unit of society and is entitled to protection by society and the State.

Article 17

1. Everyone has the right to own property alone as well as in association with others.

2. No one shall be arbitrarily deprived of his property.

Article 18

Everyone has the right to freedom of thought, conscience and religion; this right includes freedom to change his religion or belief, and freedom, either alone or in community with others and in public or private, to manifest his religion or belief in teaching, practice, worship and observance.

Article 19

Everyone has the right to freedom of opinion and expression; this right includes freedom to hold opinions without interference and to seek, receive and impart information and ideas through any media and regardless of frontiers.

Article 20

1. Everyone has the right to freedom of peaceful assembly and association.

2. No one may be compelled to belong to an association.

Article 21

1. Everyone has the right to take part in the government of his country, directly or through freely chosen representatives.

2. Everyone has the right of equal access to public service in his country.

3. The will of the people shall be the basis of the authority of government; this will shall be expressed in periodic and genuine elections which shall be by universal and equal suffrage and shall be held by secret vote or by equivalent free voting procedures.

Article 22

Everyone, as a member of society, has the right to social security and is entitled to realization, through national effort and international co-operation and in accordance with the organization and resources of each State, of the economic, social and cultural rights indispensable for his dignity and the free development of his personality.

Article 23

1. Everyone has the right to work, to free choice of employment, to just and favourable conditions of work and to protection against unemployment.

2. Everyone, without any discrimination, has the right to equal pay for equal work.

3. Everyone who works has the right to just and favourable remuneration ensuring for himself and his family an existence worthy of human dignity, and supplemented, if necessary, by other means of social protection.

4. Everyone has the right to form and to join trade unions for the protection of his interests.

Article 24

Everyone has the right to rest and leisure, including reasonable limitation of working hours and periodic holidays with pay.

Article 25

1. Everyone has the right to a standard of living adequate for the health and well-being of himself and of his family, including food, clothing, housing and medical care and necessary social services, and the right to security in the event of unemployment, sickness, disability, widowhood, old age or other lack of livelihood in circumstances beyond his control.

2. Motherhood and childhood are entitled to special care and assistance. All children, whether born in or out of wedlock, shall enjoy the same social protection.

Article 26

1. Everyone has the right to education. Education shall be free, at least in the elementary and fundamental stages. Elementary education shall be compulsory. Technical and professional education shall be made

generally available and higher education shall be equally accessible to all on the basis of merit.

2. Education shall be directed to the full development of the human personality and to the strengthening of respect for human rights and fundamental freedoms. It shall promote understanding, tolerance and friendship among all nations, racial or religious groups, and shall further the activities of the United Nations for the maintenance of peace.

3. Parents have a prior right to choose the kind of education that shall be given to their children.

Article 27

1. Everyone has the right freely to participate in the cultural life of the community, to enjoy the arts and to share in scientific advancement and its benefits.

2. Everyone has the right to the protection of the moral and material interests resulting from any scientific, literary or artistic production of which he is the author.

Article 28

Everyone is entitled to a social and international order in which the rights and freedoms set forth in this Declaration can be fully realized.

Article 29

1. Everyone has duties to the community in which alone the free and full development of his personality is possible.

2. In the exercise of his rights and freedoms, everyone shall be subject only to such limitations as are determined by law solely for the purpose of securing due recognition and respect for the rights and freedoms of others and of meeting the just requirements of morality, public order and the general welfare in a democratic society.

3. These rights and freedoms may in no case be exercised contrary to the purposes and principles of the United Nations.

Article 30

Nothing in this Declaration may be interpreted as implying for any State, group or person any right to engage in any activity or to perform any act aimed at the destruction of any of the rights and freedoms set forth herein.

III. DECLARATION ON THE GRANTING OF INDEPENDENCE TO COLONIAL COUNTRIES AND PEOPLES

THE Declaration set out below was adopted by the United Nations General Assembly in Resolution 1514 (XV) on 14 December 1960. Eighty-nine States voted for the resolution and none against: but there were nine abstentions, viz., Portugal, Spain, Union of South Africa, United Kingdom, United States, Australia, Belgium, Dominican Republic, and France. The Declaration relates the normative development in the field of human rights to the rights of national groups, and, in particular, the right of self-determination. The Declaration, in conjunction with the United Nations Charter, supports the view that self-determination is now a legal principle, and, although its precise ramifications are not yet determined, the principle has great significance as a root of particular legal developments. See also the Declaration on the Inadmissibility of Intervention in Resolution 2131 (XX) of 14 January 1966, 5 *International Legal Materials* (1966), p. 374. Generally on self-determination see Nawaz, *Duke Law Journal* (1965), pp. 82–101; Scelle, *Spiropoulos Festschrift*, 1957, pp. 385–91; Tunkin, *Droit international public, problèmes theoriques*, 1965, pp. 42–51; Whiteman, *Digest*, v, pp. 38–87; Brownlie, *Principles of Public International Law*, 1967, pp. 482–6. Resolution 1514 (XV) is in the form of an authoritative interpretation of the Charter rather than a recommendation. For comment see Waldock, 106 *Recueil des cours de l'académie de droit international* (1962, II), pp. 29–34; and Jennings, *The Acquisition of Territory in International Law*, pp. 78–87. For earlier resolutions see Resolutions 637 A (VII) of 16 December 1952 and 1314 (XIII) of 12 December 1958.

The General Assembly established as a subsidiary organ a Special Committee on the Situation with regard to the Implementation of the Declaration on the Granting of Independence by Resolution 1654 (XVI) of 27 November 1961. This consisted at first of seventeen and later of twenty-four states. In 1964 the Special Committee examined situations and made recommendations in respect to fifty-five territories. In 1963 the General Assembly decided to discontinue the Committee on information from non-self-governing territories and to transfer its functions to the Special Committee. As a result, apart from the Trusteeship Council, the Special Committee is the only body responsible for matters relating to dependent territories. The Trusteeship Council is responsible only for New Guinea, and the Trust Territory of the Pacific Islands. For some of the many resolutions based on Resolution 1514 (XV) see *Contemporary Practice of the United Kingdom* (ed. Lauterpacht), 1962—II, pp. 280–2; and *U.N. Monthly Chronicle*, June 1965, pp. 55 et seq.; and ibid., July 1965, p. 47. See further a General Assembly resolution adopted on 12 October 1970 relating to implementation of the Declaration.

TEXT

The General Assembly,

 Mindful of the determination proclaimed by the peoples of the world in the Charter of the United Nations to reaffirm faith in fundamental human rights, in the dignity and worth of the human person, in the equal rights of men and women and of nations large and small and to promote social progress and better standards of life in larger freedom,

 Conscious of the need for the creation of conditions of stability and well-being and peaceful and friendly relations based on respect for the principles of equal rights and self-determination of all peoples, and of universal respect for, and observance of, human rights and fundamental freedoms for all without distinction as to race, sex, language or religion,

 Recognizing the passionate yearning for freedom in all dependent peoples and the decisive role of such peoples in the attainment of their independence,

 Aware of the increasing conflicts resulting from the denial of or impediments in the way of the freedom of such peoples, which constitute a serious threat to world peace,

 Considering the important role of the United Nations in assisting the movement for independence in Trust and Non-Self-Governing Territories,

 Recognizing that the peoples of the world ardently desire the end of colonialism in all its manifestations,

 Convinced that the continued existence of colonialism prevents the development of international economic co-operation, impedes the social, cultural and economic development of dependent peoples and militates against the United Nations ideal of universal peace,

 Affirming that peoples may, for their own ends, freely dispose of their natural wealth and resources without prejudice to any obligations arising out of international economic co-operation, based upon the principle of mutual benefit, and international law,

 Believing that the process of liberation is irresistible and that, in order to avoid serious crises, an end must be put to colonialism and all practices of segregation and discrimination associated therewith,

 Welcoming the emergence in recent years of a large number of dependent territories into freedom and independence, and recognizing the increasingly powerful trends towards freedom in such territories which have not yet attained independence,

Convinced that all peoples have an inalienable right to complete freedom, the exercise of their sovereignty and the integrity of their national territory, *Solemnly proclaims* the necessity of bringing to a speedy and unconditional end colonialism in all its forms and manifestations;

And to this end

Declares that:

1. The subjection of peoples to alien subjugation, domination and exploitation constitutes a denial of fundamental human rights, is contrary to the Charter of the United Nations and is an impediment to the promotion of World peace and co-operation.

2. All peoples have the right to self-determination; by virtue of that right they freely determine their political status and freely pursue their economic, social and cultural development.

3. Inadequacy of political, economic, social or educational preparedness should never serve as a pretext for delaying independence.

4. All armed action or repressive measures of all kinds directed against dependent peoples shall cease in order to enable them to exercise peacefully and freely their right to complete independence, and the integrity of their national territory shall be respected.

5. Immediate steps shall be taken, in Trust and Non-Self-Governing Territories or all other territories which have not yet attained independence, to transfer all powers to the peoples of those territories, without any conditions or reservations, in accordance with their freely expressed will and desire, without any distinction as to race, creed or colour, in order to enable them to enjoy complete independence and freedom.

6. Any attempt aimed at the partial or total disruption of the national unity and the territorial integrity of a country is incompatible with the purposes and principles of the Charter of the United Nations.

7. All States shall observe faithfully and strictly the provisions of the Charter of the United Nations, the Universal Declaration of Human Rights and the present Declaration on the basis of equality, non-interference in the internal affairs of all States, and respect for the sovereign rights of all peoples and their territorial integrity.

IV. CONVENTION ON THE PREVENTION AND PUNISHMENT OF THE CRIME OF GENOCIDE, 1948

THIS agreement was adopted by the General Assembly on 9 December 1948. Forty-three States signed the Convention and there have been seventy-three ratifications and accessions. The Convention came into force on 12 January 1961. The United Kingdom has now ratified it: see the Genocide Act, United Kingdom Statutes, 1969, c. 12, in force 30 April 1970.

The text in various languages: *United Nations Treaty Series*, Vol. 78, p. 277; H.M.S.O., Misc. No. 2 (1966), Cmnd. 2904. The latter contains the English text of various reservations and declarations by States ratifying or acceding to the Convention. (See also *U.N. Multilateral Treaties in Respect of which the Secretary-General Performs Depositary Functions*, 1969, pp. 58–62.)

For further reference see Robinson, *The Genocide Convention*, 1960; Lemkin, *Axis Rule in Occupied Europe*, 1944; Anon., *Yale Law Journal*, 58 (1949), p. 1142; Whiteman, *Digest of International Law*, vol. ii, pp. 848–74.

TEXT

THE CONTRACTING PARTIES,

HAVING CONSIDERED the declaration made by the General Assembly of the United Nations in its resolution 96 (I) dated 11 December 1946 that genocide is a crime under international law, contrary to the spirit and aims of the United Nations and condemned by the civilized world;

RECOGNIZING that at all periods of history genocide has inflicted great losses on humanity; and

BEING CONVINCED that, in order to liberate mankind from such an odious scourge, international co-operation is required,

HEREBY AGREE AS HEREINAFTER PROVIDED:

Article I

The Contracting Parties confirm that genocide, whether committed in time of peace or in time of war, is a crime under international law which they undertake to prevent and to punish.

Article II

In the present Convention, genocide means any of the following acts committed with intent to destroy, in whole or in part, a national, ethnical, racial or religious group, as such:

(a) Killing members of the group;
(b) Causing serious bodily or mental harm to members of the group;
(c) Deliberately inflicting on the group conditions of life calculated to bring about its physical destruction in whole or in part;
(d) Imposing measures intended to prevent births within the group;
(e) Forcibly transferring children of the group to another group.

Article III

The following acts shall be punishable:

(a) Genocide;
(b) Conspiracy to commit genocide;
(c) Direct and public incitement to commit genocide;
(d) Attempt to commit genocide;
(e) Complicity in genocide.

Article IV

Persons committing genocide or any of the other acts enumerated in Article III shall be punished, whether they are constitutionally responsible rulers, public officials or private individuals.

Article V

The Contracting Parties undertake to enact, in accordance with their respective Constitutions, the necessary legislation to give effect to the provisions of the present Convention and, in particular, to provide effective penalties for persons guilty of genocide or of any of the other acts enumerated in Article III.

Article VI

Persons charged with genocide or any of the other acts enumerated in Article III shall be tried by a competent tribunal of the State in the territory of which the act was committed, or by such international penal tribunal as may have jurisdiction with respect to those Contracting Parties which shall have accepted its jurisdiction.

Article VII

Genocide and the other acts enumerated in Article III shall not be considered as political crimes for the purpose of extradition.

The Contracting Parties pledge themselves in such cases to grant extradition in accordance with their laws and treaties in force.

Article VIII

Any Contracting Party may call upon the competent organs of the United Nations to take such action under the Charter of the United Nations as they consider appropriate for the prevention and suppression of acts of genocide or any of the other acts enumerated in Article III.

Article IX

Disputes between the Contracting Parties relating to the interpretation, application or fulfilment of the present Convention, including those relating to the responsibility of a State for genocide or for any of the other acts enumerated in Article III, shall be submitted to the International Court of Justice at the request of any of the parties to the dispute.

Article X

The present Convention, of which the Chinese, English, French, Russian and Spanish texts are equally authentic, shall bear the date of 9 December 1948.

Article XI

The present Convention shall be open until 31 December 1949 for signature on behalf of any Member of the United Nations and of any non-member State to which an invitation to sign has been addressed by the General Assembly.

The present Convention shall be ratified, and the instruments of ratification shall be deposited with the Secretary-General of the United Nations.

After 1 January 1950 the present Convention may be acceded to on behalf of any Member of the United Nations and of any non-member State which has received an invitation as aforesaid.

Instruments of accession shall be deposited with the Secretary-General of the United Nations.

Article XII

Any Contracting Party may at any time, by notification addressed to the Secretary-General of the United Nations, extend the application of the present Convention to all or any of the territories for the conduct of whose foreign relations that Contracting Party is responsible.

Article XIII

On the day when the first twenty instruments of ratification or accession have been deposited, the Secretary-General shall draw up a *procès-verbal* and transmit a copy thereof to each Member of the United Nations and to each of the non-member States contemplated in Article XI.

The present Convention shall come into force on the ninetieth day following the date of deposit of the twentieth instrument of ratification or accession.

Any ratification or accession effected subsequent to the latter date shall become effective on the ninetieth day following the deposit of the instrument of ratification or accession.

Article XIV

The present Convention shall remain in effect for a period of ten years as from the date of its coming into force.

It shall thereafter remain in force for successive periods of five years for such Contracting Parties as have not denounced it at least six months before the expiration of the current period.

Denunciation shall be effected by a written notification addressed to the Secretary-General of the United Nations.

Article XV

If, as a result of denunciations, the number of Parties to the present Convention should become less than sixteen, the Convention shall cease to be in force as from the date on which the last of these denunciations shall become effective.

Article XVI

A request for the revision of the present Convention may be made at any time by any Contracting Party by means of a notification in writing addressed to the Secretary-General.

The General Assembly shall decide upon the steps, if any, to be taken in respect of such request.

Article XVII

The Secretary-General of the United Nations shall notify all Members of the United Nations and the non-member States contemplated in Article XI of the following:

(*a*) signatures, ratifications and accessions received in accordance with Article XI;
(*b*) Notifications received in accordance with Article XII;
(*c*) The date upon which the present Convention comes into force in accordance with Article XIII;
(*d*) Denunciations received in accordance with Article XIV;
(*e*) The abrogation of the Convention in accordance with Article XV;
(*f*) Notifications received in accordance with Article XVI.

Article XVIII

The original of the present Convention shall be deposited in the archives of the United Nations.

A certified copy of the Convention shall be transmitted to each Member of the United Nations and to each of the non-member States contemplated in Article XI.

Article XIX

The present Convention shall be registered by the Secretary-General of the United Nations on the date of its coming into force.

V. SLAVERY CONVENTION, 1926, AMENDED BY PROTOCOL, 1953

THE Slavery Convention was signed on 25 September 1926 and entered into force on 9 March 1927. Over fifty-five States have become parties. For the text in various languages: *League of Nations Treaty Series*, Vol. 60, p. 253; *U.K. Treaty Series*, No. 16 (1927), Cmd. 2910. See also *Multilateral Treaties in Respect of which the Secretary-General Performs Depositary Functions*, 1969, p. 313.

The Protocol of amendment was opened for signature on 7 December 1953, and the Slavery Convention as amended by the Protocol entered into force on 7 July 1955. Over twenty-eight States have become parties. For the text in various languages: *United Nations Treaty Series*, Vol. 212, p. 17; *U.K. Treaty Series*, No. 24 (1956), Cmd. 9797. See also *Multilateral Treaties in Respect of which the Secretary-General Performs Depositary Functions*, 1969, p. 311.

For further reference see U.N., *Report on Slavery*, Sales No. 67, XIV.2; Fawcett, *The Application of the European Convention on Human Rights*, 1969, 42–3.

There have been problems in defining slavery and associated practices, and the position has been improved by the Supplementary Convention below, pp. 128–34. See, further, the I.L.O. Conventions concerning forced labour, below.

TEXT

Article 1

For the purpose of the present Convention, the following definitions are agreed upon:

(1) Slavery is the status or condition of a person over whom any or all of the powers attaching to the right of ownership are exercised.

(2) The slave trade includes all acts involved in the capture, acquisition or disposal of a person with intent to reduce him to slavery; all acts involved in the acquisition of a slave with a view to selling or exchanging him; all acts of disposal by sale or exchange of a slave acquired with a view to being sold or exchanged, and, in general, every act of trade or transport in slaves.

Article 2

The High Contracting Parties undertake, each in respect of the territories placed under its sovereignty, jurisdiction, protection, suzerainty or tutelage, so far as they have not already taken the necessary steps:

(*a*) To prevent and suppress the slave trade;

(*b*) to bring about, progressively and as soon as possible, the complete abolition of slavery in all its forms.

Article 3

The High Contracting Parties undertake to adopt all appropriate measures with a view to preventing and suppressing the embarkation, disembarkation and transport of slaves in their territorial waters and upon all vessels flying their respective flags.

The High Contracting Parties undertake to negotiate as soon as possible a general Convention with regard to the slave trade which will give them rights and impose upon them duties of the same nature as those provided for in the Convention of 17 June, 1925,[1] relative to the International Trade in Arms (Articles 12, 20, 21, 22, 23, 24, and paragraphs 3, 4 and 5 of Section II of Annex II), with the necessary adaptations, it being understood that this general Convention will not place the ships (even of small tonnage) of any High Contracting Parties in a position different from that of the other High Contracting Parties.

It is also understood that, before or after the coming into force of this general Convention, the High Contracting Parties are entirely free to conclude between themselves, without, however, derogating from the principles laid down in the preceding paragraph, such special agreements as, by reason of their peculiar situation, might appear to be suitable in order to bring about as soon as possible the complete disappearance of the slave trade.

Article 4

The High Contracting Parties shall give to one another every assistance with the object of securing the abolition of slavery and the slave trade.

Article 5

The High Contracting Parties recognize that recourse to compulsory or forced labour may have grave consequences and undertake, each in respect of the territories placed under its sovereignty, jurisdiction, protection, suzerainty or tutelage, to take all necessary measures to prevent compul-

[1] 'Miscellaneous No. 11 (1929)', Cmd. 3448.

sory or forced labour from developing into conditions analogous to slavery.

It is agreed that:

(1) Subject to the transitional provisions laid down in paragraph (2) below, compulsory or forced labour may only be exacted for public purposes.

(2) In territories in which compulsory or forced labour for other than public purposes still survives, the High Contracting Parties shall endeavour progressively and as soon as possible to put an end to the practice. So long as such forced or compulsory labour exists, this labour shall invariably be of an exceptional character, shall always receive adequate remuneration, and shall not involve the removal of the labourers from their usual place of residence.

(3) In all cases, the responsibility for any recourse to compulsory or forced labour shall rest with the competent central authorities of the territory concerned.

Article 6

Those of the High Contracting Parties whose laws do not at present make adequate provision for the punishment of infractions of laws and regulations enacted with a view to giving effect to the purposes of the present Convention undertake to adopt the necessary measures in order that severe penalties may be imposed in respect of such infractions.

Article 7

The High Contracting Parties undertake to communicate to each other and to the Secretary-General of the United Nations any laws and regulations which they may enact with a view to the application of the provisions of the present Convention.

Article 8

The High Contracting Parties agree that disputes arising between them relating to the interpretation or application of this Convention shall, if they cannot be settled by direct negotiation, be referred for decision to the International Court of Justice. In case either or both of the States Parties to such a dispute should not be parties to the Statute of the International Court of Justice, the dispute shall be referred, at the choice of the Parties and in accordance with the constitutional procedure of each State, either to the International Court of Justice or to a court of arbitration constituted in accordance with the Convention of 18 October, 1907,[1] for the Pacific

[1] 'Miscellaneous No. 6 (1908)', Cd. 4175.

Settlement of International Disputes, or to some other court of arbitration.

Article 9

At the time of signature or of ratification or of accession, any High Contracting Party may declare that its acceptance of the present Convention does not bind some or all of the territories placed under its sovereignty, jurisdiction, protection, suzerainty or tutelage in respect of all or any provisions of the Convention; it may subsequently accede separately on behalf of any one of them or in respect of any provision to which any one of them is not a party.

Article 10

In the event of a High Contracting Party wishing to denounce the present Convention, the denunciation shall be notified in writing to the Secretary-General of the United Nations, who will at once communicate a certified true copy of the notification to all the other High Contracting Parties, informing them of the date on which it was received.

The denunciation shall only have effect in regard to the notifying State, and one year after the notification has reached the Secretary-General of the United Nations.

Denunciation may also be made separately in respect of any territory placed under its sovereignty, jurisdiction, protection, suzerainty or tutelage.

Article 11

The present Convention, which will bear this day's date and of which the French and English texts are both authentic, will remain open for signature by the States Members of the League of Nations until 1 April, 1927.

The present Convention shall be open to accession by all States, including States which are not Members of the United Nations, to which the Secretary-General of the United Nations shall have communicated a certified copy of the Convention.

Accession shall be effected by the deposit of a formal instrument with the Secretary-General of the United Nations, who shall give notice thereof to all States Parties to the Convention and to all other States contemplated in the present article, informing them of the date on which each such instrument of accession was received in deposit.

Article 12

The present Convention will be ratified and the instruments of ratification shall be deposited in the office of the Secretary-General of the United

Nations. The Secretary-General will inform all the High Contracting Parties of such deposit.

The Convention will come into operation for each State on the date of the deposit of its ratification or of its accession.

PROTOCOL AMENDING THE SLAVERY CONVENTION[1]

The States Parties to the present Protocol,

Considering that under the Slavery Convention signed at Geneva on 25 September, 1926 (hereinafter called 'the Convention') the League of Nations was invested with certain duties and functions, and

Considering that it is expedient that these duties and functions should be continued by the United Nations,

Have agreed as follows:

Article I

The States Parties to the present Protocol undertake that as between themselves they will, in accordance with the provisions of the Protocol, attribute full legal force and effect to and duly apply the amendments to the Convention set forth in the annex to the Protocol.

Article II

1. The present Protocol shall be open for signature or acceptance by any of the States Parties to the Convention to which the Secretary-General has communicated for this purpose a copy of the Protocol.

2. States may become Parties to the present Protocol by:

(*a*) Signature without reservation as to acceptance;
(*b*) Signature with reservation as to acceptance, followed by acceptance;
(*c*) Acceptance.

3. Acceptance shall be effected by the deposit of a formal instrument with the Secretary-General of the United Nations.

Article III

1. The present Protocol shall come into force on the date on which two States shall have become Parties thereto, and shall thereafter come into force in respect of each State upon the date on which it becomes a Party to the Protocol.

2. The amendments set forth in the annex to the present Protocol shall come into force when twenty-three States shall have become Parties to the Protocol, and consequently any State becoming a Party to the Convention,

[1] *United Nations Treaty Series*, Vol. 182, p. 51.

after the amendments thereto have come into force, shall become a Party to the Convention as so amended.

Article IV

In accordance with paragraph 1 of Article 102 of the Charter of the United Nations and the regulations pursuant thereto adopted by the General Assembly, the Secretary-General of the United Nations is authorized to effect registration of the present Protocol and of the amendments made in the Convention by the Protocol on the respective dates of their entry into force and to publish the Protocol and the amended text of the Convention as soon as possible after registration.

Article V

The present Protocol, of which the Chinese, English, French, Russian and Spanish texts are equally authentic, shall be deposited in the archives of the United Nations Secretariat. The texts of the Convention to be amended in accordance with the annex being authentic in the English and French languages only, the English and French texts of the annex shall be equally authentic, and the Chinese, Russian and Spanish texts shall be translations. The Secretary-General shall prepare certified copies of the Protocol, including the annex, for communication to States Parties to the Convention, as well as to all other States Members of the United Nations. He shall likewise prepare for communication to States, including States not Members of the United Nations, upon the entry into force of the amendments as provided in Article III, certified copies of the Convention as so amended.

ANNEX

To the Protocol Amending the Slavery Convention Signed at Geneva on 25 September, 1926

In Article 7 'the Secretary-General of the United Nations' *shall be substituted for* 'the Secretary-General of the League of Nations'.

In Article 8 'the International Court of Justice' *shall be substituted for* 'the Permanent Court of International Justice', and 'the Statute of the International Court of Justice' *shall be substituted for* 'the Protocol of 16 December, 1920, relating to the Permanent Court of International Justice'.

In the first and second paragraphs of Article 10 'the United Nations' *shall be substituted for* 'the League of Nations'.

The last three paragraphs of Article 11 shall be *deleted* and the following *substituted*:

'The present Convention shall be open to accession by all States, including States which are not members of the United Nations, to which the Secretary-General of the United Nations shall have communicated a certified copy of the Convention.

'Accession shall be effected by the deposit of a formal instrument with the Secretary-General of the United Nations, who shall give notice thereof to all States Parties to the Convention and to all other States contemplated in the present article, informing them of the date on which each such instrument of accession was received in deposit.'

In Article 12 'the United Nations' *shall be substituted for* 'the League of Nations'.

VI. SUPPLEMENTARY CONVENTION ON THE ABOLITION OF SLAVERY, THE SLAVE TRADE, AND INSTITUTIONS AND PRACTICES SIMILAR TO SLAVERY, 1956

THE Supplementary Convention was adopted by a United Nations Conference on 7 September 1956 and entered into force on 30 April 1957. Over seventy-five States have become parties. For the text in various languages: *United Nations Treaty Series*, Vol. 266, p. 3; *U.K. Treaty Series*, No. 59 (1957), Cmnd. 257. See also *Multilateral Treaties in Respect of which the Secretary-General Performs Depositary Functions*, 1969, p. 315.

For further reference see Joyce Gutteridge, *International and Comparative Law Quarterly*, 6 (1957), p. 449; Schreiber, *Annuaire français de droit international*, 1956, p. 547.

TEXT

PREAMBLE

The States Parties to the present Convention,

Considering that freedom is the birthright of every human being;

Mindful that the peoples of the United Nations reaffirmed in the Charter their faith in the dignity and worth of the human person;

Considering that the Universal Declaration of Human Rights, proclaimed by the General Assembly of the United Nations as a common standard of achievement for all peoples and all nations, states that no one shall be held in slavery or servitude and that slavery and the slave trade shall be prohibited in all their forms;

Recognizing that, since the conclusion of the Slavery Convention signed at Geneva on 25 September, 1926, which was designed to secure the abolition of slavery and of the slave trade, further progress has been made towards this end;

Having regard to the Forced Labour Convention of 1930 and to subsequent action by the International Labour Organization in regard to forced or compulsory labour;

Being aware, however, that slavery, the slave trade and institutions and practices similar to slavery have not yet been eliminated in all parts of the world;

Having decided, therefore, that the Convention of 1926, which remains operative, should now be augmented by the conclusion of a supplementary convention designed to intensify national as well as international efforts towards the abolition of slavery, the slave trade and institutions and practices similar to slavery;

Have agreed as follows:

Section I. Institutions and Practices Similar to Slavery

Article 1

Each of the States Parties to this Convention shall take all practicable and necessary legislative and other measures to bring about progressively and as soon as possible the complete abolition or abandonment of the following institutions and practices, where they still exist and whether or not they are covered by the definition of slavery contained in Article 1 of the Slavery Convention signed at Geneva on 25 September, 1926:

(a) debt bondage, that is to say, the status or condition arising from a pledge by a debtor of his personal services or of those of a person under his control as security for a debt, if the value of those services as reasonably assessed is not applied towards the liquidation of the debt or the length and nature of those services are not respectively limited and defined;

(b) serfdom, that is to say, the condition or status of a tenant who is by law, custom or agreement bound to live and labour on land belonging to another person and to render some determinate service to such other person, whether for reward or not, and is not free to change his status;

(c) any institution or practice whereby:

   (i) a woman, without the right to refuse, is promised or given in marriage on payment of a consideration in money or in kind to her parents, guardian, family or any other person or group; or

   (ii) the husband of a woman, his family, or his clan, has the right to transfer her to another person for value received or otherwise; or

    (iii) a woman on the death of her husband is liable to be inherited
        by another person;

(*d*) any institution or practice whereby a child or young person under
the age of eighteen years is delivered by either or both of his natural
parents or by his guardian to another person, whether for reward
or not, with a view to the exploitation of the child or young person
or of his labour.

Article 2

With a view to bringing to an end the institutions and practices mentioned
in Article 1 (*c*) of this Convention, the States Parties undertake to prescribe,
where appropriate, suitable minimum ages of marriage, to encourage the
use of facilities whereby the consent of both parties to a marriage may be
freely expressed in the presence of a competent civil or religious authority,
and to encourage the registration of marriages.

SECTION II. THE SLAVE TRADE

Article 3

1. The act of conveying or attempting to convey slaves from one country
to another by whatever means of transport, or of being accessory thereto,
shall be a criminal offence under the laws of the States Parties to this
Convention and persons convicted thereof shall be liable to very severe
penalties.

2.—(*a*) The States Parties shall take all effective measures to prevent ships
and aircraft authorized to fly their flags from conveying slaves and to
punish persons guilty of such acts or of using national flags for that
purpose.

    (*b*) The States Parties shall take all effective measures to ensure that
their ports, airfields and coasts are not used for the conveyance of slaves.

3. The States Parties to this Convention shall exchange information in
order to ensure the practical co-ordination of the measures taken by them
in combating the slave trade and shall inform each other of every case of
the slave trade, and of every attempt to commit this criminal offence, which
comes to their notice.

Article 4

Any slave who takes refuge on board any vessel of a State Party to this
Convention shall *ipso facto* be free.

Section III. Slavery and Institutions and Practices Similar to Slavery

Article 5

In a country where the abolition or abandonment of slavery, or of the institutions or practices mentioned in Article 1 of this Convention, is not yet complete, the act of mutilating, branding or otherwise marking a slave or a person of servile status in order to indicate his status, or as a punishment, or for any other reason, or of being accessory thereto, shall be a criminal offence under the laws of the States Parties to this Convention and persons convicted thereof shall be liable to punishment.

Article 6

1. The act of enslaving another person or of inducing another person to give himself or a person dependent upon him into slavery, or of attempting these acts, or being accessory thereto, or being a party to a conspiracy to accomplish any such acts, shall be a criminal offence under the laws of the States Parties to this Convention and persons convicted thereof shall be liable to punishment.

2. Subject to the provisions of the introductory paragraph of Article 1 of this Convention, the provisions of paragraph 1 of the present Article shall also apply to the act of inducing another person to place himself or a person dependent upon him into the servile status resulting from any of the institutions or practices mentioned in Article 1, to any attempt to perform such acts, to being accessory thereto, and to being a party to a conspiracy to accomplish any such acts.

Section IV. Definitions

Article 7

For the purposes of the present Convention:

(*a*) 'slavery' means, as defined in the Slavery Convention of 1926, the status or condition of a person over whom any or all of the powers attaching to the right of ownership are exercised, and 'slave' means a person in such condition or status;

(*b*) 'a person of servile status' means a person in the condition or status resulting from any of the institutions or practices mentioned in Article 1 of this Convention;

(*c*) 'slave trade' means and includes all acts involved in the capture, acquisition or disposal of a person with intent to reduce him to slavery; all acts involved in the acquisition of a slave with a view to selling or exchanging him; all acts of disposal by sale or exchange of a person acquired with a view to being sold or exchanged; and, in general, every act of trade or transport in slaves by whatever means of conveyance.

SECTION V. CO-OPERATION BETWEEN STATES PARTIES AND COMMUNICATION OF INFORMATION

Article 8

1. The States Parties to this Convention undertake to co-operate with each other and with the United Nations to give effect to the foregoing provisions.

2. The Parties undertake to communicate to the Secretary-General of the United Nations copies of any laws, regulations and administrative measures enacted or put into effect to implement the provisions of this Convention.

3. The Secretary-General shall communicate the information received under paragraph 2 of this Article to the other Parties and to the Economic and Social Council as part of the documentation for any discussion which the Council might undertake with a view to making further recommendations for the abolition of slavery, the slave trade or the institutions and practices which are the subject of this Convention.

SECTION VI. FINAL CLAUSES

Article 9

No reservations may be made to this Convention.

Article 10

Any dispute between States Parties to this Convention relating to its interpretation or application, which is not settled by negotiation, shall be referred to the International Court of Justice at the request of any one of the parties to the dispute, unless the parties concerned agree on another mode of settlement.

Article 11

1. This Convention shall be open until 1 July, 1957, for signature by any State Member of the United Nations or of a specialized agency. It shall

be subject to ratification by the signatory States, and the instruments of ratification shall be deposited with the Secretary-General of the United Nations, who shall inform each signatory and acceding State.

2. After 1 July, 1957, this Convention shall be open for accession by any State Member of the United Nations or of a specialized agency, or by any other State to which an invitation to accede has been addressed by the General Assembly of the United Nations. Accession shall be effected by the deposit of a formal instrument with the Secretary-General of the United Nations, who shall inform each signatory and acceding State.

Article 12

1. This Convention shall apply to all non-self-governing, trust, colonial and other non-metropolitan territories for the international relations of which any State Party is responsible; the Party concerned shall, subject to the provisions of paragraph 2 of this Article, at the time of signature, ratification or accession declare the non-metropolitan territory or territories to which the Convention shall apply *ipso facto* as a result of such signature, ratification or accession.

2. In any case in which the previous consent of a non-metropolitan territory is required by the constitutional laws or practices of the Party or of the non-metropolitan territory, the Party concerned shall endeavour to secure the needed consent of the non-metropolitan territory within the period of twelve months from the date of signature of the Convention by the metropolitan State, and when such consent has been obtained the Party shall notify the Secretary-General. This Convention shall apply to the territory or territories named in such notification from the date of its receipt by the Secretary-General.

3. After the expiry of the twelve-month period mentioned in the preceding paragraph, the States Parties concerned shall inform the Secretary-General of the results of the consultations with those non-metropolitan territories for whose international relations they are responsible and whose consent to the application of this Convention may have been withheld.

Article 13

1. This Convention shall enter into force on the date on which two States have become Parties thereto.

2. It shall thereafter enter into force with respect to each State and territory on the date of deposit of the instrument of ratification or accession of that State or notification of application to that territory.

Article 14

1. The application of this Convention shall be divided into successive periods of three years, of which the first shall begin on the date of entry into force of the Convention in accordance with paragraph 1 of Article 13.

2. Any State Party may denounce this Convention by a notice addressed by that State to the Secretary-General not less than six months before the expiration of the current three-year period. The Secretary-General shall notify all other Parties of each such notice and the date of receipt thereof.

3. Denunciations shall take effect at the expiration of the current three-year period.

4. In cases where, in accordance with the provisions of Article 12, this Convention has become applicable to a non-metropolitan territory of a Party, that Party may at any time thereafter, with the consent of the territory concerned, give notice to the Secretary-General of the United Nations denouncing this Convention separately in respect of that territory. The denunciation shall take effect one year after the date of the receipt of such notice by the Secretary-General, who shall notify all other Parties of such notice and the date of the receipt thereof.

Article 15

This Convention, of which the Chinese, English, French, Russian and Spanish texts are equally authentic, shall be deposited in the archives of the United Nations Secretariat. The Secretary-General shall prepare a certified copy thereof for communication to States Parties to this Convention, as well as to all other States Members of the United Nations and of the specialized agencies.

In witness whereof the undersigned, being duly authorized thereto by their respective Governments, have signed this Convention on the date appearing opposite their respective signatures.

Done at the European Office of the United Nations at Geneva, this seventh day of September, one thousand nine hundred and fifty-six.

VII. CONVENTION RELATING TO THE STATUS OF REFUGEES, 1951

THE Convention was adopted by the U.N. Conference on the Status of Refugees and Stateless Persons at Geneva, 2–25 July 1951, and entered into force on 22 April 1954. Over fifty-six States have become parties. For the text in various languages: *United Nations Treaty Series*, Vol. 189, p. 137; *U.K. Treaty Series*, No. 39 (1954), Cmd. 9171. For the declarations and reservations made by certain States on becoming parties see *Multilateral Treaties in Respect of which the Secretary-General Performs Depositary Functions*, 1969, pp. 79–87.

For further reference see Weis, *British Year Book of International Law*, Vol. 30 (1953), p. 478; the same, *American Journal of International Law*, 48 (1954), p. 193; the same, *Journal de droit international*, 87 (1960), p. 928; Grahl-Madsen, *The Status of Refugees in International Law*, 2 vols., 1966.

The Convention which follows is confined to those who became refugees 'as a result of events occurring before 1 January 1951'. This limitation will be removed by the Protocol Relating to the Status of Refugees adopted by the General Assembly of the United Nations on 16 December 1966: see Weis, *British Year Book*, Vol. 42 (1967), p. 39 (text of Protocol at p. 67). The Protocol came into force on 4 October 1967, and not less than thirty-three States are parties. For the text in various languages: *United Nations Treaty Series*, Vol. [606, p. 267]; *U.K. Treaty Series*, No. 15 (1969), Cmnd. 3906. For the declarations and reservations made by certain States on becoming parties see *Multilateral Treaties in Respect of which the Secretary-General Performs Depositary Functions*, pp. 96–7. The text of the Protocol is not reproduced here: the changes it makes in Article 1A(2) of the Convention are indicated by square brackets.

TEXT

PREAMBLE

The High Contracting Parties,

Considering that the Charter of the United Nations and the Universal Declaration of Human Rights approved on 10 December 1948 by the General Assembly have affirmed the principle that human beings shall enjoy fundamental rights and freedoms without discrimination,

Considering that the United Nations has, on various occasions, manifested its profound concern for refugees and endeavoured to assure refugees the widest possible exercise of these fundamental rights and freedoms,

Considering that it is desirable to revise and consolidate previous international agreements relating to the status of refugees and to extend the scope of and the protection accorded by such instruments by means of a new agreement,

Considering that the grant of asylum may place unduly heavy burdens on certain countries, and that a satisfactory solution of a problem of which the United Nations has recognized the international scope and nature cannot therefore be achieved without international co-operation,

Expressing the wish that all States, recognizing the social and humanitarian nature of the problem of refugees, will do everything within their power to prevent this problem from becoming a cause of tension between States,

Noting that the United Nations High Commissioner for Refugees is charged with the task of supervising international conventions providing for the protection of refugees, and recognizing that the effective co-ordination of measures taken to deal with this problem will depend upon the co-operation of States with the High Commissioner,

Have agreed as follows:

CHAPTER I. GENERAL PROVISIONS

DEFINITION OF THE TERM 'REFUGEE'

Article 1

A. For the purposes of the present Convention, the term 'refugee' shall apply to any person who:

(1) Has been considered a refugee under the Arrangements of 12 May 1926 and 30 June 1928 or under the Conventions of 28 October 1933 and 10 February 1938, the Protocol of 14 September 1939 or the Constitution of the International Refugee Organization;

Decisions of non-eligibility taken by the International Refugee Organization during the period of its activities shall not prevent the status of refugee being accorded to persons who fulfil the conditions of paragraph 2 of this section;

(2) [As a result of events occurring before 1 January 1951 and] owing to well-founded fear of being persecuted for reasons of race, religion,

nationality, membership of a particular social group or political opinion, is outside the country of his nationality and is unable or, owing to such fear, is unwilling to avail himself of the protection of that country; or who, not having a nationality and being outside the country of his former habitual residence [as a result of such events], is unable or, owing to such fear, is unwilling to return to it.

In the case of a person who has more than one nationality, the term 'the country of his nationality' shall mean each of the countries of which he is a national, and a person shall not be deemed to be lacking the protection of the country of his nationality if, without any valid reason based on well-founded fear, he has not availed himself of the protection of one of the countries of which he is a national.

B. (1) For the purposes of this Convention, the words 'events occurring before 1 January 1951' in Article 1, Section A, shall be understood to mean either

(a) 'events occurring in Europe before 1 January 1951'; or
(b) 'events occurring in Europe or elsewhere before 1 January 1951';

and each Contracting State shall make a declaration at the time of signature, ratification or accession, specifying which of these meanings it applies for the purpose of its obligations under this Convention.

(2) Any Contracting State which has adopted alternative (a) may at any time extend its obligations by adopting alternative (b) by means of a notification addressed to the Secretary-General of the United Nations.

C. This Convention shall cease to apply to any person falling under the terms of section A if:

(1) He has voluntarily re-availed himself of the protection of the country of his nationality; or

(2) Having lost his nationality, he has voluntarily reacquired it; or

(3) He has acquired a new nationality, and enjoys the protection of the country of his new nationality; or

(4) He has voluntarily re-established himself in the country which he left or outside which he remained owing to fear of persecution; or

(5) He can no longer, because the circumstances in connexion with which he has been recognized as a refugee have ceased to exist, continue to refuse to avail himself of the protection of the country of his nationality;

Provided that this paragraph shall not apply to a refugee falling under section A (1) of this article who is able to invoke compelling reasons arising out of previous persecution for refusing to avail himself of the protection of the country of nationality;

(6) Being a person who has no nationality he is, because the circumstances in connexion with which he has been recognized as a refugee have ceased to exist, able to return to the country of his former habitual residence;

Provided that this paragraph shall not apply to a refugee falling under section A (1) of this article who is able to invoke compelling reasons arising out of previous persecution for refusing to return to the country of his former habitual residence.

D. This Convention shall not apply to persons who are at present receiving from organs or agencies of the United Nations other than the United Nations High Commissioner for Refugees protection or assistance.

When such protection or assistance has ceased for any reason, without the position of such persons being definitively settled in accordance with the relevant resolutions adopted by the General Assembly of the United Nations, these persons shall *ipso facto* be entitlted to the benefits of this Convention.

E. This Convention shall not apply to a person who is recognized by the competent authorities of the country in which he has taken residence as having the rights and obligations which are attached to the possession of the nationality of that country.

F. The provisions of this Convention shall not apply to any person with respect to whom there are serious reasons for considering that:

(a) He has committed a crime against peace, a war crime, or a crime against humanity, as defined in the international instruments drawn up to make provision in respect of such crimes;
(b) He has committed a serious non-political crime outside the country of refuge prior to his admission to that country as a refugee;
(c) He has been guilty of acts contrary to the purposes and principles of the United Nations.

General Obligations

Article 2

Every refugee has duties to the country in which he finds himself, which require in particular that he conform to its laws and regulations as well as to measures taken for the maintenance of public order.

Non-discrimination

Article 3

The Contracting States shall apply the provisions of this Convention to refugees without discrimination as to race, religion or country of origin.

Religion

Article 4

The Contracting States shall accord to refugees within their territories treatment at least as favourable as that accorded to their nationals with respect to freedom to practise their religion and freedom as regards the religious education of their children.

Rights Granted Apart from this Convention

Article 5

Nothing in this Convention shall be deemed to impair any rights and benefits granted by a Contracting State to refugees apart from this Convention.

The Term 'In the same circumstances'

Article 6

For the purpose of this Convention, the term 'in the same circumstances' implies that any requirements (including requirements as to length and conditions of sojourn or residence) which the particular individual would have to fulfil for the enjoyment of the right in question, if he were not a refugee, must be fulfilled by him, with the exception of requirements which by their nature a refugee is incapable of fulfilling.

Exemption from Reciprocity

Article 7

1. Except where this Convention contains more favourable provisions, a Contracting State shall accord to refugees the same treatment as is accorded to aliens generally.

2. After a period of three years' residence, all refugees shall enjoy exemption from legislative reciprocity in the territory of the Contracting States.

3. Each Contracting State shall continue to accord to refugees the rights and benefits to which they were already entitled, in the absence of reciprocity, at the date of entry into force of this Convention for that State.

4. The Contracting States shall consider favourably the possibility of according to refugees, in the absence of reciprocity, rights and benefits beyond those to which they are entitled according to paragraphs 2 and 3, and to extending exemption from reciprocity to refugees who do not fulfil the conditions provided for in paragraphs 2 and 3.

5. The provisions of paragraphs 2 and 3 apply both to the rights and benefits referred to in Articles 13, 18, 19, 21 and 22 of this Convention and to rights and benefits for which this Convention does not provide.

Exemption from Exceptional Measures
Article 8

With regard to exceptional measures which may be taken against the person, property or interests of nationals of a foreign State, the Contracting States shall not apply such measures to a refugee who is formally a national of the said State solely on account of such nationality. Contracting States which, under their legislation, are prevented from applying the general principle expressed in this article, shall, in appropriate cases, grant exemptions in favour of such refugees.

Provisional Measures
Article 9

Nothing in this Convention shall prevent a Contracting State, in time of war or other grave and exceptional circumstances, from taking provisionally measures which it considers to be essential to the national security in the case of a particular person, pending a determination by the Contracting State that that person is in fact a refugee and that the continuance of such measures is necessary in his case in the interests of national security.

Continuity of Residence
Article 10

1. Where a refugee has been forcibly displaced during the Second World War and removed to the territory of a Contracting State, and is resident there, the period of such enforced sojourn shall be considered to have been lawful residence within that territory.

2. Where a refugee has been forcibly displaced during the Second World War from the territory of a Contracting State and has, prior to the date of entry into force of this Convention, returned there for the purpose of taking up residence, the period of residence before and after such en-

forced displacement shall be regarded as one uninterrupted period for any purposes for which uninterrupted residence is required.

Refugee Seamen

Article 11

In the case of refugees regularly serving as crew members on board a ship flying the flag of a Contracting State, that State shall give sympathetic consideration to their establishment on its territory and the issue of travel documents to them or their temporary admission to its territory particularly with a view to facilitating their establishment in another country.

CHAPTER II. JURIDICAL STATUS

Personal Status

Article 12

1. The personal status of a refugee shall be governed by the law of the country of his domicile or, if he has no domicile, by the law of the country of his residence.
2. Rights previously acquired by a refugee and dependent on personal status, more particularly rights attaching to marriage, shall be respected by a Contracting State, subject to compliance, if this be necessary, with the formalities required by the law of that State, provided that the right in question is one which would have been recognized by the law of that State had he not become a refugee.

Movable and Immovable Property

Article 13

The Contracting States shall accord to a refugee treatment as favourable as possible and, in any event, not less favourable than that accorded to aliens generally in the same circumstances, as regards the acquisition of movable and immovable property and other rights pertaining thereto, and to leases and other contracts relating to movable and immovable property.

Artistic Rights and Industrial Property

Article 14

In respect of the protection of industrial property, such as inventions, designs or models, trade marks, trade names, and of rights in literary, artistic and scientific works, a refugee shall be accorded in the country in which he has his habitual residence the same protection as is accorded to nationals of that country. In the territory of any other Contracting State, he shall be accorded the same protection as is accorded in that territory to nationals of the country in which he has his habitual residence.

Right of Association

Article 15

As regards non-political and non-profit-making associations and trade unions the Contracting States shall accord to refugees lawfully staying in their territory the most favourable treatment accorded to nationals of a foreign country, in the same circumstances.

Access to Courts

Article 16

1. A refugee shall have free access to the courts of law on the territory of all Contracting States.

2. A refugee shall enjoy in the Contracting State in which he has his habitual residence the same treatment as a national in matters pertaining to access to the courts, including legal assistance and exemption from *cautio judicatum solvi.*

3. A refugee shall be accorded in the matters referred to in paragraph 2 in countries other than that in which he has his habitual residence the treatment granted to a national of the country of his habitual residence.

CHAPTER III. GAINFUL EMPLOYMENT

Wage-earning Employment

Article 17

1. The Contracting States shall accord to refugees lawfully staying in their territory the most favourable treatment accorded to nationals of a foreign country in the same circumstances, as regards the right to engage in wage-earning employment.

2. In any case, restrictive measures imposed on aliens or the employment of aliens for the protection of the national labour market shall not be applied to a refugee who was already exempt from them at the date of entry into force of this Convention for the Contracting State concerned, or who fulfils one of the following conditions:

(*a*) He has completed three years' residence in the country.

(*b*) He has a spouse possessing the nationality of the country of residence. A refugee may not invoke the benefit of this provision if he has abandoned his spouse;

(*c*) He has one or more children possessing the nationality of the country of residence.

3. The Contracting States shall give sympathetic consideration to assimilating the rights of all refugees with regard to wage-earning employment to those of nationals, and in particular of those refugees who have entered their territory pursuant to programmes of labour recruitment or under immigration schemes.

Self-employment
Article 18

The Contracting States shall accord to a refugee lawfully in their territory treatment as favourable as possible and, in any event, not less favourable than that accorded to aliens generally in the same circumstances, as regards the right to engage on his own account in agriculture, industry, handicrafts and commerce and to establish commercial and industrial companies.

Liberal Professions
Article 19

1. Each Contracting State shall accord to refugees lawfully staying in their territory who hold diplomas recognized by the competent authorities of that State, and who are desirous of practising a liberal profession, treatment as favourable as possible and, in any event, not less favourable than that accorded to aliens generally in the same circumstances.

2. The Contracting States shall use their best endeavours consistently with their laws and constitutions to secure the settlement of such refugees in the territories, other than the metropolitan territory, for whose international relations they are responsible.

CHAPTER IV. WELFARE
Rationing
Article 20

Where a rationing system exists, which applies to the population at large and regulates the general distribution of products in short supply, refugees shall be accorded the same treatment as nationals.

Housing
Article 21

As regards housing, the Contracting States, in so far as the matter is regulated by laws or regulations or is subject to the control of public authorities, shall accord to refugees lawfully staying in their territory treatment as favourable as possible and, in any event, not less favourable than that accorded to aliens generally in the same circumstances.

Public Education
Article 22

1. The Contracting States shall accord to refugees the same treatment as is accorded to nationals with respect to elementary education.

2. The Contracting States shall accord to refugees treatment as favourable as possible, and, in any event, not less favourable than that accorded to aliens generally in the same circumstances, with respect to education other than elementary education and, in particular, as regards access to studies, the recognition of foreign school certificates, diplomas and degrees, the remission of fees and charges and the award of scholarships.

Public Relief
Article 23

The Contracting States shall accord to refugees lawfully staying in their territory the same treatment with respect to public relief and assistance as is accorded to their nationals.

Labour Legislation and Social Security
Article 24

1. The Contracting States shall accord to refugees lawfully staying in their territory the same treatment as is accorded to nationals in respect of the following matters:

(*a*) In so far as such matters are governed by laws or regulations or are subject to the control of administrative authorities: remuneration, including family allowances where these form part of remuneration, hours of work, overtime arrangements, holidays with pay, restrictions on home work, minimum age of employment, apprenticeship and training, women's work and the work of young persons, and the enjoyment of the benefits of collective bargaining;

(*b*) Social security (legal provisions in respect of employment injury, occupational diseases, maternity, sickness, disability, old age, death, unemployment, family responsibilities and any other contingency which, according to national laws or regulations, is covered by a social security scheme), subject to the following limitations:

(i) There may be appropriate arrangements for the maintenance of acquired rights and rights in course of acquisition;

(ii) National laws or regulations of the country of residence may prescribe special arrangements concerning benefits or portions of benefits which are payable wholly out of public funds, and concerning allowances paid to persons who do not fulfil the contribution conditions prescribed for the award of a normal pension.

2. The right to compensation for the death of a refugee resulting from employment injury or from occupational disease shall not be affected by the fact that the residence of the beneficiary is outside the territory of the Contracting State.

3. The Contracting States shall extend to refugees the benefits of agreements concluded between them, or which may be concluded between them in the future, concerning the maintenance of acquired rights in the process of acquisition in regard to social security, subject only to the conditions which apply to nationals of the States signatory to the agreements in question.

4. The Contracting States will give sympathetic consideration to extending to refugees so far as possible the benefits of similar agreements which may at any time be in force between such Contracting States and non-contracting States.

CHAPTER V. ADMINISTRATIVE MEASURES

Administrative Assistance

Article 25

1. When the exercise of a right by a refugee would normally require the assistance of authorities of a foreign country to whom he cannot have recourse, the Contracting States in whose territory he is residing shall arrange that such assistance be afforded to him by their own authorities or by an international authority.

2. The authority or authorities mentioned in paragraph 1 shall deliver or cause to be delivered under their supervision to refugees such documents or certifications as would normally be delivered to aliens by or through their national authorities.

3. Documents or certifications so delivered shall stand in the stead of the official instruments delivered to aliens by or through their national authorities, and shall be given credence in the absence of proof to the contrary.

4. Subject to such exceptional treatment as may be granted to indigent persons, fees may be charged for the services mentioned herein, but such fees shall be moderate and commensurate with those charged to nationals for similar services.

5. The provisions of this article shall be without prejudice to articles 27 and 28.

Freedom of Movement
Article 26

Each Contracting State shall accord to refugees lawfully in its territory the right to choose their place of residence and to move freely within its territory, subject to any regulations applicable to aliens generally in the same circumstances.

Identity Papers
Article 27

The Contracting States shall issue identity papers to any refugee in their territory who does not possess a valid travel document.

Travel Documents
Article 28

1. The Contracting States shall issue to refugees lawfully staying in their territory travel documents for the purpose of travel outside their territory, unless compelling reasons of national security or public order otherwise require, and the provisions of the Schedule to this Convention shall apply with respect to such documents. The Contracting States may issue such a travel document to any other refugee in their territory; they shall in particular give sympathetic consideration to the issue of such a travel document to refugees in their territory who are unable to obtain a travel document from the country of their lawful residence.

2. Travel documents issued to refugees under previous international agreements by parties thereto shall be recognized and treated by the Contracting States in the same way as if they had been issued pursuant to this article.

Fiscal Charges

Article 29

1. The Contracting States shall not impose upon refugees duties, charges or taxes, of any description whatsoever, other or higher than those which are or may be levied on their nationals in similar situations.

2. Nothing in the above paragraph shall prevent the application to refugees of the laws and regulations concerning charges in respect of the issue to aliens of administrative documents including identity papers.

Transfer of Assets

Article 30

1. A Contracting State shall, in conformity with its laws and regulations, permit refugees to transfer assets which they have brought into its territory, to another country where they have been admitted for the purposes of resettlement.

2. A Contracting State shall give sympathetic consideration to the application of refugees for permission to transfer assets wherever they may be and which are necessary for their resettlement in another country to which they have been admitted.

Refugees Unlawfully in the Country of Refuge

Article 31

1. The Contracting States shall not impose penalties, on account of their illegal entry or presence, on refugees who, coming directly from a territory where their life or freedom was threatened in the sense of Article 1, enter or are present in their territory without authorization, provided they present themselves without delay to the authorities and show good cause for their illegal entry or presence.

2. The Contracting States shall not apply to the movements of such refugees restrictions other than those which are necessary and such restrictions shall only be applied until their status in the country is regularized or they obtain admission into another country. The Contracting States shall allow such refugees a reasonable period and all the necessary facilities to obtain admission into another country.

Expulsion

Article 32

1. The Contracting States shall not expel a refugee lawfully in their territory save on grounds of national security or public order.

2. The expulsion of such a refugee shall be only in pursuance of a decision reached in accordance with due process of law. Except where compelling reasons of national security otherwise require, the refugee shall be allowed to submit evidence to clear himself, and to appeal to and be represented for the purpose before competent authority or a person or persons specially designated by the competent authority.

3. The Contracting States shall allow such a refugee a reasonable period within which to seek legal admission into another country. The Contracting States reserve the right to apply during that period such internal measures as they may deem necessary.

Prohibition of Expulsion or Return ('Refoulement')

Article 33

1. No Contracting State shall expel or return ('refouler') a refugee in any manner whatsoever to the frontiers of territories where his life or freedom would be threatened on account of his race, religion, nationality, membership of a particular social group or political opinion.
2. The benefit of the present provision may not, however, be claimed by a refugee whom there are reasonable grounds for regarding as a danger to the security of the country in which he is, or who, having been convicted by a final judgment of a particularly serious crime, constitutes a danger to the community of that country.

Naturalization

Article 34

The Contracting States shall as far as possible facilitate the assimilation and naturalization of refugees. They shall in particular make every effort to expedite naturalization proceedings and to reduce as far as possible the charges and costs of such proceedings.

Chapter VI. Executory and Transitory Provisions

Co-operation of the National Authorities with the United Nations

Article 35

1. The Contracting States undertake to co-operate with the Office of the United Nations High Commissioner for Refugees, or any other agency of

the United Nations which may succeed it, in the exercise of its functions, and shall in particular facilitate its duty of supervising the application of the provisions of this Convention.

2. In order to enable the Office of the High Commissioner or any other agency of the United Nations which may succeed it, to make reports to the competent organs of the United Nations, the Contracting States undertake to provide them in the appropriate form with information and statistical data requested concerning:

(a) The condition of refugees,
(b) The implementation of this Convention, and
(c) Laws, regulations and decrees which are, or may hereafter be, in force relating to refugees.

Information on National Legislation

Article 36

The Contracting States shall communicate to the Secretary-General of the United Nations the laws and regulations which they may adopt to ensure the application of this Convention.

Relation to Previous Conventions

Article 37

Without prejudice to Article 28, paragraph 2, of this Convention, this Convention replaces, as between parties to it, the Arrangements of 5 July 1922, 31 May 1924, 12 May 1926, 30 June 1928 and 30 July 1935, the Conventions of 28 October 1933 and 10 February 1938, the Protocol of 14 September 1939 and the Agreement of 15 October 1946.

CHAPTER VII. FINAL CLAUSES

Settlement of Disputes

Article 38

Any dispute between parties to this Convention relating to its interpretation or application, which cannot be settled by other means, shall be referred to the International Court of Justice at the request of any one of the parties to the dispute.

Signature, Ratification and Accession

Article 39

1. This Convention shall be opened for signature at Geneva on 28 July 1951 and shall thereafter be deposited with the Secretary-General of the

United Nations. It shall be open for signature at the European Office of the United Nations from 28 July to 31 August 1951 and shall be re-opened for signature at the Headquarters of the United Nations from 17 September 1951 to 31 December 1952.

2. This Convention shall be open for signature on behalf of all States Members of the United Nations, and also on behalf of any other State invited to attend the Conference of Plenipotentiaries on the Status of Refugees and Stateless Persons or to which an invitation to sign will have been addressed by the General Assembly. It shall be ratified and the instruments of ratification shall be deposited with the Secretary-General of the United Nations.

3. This Convention shall be open from 28 July 1951 for accession by the States referred to in paragraph 2 of this article. Accession shall be effected by the deposit of an instrument of accession with the Secretary-General of the United Nations.

Territorial Application Clause
Article 40

1. Any State may, at the time of signature, ratification or accession, declare that this Convention shall extend to all or any of the territories for the international relations of which it is responsible. Such a declaration shall take effect when the Convention enters into force for the State concerned.

2. At any time thereafter any such extension shall be made by notification addressed to the Secretary-General of the United Nations and shall take effect as from the ninetieth day after the day of receipt by the Secretary-General of the United Nations of this notification, or as from the date of entry into force of the Convention for the State concerned, whichever is the later.

3. With respect to those territories to which this Convention is not extended at the time of signature, ratification or accession, each State concerned shall consider the possibility of taking the necessary steps in order to extend the application of this Convention to such territories, subject, where necessary for constitutional reasons, to the consent of the Governments of such territories.

Federal Clause
Article 41

In the case of a Federal or non-unitary State, the following provisions shall apply:

(a) With respect to those articles of this Convention that come within the legislative jurisdiction of the federal legislative authority, the obligations of the Federal Government shall to this extent be the same as those of Parties which are not Federal States;

(b) With respect to those articles of this Convention that come within the legislative jurisdiction of constituent states, provinces or cantons which are not, under the constitutional system of the federation, bound to take legislative action, the Federal Government shall bring such articles with a favourable recommendation to the notice of the appropriate authorities of states, provinces or cantons at the earliest possible moment.

(c) A Federal State Party to this Convention shall, at the request of any other Contracting State transmitted through the Secretary-General of the United Nations, supply a statement of the law and practice of the Federation and its constituent units in regard to any particular provision of the Convention showing the extent to which effect has been given to that provision by legislative or other action.

Reservations

Article 42

1. At the time of signature, ratification or accession, any State may make reservations to articles of the Convention other than to articles 1, 3, 4, 16 (1), 33, 36–46 inclusive.

2. Any State making a reservation in accordance with paragraph 1 of this Article may at any time withdraw the reservation by a communication to that effect addressed to the Secretary-General of the United Nations.

Entry into Force

Article 43

1. This Convention shall come into force on the ninetieth day following the day of deposit of the sixth instrument of ratification or accession.

2. For each State ratifying or acceding to the Convention after the deposit of the sixth instrument of ratification or accession, the Convention shall enter into force on the ninetieth day following the date of deposit by such State of its instrument of ratification or accession.

Denunciation

Article 44

1. Any Contracting State may denounce this Convention at any time by a notification addressed to the Secretary-General of the United Nations.

6+B.D.H.R.

2. Such denunciation shall take effect for the Contracting State concerned one year from the date upon which it is received by the Secretary-General of the United Nations.

3. Any State which has made a declaration or notification under Article 40 may, at any time thereafter, by a notification to the Secretary-General of the United Nations, declare that the Convention shall cease to extend to such territory one year after the date of receipt of the notification by the Secretary-General.

Revision

Article 45

1. Any Contracting State may request revision of this Convention at any time by a notification addressed to the Secretary-General of the United Nations.

2. The General Assembly of the United Nations shall recommend the steps, if any, to be taken in respect of such request.

Notifications by the Secretary-General of the United Nations

Article 46

The Secretary-General of the United Nations shall inform all Members of the United Nations and non-member States referred to in Article 39:

- (*a*) Of declarations and notifications in accordance with section B of Article 1;
- (*b*) Of signatures, ratifications and accessions in accordance with Article 39;
- (*c*) Of declarations and notifications in accordance with Article 40;
- (*d*) Of reservations and withdrawals in accordance with Article 42;
- (*e*) Of the date on which this Convention will come into force in accordance with Article 43;
- (*f*) Of denunciations and notifications in accordance with Article 44;
- (*g*) Of requests for revision in accordance with Article 45.

In faith whereof the undersigned, duly authorized, have signed this Convention on behalf of their respective Governments;

Done at Geneva, this twenty-eighth day of July, one thousand nine hundred and fifty-one, in a single copy, of which the English and French texts are equally authentic and which shall remain deposited in the archives of the United Nations, and certified true copies of which shall be delivered to all Members of the United Nations and to the non-member States referred to in Article 39.

VIII. CONVENTION RELATING TO THE STATUS OF STATELESS PERSONS, 1954

STATELESSNESS has become a very serious problem, and measures to reduce its incidence have not readily found favour with States (see the Convention set out below). The persistence of statelessness has necessitated the creation of a regime which will give stateless persons a stable basis of life in host countries. The Convention concerning the status of stateless persons was adopted by a U.N. Conference, New York, 13–23 September 1954, and came into force on 6 June 1960. The text in several languages appears in *United Nations Treaty Series*, Vol. 360, p. 117; and *U.K. Treaty Series*, Misc. No. 41, 1960, Cmnd. 1098. Twenty-two States signed the Convention, and over twenty have become parties. For declarations and reservations by parties see U.N., *Multilateral Treaties in Respect of which the Secretary-General Performs Depositary Functions*, 1969, pp. 88–93.

For further reference see United Nations, Dept. of Social Affairs, *A Study of Statelessness*, 1949, Sales No. 1949, XIV.2; Weis, *International and Comparative Law Quarterly*, 10 (1961), p. 255.

TEXT

PREAMBLE

The High Contracting Parties,

Considering that the Charter of the United Nations and the Universal Declaration of Human Rights approved on 10 December 1948 by the General Assembly of the United Nations have affirmed the principle that human beings shall enjoy fundamental rights and freedoms without discrimination,

Considering that the United Nations has, on various occasions, manifested its profound concern for stateless persons and endeavoured to assure stateless persons the widest possible exercise of these fundamental rights and freedoms,

Considering that only those stateless persons who are also refugees are covered by the Convention relating to the Status of Refugees of 28 July

1951, and that there are many stateless persons who are not covered by that Convention,

Considering that it is desirable to regulate and improve the status of stateless persons by an international agreement.

Have agreed as follows:

CHAPTER I. GENERAL PROVISIONS

Definition of the term 'Stateless Person'

Article 1

1. For the purpose of this Convention, the term 'stateless person' means a person who is not considered as a national by any State under the operation of its law.

2. This Convention shall not apply:

(i) To persons who are at present receiving from organs or agencies of the United Nations other than the United Nations High Commissioner for Refugees protection or assistance so long as they are receiving such protection or assistance;

(ii) To persons who are recognized by the competent authorities of the country in which they have taken residence as having the rights and obligations which are attached to the possession of the nationality of that country;

(iii) To persons with respect to whom there are serious reasons for considering that:

(a) They have committed a crime against peace, a war crime, or a crime against humanity, as defined in the international instruments drawn up to make provisions in respect of such crimes;

(b) They have committed a serious non-political crime outside the country of their residence prior to their admission to that country;

(c) They have been guilty of acts contrary to the purposes and principles of the United Nations.

General obligations

Article 2

Every stateless person has duties to the country in which he finds himself, which require in particular that he conform to its laws and regulations as well as to measures taken for the maintenance of public order.

Non-discrimination

Article 3

The Contracting States shall apply the provisions of this Convention to stateless persons without discrimination as to race, religion or country of origin.

Religion

Article 4

The Contracting States shall accord to stateless persons within their territories treatment at least as favourable as that accorded to their nationals with respect to freedom to practise their religion and freedom as regards the religious education of their children.

Rights Granted Apart from this Convention

Article 5

Nothing in this Convention shall be deemed to impair any rights and benefits granted by a Contracting State to stateless persons apart from this Convention.

The Term 'In the same Circumstances'

Article 6

For the purpose of this Convention, the term 'in the same circumstances' implies that any requirements (including requirements as to length and conditions of sojourn or residence) which the particular individual would have to fulfil for the enjoyment of the right in question, if he were not a stateless person, must be fulfilled by him, with the exception of requirements which by their nature a stateless person is incapable of fulfilling.

Exemption from Reciprocity

Article 7

1. Except where this Convention contains more favourable provisions, a Contracting State shall accord to stateless persons the same treatment as is accorded to aliens generally.

2. After a period of three years' residence, all stateless persons shall enjoy exemption from legislative reciprocity in the territory of the Contracting States.

3. Each Contracting State shall continue to accord to stateless persons the rights and benefits to which they were already entitled, in the absence of reciprocity, at the date of entry into force of this Convention for that State.

4. The Contracting States shall consider favourably the possibility of according to stateless persons, in the absence of reciprocity, rights and benefits beyond those to which they are entitled according to paragraphs 2 and 3, and to extending exemption from reciprocity to stateless persons who do not fulfil the conditions provided for in paragraphs 2 and 3.

5. The provisions of paragraphs 2 and 3 apply both to the rights and benefits referred to in articles 13, 18, 19, 21 and 22 of this Convention and to rights and benefits for which this Convention does not provide.

Exemption from Exceptional Measures
Article 8

With regard to exceptional measures which may be taken against the person, property or interests of nationals or former nationals of a foreign State, the Contracting States shall not apply such measures to a stateless person solely on account of his having previously possessed the nationality of the foreign State in question. Contracting States which, under their legislation, are prevented from applying the general principle expressed in this article shall, in appropriate cases, grant exemptions in favour of such stateless persons.

Provisional Measures
Article 9

Nothing in this Convention shall prevent a Contracting State, in time of war or other grave and exceptional circumstances, from taking provisionally measures which it considers to be essential to the national security in the case of a particular person, pending a determination by the Contracting State that that person is in fact a stateless person and that the continuance of such measures is necessary in his case in the interests of national security.

Continuity of Residence
Article 10

1. Where a stateless person has been forcibly displaced during the Second World War and removed to the territory of a Contracting State, and is resident there, the period of such enforced sojourn shall be considered to have been lawful residence within that territory.

2. Where a stateless person has been forcibly displaced during the Second World War from the territory of a Contracting State and has, prior to the date of entry into force of this Convention, returned there for the purpose of taking up residence, the period of residence before and after such

enforced displacement shall be regarded as one uninterrupted period for any purpose for which uninterrupted residence is required.

Stateless Seamen

Article 11

In the case of stateless persons regularly serving as crew members on board a ship flying the flag of a Contracting State, that State shall give sympathetic consideration to their establishment on its territory and the issue of travel documents to them or their temporary admission to its territory particularly with a view to facilitating their establishment in another country.

CHAPTER II. JURIDICAL STATUS

Personal Status

Article 12

1. The personal status of a stateless person shall be governed by the law of the country of his domicile or, if he has no domicile, by the law of the country of his residence.

2. Rights previously acquired by a stateless person and dependent on personal status, more particularly rights attaching to marriage, shall be respected by a Contracting State, subject to compliance, if this be necessary, with the formalities required by the law of that State, provided that the right in question is one which would have been recognized by the law of that State had he not become stateless.

Movable and Immovable Property

Article 13

The Contracting States shall accord to a stateless person treatment as favourable as possible and, in any event, not less favourable than that accorded to aliens generally in the same circumstances, as regards the acquisition of movable and immovable property and other rights pertaining thereto, and to leases and other contracts relating to movable and immovable property.

Artistic Rights and Industrial Property

Article 14

In respect of the protection of industrial property, such as inventions, designs or models, trade marks, trade names, and of rights in literary, artistic and scientific works, a stateless person shall be accorded in the country in which he has his habitual residence the same protection as is accorded to nationals of that country. In the territory of any other Contracting State, he shall be accorded the same protection as is accorded in that territory to nationals of the country in which he has his habitual residence.

Right of Association
Article 15

As regards non-political and non-profit-making associations and trade unions the Contracting States shall accord to stateless persons lawfully staying in their territory treatment as favourable as possible, and in any event, not less favourable than that accorded to aliens generally in the same circumstances.

Access to Courts
Article 16

1. A stateless person shall have free access to the Courts of Law on the territory of all Contracting States.

2. A stateless person shall enjoy in the Contracting State in which he has his habitual residence the same treatment as a national in matters pertaining to access to the Courts, including legal assistance and exemption from *cautio judicatum solvi*.

3. A stateless person shall be accorded in the matters referred to in paragraph 2 in countries other than that in which he has his habitual residence the treatment granted to a national of the country of his habitual residence.

CHAPTER III. GAINFUL EMPLOYMENT

Wage-earning Employment
Article 17

1. The Contracting States shall accord to stateless persons lawfully staying in their territory treatment as favourable as possible and, in any event, not less favourable than that accorded to aliens generally in the same circumstances, as regards the right to engage in wage-earning employment.

2. The Contracting States shall give sympathetic consideration to

assimilating the rights of all stateless persons with regard to wage-earning employment to those of nationals, and in particular of those stateless persons who have entered their territory pursuant to programmes of labour recruitment or under immigration schemes.

Self-employment
Article 18

The Contracting States shall accord to a stateless person lawfully in their territory treatment as favourable as possible and, in any event, not less favourable than that accorded to aliens generally in the same circumstances, as regards the right to engage on his own account in agriculture, industry, handicrafts and commerce and to establish commercial and industrial companies.

Liberal Professions
Article 19

Each Contracting State shall accord to stateless persons lawfully staying in their territory who hold diplomas recognized by the competent authorities of that State, and who are desirous of practising a liberal profession, treatment as favourable as possible and, in any event, not less favourable than that accorded to aliens generally in the same circumstances.

CHAPTER IV. WELFARE

Rationing
Article 20

Where a rationing system exists, which applies to the population at large and regulates the general distribution of products in short supply, stateless persons shall be accorded the same treatment as nationals.

Housing
Article 21

As regards housing, the Contracting States, in so far as the matter is regulated by laws or regulations or is subject to the control of public authorities, shall accord to stateless persons lawfully staying in their territory treatment as favourable as possible and, in any event, not less favourable than that accorded to aliens generally in the same circumstances.

6*

Public Education

Article 22

1. The Contracting States shall accord to stateless persons the same treatment as is accorded to nationals with respect to elementary education.
2. The Contracting States shall accord to stateless persons treatment as favourable as possible and, in any event, not less favourable than that accorded to aliens generally in the same circumstances, with respect to education other than elementary education and, in particular, as regards access to studies, the recognition of foreign school certificates, diplomas and degrees, the remission of fees and charges and the award of scholarships.

Public Relief

Article 23

The Contracting States shall accord to stateless persons lawfully staying in their territory the same treatment with respect to public relief and assistance as is accorded to their nationals.

Labour Legislation and Social Security

Article 24

1. The Contracting States shall accord to stateless persons lawfully staying in their territory the same treatment as is accorded to nationals in respect of the following matters:

(*a*) In so far as such matters are governed by laws or regulations or are subject to the control of administrative authorities: remuneration, including family allowances where these form part of remuneration, hours of work, overtime arrangements, holidays with pay, restrictions on home work, minimum age of employment, apprenticeship and training, women's work and the work of young persons, and the enjoyment of the benefits of collective bargaining;

(*b*) Social security (legal provisions in respect of employment injury, occupational diseases, maternity, sickness, disability, old age, death, unemployment, family responsibilities and any other contingency which, according to national laws or regulations, is covered by a social security scheme), subject to the following limitations:

(i) There may be appropriate arrangements for the maintenance of acquired rights and rights in course of acquisition;

(ii) National laws or regulations of the country of residence may prescribe special arrangements concerning benefits or portions of benefits which are payable wholly out of public funds, and concerning allowances paid to persons who do not fulfil the contribution conditions prescribed for the award of a normal pension.

2. The right to compensation for the death of a stateless person resulting from employment injury or from occupational disease shall not be affected by the fact that the residence of the beneficiary is outside the territory of the Contracting State.

3. The Contracting States shall extend to stateless persons the benefits of agreements concluded between them, or which may be concluded between them in the future, concerning the maintenance of acquired rights and rights in the process of acquisition in regard to social security, subject only to the conditions which apply to nationals of the States signatory to the agreements in question.

4. The Contracting States will give sympathetic consideration to extending to stateless persons so far as possible the benefits of similar agreements which may at any time be in force between such Contracting States and non-contracting States.

CHAPTER V. ADMINISTRATIVE MEASURES

Administrative Assistance

Article 25

1. When the exercise of a right by a stateless person would normally require the assistance of authorities of a foreign country to whom he cannot have recourse, the Contracting State in whose territory he is residing shall arrange that such assistance be afforded to him by their own authorities.

2. The authority or authorities mentioned in paragraph 1 shall deliver or cause to be delivered under their supervision to stateless persons such documents or certifications as would normally be delivered to aliens by or through their national authorities.

3. Documents or certifications so delivered shall stand in the stead of the official instruments delivered to aliens by or through their national authorities, and shall be given credence in the absence of proof to the contrary.

4. Subject to such exceptional treatment as may be granted to indigent persons, fees may be charged for the services mentioned herein, but such

fees shall be moderate and commensurate with those charged to nationals for similar services.

5. The provisions of this article shall be without prejudice to articles 27 and 28.

Freedom of Movement
Article 26

Each Contracting State shall accord to stateless persons lawfully in its territory the right to choose their place of residence and to move freely within its territory, subject to any regulations applicable to aliens generally in the same circumstances.

Identity Papers
Article 27

The Contracting States shall issue identity papers to any stateless person in their territory who does not possess a valid travel document.

Travel Documents
Article 28

The Contracting States shall issue to stateless persons lawfully staying in their territory travel documents for the purpose of travel outside their territory, unless compelling reasons of national security or public order otherwise require, and the provisions of the Schedule to this Convention shall apply with respect to such documents. The Contracting States may issue such a travel document to any other stateless person in their territory; they shall in particulr give sympathetic consideration to the issue of such a travel document to stateless persons in their territory who are unable to obtain a travel document from the country of their lawful residence.

Fiscal Charges
Article 29

1. The Contracting States shall not impose upon stateless persons duties, charges or taxes, of any description whatsoever, other or higher than those which are or may be levied on their nationals in similar situations.

2. Nothing in the above paragraph shall prevent the application to stateless persons of the laws and regulations concerning charges in respect of the issue to aliens of administrative documents including identity papers.

Transfer of Assets

Article 30

1. A Contracting State shall, in conformity with its laws and regulations, permit stateless persons to transfer assets which they have brought into its territory, to another country where they have been admitted for the purpose of resettlement.

2. A Contracting State shall give sympathetic consideration to the application of stateless persons for permission to transfer assets wherever they may be and which are necessary for their resettlement in another country to which they have been admitted.

Expulsion

Article 31

1. The Contracting States shall not expel a stateless person lawfully in their territory save on grounds of national security or public order.

2. The expulsion of such a stateless person shall be only in pursuance of a decision reached in accordance with due process of law. Except where compelling reasons of national security otherwise require, the stateless person shall be allowed to submit evidence to clear himself, and to appeal to and be represented for the purpose before competent authority or a person or persons specially designated by the competent authority.

3. The Contracting States shall allow such a stateless person a reasonable period within which to seek legal admission into another country. The Contracting States reserve the right to apply during that period such internal measures as they may deem necessary.

Naturalization

Article 32

The Contracting States shall as far as possible facilitate the assimilation and naturalization of stateless persons. They shall in particular make every effort to expedite naturalization proceedings and to reduce as far as possible the charges and costs of such proceedings.

CHAPTER VI. FINAL CLAUSES

Information on National Legislation

Article 33

The Contracting States shall communicate to the Secretary-General of the United Nations the laws and regulations which they may adopt to ensure the application of this Convention.

Settlement of Disputes
Article 34

Any dispute between parties to this Convention relating to its interpretation or application, which cannot be settled by other means, shall be referred to the International Court of Justice at the request of any one of the parties to the dispute.

Signature, Ratification and Accession
Article 35

1. This Convention shall be open for signature at the Headquarters of the United Nations until 31 December 1955.

2. It shall be open for signature on behalf of:
   (*a*) Any State Member of the United Nations;
   (*b*) Any other State invited to attend the United Nations Conference on the Status of Stateless Persons; and
   (*c*) Any State to which an invitation to sign or to accede may be addressed by the General Assembly of the United Nations.

3. It shall be ratified and the instruments of ratification shall be deposited with the Secretary-General of the United Nations.

4. It shall be open for accession by the States referred to in paragraph 2 of this article. Accession shall be effected by the deposit of an instrument of accession with the Secretary-General of the United Nations.

Territorial Application Clause
Article 36

1. Any State may, at the time of signature, ratification or accession, declare that this Convention shall extend to all or any of the territories for the international relations of which it is responsible. Such a declaration shall take effect when the Convention enters into force for the State concerned.

2. At any time thereafter any such extension shall be made by notification addressed to the Secretary-General of the United Nations and shall take effect as from the ninetieth day after the day of receipt by the Secretary-General of the United Nations of this notification, or as from the date of entry into force of the Convention for the State concerned, whichever is the later.

3. With respect to those territories to which this Convention is not extended at the time of signature, ratification or accession, each State concerned shall consider the possibility of taking the necessary steps in order to extend the application of this Convention to such territories, subject, where necessary for constitutional reasons, to the consent of the Governments of such territories.

Federal Clause

Article 37

In the case of a Federal or non-unitary State, the following provisions shall apply:

(*a*) With respect to those articles of this Convention that come within the legislative jurisdiction of the federal legislative authority, the obligations of the Federal Government shall to this extent be the same as those of Parties which are not Federal States;

(*b*) With respect to those articles of this Convention that come within the legislative jurisdiction of constituent States, provinces or cantons which are not, under the constitutional system of the Federation, bound to take legislative action, the Federal Government shall bring such articles with a favourable recommendation to the notice of the appropriate authorities of States, provinces or cantons at the earliest possible moment.

(*c*) A Federal State Party to this Convention shall, at the request of any other Contracting State transmitted through the Secretary-General of the United Nations, supply a statement of the law and practice of the Federation and its constituent units in regard to any particular provision of the Convention showing the extent to which effect has been given to that provision by legislative or other action.

Reservations

Article 38

1. At the time of signature, ratification or accession, any State may make reservations to articles of the Convention other than to articles 1, 3, 4, 16 (1) and 33 to 42 inclusive.

2. Any State making a reservation in accordance with paragraph 1 of this article may at any time withdraw the reservation by a communication to that effect addressed to the Secretary-General of the United Nations.

Entry into Force

Article 39

1. This Convention shall come into force on the ninetieth day following the day of deposit of the sixth instrument of ratification or accession.

2. For each State ratifying or acceding to the Convention after the deposit of the sixth instrument of ratification or accession, the Convention shall enter into force on the ninetieth day following the date of deposit by such State of its instrument of ratification or accession.

Denunciation

Article 40

1. Any Contracting State may denounce this Convention at any time by a notification addressed to the Secretary-General of the United Nations.

2. Such denunciation shall take effect for the Contracting State concerned one year from the date upon which it is received by the Secretary-General of the United Nations.

3. Any State which has made a declaration or notification under Article 36 may, at any time thereafter, by a notification to the Secretary-General of the United Nations, declare that the Convention shall cease to extend to such territory one year after the date of receipt of the notification by the Secretary-General.

Revision

Article 41

1. Any Contracting State may request revision of this Convention at any time by a notification addressed to the Secretary-General of the United Nations.

2. The General Assembly of the United Nations shall recommend the steps, if any, to be taken in respect of such request.

Notifications by the Secretary-General of the United Nations

Article 42

The Secretary-General of the United Nations shall inform all Members of the United Nations and non-Member States referred to in article 35:

(*a*) Of signatures, ratifications and accessions in accordance with article 35;

(*b*) Of declarations and notifications in accordance with article 36;

(*c*) Of reservations and withdrawals in accordance with article 38;

(*d*) Of the date on which this Convention will come into force in accordance with article 39;

(*e*) Of denunciations and notifications in accordance with article 40;

(*f*) Of requests for revision in accordance with article 41.

In faith whereof the undersigned, duly authorized, have signed this Convention on behalf of their respective Governments.

Done at New York, this twenty-eighth day of September, one thousand nine hundred and fifty-four, in a single copy, of which the English, French and Spanish texts are equally authentic and which shall remain deposited in the archives of the United Nations, and certified true copies of which shall be delivered to all Members of the United Nations and to the non-Member States referred to in article 35.

SCHEDULE

Paragraph 1

1. The travel document referred to in article 28 of this Convention shall indicate that the holder is a stateless person under the terms of the Convention of 28 September 1954.

2. The document shall be made out in at least two languages, one of which shall be English or French.

3. The Contracting States will consider the desirability of adopting the model travel document attached hereto.

Paragraph 2

Subject to the regulations obtaining in the country of issue, children may be included in the travel document of a parent or, in exceptional circumstances, of another adult.

Paragraph 3

The fees charged for issue of the document shall not exceed the lowest scale of charges for national passports.

Paragraph 4

Save in special or exceptional cases, the document shall be made valid for the largest possible number of countries.

Paragraph 5

The document shall have a validity of not less than three months and not more than two years.

Paragraph 6

1. The renewal or extension of the validity of the document is a matter for the authority which issued it, so long as the holder has not established lawful residence in another territory and resides lawfully in the territory of the said authority. The issue of a new document is, under the same conditions, a matter for the authority which issued the former document.

2. Diplomatic or consular authorities may be authorized to extend, for a period not exceeding six months, the validity of travel documents issued by their Governments.

3. The Contracting States shall give sympathetic consideration to renewing or extending the validity of travel documents or issuing new documents to stateless persons no longer lawfully resident in their territory who are unable to obtain a travel document from the country of their lawful residence.

Paragraph 7

The Contracting States shall recognize the validity of the documents issued in accordance with the provisions of article 28 of this Convention.

Paragraph 8

The competent authorities of the country to which the stateless person desires to proceed shall, if they are prepared to admit him and if a visa is required, affix a visa on the document of which he is the holder.

Paragraph 9

1. The Contracting States undertake to issue transit visas to stateless persons who have obtained visas for a territory of final destination.

2. The issue of such visas may be refused on grounds which would justify refusal of a visa to any alien.

Paragraph 10

The fees for the issue of exit, entry or transit visas shall not exceed the lowest scale of charges for visas on foreign passports.

Paragraph 11

When a stateless person has lawfully taken up residence in the territory of another Contracting State, the responsibility for the issue of a new document, under the terms and conditions of article 28 shall be that of the competent authority of that territory, to which the stateless person shall be entitled to apply.

Paragraph 12

The authority issuing a new document shall withdraw the old document and shall return it to the country of issue if it is stated in the document that it should be so returned; otherwise it shall withdraw and cancel the document.

Paragraph 13

1. A travel document issued in accordance with article 28 of this Convention shall, unless it contains a statement to the contrary, entitle the holder to re-enter the territory of the issuing State at any time during the period of its validity. In any case the period during which the holder may return to the country issuing the document shall not be less than three months, except when the country to which the stateless person proposes to travel does not insist on the travel document according the right of re-entry.

2. Subject to the provisions of the preceding sub-paragraph, a Contracting State may require the holder of the document to comply with such formalities as may be prescribed in regard to exit from or return to its territory.

Paragraph 14

Subject only to the terms of paragraph 13, the provisions of this Schedule in no way affect the laws and regulations governing the conditions of admission to, transit through, residence and establishment in, and departure from, the territories of the Contracting States.

Paragraph 15

Neither the issue of the document nor the entries made thereon determine or affect the status of the holder, particularly as regards nationality.

Paragraph 16

The issue of the document does not in any way entitle the holder to the protection of the diplomatic or consular authorities of the country of issue, and does not *ipso facto* confer on these authorities a right of protection.

[Model Travel Document omitted.]

IX. CONVENTION ON THE REDUCTION OF STATELESSNESS, 1961

THIS is not yet in force. The Convention was adopted by the U.N. Conference on the Elimination or Reduction of Future Statelessness, 24 March–18 April 1959 and 15–28 August 1961. The official source of the text is U.N. Document A/CONF. 9/15, 1961. So far there have been five signatures and only one ratification.

For further reference see U.N., *Multilateral Treaties in Respect of which the Secretary-General Performs Depositary Functions*, 1969, pp. 94–5.

TEXT

The Contracting States,

Acting in pursuance of resolution 896 (IX), adopted by the General Assembly of the United Nations on 4 December 1954,

Considering it desirable to reduce statelessness by international agreement,

Have agreed as follows:

Article 1

1. A contracting State shall grant its nationality to a person born in its territory who would otherwise be stateless. Such nationality shall be granted:

(*a*) At birth, by operation of law, or

(*b*) Upon an application being lodged with the appropriate authority, by or on behalf of the person concerned, in the manner prescribed by the national law. Subject to the provisions of paragraph 2 of this Article, no such application may be rejected.

A contracting State which provides for the grant of its nationality in accordance with sub-paragraph (*b*) of this paragraph may also provide for the grant of its nationality by operation of law at such age and subject to such conditions as may be prescribed by the national law.

2. A contracting State may make the grant of its nationality in accordance with sub-paragraph (*b*) of paragraph 1 of this article subject to one or more of the following conditions:

(*a*) That the application is lodged during a period, fixed by the contracting State, beginning not later than at the age of eighteen years and ending not earlier than at the age of twenty-one years, so, however, that the person concerned shall be allowed at least one year during which he may himself make the application without having to obtain legal authorization to do so;

(*b*) That the person concerned has habitually resided in the territory of the contracting State for such period as may be fixed by that State, not exceeding five years immediately preceding the lodging of the application nor ten years in all;

(*c*) That the person concerned has neither been convicted of an offence against national security nor has been sentenced to imprisonment for a term of five years or more on a criminal charge;

(*d*) That the person concerned has always been stateless.

3. Notwithstanding the provisions of paragraphs 1 (*b*) and 2 of this Article, a child born in wedlock in the territory of a contracting State, whose mother has the nationality of that State, shall acquire at birth that nationality if it otherwise would be stateless.

4. A contracting State shall grant its nationality to a person who would otherwise be stateless and who is unable to acquire the nationality of the contracting State in whose territory he was born because he has passed the age for lodging his application or has not fulfilled the required residence conditions, if the nationality of one of his parents at the time of the person's birth was that of the contracting State first above mentioned. If his parents did not possess the same nationality at the time of his birth, the question whether the nationality of the person concerned should follow that of the father or that of the mother shall be determined by the national law of such contracting State. If application for such nationality is required, the application shall be made to the appropriate authority by or on behalf of the applicant in the manner prescribed by the national law. Subject to the provisions of paragraph 5 of this article, such application shall not be refused.

5. The contracting State may make the grant of its nationality in accordance with the provisions of paragraph 4 of this article subject to one or more of the following conditions:

(*a*) That the application is lodged before the applicant reaches an age, being not less than twenty-three years, fixed by the contracting State;

(b) That the person concerned has habitually resided in the territory of the contracting State for such period immediately preceding the lodging of the application, not exceeding three years, as may be fixed by that State;

(c) That the person concerned has always been stateless.

Article 2

A foundling found in the territory of a contracting State shall, in the absence of proof to the contrary, be considered to have been born within that territory of parents possessing the nationality of that State.

Article 3

For the purpose of determining the obligations of contracting States under this convention, birth on a ship or in an aircraft shall be deemed to have taken place in the territory of the State whose flag the ship flies or in the territory of the State in which the aircraft is registered, as the case may be.

Article 4

1. A contracting State shall grant its nationality to a person, not born in the territory of a contracting State, who would otherwise be stateless, if the nationality of one of his parents at the time of the person's birth was that of that State. If his parents did not possess the same nationality at the time of his birth, the question whether the nationality of the person concerned should follow that of the father or that of the mother shall be determined by the national law of such contracting State. Nationality granted in accordance with the provisions of this paragraph shall be granted:

(a) At birth, by operation of law, or

(b) Upon an application being lodged with the appropriate authority, by or on behalf of the person concerned, in the manner prescribed by the national law. Subject to the provisions of paragraph 2 of this article, no such application may be rejected.

2. A contracting State may make the grant of its nationality in accordance with the provisions of paragraph 1 of this article subject to one or more of the following conditions:

(a) That the application is lodged before the applicant reaches an age, being not less than twenty-three years, fixed by the contracting State;

(b) That the person concerned has habitually resided in the territory of the contracting State for such period immediately preceding the lodging of the application, not exceeding three years, as may be fixed by that State;

(c) That the person concerned has not been convicted of an offence against national security;

(d) That the person concerned has always been stateless.

Article 5

1. If the law of a contracting State entails loss of nationality as a consequence of any change in the personal status of a person such as marriage, termination of marriage, legitimation, recognition or adoption, such loss shall be conditional upon possession or acquisition of another nationality.

2. If, under the law of a contracting State, a child born out of wedlock loses the nationality of that State in consequence of a recognition of affiliation, he shall be given an opportunity to recover that nationality by written application to the appropriate authority, and the conditions governing such application shall not be more rigorous than those laid down in paragraph 2 of article 1 of this Convention.

Article 6

If the law of a contracting State provides for loss of its nationality by a person's spouse or children as a consequence of that person losing or being deprived of that nationality, such loss shall be conditional upon their possession or acquisition of another nationality.

Article 7

1. (a) If the law of a contracting State permits renunciation of nationality, such renunciation shall not result in loss of nationality unless the person concerned possesses or acquires another nationality.

(b) The provisions of sub-paragraph (a) of this paragraph shall not apply where their application would be inconsistent with the principles stated in articles 13 and 14 of the Universal Declaration of Human Rights approved on 10 December 1948 by the General Assembly of the United Nations.

2. A national of a contracting State who seeks naturalization in a foreign country shall not lose his nationality unless he acquires or has been accorded assurance of acquiring the nationality of that foreign country.

3. Subject to the provisions of paragraphs 4 and 5 of this article, a national of a contracting State shall not lose his nationality, so as to become stateless, on the ground of departure, residence abroad, failure to register or on any similar ground.

4. A naturalized person may lose his nationality on account of residence abroad for a period, not less than seven consecutive years, specified by the law of the contracting State concerned if he fails to declare to the appropriate authority his intention to retain his nationality.

5. In the case of a national of a contracting State, born outside its territory, the law of that State may make the retention of its nationality after the expiry of one year from his attaining his majority conditional upon residence at that time in the territory of the State or registration with the appropriate authority.

6. Except in the circumstances mentioned in this Article, a person shall not lose the nationality of a contracting State, if such loss would render him stateless, notwithstanding that such loss is not expressly prohibited by any other provision of this convention.

Article 8

1. A contracting State shall not deprive a person of its nationality if such deprivation would render him stateless.

2. Notwithstanding the provisions of paragraph 1 of this article, a person may be deprived of the nationality of a contracting State:

(a) In the circumstances in which, under paragraphs 4 and 5 of article 7, it is permissible that a person should lose his nationality;

(b) Where the nationality has been obtained by misrepresentation or fraud.

3. Notwithstanding the provisions of paragraph 1 of this article, a contracting State may retain the right to deprive a person of his nationality, if at the time of signature, ratification or accession it specifies its retention of such right on one or more of the following grounds, being grounds existing in its national law at that time:

(a) That, inconsistently with his duty of loyalty to the contracting State, the person

(i) has, in disregard of an express prohibition by the contracting State rendered or continued to render services to, or received or continued to receive emoluments from, another State, or

    (ii) has conducted himself in a manner seriously prejudicial to the vital interests of the State;

  (b) That the person has taken an oath, or made a formal declaration, of allegiance to another State, or given definite evidence of his determination to repudiate his allegiance to the contracting State.

4. A contracting State shall not exercise a power of deprivation permitted by paragraphs 2 or 3 of this article except in accordance with law, which shall provide for the person concerned the right to a fair hearing by a court or other independent body.

Article 9

A contracting State may not deprive any person or group of persons of their nationality on racial, ethnic, religious or political grounds.

Article 10

1. Every treaty between contracting States providing for the transfer of territory shall include provisions designed to secure that no person shall become stateless as a result of the transfer. A contracting State shall use its best endeavours to secure that any such treaty made by it with a state which is not a party to this convention includes such provisions.

2. In the absence of such provisions a contracting State to which territory is transferred or which otherwise acquires territory shall confer its nationality on such persons as would otherwise become stateless as a result of the transfer or acquisition.

Article 11

The contracting States shall promote the establishment within the framework of the United Nations, as soon as may be after the deposit of the sixth instrument of ratification or accession, of a body to which a person claiming the benefit of this convention may apply for the examination of his claim and for assistance in presenting it to the appropriate authority.

Article 12

1. In relation to a contracting State which does not, in accordance with the provisions of paragraph 1 of article 1 or of article 4 of this Convention, grant its nationality at birth by operation of law, the provisions of paragraph 1 of article 4, as the case may be, shall apply to persons born before as well as to persons born after the entry into force of this convention.

2. The provisions of paragraph 4 of article 1 of this convention shall

apply to persons born before as well as to persons born after its entry into force.

3. The provisions of article 2 of this convention shall apply only to foundlings found in the territory of a contracting State after the entry into force of the convention for that State.

Article 13

This convention shall not be construed as affecting any provisions more conducive to the reduction of statelessness which may be contained in the law of any contracting State now or hereafter in force, or may be contained in any other convention, treaty or agreement now or hereafter in force between two or more contracting States.

Article 14

Any dispute between contracting States concerning the interpretation or application of this convention which cannot be settled by other means shall be submitted to the International Court of Justice at the request of any one of the parties to the dispute.

Article 15

1. This convention shall apply to all non–self–governing, trust, colonial and other non–metropolitan territories for the international relations of which any contracting State is responsible; the contracting State concerned shall, subject to the provisions of paragraph 2 of this article, at the time of signature, ratification or accession, declare the non–metropolitan territory or territories to which the convention shall apply *ipso facto* as a result of such signature, ratification or accession.

2. In any case in which, for the purpose of nationality, a non–metropolitan territory is not treated as one with the metropolitan territory, or in any case in which the previous consent of a non–metropolitan territory is required by the constitutional laws or practices of the contracting State or of the non–metropolitan territory for the application of the convention to that territory, that contracting State shall endeavour to secure the needed consent of the non–metropolitan territory within the period of twelve months from the date of signature of the convention by that contracting State, and when such consent has been obtained the contracting State shall notify the Secretary–General of the United Nations. This convention shall apply to the territory or territories named in such notification from the date of its receipt by the Secretary–General.

3. After the expiry of the twelve-month period mentioned in paragraph 2 of this article, the contracting States concerned shall inform the Secretary-General of the results of the consultations with those non-metropolitan territories for whose international relations they are responsible and whose consent to the application of this convention may have been withheld.

Article 16

1. This convention shall be open for signature at the Headquarters of the United Nations from 30 August 1961 to 31 May 1962.

2. This convention shall be open for signature on behalf of:

(*a*) Any State Member of the United Nations;

(*b*) Any other State invited to attend the United Nations Conference on the Elimination or Reduction of Future Statelessness;

(*c*) Any State to which an invitation to sign or to accede may be addressed by the General Assembly of the United Nations.

3. This convention shall be ratified and the instruments of ratification shall be deposited with the Secretary-General of the United Nations.

4. This convention shall be open for accession by the States referred to in paragraph 2 of this article. Accession shall be effected by the deposit of an instrument of accession with the Secretary-General of the United Nations.

Article 17

1. At the time of signature, ratification or accession any State may make a reservation in respect of articles 11, 14 or 15.

2. No other reservations to this convention shall be admissible.

Article 18

1. This convention shall enter into force two years after the date of the deposit of the sixth instrument of ratification or accession.

2. For each State ratifying or acceding to this convention after the deposit of the sixth instrument of ratification or accession, it shall enter into force on the ninetieth day after the deposit by such State of its instrument of ratification or accession or on the date on which this convention enters into force in accordance with the provisions of paragraph 1 of this article, whichever is the later.

Article 19

1. Any contracting State may denounce this convention at any time by a written notification addressed to the Secretary-General of the United Nations. Such denunciation shall take effect for the contracting State concerned one year after the date of its receipt by the Secretary-General.

2. In cases where, in accordance with the provisions of article 15, this convention has become applicable to a non-metropolitan territory of a contracting State, that State may at any time thereafter, with the consent of the territory concerned, give notice to the Secretary-General of the United Nations denouncing this convention separately in respect of that territory. The denunciation shall take effect one year after the date of the receipt of such notice by the Secretary-General, who shall notify all other contracting States of such notice and the date or receipt thereof.

Article 20

1. The Secretary-General of the United Nations shall notify all Members of the United Nations and the non-member States referred to in article 16 of the following particulars:

    (*a*) Signatures, ratifications and accessions under article 16;
    (*b*) Reservations under article 17;
    (*c*) The date upon which this convention enters into force in pursuance of article 18;
    (*d*) Denunciations under article 19.

2. The Secretary-General of the United Nations shall, after the deposit of the sixth instrument of ratification or accession at the latest, bring to the attention of the General Assembly the question of the establishment, in accordance with article 11, of such a body as therein mentioned.

Article 21

This convention shall be registered by the Secretary-General of the United Nations on the date of its entry into force.

In witness whereof the undersigned Plenipotentiaries have signed this Convention.

Done at New York, this thirtieth day of August, one thousand nine hundred and sixty-one, in a single copy, of which the Chinese, English, French, Russian and Spanish texts are equally authentic and which shall be deposited in the archives of the United Nations, and certified copies of which shall be delivered by the Secretary-General of the United Nations to all Members of the United Nations and to the non-member States referred to in article 16 of this Convention.

X. CONVENTION ON THE POLITICAL RIGHTS OF WOMEN, 1953

THE Convention was opened for signature on 31 March 1953 and entered into force on 7 July 1954. Not less than sixty-five States have become parties. For the text in various languages: *United Nations Treaty Series*, Vol. 193, p. 135; *U.K. Treaty Series*, No. 101 (1967), Cmnd. 3449. For the declarations and reservations made by certain States on becoming parties see *Multilateral Treaties in Respect of which the Secretary-General Performs Depositary Functions*, 1969, pp. 298–302.

See, further, *Convention on the Political Rights of Women: History and Commentary*, ST/SOA/27, U.N. Sales No. 1955, IV, 17; and *Yearbook on Human Rights*, 1948, p. 439 (Bogota Convention).

TEXT

The Contracting Parties,

Desiring to implement the principle of equality of rights for men and women contained in the Charter of the United Nations,

Recognizing that everyone has the right to take part in the government of his country, directly or indirectly through freely chosen representatives, and has the right to equal access to public service in his country, and desiring to equalize the status of men and women in the enjoyment and exercise of political rights, in accordance with the provisions of the Charter of the United Nations and of the Universal Declaration of Human Rights.

Having resolved to conclude a Convention for this purpose,

Hereby agree as hereinafter provided:

Article I

Women shall be entitled to vote in all elections on equal terms with men, without any discrimination.

Article II

Women shall be eligible for election to all publicly elected bodies, established by national law, on equal terms with men, without any discrimination.

Article III

Women shall be entitled to hold public office and to exercise all public functions, established by national law, on equal terms with men, without any discrimination.

Article IV

1. This Convention shall be open for signature on behalf of any Member of the United Nations and also on behalf of any other State to which an invitation has been addressed by the General Assembly.

2. This Convention shall be ratified and the instruments of ratification shall be deposited with the Secretary-General of the United Nations.

Article V

1. This Convention shall be open for accession to all States referred to in paragraph 1 of Article IV.

2. Accession shall be effected by the deposit of an instrument of accession with the Secretary-General of the United Nations.

Article VI

1. This Convention shall come into force on the ninetieth day following the date of deposit of the sixth instrument of ratification or accession.

2. For each State ratifying or acceding to the Convention after the deposit of the sixth instrument of ratification or accession the Convention shall enter into force on the ninetieth day after deposit by such State of its instrument of ratification or accession.

Article VII

In the event that any State submits a reservation to any of the articles of this Convention at the time of signature, ratification or accession, the Secretary-General shall communicate the text of the reservation to all States which are or may become parties to this Convention. Any State which objects to the reservation may, within a period of ninety days from the date of the said communication (or upon the date of its becoming a party to the Convention), notify the Secretary-General that it does not accept it. In such case, the Convention shall not enter into force as between such State and the State making the reservation.

Article VIII

1. Any State may denounce this Convention by written notification to the Secretary-General of the United Nations. Denunciation shall take effect one year after the date of receipt of the notification by the Secretary-General.

2. This Convention shall cease to be in force as from the date when the denunciation which reduces the number of parties to less than six becomes effective.

Article IX

Any dispute which may arise between any two or more Contracting States concerning the interpretation or application of this Convention which is not settled by negotiation, shall at the request of any one of the parties to the dispute be referred to the International Court of Justice for decision unless they agree to another mode of settlement.

Article X

The Secretary-General of the United Nations shall notify all Members of the United Nations and the non-member States contemplated in paragraph 1 of article IV of this Convention of the following:

(*a*) Signatures and instruments of ratifications received in accordance with article IV;

(*b*) Instruments of accession received in accordance with article V;

(*c*) The date upon which this Convention enters into force in accordance with article VI;

(*d*) Communications and notifications received in accordance with article VII;

(*e*) Notifications of denunciation received in accordance with paragraph 1 of article VIII;

(*f*) Abrogation in accordance with paragraph 2 of article VIII.

Article XI

1. This Convention, of which the Chinese, English, French, Russian and Spanish texts shall be equally authentic, shall be deposited in the archives of the United Nations.

2. The Secretary-General of the United Nations shall transmit a certified copy to all Members of the United Nations and to the non-member States contemplated in paragraph 1 of article IV.

In faith whereof the undersigned, being duly authorized thereto by their respective Governments, have signed the present Convention, opened for signature at New York, on the thirty-first day of March, one thousand nine hundred and fifty-three.

XI. DECLARATION ON ELIMINATION OF DISCRIMINATION AGAINST WOMEN, 1967

THE text which follows was adopted unanimously by the United Nations General Assembly on 7 November 1967. The declaration was prepared by the Commission on Status of Women and the Third Committee of the General Assembly.

See, further, *Yearbook of the United Nations*, 1967, p. 520.

Reference should also be made to the I.L.O. Convention Concerning Equal Remuneration for Men and Women Workers for Work of Equal Value, below.

TEXT

The General Assembly,

Considering that the peoples of the United Nations have, in the Charter, reaffirmed their faith in fundamental human rights, in the dignity and worth of the human person and in the equal rights of men and women,

Considering that the Universal Declaration on Human Rights asserts the principle of non-discrimination and proclaims that all human beings are born free and equal in dignity and rights and that everyone is entitled to all the rights and freedoms set forth therein, without distinction of any kind, including any distinction as to sex,

Taking into account the resolutions, declarations, conventions and recommendations of the United Nations and the specialized agencies designed to eliminate all forms of discrimination and to promote equal rights for men and women,

Concerned that, despite the Charter of the United Nations, the Universal Declaration of Human Rights, the International Covenants on Human Rights and other instruments of the United Nations and the specialized agencies and despite the progress made in the matter of equality of rights, there continues to exist considerable discrimination against women,

Considering that discrimination against women is incompatible with human dignity and with the welfare of the family and of society, prevents their participation, on equal terms with men, in the political, social, economic and cultural life of their countries and is an obstacle to the full development of the potentialities of women in the service of their countries and of humanity,

Bearing in mind the great contribution made by women to social, political, economic and cultural life and the part they play in the family and particularly in the rearing of children,

Convinced that the full and complete development of a country, the welfare of the world and the cause of peace require the maximum participation of women as well as men in all fields,

Considering that it is necessary to ensure the universal recognition in law and in fact of the principle of equality of men and women,

Solemnly proclaims this Declaration:

Article 1

Discrimination against women, denying or limiting as it does their equality of rights with men, is fundamentally unjust and constitutes an offence against human dignity.

Article 2

All appropriate measures shall be taken to abolish existing laws, customs, regulations and practices which are discriminatory against women, and to establish adequate legal protection for equal rights of men and women, in particular:

(a) The principle of equality of rights shall be embodied in the constitution or otherwise guaranteed by law;

(b) The international instruments of the United Nations and the specialized agencies relating to the elimination of discrimination against women shall be ratified or acceded to and fully implemented as soon as practicable.

Article 3

All appropriate measures shall be taken to educate public opinion and to direct national aspirations towards the eradication of prejudice and the abolition of customary and all other practices which are based on the idea of the inferiority of women.

Article 4

All appropriate measures shall be taken to ensure to women on equal terms with men, without any discrimination:

(a) The right to vote in all elections and be eligible for election to all publicly elected bodies;

(*b*) The right to vote in all public referenda;

(*c*) The right to hold public office and to exercise all public functions. Such rights shall be guaranteed by legislation.

Article 5

Women shall have the same rights as men to acquire, change or retain their nationality. Marriage to an alien shall not automatically affect the nationality of the wife either by rendering her stateless or by forcing upon her the nationality of her husband.

Article 6

1. Without prejudice to the safeguarding of the unity and the harmony of the family, which remains the basic unit of any society, all appropriate measures, particularly legislative measures, shall be taken to ensure to women, married or unmarried, equal rights with men in the field of civil law, and in particular:

(*a*) The right to acquire, administer, enjoy, dispose of and inherit property, including property acquired during marriage;

(*b*) The right to equality in legal capacity and the exercise thereof;

(*c*) The same rights as men with regard to the law on the movement of persons.

2. All appropriate measures shall be taken to ensure the principle of equality of status of the husband and wife, and in particular:

(*a*) Women shall have the same right as men to free choice of a spouse and to enter into marriage only with their free and full consent;

(*b*) Women shall have equal rights with men during marriage and at its dissolution. In all cases the interest of the children shall be paramount;

(*c*) Parents shall have equal rights and duties in matters relating to their children. In all cases the interest of the children shall be paramount.

3. Child marriage and the betrothal of young girls before puberty shall be prohibited, and effective action, including legislation, shall be taken to specify a minimum age for marriage and to make the registration of marriages in an official registry compulsory.

Article 7

All provisions of penal codes which constitute discrimination against women shall be repealed.

Article 8

All appropriate measures, including legislation, shall be taken to combat all forms of traffic in women and exploitation of prostitution of women.

Article 9

All appropriate measures shall be taken to ensure to girls and women, married or unmarried, equal rights with men in education at all levels, and in particular:

(*a*) Equal conditions of access to, and study in, educational institutions of all types, including universities and vocational, technical and professional schools;

(*b*) The same choice of curricula, the same examinations, teaching staff with qualifications of the same standard, and school premises and equipment of the same quality, whether the institutions are co-educational or not;

(*c*) Equal opportunities to benefit from scholarships and other study grants;

(*d*) Equal opportunities for access to programmes of continuing education, including adult literacy programmes;

(*e*) Access to educational information to help in ensuring the health and well-being of families.

Article 10

1. All appropriate measures shall be taken to ensure to women, married or unmarried, equal rights with men in the field of economic and social life, and in particular:

(*a*) The right, without discrimination on grounds of marital status or any other grounds, to receive vocational training, to work, to free choice of profession and employment, and to professional and vocational advancement;

(*b*) The right to equal remuneration with men and to equality of treatment in respect of work of equal value;

(*c*) The right to leave with pay, retirement privileges and provision for security in respect to unemployment, sickness, old age or other incapacity to work;

(*d*) The right to receive family allowances on equal terms with men.

2. In order to prevent discrimination against women on account of marriage or maternity and to ensure their effective right to work, measures shall be taken to prevent their dismissal in the event of marriage or

maternity and to provide paid maternity leave, with the guarantee of returning to former employment, and to provide the necessary social services, including child-care facilities.

3. Measures taken to protect women in certain types of work, for reasons inherent in their physical nature, shall not be regarded as discriminatory.

Article 11

1. The principle of equality of rights of men and women demands implementation in all States in accordance with the principles of the Charter of the United Nations and of the Universal Declaration of Human Rights.

2. Governments, non-governmental organizations and individuals are urged, therefore, to do all in their power to promote the implementation of the principles contained in this Declaration.

XII. DECLARATION OF THE RIGHTS
OF THE CHILD, 1959

THE United Nations General Assembly adopted the Declaration unanimously on 20 November 1959. The rights of the child are also the subject of Article 24 of the Covenant on Civil and Political Rights, below.

See, further, *Yearbook of the United Nations*, 1959, p. 198; 1963, pp. 317–19, 322–3.

TEXT

PREAMBLE

Whereas the peoples of the United Nations have, in the Charter, re-affirmed their faith in fundamental human rights and in the dignity and worth of the human person, and have determined to promote social progress and better standards of life in larger freedom,

Whereas the United Nations has, in the Universal Declaration of Human Rights, proclaimed that everyone is entitled to all the rights and freedoms set forth therein, without distinction of any kind, such as race, colour, sex, language, religion, political or other opinion, national or social origin, property, birth or other status,

Whereas the child by reason of his physical and mental immaturity, needs special safeguards and care, including appropriate legal protection, before as well as after birth,

Whereas the need for such special safeguards has been stated in the Geneva Declaration of the Rights of the Child of 1924, and recognized in the Universal Declaration of Human Rights and in the statutes of specialized agencies and international organizations concerned with the welfare of children,

Whereas mankind owes to the child the best it has to give,

Now therefore,

The General Assembly

Proclaims this Declaration of the Rights of the Child to the end that he may have a happy childhood and enjoy for his own good and for the good of society the rights and freedoms herein set forth, and calls upon parents, upon men and women as individuals, and upon voluntary organizations, local authorities and national Governments to recognize these rights and strive for their observance by legislative and other measures progressively taken in accordance with the following principles:

Principle 1

The child shall enjoy all the rights set forth in this Declaration. Every child, without any exception whatsoever, shall be entitled to these rights, without distinction or discrimination on account of race, colour, sex, language, religion, political or other opinion, national or social origin, property, birth or other status, whether of himself or of his family.

Principle 2

The child shall enjoy special protection, and shall be given opportunities and facilities, by law and by other means, to enable him to develop physically, mentally, morally, spiritually and socially in a healthy and normal manner and in conditions of freedom and dignity. In the enactment of laws for this purpose, the best interests of the child shall be the paramount considerations.

Principle 3

The child shall be entitled from his birth to a name and a nationality.

Principle 4

The child shall enjoy the benefits of social security. He shall be entitled to grow and develop in health; to this end, special care and protection shall be provided both to him and to his mother, including adequate pre-natal and post-natal care. The child shall have the right to adequate nutrition, housing, recreation and medical services.

Principle 5

The child who is physically, mentally or socially handicapped shall be given the special treatment, education and care required by his particular condition.

Principle 6

The child, for the full and harmonious development of his personality, needs love and understanding. He shall, wherever possible, grow up in the care and under the responsibility of his parents, and, in any case, in an atmosphere of affection and of moral and material security; a child of tender years shall not, save in exceptional circumstances, be separated from his mother. Society and the public authorities shall have the duty to extend particular care to children without a family and to those without adequate means of support. Payment of State and other assistance towards the maintenance of children of large families is desirable.

Principle 7

The child is entitled to receive education, which shall be free and compulsory, at least in the elementary stages. He shall be given an education which will promote his general culture, and enable him, on a basis of equal opportunity, to develop his abilities, his individual judgement, and his sense of moral and social responsibility, and to become a useful member of society.

The best interests of the child shall be the guiding principle of those responsible for his education and guidance; that responsibility lies in the first place with his parents.

The child shall have full opportunity for play and recreation, which should be directed to the same purposes as education; society and the public authorities shall endeavour to promote the enjoyment of this right.

Principle 8

The child shall in all circumstances be among the first to receive protection and relief.

Principle 9

The child shall be protected against all forms of neglect, cruelty and exploitation. He shall not be the subject of traffic, in any form.

The child shall not be admitted to employment before an appropriate minimum age; he shall in no case be caused or permitted to engage in any occupation or employment which would prejudice his health or education, or interfere with his physical, mental or moral development.

Principle 10

The child shall be protected from practices which may foster racial, religious and any other form of discrimination. He shall be brought up in a spirit of understanding, tolerance, friendship among peoples, peace and universal brotherhood, and in full consciousness that his energy and talents should be devoted to the service of his fellow men.

XIII. DRAFT CONVENTION ON THE ELIMINATION OF ALL FORMS OF RELIGIOUS INTOLERANCE, 1967

THIS was prepared by the Human Rights Commission and the Social Committee of the Economic and Social Council. The draft Convention was transmitted to the General Assembly by the Economic and Social Council in 1967. The General Assembly has not yet completed consideration of the draft Convention. The project at present bears the title: draft International Convention on the Elimination of All Forms of Intolerance and of Discrimination based on Religion or Belief.

For further reference see *Yearbook of the United Nations*, 1967, pp. 488–90; Krishnaswami, *Study of Discrimination in the Matter of Religious Rights and Practices*, United Nations, 1960.

TEXT

PREAMBLE

The States Parties to the present Convention,

Considering that one of the basic principles of the Charter of the United Nations is that of the dignity and equality inherent in all human beings, and that all States Members have pledged themselves to take joint and separate action in co-operation with the Organization to promote and encourage universal respect for and observance of human rights and fundamental freedoms for all, without distinction as to race, sex, language or religion,

Considering that the Universal Declaration of Human Rights proclaims the principle of non-discrimination and the right to freedom of thought, conscience, religion and belief,

Considering that the disregard and infringement of human rights and fundamental freedoms, and in particular of the right of freedom of thought conscience, religion and belief, have brought great suffering to mankind,

Considering that religion or belief, for anyone who professes either, is a

7*

fundamental element in his conception of life, and that freedom to practise religion as well as to manifest a belief should be fully respected and guaranteed,

Considering it essential that Governments, organizations and private persons should strive to promote through education, and by other means, understanding, tolerance and respect in matters relating to freedom of religion and belief,

Noting with satisfaction the coming into force of conventions concerning discrimination, *inter alia*, on the ground of religion, such as the Convention concerning Discrimination in Respect of Employment and Occupation adopted by the International Labour Organization in 1958, the Convention against Discrimination in Education adopted by the United Nations Educational, Scientific and Cultural Organization in 1960, and the United Nations Convention on the Prevention and Punishment of the Crime of Genocide, adopted in 1948,

Concerned by manifestations of intolerance in such matters still in evidence in some areas of the world,

Resolved to adopt all necessary measures for eliminating speedily such intolerance in all its forms and manifestations and to prevent and combat discrimination on the ground of religion or belief,

Have agreed as follows:

Article I

For the purpose of this Convention:

(a) The expression 'religion or belief' shall include theistic, non-theistic and atheistic beliefs;

(b) The expression 'discrimination on the ground of religion or belief' shall mean any distinction, exclusion, restriction or preference based on religion or belief which has the purpose or effect of nullifying or impairing the recognition, enjoyment or exercise, on equal footing, of human rights and fundamental freedoms in the political, economic, social, cultural or any other field of public life;

(c) The expression 'religious intolerance' shall mean intolerance in matters of religion or belief;

(d) Neither the establishment of a religion nor the recognition of a religion or belief by a State nor the separation of Church from State shall by itself be considered religious intolerance or discrimination on the ground of religion or belief; provided that this paragraph shall not be construed as permitting violation of specific provisions of this Convention.

Article II

States Parties recognize that the religion or belief of an individual is a matter for his own conscience and must be respected accordingly. They condemn all forms of religious intolerance and all discrimination on the ground of religion or belief and undertake to promote and implement policies which are designed to protect freedom of thought, conscience, religion or belief, to secure religious tolerance and to eliminate all discrimination on the ground of religion or belief.

Article III

1. States Parties undertake to ensure to everyone within their jurisdiction the right to freedom of thought, conscience, religion or belief. This right shall include:

(a) Freedom to adhere or not to adhere to any religion or belief and to change his religion or belief in accordance with the dictates of his conscience without being subjected either to any of the limitations referred to in Article XII or to any coercion likely to impair his freedom of choice or decision in the matter, provided that this sub-paragraph shall not be interpreted as extending to manifestations of religion or belief;

(b) Freedom to manifest his religion or belief either alone or in community with others, and in public or in private, without being subjected to any discrimination on the ground of religion or belief;

(c) Freedom to express opinions on questions concerning a religion or belief.

2. States Parties shall in particular ensure to everyone within their jurisdiction:

(a) Freedom to worship, to hold assemblies related to religion or belief and to establish and maintain places of worship or assembly for these purposes;

(b) Freedom to teach, to disseminate and to learn his religion or belief and its sacred languages or traditions, to write, print and publish religious books and texts, and to train personnel intending to devote themselves to its practices or observances;

(c) Freedom to practise his religion or belief by establishing and maintaining charitable and educational institutions and by expressing in public life the implications of religion or belief;

(d) Freedom to observe the rituals, dietary and other practices of his religion or belief and to produce or if necessary import the objects, foods and other articles and facilities customarily used in its observances and practices;

(e) Freedom to make pilgrimages and other journeys in connexion with his religion or belief, whether inside or outside his country;

(f) Equal legal protection for the places of worship or assembly, the rites, ceremonies and activities, and the places of disposal of the dead associated with his religion or belief;

(g) Freedom to organize and maintain local, regional, national and international associations in connexion with his religion or belief, to participate in the activities, and to communicate with his co-religionists and believers;

(h) Freedom from compulsion to take an oath of religious nature.

Article IV

1. States Parties undertake to respect the right of parents and, where applicable, legal guardians, to bring up in the religion or belief of their choice their children or wards who are as yet incapable of exercising the freedom of choice guaranteed under article III, paragraph 1 (a).

2. The exercise of this right carries with it the duty of parents and legal guardians to inculcate in their children or wards tolerance for the religion or belief of others, and to protect them from any precepts or practices based on religious intolerance or discrimination on the ground of religion or belief.

3. In the case of a child who has been deprived of his parents, their expressed or presumed wishes shall be duly taken into account.

4. In applying the provisions of this article, the best interests of the child shall be the guiding principle for those who are responsible for his upbringing and education.

Article V

States Parties shall ensure to everyone freedom to enjoy and to exercise political, civic, economic, social and cultural rights without discrimination on the ground of religion or belief.

Article VI

States Parties undertake to adopt immediate and effective measures, particularly in the fields of teaching, education, culture and information, with a view to combating prejudices as, for example, anti-Semitism and other manifestations which lead to religious intolerance and to discrimination on the ground of religion or belief, and to promoting and encouraging in the interest of universal peace, understanding, tolerance, co-operation and friendship among nations, groups and individuals, irrespective of differences in religion or belief, in accordance with the purposes and principles of the Charter of the United Nations, the Universal Declaration of Human Rights and this Convention.

Article VII

1. In compliance with the fundamental obligations laid down in article II, States Parties shall take effective measures to prevent and eliminate discrimination on the ground of religion or belief, including the enactment or abrogation of laws or regulations where necessary to prohibit such discrimination by any person, group or organization.
2. States Parties undertake not to pursue any policy or enact or retain laws or regulations restricting or impeding freedom of conscience, religion or belief or the free and open exercise thereof, nor discriminate against any person, group or organization on account of membership or non-membership in, practice or non-practice of, or adherence or non-adherence to any religion or belief.

Article VIII

States Parties undertake to ensure to everyone equality before the law without any discrimination in the exercise of the right to freedom of thought, conscience, religion or belief, and the right to equal protection of the law against any discrimination on the ground of religion or belief.

Article IX

States Parties shall ensure equal protection of the law against promotion of or incitement to religious intolerance or discrimination on the ground of religion or belief. Any act of violence against the adherents of any religion or belief or against the means used for its practice, any incitement to such acts or incitement to hatred likely to result in acts of violence against any religion or belief or its adherents, shall be considered as offences punishable by law. Membership in an organization based on religion or belief does not remove the responsibility for the abovementioned acts.

Article X

States Parties shall ensure to everyone within their jurisdiction effective protection and remedies, through the competent national tribunals and other State institutions, against any acts, including acts of discrimination on the ground of religion or belief, which violate his human rights and fundamental freedoms contrary to this Convention, as well as the right to seek from such tribunals just and adequate reparation or satisfaction for any damage suffered as a result of such acts.

Article XI

Nothing in this Convention shall be interpreted as giving to any person, group, organization or institution the right to engage in activities aimed at prejudicing national security, friendly relations between nations or the purposes and principles of the United Nations.

Article XII

Nothing in this Convention shall be construed to preclude a State Party from prescribing by law such limitations as are necessary to protect public safety, order, health or morals, or the individual rights and freedoms of others, or the general welfare in a democratic society.

PART THREE

IMPLEMENTATION AND STANDARD-SETTING IN CONVENTIONS SPONSORED BY THE UNITED NATIONS

INTRODUCTION

THE documents that follow are concerned with standard-setting, and at the same time provide for measures of implementation apart from the ordinary working of the national legal systems of individual States parties to the conventions. The International Covenants are intended to supersede the Universal Declaration of Human Rights, since the Covenants, when they enter into force, will have undoubted legal force as treaties for the parties to them. On the Covenants see Ganji, *International Protection of Human Rights*, 1962; Schwelb, *American Journal of International Law*, 62 (1968), p. 827; Schwelb, in Eide and Schou (eds.), *International Protection of Human Rights*, 1967, p. 103; Capotorti, in the same work, p. 131.

I. INTERNATIONAL COVENANT ON ECONOMIC, SOCIAL, AND CULTURAL RIGHTS, 1966

THIS appears in the annex to a resolution adopted by the United Nations General Assembly on 16 December 1966. It was signed by thirty-nine States, but so far has attracted only one ratification.

TEXT

PREAMBLE

The States Parties to the present Covenant,

Considering that, in accordance with the principles proclaimed in the Charter of the United Nations, recognition of the inherent dignity and of the equal and inalienable rights of all members of the human family is the foundation of freedom, justice and peace in the world,

Recognizing that these rights derive from the inherent dignity of the human person,

Recognizing that, in accordance with the Universal Declaration of Human Rights, the ideal of free human beings enjoying freedom from fear and want can only be achieved if conditions are created whereby everyone may enjoy his economic, social and cultural rights, as well as his civil and political rights,

Considering the obligation of States under the Charter of the United Nations to promote universal respect for, and observance of, human rights and freedoms,

Realizing that the individual, having duties to other individuals and to the community to which he belongs, is under a responsibility to strive for the promotion and observance of the rights recognized in the present Covenant,

Agree upon the following articles:

PART I

Article 1

1. All peoples have the right of self-determination. By virtue of that right

they freely determine their political status and freely pursue their economic, social and cultural development.

2. All peoples may, for their own ends, freely dispose of their natural wealth and resources without prejudice to any obligations arising out of international economic co-operation, based upon the principle of mutual benefit, and international law. In no case may a people be deprived of its own means of subsistence.

3. The States Parties to the present Covenant, including those having responsibility for the administration of Non-Self-Governing and Trust Territories, shall promote the realization of the right of self-determination, and shall respect that right, in conformity with the provisions of the Charter of the United Nations.

PART II

Article 2

1. Each State Party to the present Covenant undertakes to take steps, individually and through international assistance and co-operation, especially economic and technical, to the maximum of its available resources, with a view to achieving progressively the full realization of the rights recognized in the present Covenant by all appropriate means, including particularly the adoption of legislative measures.

2. The States Parties to the present Covenant undertake to guarantee that the rights enunciated in the present Covenant will be exercised without discrimination of any kind as to race, colour, sex, language, religion, political or other opinion, national or social origin, property, birth or other status.

3. Developing countries, with due regard to human rights and their national economy, may determine to what extent they would guarantee the economic rights recognized in the present Covenant to non-nationals.

Article 3

The States Parties to the present Covenant undertake to ensure the equal right of men and women to the enjoyment of all economic, social and cultural rights set forth in the present Covenant.

Article 4

The States Parties to the present Covenant recognize that, in the enjoyment of those rights provided by the State in conformity with the present Covenant, the State may subject such rights only to such limitations as are determined by law only in so far as this may be compatible with the nature of these rights and solely for the purpose of promoting the general welfare in a democratic society.

Article 5

1. Nothing in the present Covenant may be interpreted as implying for any State, group or person any right to engage in any activity or to perform any act aimed at the destruction of any of the rights or freedoms recognized herein, or at their limitation to a greater extent than is provided for in the present Covenant.

2. No restriction upon or derogation from any of the fundamental human rights recognized or existing in any country in virtue of law, conventions, regulations or custom shall be admitted on the pretext that the present Covenant does not recognize such rights or that it recognizes them to a lesser extent.

Part III

Article 6

1. The States Parties to the present Covenant recognize the right to work, which includes the right of everyone to the opportunity to gain his living by work which he freely chooses or accepts, and will take appropriate steps to safeguard this right.

2. The steps to be taken by a State Party to the present Covenant to achieve the full realization of this right shall include technical and vocational guidance and training programmes, policies and techniques to achieve steady economic, social and cultural development and full and productive employment under conditions safeguarding fundamental political and economic freedoms to the individual.

Article 7

The States Parties to the present Covenant recognize the right of everyone to the enjoyment of just and favourable conditions of work, which ensure, in particular:

(*a*) Remuneration which provides all workers, as a minimum with:
  (i) Fair wages and equal remuneration for work of equal value without distinction of any kind, in particular women being guaranteed conditions of work not inferior to those enjoyed by men, with equal pay for equal work;

(ii) A decent living for themselves and their families in accordance with the provisions of the present Covenant;

(*b*) Safe and healthy working conditions;

(*c*) Equal opportunity for everyone to be promoted in his employment to an appropriate higher level, subject to no considerations other than those of seniority and competence;

(*d*) Rest, leisure and reasonable limitation of working hours and periodic holidays with pay, as well as remuneration for public holidays.

Article 8

1. The States Parties to the present Covenant undertake to ensure:

(*a*) The right of everyone to form trade unions and join the trade union of his choice, subject only to the rules of the organization concerned, for the promotion and protection of his economic and social interests. No restrictions may be placed on the exercise of this right other than those prescribed by law and which are necessary in a democratic society in the interests of national security or public order or for the protection of the rights and freedoms of others;

(*b*) The right of trade unions to establish national federations or confederations and the right of the latter to form or join international trade union organizations;

(*c*) The right of trade unions to function freely subject to no limitations other than those prescribed by law and which are necessary in a democratic society in the interests of national security or public order or for the protection of the rights and freedoms of others;

(*d*) The right to strike, provided that it is exercised in conformity with the laws of the particular country.

2. This article shall not prevent the imposition of lawful restrictions on the exercise of these rights by members of the armed forces or of the police or of the administration of the State.

3. Nothing in this article shall authorize States Parties to the International Labour Organization Convention of 1948 concerning Freedom of Association and Protection of the Right to Organize to take legislative measures which would prejudice, or apply the law in such a manner as would prejudice, the guarantees provided for in that Convention.

Article 9

The States Parties to the present Covenant recognize the right of everyone to social security, including social insurance.

Article 10

The States Parties to the present Covenant recognize that:

1. The widest possible protection and assistance should be accorded to the family, which is the natural and fundamental group unit of society, particularly for its establishment and while it is responsible for the care and education of dependent children. Marriage must be entered into with the free consent of the intending spouses.

2. Special protection should be accorded to mothers during a reasonable period before and after childbirth. During such period working mothers should be accorded paid leave or leave with adequate social security benefits.

3. Special measures of protection and assistance should be taken on behalf of all children and young persons without any discrimination for reasons of parentage or other conditions. Children and young persons should be protected from economic and social exploitation. Their employment in work harmful to their morals or health or dangerous to life or likely to hamper their normal development should be punishable by law. States should also set age limits below which the paid employment of child labour should be prohibited and punishable by law.

Article 11

1. The States Parties to the present Covenant recognize the right of everyone to an adequate standard of living for himself and his family, including adequate food, clothing and housing, and to the continuous improvement of living conditions. The States Parties will take appropriate steps to ensure the realization of this right, recognizing to this effect the essential importance of international co-operation based on free consent.

2. The States Parties to the present Covenant, recognizing the fundamental right of everyone to be free from hunger, shall take, individually and through international co-operation, the measures, including specific programmes, which are needed:

(*a*) To improve methods of production, conservation and distribution of food by making full use of technical and scientific knowledge, by disseminating knowledge of the principles of nutrition and by developing or reforming agrarian systems in such a way as to achieve the most efficient development and utilization of natural resources;

(*b*) Taking into account the problems of both food-importing and food-exporting countries, to ensure an equitable distribution of world food supplies in relation to need.

Article 12

1. The States Parties to the present Covenant recognize the right of everyone to the enjoyment of the highest attainable standard of physical and mental health.

2. The steps to be taken by the States Parties to the present Covenant to achieve the full realization of this right shall include those necessary for:

 (a) The provision for the reduction of the stillbirth-rate and of infant mortality and for the healthy development of the child;

 (b) The improvement of all aspects of environmental and industrial hygiene;

 (c) The prevention, treatment and control of epidemic, endemic, occupational and other diseases;

 (d) The creation of conditions which would assure to all medical service and medical attention in the event of sickness.

Article 13

1. The States Parties to the present Covenant recognize the right of everyone to education. They agree that education shall be directed to the full development of the human personality and the sense of its dignity, and shall strengthen the respect for human rights and fundamental freedoms. They further agree that education shall enable all persons to participate effectively in a free society, promote understanding, tolerance and friendship among all nations and all racial, ethnic or religious groups, and further the activities of the United Nations for the maintenance of peace.

2. The States Parties to the present Covenant recognize that, with a view to achieving the full realization of this right:

 (a) Primary education shall be compulsory and available free to all;

 (b) Secondary education in its different forms, including technical and vocational secondary education, shall be made generally available and accessible to all by every appropriate means, and in particular by the progressive introduction of free education;

 (c) Higher education shall be made equally accessible to all, on the basis of capacity, by every appropriate means, and in particular by the progressive introduction of free education;

 (d) Fundamental education shall be encouraged or intensified as far as possible for those persons who have not received or completed the whole period of their primary education;

(e) The development of a system of schools at all levels shall be actively pursued, an adequate fellowship system shall be established, and the material conditions of teaching staff shall be continuously improved.

3. The States Parties to the present Covenant undertake to have respect for the liberty of parents and, when applicable, legal guardians, to choose for their children schools, other than those established by the public authorities, which conform to such minimum educational standards as may be laid down or approved by the State and to ensure the religious and moral education of their children in conformity with their own convictions.

4. No part of this article shall be construed so as to interfere with the liberty of individuals and bodies to establish and direct educational institutions, subject always to the observance of the principles set forth in paragraph 1 of this Article and to the requirement that the education given in such institutions shall conform to such minimum standards as may be laid down by the State.

Article 14

Each State Party to the present Covenant which, at the time of becoming a Party, has not been able to secure in its metropolitan territory or other territories under its jurisdiction compulsory primary education, free of charge, undertakes, within two years, to work out and adopt a detailed plan of action for the progressive implementation, within a reasonable number of years, to be fixed in the plan, of the principle of compulsory education free of charge for all.

Article 15

1. The States Parties to the present Covenant recognize the right of everyone:

(a) To take part in cultural life;

(b) To enjoy the benefits of scientific progress and its applications;

(c) To benefit from the protection of the moral and material interests resulting from any scientific, literary or artistic production of which he is the author.

2. The steps to be taken by the States Parties to the present Covenant to achieve the full realization of this right shall include those necessary

for the conservation, the development and the diffusion of science and culture.

3. The States Parties to the present Covenant undertake to respect the freedom indispensable for scientific research and creative activity.

4. The States Parties to the present Covenant recognize the benefits to be derived from the encouragement and development of international contacts and co-operation in the scientific and cultural fields.

PART IV

Article 16

1. The States Parties to the present Covenant undertake to submit in conformity with this part of the Covenant reports on the measures which they have adopted and the progress made in achieving the observance of the rights recognized herein.

2. (*a*) All reports shall be submitted to the Secretary-General of the United Nations, who shall transmit copies to the Economic and Social Council for consideration in accordance with the provisions of the present Covenant.

(*b*) The Secretary-General of the United Nations shall also transmit to the specialized agencies copies of the reports, or any relevant parts therefrom, from States Parties to the present Covenant which are also members of these specialized agencies in so far as these reports, or parts therefrom, relate to any matters which fall within the responsibilities of the said agencies in accordance with their constitutional instruments.

Article 17

1. The States Parties to the present Covenant shall furnish their reports in stages, in accordance with a programme to be established by the Economic and Social Council within one year of the entry into force of the present Covenant after consultation with the States Parties and the specialized agencies concerned.

2. Reports may indicate factors and difficulties affecting the degree of fulfilment of obligations under the present Covenant.

3. Where relevant information has previously been furnished to the United Nations or to any specialized agency by any State Party to the present Covenant, it will not be necessary to reproduce that information, but a precise reference to the information so furnished will suffice.

Article 18

Pursuant to its responsibilities under the Charter of the United Nations in the field of human rights and fundamental freedoms, the Economic and Social Council may make arrangements with the specialized agencies in respect of their reporting to it on the progress made in achieving the observance of the provisions of the present Covenant falling within the scope of their activities. These reports may include particulars of decisions and recommendations on such implementation adopted by their competent organs.

Article 19

The Economic and Social Council may transmit to the Commission on Human Rights for study and general recommendation or as appropriate for information the reports concerning human rights submitted by States in accordance with Articles 16 and 17, and those concerning human rights submitted by the specialized agencies in accordance with Article 18.

Article 20

The States Parties to the present Covenant and the specialized agencies concerned may submit comments to the Economic and Social Council on any general recommendation under Article 19 or reference to such general recommendation in any report of the Commission on Human Rights or any documentation referred to therein.

Article 21

The Economic and Social Council may submit from time to time to the General Assembly reports with recommendations of a general nature and a summary of the information received from the States Parties to the present Covenant and the specialized agencies on the measures taken and the progress made in achieving general observance of the rights recognized in the present Covenant.

Article 22

The Economic and Social Council may bring to the attention of other organs of the United Nations, their subsidiary organs and specialized agencies concerned with furnishing technical assistance any matters arising out of the reports referred to in this part of the present Covenant which may assist such bodies in deciding, each within its field of competence, on the advisability of international measures likely to contribute to the effective progressive implementation of the present Covenant.

Article 23

The States Parties to the present Covenant agree that international action for the achievement of the rights recognized in the present Covenant includes such methods as the conclusion of conventions, the adoption of recommendations, the furnishing of technical assistance and the holding of regional meetings and technical meetings for the purpose of consultation and study organized in conjunction with the Governments concerned.

Article 24

Nothing in the present Covenant shall be interpreted as impairing the provisions of the Charter of the United Nations and of the constitutions of the specialized agencies which define the respective responsibilities of the various organs of the United Nations and of the specialized agencies in regard to the matters dealt with in the present Covenant.

Article 25

Nothing in the present Covenant shall be interpreted as impairing the inherent right of all peoples to enjoy and utilize fully and freely their natural wealth and resources.

PART V

Article 26

1. The present Covenant is open for signature by any State Member of the United Nations or member of any of its specialized agencies, by any State Party to the Statute of the International Court of Justice, and by any other State which has been invited by the General Assembly of the United Nations to become a party to the present Covenant.

2. The present Covenant is subject to ratification. Instruments of ratification shall be deposited with the Secretary-General of the United Nations.

3. The present Covenant shall be open to accession by any State referred to in paragraph 1 of this Article.

4. Accession shall be effected by the deposit of an instrument of accession with the Secretary-General of the United Nations.

5. The Secretary-General of the United Nations shall inform all States which have signed the present Covenant or acceded to it of the deposit of each instrument of ratification or accession.

Article 27

1. The present Covenant shall enter into force three months after the date of the deposit with the Secretary-General of the United Nations of the thirty-fifth instrument of ratification or instrument of accession.

2. For each State ratifying the present Covenant or acceding to it after the deposit of the thirty-fifth instrument of ratification or instrument of accession, the present Covenant shall enter into force three months after the date of the deposit of its own instrument of ratification or instrument of accession.

Article 28

The provisions of the present Covenant shall extend to all parts of federal States without any limitations or exceptions.

Article 29

1. Any State Party to the present Covenant may propose an amendment and file it with the Secretary-General of the United Nations. The Secretary-General shall thereupon communicate any proposed amendments to the States Parties to the present Covenant with a request that they notify him whether they favour a conference of States Parties for the purpose of considering and voting upon the proposals. In the event that at least one third of the States Parties favours such a conference, the Secretary-General shall convene the conference under the auspices of the United Nations. Any amendment adopted by a majority of the States Parties present and voting at the conference shall be submitted to the General Assembly of the United Nations for approval.

2. Amendments shall come into force when they have been approved by the General Assembly of the United Nations and accepted by a two-thirds majority of the States Parties to the present Covenant in accordance with their respective constitutional processes.

3. When amendments come into force they shall be binding on those States Parties which have accepted them, other States Parties still being bound by the provisions of the present Covenant and any earlier amendment which they have accepted.

Article 30

Irrespective of the notifications made under Article 26, paragraph 5, the Secretary-General of the United Nations shall inform all States referred to in paragraph 1 of the same article of the following particulars:

(*a*) Signatures, ratifications and accessions under Article 26;

(*b*) The date of the entry into force of the present Covenant under Article 27 and the date of the entry into force of any amendments under Article 29.

Article 31

1. The present Covenant, of which the Chinese, English, French, Russian and Spanish texts are equally authentic, shall be deposited in the archives of the United Nations.

2. The Secretary-General of the United Nations shall transmit certified copies of the present Covenant to all States referred to in Article 26.

II. INTERNATIONAL COVENANT ON CIVIL AND POLITICAL RIGHTS, 1966

THIS was adopted at the same time as the last Covenant. It was signed by thirty-eight States, but so far has attracted only one ratification.

With respect to inter-state complaints under the optional procedure provided for in Article 41 there is an overlap with the procedure under Article 24 of the European Convention on Human Rights, below. See further on this issue Resolution (70) 17 of the Committee of Ministers of the Council of Europe, adopted by the Ministers' Deputies on 15 May 1970.

TEXT

PREAMBLE

The States Parties to the present Covenant,

Considering that, in accordance with the principles proclaimed in the Charter of the United Nations, recognition of the inherent dignity and of the equal and inalienable rights of all members of the human family is the foundation of freedom, justice and peace in the world,

Recognizing that these rights derive from the inherent dignity of the human person,

Recognizing that, in accordance with the Universal Declaration of Human Rights, the ideal of free human beings enjoying civil and political freedom and freedom from fear and want can only be achieved if conditions are created whereby everyone may enjoy his civil and political rights, as well as his economic, social and cultural rights,

Considering the obligation of States under the Charter of the United Nations to promote universal respect for, and observance of, human rights and freedoms,

Realizing that the individual, having duties to other individuals and to the community to which he belongs, is under a responsibility to strive for the promotion and observance of the rights recognized in the present Covenant,

Agree upon the following articles:

PART I

Article 1

1. All peoples have the right of self-determination. By virtue of that right they freely determine their political status and freely pursue their economic, social and cultural development.

2. All peoples may, for their own ends, freely dispose of their natural wealth and resources without prejudice to any obligations arising out of international economic co-operation, based upon the principle of mutual benefit, and international law. In no case may a people be deprived of its own means of subsistence.

3. The States Parties to the present Covenant, including those having responsibility for the administration of Non-Self-Governing and Trust Territories, shall promote the realization of the right of self-determination, and shall respect that right, in conformity with the provisions of the Charter of the United Nations.

PART II

Article 2

1. Each State Party to the present Covenant undertakes to respect and to ensure to all individuals within its territory and subject to its jurisdiction the rights recognized in the present Covenant, without distinction of any kind, such as race, colour, sex, language, religion, political or other opinion, national or social origin, property, birth or other status.

2. Where not already provided for by existing legislative or other measures, each State Party to the present Covenant undertakes to take the necessary steps, in accordance with its constitutional processes and with the provisions of the present Covenant, to adopt such legislative or other measures as may be necessary to give effect to the rights recognized in the present Covenant.

3. Each State Party to the present Covenant undertakes:

(a) To ensure that any person whose rights or freedoms as herein recognized are violated shall have an effective remedy, notwithstanding that the violation has been committed by persons acting in an official capacity;

(b) To ensure that any person claiming such a remedy shall have his right thereto determined by competent judicial, administrative or legislative authorities, or by any other competent authority provided for by the legal system of the State, and to develop the possibilities of judicial remedy;

(c) To ensure that the competent authorities shall enforce such remedies when granted.

Article 3

The States Parties to the present Covenant undertake to ensure the equal right of men and women to the enjoyment of all civil and political rights set forth in the present Covenant.

Article 4

1. In time of public emergency which threatens the life of the nation and the existence of which is officially proclaimed, the State Parties to the present Covenant may take measures derogating from their obligations under the present Covenant to the extent strictly required by the exigencies of the situation, provided that such measures are not inconsistent with their other obligations under international law and do not involve discrimination solely on the ground of race, colour, sex, language, religion or social origin.

2. No derogation from Articles 6, 7, 8 (paragraphs 1 and 2), 11, 15, 16 and 18 may be made under this provision.

3. Any State Party to the present Covenant availing itself of the right of derogation shall immediately inform the other States Parties to the present Covenant, through the intermediary of the Secretary-General of the United Nations of the provisions from which it has derogated and of the reasons by which it was actuated. A further communication shall be made, through the same intermediary on the date on which it terminates such derogation.

Article 5

1. Nothing in the present Covenant may be interpreted as implying for any State, group or person any right to engage in any activity or perform any act aimed at the destruction of any of the rights and freedoms recognized herein or at their limitation to a greater extent than is provided for in the present Covenant.

2. There shall be no restriction upon or derogation from any of the fundamental human rights recognized or existing in any State Party to the present Covenant pursuant to law, conventions, regulations or custom on the pretext that the present Covenant does not recognize such rights or that it recognizes them to a lesser extent.

PART III

Article 6

1. Every human being has the inherent right to life. This right shall be protected by law. No one shall be arbitrarily deprived of his life.

2. In countries which have not abolished the death penalty, sentence of death may be imposed only for the most serious crimes in accordance with the law in force at the time of the commission of the crime and not contrary to the provisions of the present Covenant and to the Convention on the Prevention and Punishment of the Crime of Genocide. This penalty can only be carried out pursuant to a final judgement rendered by a competent court.

3. When deprivation of life constitutes the crime of genocide, it is understood that nothing in this article shall authorize any State Party to the present Covenant to derogate in any way from any obligation assumed under the provisions of the Convention on the Prevention and Punishment of the Crime of Genocide.

4. Anyone sentenced to death shall have the right to seek pardon or commutation of the sentence. Amnesty, pardon or commutation of the sentence of death may be granted in all cases.

5. Sentence of death shall not be imposed for crimes committed by persons below eighteen years of age and shall not be carried out on pregnant women.

6. Nothing in this article shall be invoked to delay or to prevent the abolition of capital punishment by any State Party to the present Covenant.

Article 7

No one shall be subjected to torture or to cruel, inhuman or degrading treatment or punishment. In particular, no one shall be subjected without his free consent to medical or scientific experimentation.

Article 8

1. No one shall be held in slavery; slavery and the slave-trade in all their forms shall be prohibited.

2. No one shall be held in servitude.

3. (*a*) No one shall be required to perform forced or compulsory labour;
   (*b*) Paragraph 3 (*a*) shall not be held to preclude, in countries where imprisonment with hard labour may be imposed as a punishment for a

crime, the performance of hard labour in pursuance of a sentence to such punishment by a competent court;

(*c*) For the purpose of this paragraph the term 'forced or compulsory labour' shall not include:

(i) Any work or service, not referred to in sub-paragraph (*b*), normally required of a person who is under detention in consequence of a lawful order of a court, or of a person during conditional release from such detention;

(ii) Any service of a military character and, in countries where conscientious objection is recognized, any national service required by law of conscientious objectors;

(iii) Any service exacted in cases of emergency or calamity threatening the life or well-being of the community;

(iv) Any work or service which forms part of normal civil obligations.

Article 9

1. Everyone has the right to liberty and security of person. No one shall be subjected to arbitrary arrest or detention. No one shall be deprived of his liberty except on such grounds and in accordance with such procedure as are established by law.

2. Anyone who is arrested shall be informed, at the time of arrest, of the reasons for his arrest and shall be promptly informed of any charges against him.

3. Anyone arrested or detained on a criminal charge shall be brought promptly before a judge or other officer authorized by law to exercise judicial power and shall be entitled to trial within a reasonable time or to release. It shall not be the general rule that persons awaiting trial shall be detained in custody, but release may be subject to guarantees to appear for trial, at any other stage of the judicial proceedings, and, should occasion arise, for execution of the judgement.

4. Anyone who is deprived of his liberty by arrest or detention shall be entitled to take proceedings before a court, in order that that court may decide without delay on the lawfulness of his detention and order his release if the detention is not lawful.

5. Anyone who has been the victim of unlawful arrest or detention shall have an enforceable right to compensation.

Article 10

1. All persons deprived of their liberty shall be treated with humanity and with respect for the inherent dignity of the human person.

2. (*a*) Accused persons shall, save in exceptional circumstances, be segregated from convicted persons and shall be subject to separate treatment appropriate to their status as unconvicted persons;

(*b*) Accused juvenile persons shall be separated from adults and brought as speedily as possible for adjudication.

3. The penitentiary system shall comprise treatment of prisoners the essential aim of which shall be their reformation and social rehabilitation. Juvenile offenders shall be segregated from adults and be accorded treatment appropriate to their age and legal status.

Article 11

No one shall be imprisoned merely on the ground of inability to fulfil a contractual obligation.

Article 12

1. Everyone lawfully within the territory of a State shall, within that territory, have the right to liberty of movement and freedom to choose his residence.

2. Everyone shall be free to leave any country, including his own.

3. The above-mentioned rights shall not be subject to any restrictions except those which are provided by law, are necessary to protect national security, public order (*ordre public*), public health or morals or the rights and freedoms of others, and are consistent with the other rights recognized in the present Covenant.

4. No one shall be arbitrarily deprived of the right to enter his own country.

Article 13

An alien lawfully in the territory of a State Party to the present Covenant may be expelled therefrom only in pursuance of a decision reached in accordance with law and shall, except where compelling reasons of national security otherwise require, be allowed to submit the reasons against his expulsion and to have his case reviewed by, and be represented for the purpose before, the competent authority or a person or persons especially designated by the competent authority.

Article 14

1. All persons shall be equal before the courts and tribunals. In the determination of any criminal charge against him, or of his rights and

obligations in a suit at law, everyone shall be entitled to a fair and public hearing by a competent, independent and impartial tribunal established by law. The Press and the public may be excluded from all or part of a trial for reasons of morals, public order (*ordre public*) or national security in a democratic society, or when the interest of the private lives of the parties so requires, or to the extent strictly necessary in the opinion of the court in special circumstances where publicity would prejudice the interests of justice; but any judgement rendered in a criminal case or in a suit at law shall be made public except where the interest of juvenile persons otherwise requires or the proceedings concern matrimonial disputes or the guardianship of children.

2. Everyone charged with a criminal offence shall have the right to be presumed innocent until proved guilty according to law.

3. In the determination of any criminal charge against him, everyone shall be entitled to the following minimum guarantees, in full equality:

(*a*) To be informed promptly and in detail in a language which he understands of the nature and cause of the charge against him;

(*b*) To have adequate time and facilities for the preparation of his defence and to communicate with counsel of his own choosing;

(*c*) To be tried without undue delay;

(*d*) To be tried in his presence, and to defend himself in person or through legal assistance of his own choosing; to be informed, if he does not have legal assistance, of this right; and to have legal assistance assigned to him, in any case where the interests of justice so require, and without payment by him in any such case if he does not have sufficient means to pay for it;

(*e*) To examine, or have examined, the witnesses against him and to obtain the attendance and examination of witnesses on his behalf under the same conditions as witnesses against him;

(*f*) To have the free assistance of an interpreter if he cannot understand or speak the language used in court;

(*g*) Not to be compelled to testify against himself or to confess guilt.

4. In the case of juvenile persons, the procedure shall be such as will take account of their age and the desirability of promoting their rehabilitation.

5. Everyone convicted of a crime shall have the right to his conviction and sentence being reviewed by a higher tribunal according to law.

6. When a person has by a final decision been convicted of a criminal offence and when subsequently his conviction has been reversed or he has been pardoned on the ground that a new or newly discovered fact

shows conclusively that there has been a miscarriage of justice, the person who has suffered punishment as a result of such conviction shall be compensated according to law, unless it is proved that the non-disclosure of the unknown fact in time is wholly or partly attributable to him.

7. No one shall be liable to be tried or punished again for an offence for which he has already been finally convicted or acquitted in accordance with the law and penal procedure of each country.

Article 15

1. No one shall be held guilty of any criminal offence on account of any act or omission which did not constitute a criminal offence, under national or international law, at the time when it was committed. Nor shall a heavier penalty be imposed than the one that was applicable at the time when the criminal offence was committed. If, subsequent to the commission of the offence, provision is made by law for the imposition of a lighter penalty, the offender shall benefit thereby.

2. Nothing in this article shall prejudice the trial and punishment of any person for any act or omission which, at the time when it was committed, was criminal according to the general principles of law recognized by the community of nations.

Article 16

Everyone shall have the right to recognition everywhere as a person before the law.

Article 17

1. No one shall be subjected to arbitrary or unlawful interference with his privacy, family, home or correspondence, nor to unlawful attacks on his honour and reputation.

2. Everyone has the right to the protection of the law against such inter-ference or attacks.

Article 18

1. Everyone shall have the right to freedom of thought, conscience and religion. This right shall include freedom to have or to adopt a religion or belief of his choice, and freedom, either individually or in community with others and in public or private, to manifest his religion or belief in worship, observance, practice and teaching.

2. No one shall be subject to coercion which would impair his freedom to have or to adopt a religion or belief of his choice.

3. Freedom to manifest one's religion or beliefs may be subject only to such limitations as are prescribed by law and are necessary to protect public safety, order, health, or morals or the fundamental rights and freedoms of others.

4. The States Parties to the present Covenant undertake to have respect for the liberty of parents and, when applicable, legal guardians to ensure the religious and moral education of their children in conformity with their own convictions.

Article 19

1. Everyone shall have the right to hold opinions without interference.

2. Everyone shall have the right to freedom of expression; this right shall include freedom to seek, receive and impart information and ideas of all kinds, regardless of frontiers, either orally, in writing or in print, in the form of art, or through any other media of his choice.

3. The exercise of the rights provided for in paragraph 2 of this Article carries with it special duties and responsibilities. It may therefore be subject to certain restrictions, but these shall only be such as are provided by law and are necessary:

(a) For respect of the rights or reputations of others;
(b) For the protection of national security or of public order (*ordre public*), or of public health or morals.

Article 20

1. Any propaganda for war shall be prohibited by law.

2. Any advocacy of national, racial or religious hatred that constitutes incitement to discrimination, hostility or violence shall be prohibited by law.

Article 21

The right of peaceful assembly shall be recognized. No restrictions may be placed on the exercise of this right other than those imposed in conformity with the law and which are necessary in a democratic society in the interests of national security or public safety, public order (*ordre public*), the protection of public health or morals or the protection of the rights and freedoms of others.

Article 22

1. Everyone shall have the right to freedom of association with others, including the right to form and join trade unions for the protection of his interests.

2. No restrictions may be placed on the exercise of this right other than those which are prescribed by law and which are necessary in a democratic society in the interests of national security or public safety, public order (*ordre public*), the protection of public health or morals or the protection of the rights and freedoms of others. This Article shall not prevent the imposition of lawful restrictions on members of the armed forces and of the police in their exercise of this right.

3. Nothing in this article shall authorize States Parties to the International Labour Organization Convention of 1948 concerning Freedom of Association and Protection of the Right to Organize to take legislative measures which would prejudice, or to apply the law in such a manner as to prejudice, the guarantees provided for in that Convention.

Article 23

1. The family is the natural and fundamental group unit of society and is entitled to protection by society and the State.

2. The right of men and women of marriageable age to marry and to found a family shall be recognized.

3. No marriage shall be entered into without the free and full consent of the intending spouses.

4. States Parties to the present Covenant shall take appropriate steps to ensure equality of rights and responsibilities of spouses as to marriage, during marriage and at its dissolution. In the case of dissolution, provision shall be made for the necessary protection of any children.

Article 24

1. Every child shall have, without any discrimination as to race, colour, sex, language, religion, national or social origin, property or birth, the right to such measures of protection as are required by his status as a minor, on the part of his family, society and the State.

2. Every child shall be registered immediately after birth and shall have a name.

3. Every child has the right to acquire a nationality.

Article 25

Every citizen shall have the right and the opportunity, without any of the distinctions mentioned in Article 2 and without unreasonable restrictions:

(*a*) To take part in the conduct of public affairs, directly or through freely chosen representatives;

(*b*) To vote and to be elected at genuine periodic elections which shall be by universal and equal suffrage and shall be held by secret ballot, guaranteeing the free expression of the will of the electors;

(*c*) To have access, on general terms of equality, to public service in his country.

Article 26

All persons are equal before the law and are entitled without any discrimination to the equal protection of the law. In this respect, the law shall prohibit any discrimination and guarantee to all persons equal and effective protection against discrimination on any ground such as race, colour, sex, language, religion, political or other opinion, national or social origin, property, birth or other status.

Article 27

In those States in which ethnic, religious or linguistic minorities exist, persons belonging to such minorities shall not be denied the right, in community with the other members of their group, to enjoy their own culture, to profess and practise their own religion, or to use their own language.

Part IV

Article 28

1. There shall be established a Human Rights Committee (hereafter referred to in the present Covenant as the Committee). It shall consist of eighteen members and shall carry out the functions hereinafter provided.

2. The Committee shall be composed of nationals of the States Parties to the present Covenant who shall be persons of high moral character and recognized competence in the field of human rights, consideration being given to the usefulness of the participation of some persons having legal experience.

3. The members of the Committee shall be elected and shall serve in their personal capacity.

Article 29

1. The members of the Committee shall be elected by secret ballot from a list of persons possessing the qualifications prescribed in Article 28 and nominated for the purpose by the States Parties to the present Covenant.

2. Each State Party to the present Covenant may nominate not more than two persons. These persons shall be nationals of the nominating State.

3. A person shall be eligible for renomination.

Article 30

1. The initial election shall be held no later than six months after the date of the entry into force of the present Covenant.

2. At least four months before the date of each election to the Committee, other than an election to fill a vacancy declared in accordance with Article 34, the Secretary-General of the United Nations shall address a written invitation to the States Parties to the present Covenant to submit their nominations for membership of the Committee within three months.

3. The Secretary-General of the United Nations shall prepare a list in alphabetical order of all the persons thus nominated, with an indication of the States Parties which have nominated them, and shall submit it to the States Parties to the present Covenant no later than one month before the date of each election.

4. Elections of the members of the Committee shall be held at a meeting of the States Parties to the present Covenant convened by the Secretary-General of the United Nations at the Headquarters of the United Nations. At that meeting, for which two thirds of the States Parties to the present Covenant shall constitute a quorum, the persons elected to the Committee shall be those nominees who obtain the largest number of votes and an absolute majority of the votes of the representatives of States Parties present and voting.

Article 31

1. The Committee may not include more than one national of the same State.

2. In the election of the Committee, consideration shall be given to equitable geographical distribution of membership and to the representation of the different forms of civilization and of the principal legal systems.

Article 32

1. The members of the Committee shall be elected for a term of four years. They shall be eligible for re-election if renominated. However, the terms of nine of the members elected at the first election shall expire at the end of two years; immediately after the first election, the names of these nine members shall be chosen by lot by the Chairman of the meeting referred to in Article 30, paragraph 4.

2. Elections at the expiry of office shall be held in accordance with the preceding articles of this part of the present Covenant.

Article 33

1. If, in the unanimous opinion of the other members, a member of the Committee has ceased to carry out his functions for any cause other than absence of a temporary character, the Chairman of the Committee shall notify the Secretary-General of the United Nations, who shall then declare the seat of that member to be vacant.

2. In the event of the death or the resignation of a member of the Committee, the Chairman shall immediately notify the Secretary-General of the United Nations, who shall declare the seat vacant from the date of death or the date on which the resignation takes effect.

Article 34

1. When a vacancy is declared in accordance with Article 33 and if the term of office of the member to be replaced does not expire within six months of the declaration of the vacancy, the Secretary-General of the United Nations shall notify each of the States Parties to the present Covenant, which may within two months submit nominations in accordance with Article 29 for the purpose of filling the vacancy.

2. The Secretary-General of the United Nations shall prepare a list in alphabetical order of the persons thus nominated and shall submit it to the States Parties to the present Covenant. The election to fill the vacancy shall then take place in accordance with the relevant provisions of this part of the present Covenant.

3. A member of the Committee elected to fill a vacancy declared in accordance with Article 33 shall hold office for the remainder of the term of the member who vacated the seat on the Committee under the provisions of that Article.

8*

Article 35

The members of the Committee shall, with the approval of the General Assembly of the United Nations, receive emoluments from United Nations resources on such terms and conditions as the General Assembly may decide, having regard to the importance of the Committee's responsibilities.

Article 36

The Secretary-General of the United Nations shall provide the necessary staff and facilities for the effective performance of the functions of the Committee under the present Covenant.

Article 37

1. The Secretary-General of the United Nations shall convene the initial meeting of the Committee at the Headquarters of the United Nations.

2. After its initial meeting, the Committee shall meet at such times as shall be provided in its rules of procedure.

3. The Committee shall normally meet at the Headquarters of the United Nations or at the United Nations Office at Geneva.

Article 38

Every member of the Committee shall, before taking up his duties, make a solemn declaration in open committee that he will perform his functions impartially and conscientiously.

Article 39

1. The Committee shall elect its officers for a term of two years. They may be re-elected.

2. The Committee shall establish its own rules of procedure, but these rules shall provide, *inter alia*, that:

    (*a*) Twelve members shall constitute a quorum;
    (*b*) Decisions of the Committee shall be made by a majority vote of the members present.

Article 40

1. The States Parties to the present Covenant undertake to submit reports on the measures they have adopted which give effect to the rights

recognized herein and on the progress made in the enjoyment of those rights:

(a) Within one year of the entry into force of the present Covenant for the States Parties concerned;

(b) Thereafter whenever the Committee so requests.

2. All reports shall be submitted to the Secretary-General of the United Nations, who shall transmit them to the Committee for consideration. Reports shall indicate the factors and difficulties, if any, affecting the implementation of the present Covenant.

3. The Secretary-General of the United Nations may, after consultation with the Committee, transmit to the specialized agencies concerned copies of such parts of the reports as may fall within their field of competence.

4. The Committee shall study the reports submitted by the States Parties to the present Covenant. It shall transmit its reports, and such general comments as it may consider appropriate, to the States Parties. The Committee may also transmit to the Economic and Social Council these comments along with the copies of the reports it has received from States Parties to the present Covenant.

5. The States Parties to the present Covenant may submit to the Committee observations on any comments that may be made in accordance with paragraph 4 of this Article.

Article 41

1. A State Party to the present Covenant may at any time declare under this article that it recognizes the competence of the Committee to receive and consider communications to the effect that a State Party claims that another State Party is not fulfilling its obligations under the present Covenant. Communications under this Article may be received and considered only if submitted by a State Party which has made a declaration recognizing in regard to itself the competence of the Committee. No communication shall be received by the Committee if it concerns a State Party which has not made such a declaration. Communications received under this article shall be dealt with in accordance with the following procedure:

(a) If a State Party to the present Covenant considers that another State Party is not giving effect to the provisions of the present Covenant, it may, by written communication, bring the matter to the attention of that State Party. Within three months after the receipt of the communication, the receiving State shall afford the State which sent the communication an explanation or any other statement in writing clarifying the matter, which should include, to the extent possible and pertinent, reference to domestic procedures and remedies taken, pending, or available in the matter.

(b) If the matter is not adjusted to the satisfaction of both States Parties concerned within six months after the receipt by the receiving State of the initial communication, either State shall have the right to refer the matter to the Committee, by notice given to the Committee and to the other State.

(c) The Committee shall deal with a matter referred to it only after it has ascertained that all available domestic remedies have been invoked and exhausted in the matter, in conformity with the generally recognized principles of international law. This shall not be the rule where the application of the remedies is unreasonably prolonged.

(d) The Committee shall hold closed meetings when examining communications under this Article.

(e) Subject to the provisions of sub-paragraph (c), the Committee shall make available its good offices to the States Parties concerned with a view to a friendly solution of the matter on the basis of respect for human rights and fundamental freedoms as recognized in the present Covenant.

(f) In any matter referred to it, the Committee may call upon the States Parties concerned, referred to in sub-paragraph (b), to supply any relevant information.

(g) The States Parties concerned, referred to in sub-paragraph (b), shall have the right to be represented when the matter is being considered in the Committee and to make submissions orally and/or in writing.

(h) The Committee shall, within twelve months after the date of receipt of notice under sub-paragraph (b), submit a report:

  (i) If a solution within the terms of sub-paragraph (e) is reached, the Committee shall confine its report to a brief statement of the facts and of the solution reached;

  (ii) If a solution within the terms of sub-paragraph (e) is not reached, the Committee shall confine its report to a brief statement of the facts; the written submissions and record of the oral submissions made by the States Parties concerned shall be attached to the report.

In every matter, the report shall be communicated to the States Parties concerned.

2. The provisions of this article shall come into force when ten States Parties to the present Covenant have made declarations under paragraph I of this article. Such declarations shall be deposited by the States Parties with the Secretary-General of the United Nations, who shall transmit copies thereof to the other States Parties. A declaration may be withdrawn at any time by notification to the Secretary-General. Such a withdrawal shall not prejudice the consideration of any matter which is the subject of a communication already transmitted under this Article; no further communication by any State Party shall be received after the notification of withdrawal of the declaration has been received by the Secretary-General, unless the State Party concerned has made a new declaration.

Article 42

1. (*a*) If a matter referred to the Committee in accordance with Article 41 is not resolved to the satisfaction of the States Parties concerned, the Committee may, with the prior consent of the States Parties concerned, appoint an *ad hoc* Conciliation Commission (hereinafter referred to as the Commission). The good offices of the Commission shall be made available to the States Parties concerned with a view to an amicable solution of the matter on the basis of respect for the present Covenant;

(*b*) The Commission shall consist of five persons acceptable to the States Parties concerned. If the States Parties concerned fail to reach agreement within three months on all or part of the composition of the Commission the members of the Commission concerning whom no agreement has been reached shall be elected by secret ballot by a two-thirds majority vote of the Committee from among its members.

2. The members of the Commission shall serve in their personal capacity. They shall not be nationals of the States Parties concerned, or of a State not party to the present Covenant, or of a State Party which has not made a declaration under Article 41.

3. The Commission shall elect its own Chairman and adopt its own rules of procedure.

4. The meetings of the Commission shall normally be held at the Headquarters of the United Nations or at the United Nations Office at Geneva. However, they may be held at such other convenient places as the Commission may determine in consultation with the Secretary-General of the United Nations and the States Parties concerned.

5. The secretariat provided in accordance with Article 36 shall also service the commissions appointed under this Article.

6. The information received and collated by the Committee shall be made available to the Commission and the Commission may call upon the States Parties concerned to supply any other relevant information.

7. When the Commission has fully considered the matter, but in any event not later than twelve months after having been seized of the matter, it shall submit to the Chairman of the Committee a report for communication to the States Parties concerned.

(a) If the Commission is unable to complete its consideration of the matter within twelve months, it shall confine its report to a brief statement of the status of its consideration of the matter.

(b) If an amicable solution to the matter on the basis of respect for human rights as recognized in the present Covenant is reached, the Commission shall confine its report to a brief statement of the facts and of the solution reached.

(c) If a solution within the terms of sub-paragraph (b) is not reached, the Commission's report shall embody its findings on all questions of fact relevant to the issues between the States Parties concerned, and its views on the possibilities of an amicable solution of the matter. This report shall also contain the written submissions and a record of the oral submissions made by the States Parties concerned.

(d) If the Commission's report is submitted under sub-paragraph (c), the States Parties concerned shall, within three months of the receipt of the report, notify the Chairman of the Committee whether or not they accept the contents of the report of the Commission.

8. The provisions of this Article are without prejudice to the responsibilities of the Committee under Article 41.

9. The States Parties concerned shall share equally all the expenses of the members of the Commission in accordance with estimates to be provided by the Secretary-General of the United Nations.

10. The Secretary-General of the United Nations shall be empowered to pay the expenses of the members of the Commission, if necessary, before reimbursement by the States Parties concerned, in accordance with paragraph 9 of this Article.

Article 43

The members of the Committee, and of the *ad hoc* conciliation commissions which may be appointed under Article 42, shall be entitled to the facilities, privileges and immunities of experts on mission for the United Nations as laid down in the relevant sections of the Convention on the Privileges and Immunities of the United Nations.

Article 44

The provisions for the implementation of the present Covenant shall apply without prejudice to the procedures prescribed in the field of human rights by or under the constituent instruments and the conventions of the United Nations and of the specialized agencies and shall not prevent the States Parties to the present Covenant from having recourse to other procedures for settling a dispute in accordance with general or special international agreements in force between them.

Article 45

The Committee shall submit to the General Assembly of the United Nations through the Economic and Social Council, an annual report on its activities.

PART V

Article 46

Nothing in the present Covenant shall be interpreted as impairing the provisions of the Charter of the United Nations and of the constitutions of the specialized agencies which define the respective responsibilities of the various organs of the United Nations and of the specialized agencies in regard to the matters dealt with in the present Covenant.

Article 47

Nothing in the present Covenant shall be interpreted as impairing the inherent right of all peoples to enjoy and utilize fully and freely their natural wealth and resources.

PART VI

Article 48

1. The present Covenant is open for signature by any State Member of the United Nations or member of any of its specialized agencies, by any State Party to the Statute of the International Court of Justice, and by any other State which has been invited by the General Assembly of the United Nations to become a party to the present Covenant.

2. The present Covenant is subject to ratification. Instruments of ratification shall be deposited with the Secretary-General of the United Nations.

3. The present Covenant shall be open to accession by any State referred to in paragraph 1 of this Article.

4. Accession shall be effected by the deposit of an instrument of accession with the Secretary-General of the United Nations.

5. The Secretary-General of the United Nations shall inform all States which have signed this Covenant or acceded to it of the deposit of each instrument of ratification or accession.

Article 49

1. The present Covenant shall enter into force three months after the date of the deposit with the Secretary-General of the United Nations of the thirty-fifth instrument of ratification or instrument of accession.

2. For each State ratifying the present Covenant or acceding to it after the deposit of the thirty-fifth instrument of ratification or instrument of accession, the present Covenant shall enter into force three months after the date of the deposit of its own instrument of ratification or instrument of accession.

Article 50

The provisions of the present Covenant shall extend to all parts of federal States without any limitations or exceptions.

Article 51

1. Any State Party to the present Covenant may propose an amendment and file it with the Secretary-General of the United Nations. The Secretary-General of the United Nations shall thereupon communicate any proposed amendments to the States Parties to the present Covenant with a request that they notify him whether they favour a conference of States Parties for the purpose of considering and voting upon the proposals. In the event that at least one third of the States Parties favours such a conference, the Secretary-General shall convene the conference under the auspices of the United Nations. Any amendment adopted by a majority of the States Parties present and voting at the conference shall be submitted to the General Assembly of the United Nations for approval.

2. Amendments shall come into force when they have been approved by

the General Assembly of the United Nations and accepted by a two-thirds majority of the States Parties to the present Covenant in accordance with their respective constitutional processes.

3. When amendments come into force, they shall be binding on those States Parties which have accepted them, other States Parties still being bound by the provisions of the present Covenant and any earlier amendment which they have accepted.

Article 52

Irrespective of the notifications made under Article 48, paragraph 5, the Secretary-General of the United Nations shall inform all States referred to in paragraph 1 of the same article of the following particulars:

(a) Signatures, ratifications and accessions under Article 48;
(b) The date of the entry into force of the present Covenant under Article 49 and the date of the entry into force of any amendments under Article 51.

Article 53

1. The present Covenant, of which the Chinese, English, French, Russian and Spanish texts are equally authentic, shall be deposited in the archives of the United Nations.

2. The Secretary-General of the United Nations shall transmit certified copies of the present Covenant to all States referred to in Article 48.

III. OPTIONAL PROTOCOL TO THE INTERNATIONAL COVENANT ON CIVIL AND POLITICAL RIGHTS, 1966

THIS was signed by fourteen States, and has been ratified by one so far. It adds to the machinery for implementing the Covenant. On the right of petition by individuals see also the Trusteeship System of the United Nations Charter, the European Convention, below, and the American Convention, below.

TEXT

The States Parties to the present Protocol,

Considering that in order further to achieve the purposes of the Covenant on Civil and Political Rights (hereinafter referred to as the Covenant) and the implementation of its provisions it would be appropriate to enable the Human Rights Committee set up in Part IV of the Covenant (hereinafter referred to as the Committee) to receive and consider, as provided in the present Protocol, communications from individuals claiming to be victims of violations of any of the rights set forth in the Covenant,

Have agreed as follows:

Article 1

A State Party to the Covenant that becomes a party to the present Protocol recognizes the competence of the Committee to receive and consider communications from individuals subject to its jurisdiction who claim to be victims of a violation by that State Party of any of the rights set forth in the Covenant. No communication shall be received by the Committee if it concerns a State Party to the Covenant which is not a party to the present Protocol.

Article 2

Subject to the provisions of Article 1, individuals who claim that any of their rights enumerated in the Covenant have been violated and who have exhausted all available domestic remedies may submit a written communication to the Committee for consideration.

Article 3

The Committee shall consider inadmissible any communication under the present Protocol which is anonymous, or which it considers to be an abuse of the right of submission of such communications or to be incompatible with the provisions of the Covenant.

Article 4

1. Subject to the provisions of Article 3, the Committee shall bring any communications submitted to it under the present Protocol to the attention of the State Party to the present Protocol alleged to be violating any provision of the Covenant.

2. Within six months, the receiving State shall submit to the Committee written explanations or statements clarifying the matter and the remedy, if any, that may have been taken by that State.

Article 5

1. The Committee shall consider communications received under the present Protocol in the light of all written information made available to it by the individual and by the State Party concerned.

2. The Committee shall not consider any communication from an individual unless it has ascertained that:

> (a) The same matter is not being examined under another procedure of international investigation or settlement;
> (b) The individual has exhausted all available domestic remedies. This shall not be the rule where the application of the remedies is unreasonably prolonged.

3. The Committee shall hold closed meetings when examining communications under the present Protocol.

4. The Committee shall forward its views to the State Party concerned and to the individual.

Article 6

The Committee shall include in its annual report under Article 45 of the Covenant a summary of its activities under the present Protocol.

Article 7

Pending the achievement of the objectives of resolution 1514 (XV) adopted by the General Assembly of the United Nations on 14 December 1960 concerning the Declaration on the Granting of Independence to Colonial Countries and Peoples, the provisions of the present Protocol shall in no way limit the right of petition granted to these peoples by the Charter of the United Nations and other international conventions and instruments under the United Nations and its specialized agencies.

Article 8

1. The present Protocol is open for signature by any State which has signed the Covenant.

2. The present Protocol is subject to ratification by any State which has ratified or acceded to the Covenant. Instruments of ratification shall be deposited with the Secretary-General of the United Nations.

3. The present Protocol shall be open to accession by any State which has ratified or acceded to the Covenant.

4. Accession shall be effected by the deposit of an instrument of accession with the Secretary-General of the United Nations.

5. The Secretary-General of the United Nations shall inform all States which have signed the present Protocol or acceded to it of the deposit of each instrument of ratification or accession.

Article 9

1. Subject to the entry into force of the Covenant, the present Protocol shall enter into force three months after the date of the deposit with the Secretary-General of the United Nations of the tenth instrument of ratification or instrument of accession.

2. For each State ratifying the present Protocol or acceding to it after the deposit of the tenth instrument of ratification or instrument of accession, the present Protocol shall enter into force three months after the date of the deposit of its own instrument of ratification or instrument of accession.

Article 10

The provisions of the present Protocol shall extend to all parts of federal States without any limitations or exceptions.

Article 11

1. Any State Party to the present Protocol may propose an amendment and file it with the Secretary-General of the United Nations. The Secretary-General shall thereupon communicate any proposed amendments to the States Parties to the present Protocol with a request that they notify him whether they favour a conference of States Parties for the purpose of considering and voting upon the proposal. In the event that at least one third of the States Parties favours such a conference, the Secretary-General shall convene the conference under the auspices of the United Nations. Any amendment adopted by a majority of the States Parties present and voting at the conference shall be submitted to the General Assembly of the United Nations for approval.

2. Amendments shall come into force when they have been approved by the General Assembly of the United Nations and accepted by a two-thirds majority of the States Parties to the present Protocol in accordance with their respective constitutional processes.

3. When amendments come into force, they shall be binding on those States Parties which have accepted them, other States Parties still being bound by the provisions of the present Protocol and any earlier amendment which they have accepted.

Article 12

1. Any State Party may denounce the present Protocol at any time by written notification addressed to the Secretary-General of the United Nations. Denunciation shall take effect three months after the date of receipt of the notification by the Secretary-General.

2. Denunciation shall be without prejudice to the continued application of the provisions of the present Protocol to any communication submitted under Article 2 before the effective date of denunciation.

Article 13

Irrespective of the notifications made under Article 8, paragraph 5, of the present Protocol, the Secretary-General of the United Nations shall inform all States referred to in Article 48, paragraph 1, of the Covenant of the following particulars:

(*a*) Signatures, ratifications and accessions under Article 8;
(*b*) The date of the entry into force of the present Protocol under Article 9 and the date of the entry into force of any amendments under Article 11;
(*c*) Denunciations under Article 12.

Article 14

1. The present Protocol, of which the Chinese, English, French, Russian and Spanish texts are equally authentic, shall be deposited in the archives of the United Nations.

2. The Secretary-General of the United Nations shall transmit certified copies of the present Protocol to all States referred to in Article 48 of the Covenant.

IV. INTERNATIONAL CONVENTION ON THE ELIMINATION OF ALL FORMS OF RACIAL DISCRIMINATION, 1966

THE great theme which pervades the provisions of the U.N. Charter and other instruments, both national and international, concerned with human rights and civil liberties, is that of equality. It has slowly come to be recognized that racial discrimination and resulting conflict are a major issue in world affairs. The Convention, opened for signature on 7 March 1966, was adopted by the General Assembly of the United Nations on 21 December 1965. It has been signed by seventy-one States and over twenty-nine States have become parties. For the text in various languages see *U.K. Treaty Series*, Misc. No. 77, 1969, Cmnd. 4108.

For further reference see U.N., *Multilateral Treaties in Respect of which the Secretary-General Performs Depositary Functions*, 1969, pp. 64–7; Philip Mason, *Patterns of Dominance*, 1970; Schwelb, *International and Comparative Law Quarterly*, 15 (1966), p. 996.

The link between the issue of racial equality and decolonization is established in the resolution of the General Assembly of the United Nations (printed as an annex below) Resolution 2106 (XX), B, associated with the adoption by the General Assembly of the Convention itself. See further Resolution 2547 (XXIV) adopted by the General Assembly on 15 December 1969.

TEXT

The States Parties to this Convention,

Considering that the Charter of the United Nations is based on the principles of the dignity and equality inherent in all human beings, and that all Member States have pledged themselves to take joint and separate action, in co-operation with the Organization, for the achievement of one of the purposes of the United Nations which is to promote and encourage universal respect for and observance of human rights and fundamental freedoms for all, without distinction as to race, sex, language or religion,

Considering that the Universal Declaration of Human Rights proclaims that all human beings are born free and equal in dignity and rights and that everyone is entitled to all the rights and freedoms set out therein, without distinction of any kind, in particular as to race, colour or national origin,

Considering that all human beings are equal before the law and are entitled to equal protection of the law against any discrimination and against any incitement to discrimination,

Considering that the United Nations has condemned colonialism and all practices of segregation and discrimination associated therewith, in whatever form and wherever they exist, and that the Declaration on the Granting of Independence to Colonial Countries and Peoples of 14 December 1960 (General Assembly resolution 1514 (XV)) has affirmed and solemnly proclaimed the necessity of bringing them to a speedy and unconditional end,

Considering that the United Nations Declaration on the Elimination of All Forms of Racial Discrimination of 20 November 1963 (General Assembly resolution 1940 (XVIII)) solemnly affirms the necessity of speedily eliminating racial discrimination throughout the world in all its forms and manifestations and of securing understanding of and respect for the dignity of the human person,

Convinced that any doctrine of superiority based on racial differentiation is scientifically false, morally condemnable, socially unjust and dangerous, and that there is no justification for racial discrimination, in theory or in practice, anywhere,

Reaffirming that discrimination between human beings on the grounds of race, colour or ethnic origin is an obstacle to friendly and peaceful relations among nations and is capable of disturbing peace and security among peoples and the harmony of persons living side by side even within one and the same State,

Convinced that the existence of racial barriers is repugnant to the ideals of any human society,

Alarmed by manifestations of racial discrimination still in evidence in some areas of the world and by governmental policies based on racial superiority or hatred, such as policies of *apartheid*, segregation or separation,

Resolved to adopt all necessary measures for speedily eliminating racial discrimination in all its forms and manifestations, and to prevent and combat racist doctrines and practices in order to promote understanding between races and to build an international community free from all forms of racial segregation and racial discrimination,

Bearing in mind the Convention concerning Discrimination in respect of Employment and Occupation adopted by the International Labour Organization in 1958, and the Convention against Discrimination in

Education adopted by the United Nations Educational, Scientific and Cultural Organization in 1960,

Desiring to implement the principles embodied in the United Nations Declaration on the Elimination of All Forms of Racial Discrimination and to secure the earliest adoption of practical measures to that end,

Have agreed as follows:

PART I

Article 1

1. In this Convention, the term 'racial discrimination' shall mean any distinction, exclusion, restriction or preference based on race, colour, descent, or national or ethnic origin which has the purpose or effect of nullifying or impairing the recognition, enjoyment or exercise, on an equal footing, of human rights and fundamental freedoms in the political, economic, social, cultural or any other field of public life.

2. This Convention shall not apply to distinctions, exclusions, restrictions or preferences made by a State Party to this Convention between citizens and non-citizens.

3. Nothing in this Convention may be interpreted as affecting in any way the legal provisions of States Parties concerning nationality, citizenship or naturalization, provided that such provisions do not discriminate against any particular nationality.

4. Special measures taken for the sole purpose of securing adequate advancement of certain racial or ethnic groups or individuals requiring such protection as may be necessary in order to ensure such groups or individuals equal enjoyment or exercise of human rights and fundamental freedoms shall not be deemed racial discrimination, provided, however, that such measures do not, as a consequence, lead to the maintenance of separate rights for different racial groups and that they shall not be continued after the objectives for which they were taken have been achieved.

Article 2

1. States Parties condemn racial discrimination and undertake to pursue by all appropriate means and without delay a policy of eliminating racial discrimination in all its forms and promoting understanding among all races, and, to this end:

(*a*) Each State Party undertakes to engage in no act or practice of racial discrimination against persons, groups of persons or institutions and to ensure that all public authorities and public institutions, national and local, shall act in conformity with this obligation;

(b) Each State Party undertakes not to sponsor, defend or support racial discrimination by any persons or organizations;

(c) Each State Party shall take effective measures to review governmental, national and local policies, and to amend, rescind or nullify any laws and regulations which have the effect of creating or perpetuating racial discrimination wherever it exists;

(d) Each State Party shall prohibit and bring to an end, by all appropriate means, including legislation as required by circumstances, racial discrimination by any persons, group or organization;

(e) Each State Party undertakes to encourage, where appropriate, integrationist multi-racial organizations and movements and other means of eliminating barriers between races, and to discourage anything which tends to strengthen racial division.

2. States Parties shall, when the circumstances so warrant, take, in the social, economic, cultural and other fields, special and concrete measures to ensure the adequate development and protection of certain racial groups or individuals belonging to them, for the purpose of guaranteeing them the full and equal enjoyment of human rights and fundamental freedoms. These measures shall in no case entail as a consequence the maintenance of unequal or separate rights for different racial groups after the objectives for which they were taken have been achieved.

Article 3

States Parties particularly condemn racial segregation and *apartheid* and undertake to prevent, prohibit and eradicate all practices of this nature in territories under their jurisdiction.

Article 4

States Parties condemn all propaganda and all organizations which are based on ideas or theories of superiority of one race or group of persons of one colour or ethnic origin, or which attempt to justify or promote racial hatred and discrimination in any form, and undertake to adopt immediate and positive measures designed to eradicate all incitement to, or acts of, such discrimination and, to this end, with due regard to the principles embodied in the Universal Declaration of Human Rights and the rights expressly set forth in Article 5 of this Convention, *inter alia*:

(*a*) Shall declare an offence punishable by law all dissemination of ideas based on racial superiority or hatred, incitement to racial discrimination, as well as all acts of violence or incitement to such acts against any race or group of persons of another colour or ethnic origin, and also the provision of any assistance to racist activities, including the financing thereof;

(*b*) Shall declare illegal and prohibit organizations, and also organized and all other propaganda activities, which promote and incite racial discrimination, and shall recognize participation in such organizations or activities as an offence punishable by law;

(*c*) Shall not permit public authorities or public institutions, national or local, to promote or incite racial discrimination.

Article 5

In compliance with the fundamental obligations laid down in Article 2 of this Convention, States Parties undertake to prohibit and to eliminate racial discrimination in all its forms and to guarantee the right of everyone, without distinction as to race, colour, or national or ethnic origin, to equality before the law, notably in the enjoyment of the following rights:

(*a*) The right to equal treatment before the tribunals and all other organs administering justice;

(*b*) The right to security of person and protection by the State against violence or bodily harm, whether inflicted by government officials or by any individual, group or institution;

(*c*) Political rights, in particular the rights to participate in elections— to vote and to stand for election—on the basis of universal and equal suffrage, to take part in the Government as well as in the conduct of public affairs at any level and to have equal access to public service;

(*d*) Other civil rights, in particular:

   (i) The right to freedom of movement and residence within the border of the State;

   (ii) The right to leave any country, including one's own, and to return to one's country;

   (iii) The right to nationality;

   (iv) The right to marriage and choice of spouse;

   (v) The right to own property alone as well as in association with others;

   (vi) The right to inherit;

(vii) The right to freedom of thought, conscience and religion;
(viii) The right to freedom of opinion and expression;
(ix) The right to freedom of peaceful assembly and association;
(e) Economic, social and cultural rights, in particular:
  (i) The rights to work, to free choice of employment, to just and favourable conditions of work, to protection against unemployment, to equal pay for equal work, to just and favourable remuneration;
  (ii) The right to form and join trade unions;
  (iii) The right to housing;
  (iv) The right to public health, medical care, social security and social services;
  (v) The right to education and training;
  (vi) The right to equal participation in cultural activities;
(f) The right of access to any place or service intended for use by the general public, such as transport, hotels, restaurants, cafés, theatres and parks.

Article 6

States Parties shall assure to everyone within their jurisdiction effective protection and remedies, through the competent national tribunals and other State institutions, against any acts of racial discrimination which violate his human rights and fundamental freedoms contrary to this Convention, as well as the right to seek from such tribunals just and adequate reparation or satisfaction for any damage suffered as a result of such discrimination.

Article 7

States Parties undertake to adopt immediate and effective measures, particularly in the fields of teaching, education, culture and information, with a view to combating prejudices which lead to racial discrimination and to promoting understanding, tolerance and friendship among nations and racial or ethnical groups, as well as to propagating the purposes and principles of the Charter of the United Nations, the Universal Declaration of Human Rights, the United Nations Declaration on the Elimination of All Forms of Racial Discrimination, and this Convention.

PART II

Article 8

1. There shall be established a Committee on the Elimination of Racial Discrimination (hereinafter referred to as the Committee) consisting of

eighteen experts of high moral standing and acknowledged impartiality elected by States Parties from among their nationals, who shall serve in their personal capacity, consideration being given to equitable geographical distribution and to the representation of the different forms of civilization as well as of the principal legal systems.

2. The members of the Committee shall be elected by secret ballot from a list of persons nominated by the States Parties. Each State Party may nominate one person from among its own nationals.

3. The initial election shall be held six months after the date of the entry into force of this Convention. At least three months before the date of each election the Secretary-General of the United Nations shall address a letter to the States Parties inviting them to submit their nominations within two months. The Secretary-General shall prepare a list in alphabetical order of all persons thus nominated, indicating the States Parties which have nominated them, and shall submit it to the States Parties.

4. Elections of the members of the Committee shall be held at a meeting of States Parties convened by the Secretary-General at United Nations Headquarters. At that meeting, for which two-thirds of the States Parties shall constitute a quorum, the persons elected to the Committee shall be those nominees who obtain the largest number of votes and an absolute majority of the votes of the representatives of States Parties present and voting.

5. (*a*) The members of the Committee shall be elected for a term of four years. However, the terms of nine of the members elected at the first election shall expire at the end of two years; immediately after the first election the names of these nine members shall be chosen by lot by the Chairman of the Committee.

(*b*) For the filling of casual vacancies, the State Party whose expert has ceased to function as a member of the Committee shall appoint another expert from among its nationals, subject to the approval of the Committee.

6. States Parties shall be responsible for the expenses of the members of the Committee while they are in performance of Committee duties.

Article 9

1. States Parties undertake to submit to the Secretary-General of the United Nations, for consideration by the Committee, a report on the legislative, judicial, administrative or other measures which they have adopted and which give effect to the provisions of this Convention:

(*a*) within one year after the entry into force of the Convention for the State concerned; and (*b*) thereafter every two years and whenever the Committee so requests. The Committee may request further information from the States Parties.

2. The Committee shall report annually, through the Secretary-General, to the General Assembly of the United Nations on its activities and may make suggestions and general recommendations based on the examination of the reports and information received from the States Parties. Such suggestions and general recommendations shall be reported to the General Assembly together with comments, if any, from States Parties.

Article 10

1. The Committee shall adopt its own rules of procedure.

2. The Committee shall elect its officers for a term of two years.

3. The secretariat of the Committee shall be provided by the Secretary-General of the United Nations.

4. The meetings of the Committee shall normally be held at United Nations Headquarters.

Article 11

1. If a State Party considers that another State Party is not giving effect to the provisions of this Convention, it may bring the matter to the attention of the Committee. The Committee shall then transmit the communication to the State Party concerned. Within three months, the receiving State shall submit to the Committee written explanations or statements clarifying the matter and the remedy, if any, that may have been taken by that State.

2. If the matter is not adjusted to the satisfaction of both parties, either by bilateral negotiations or by any other procedure open to them, within six months after the receipt by the receiving State of the initial communication, either State shall have the right to refer the matter again to the Committee by notifying the Committee and also the other State.

3. The Committee shall deal with a matter referred to it in accordance with paragraph 2 of this Article after it has ascertained that all available domestic remedies have been invoked and exhausted in the case, in conformity with the generally recognized principles of international law. This shall not be the rule where the application of the remedies is unreasonably prolonged.

4. In any matter referred to it, the Committee may call upon the States Parties concerned to supply any other relevant information.

5. When any matter arising out of this article is being considered by the Committee, the States Parties concerned shall be entitled to send a representative to take part in the proceedings of the Committee, without voting rights, while the matter is under consideration.

Article 12

1. (*a*) After the Committee has obtained and collated all the information it deems necessary, the Chairman shall appoint an *ad hoc* Conciliation Commission (hereinafter referred to as the Commission) comprising five persons who may or may not be members of the Committee. The members of the Commission shall be appointed with the unanimous consent of the parties to the dispute, and its good offices shall be made available to the States concerned with a view to an amicable solution of the matter on the basis of respect for this Convention.

(*b*) If the States Parties to the dispute fail to reach agreement within three months on all or part of the composition of the Commission, the members of the Commission not agreed upon by the States parties to the dispute shall be elected by secret ballot by a two-thirds majority vote of the Committee from among its own members.

2. The members of the Commission shall serve in their personal capacity. They shall not be nationals of the States parties to the dispute or of a State not Party to this Convention.

3. The Commission shall elect its own Chairman and adopt its own rules of procedure.

4. The meetings of the Commission shall normally be held at United Nations Headquarters or at any other convenient place as determined by the Commission.

5. The secretariat provided in accordance with Article 10, paragraph 3, of this Convention shall also service the Commission whenever a dispute among States Parties brings the Commission into being.

6. The States parties to the dispute shall share equally all the expenses of the members of the Commission in accordance with estimates to be provided by the Secretary-General of the United Nations.

7. The Secretary-General shall be empowered to pay the expenses of the members of the Commission, if necessary, before reimbursement by the States parties to the dispute in accordance with paragraph 6 of this Article.

8. The information obtained and collated by the Committee shall be made available to the Commission, and the Commission may call upon the States concerned to supply any other relevant information.

Article 13

1. When the Commission has fully considered the matter, it shall prepare and submit to the Chairman of the Committee a report embodying its findings on all questions of fact relevant to the issue between the parties and containing such recommendations as it may think proper for the amicable solution of the dispute.

2. The Chairman of the Committee shall communicate the report of the Commission to each of the States parties to the dispute. These States shall, within three months, inform the Chairman of the Committee whether or not they accept the recommendations contained in the report of the Commission.

3. After the period provided for in paragraph 2 of this Article, the Chairman of the Committee shall communicate the report of the Commission and the declarations of the States Parties concerned to the other States Parties to this Convention.

Article 14

1. A State Party may at any time declare that it recognizes the competence of the Committee to receive and consider communications from individuals or groups of individuals within its jurisdiction claiming to be victims of a violation by that State Party of any of the rights set forth in this Convention. No communication shall be received by the Committee if it concerns a State Party which has not made such a declaration.

2. Any State Party which makes a declaration as provided for in paragraph 1 of this Article may establish or indicate a body within its national legal order which shall be competent to receive and consider petitions from individuals and groups of individuals within its jurisdiction who claim to be victims of a violation of any of the rights set forth in this Convention and who have exhausted other available local remedies.

3. A declaration made in accordance with paragraph 1 of this Article and the name of any body established or indicated in accordance with paragraph 2 of this Article shall be deposited by the State Party concerned with the Secretary-General of the United Nations, who shall transmit copies thereof to the other States Parties. A declaration may be withdrawn at any time by notification to the Secretary-General, but such a

withdrawal shall not affect communications pending before the Committee.

4. A register of petitions shall be kept by the body established or indicated in accordance with paragraph 2 of this Article, and certified copies of the register shall be filed annually through appropriate channels with the Secretary-General on the understanding that the contents shall not be publicly disclosed.

5. In the event of failure to obtain satisfaction from the body established or indicated in accordance with paragraph 2 of this Article, the petitioner shall have the right to communicate the matter to the Committee within six months.

6. (a) The Committee shall confidentially bring any communication referred to it to the attention of the State Party alleged to be violating any provision of this Convention, but the identity of the individual or groups of individuals concerned shall not be revealed without his or their express consent. The Committee shall not receive anonymous communications.

(b) Within three months, the receiving State shall submit to the Committee written explanations or statements clarifying the matter and the remedy, if any, that may have been taken by that State.

7. (a) The Committee shall consider communications in the light of all information made available to it by the State Party concerned and by the petitioner. The Committee shall not consider any communication from a petitioner unless it has ascertained that the petitioner has exhausted all available domestic remedies. However, this shall not be the rule where the application of the remedies is unreasonably prolonged.

(b) The Committee shall forward its suggestions and recommendations, if any, to the State Party concerned and to the petitioner.

8. The Committee shall include in its annual report a summary of such communications and, where appropriate, a summary of the explanations and statements of the States Parties concerned and of its own suggestions and recommendations.

9. The Committee shall be competent to exercise the functions provided for in this Article only when at least ten States Parties to this Convention are bound by declarations in accordance with paragraph 1 of this Article.

Article 15

1. Pending the achievement of the objectives of the Declaration on the Granting of Independence to Colonial Countries and Peoples, contained in General Assembly resolution 1514 (XV) of 14 December 1960, the

provisions of this Convention shall in no way limit the right of petition granted to these peoples by other international instruments or by the United Nations and its specialized agencies.

2. (*a*) The Committee established under Article 8, paragraph 1, of this Convention shall receive copies of the petitions from, and submit expressions of opinion and recommendations on these petitions to, the bodies of the United Nations which deal with matters directly related to the principles and objectives of this Convention in their consideration of petitions from the inhabitants of Trust and Non-Self-Governing Territories and all other territories to which General Assembly resolution 1514 (XV) applies, relating to matters covered by this Convention which are before these bodies.

(*b*) The Committee shall receive from the competent bodies of the United Nations copies of the reports concerning the legislative, judicial, administrative or other measures directly related to the principles and objectives of this Convention applied by the administering Powers within the Territories mentioned in sub-paragraph (*a*) of this paragraph, and shall express opinions and make recommendations to these bodies.

3. The Committee shall include in its report to the General Assembly a summary of the petitions and reports it has received from United Nations bodies, and the expressions of opinion and recommendations of the Committee relating to the said petitions and reports.

4. The Committee shall request from the Secretary-General of the United Nations all information relevant to the objectives of this Convention and available to him regarding the Territories mentioned in paragraph 2 (*a*) of this Article.

Article 16

The provisions of this Convention concerning the settlement of disputes or complaints shall be applied without prejudice to other procedures for settling disputes or complaints in the field of discrimination laid down in the constituent instruments of, or in conventions adopted by, the United Nations and its specialized agencies, and shall not prevent the States Parties from having recourse to other procedures for settling a dispute in accordance with general or special international agreements in force between them.

PART III

Article 17

1. This Convention is open for signature by any State Member of the

United Nations or member of any of its specialized agencies, by any State Party to the Statute of the International Court of Justice, and by any other State which has been invited by the General Assembly of the United Nations to become a Party to this Convention.

2. This Convention is subject to ratification. Instruments of ratification shall be deposited with the Secretary-General of the United Nations.

Article 18

1. This Convention shall be open to accession by any State referred to in Article 17, paragraph 1, of the Convention.

2. Accession shall be effected by the deposit of an instrument of accession with the Secretary-General of the United Nations.

Article 19

1. This Convention shall enter into force on the thirtieth day after the date of the deposit with the Secretary-General of the United Nations of the twenty-seventh instrument of ratification or instrument of accession.

2. For each State ratifying this Convention or acceding to it after the deposit of the twenty-seventh instrument of ratification or instrument of accession, the Convention shall enter into force on the thirtieth day after the date of the deposit of its own instrument of ratification or instrument of accession.

Article 20

1. The Secretary-General of the United Nations shall receive and circulate to all States which are or may become Parties to this Convention reservations made by States at the time of ratification or accession. Any State which objects to the reservation shall, within a period of ninety days from the date of the said communication, notify the Secretary-General that it does not accept it.

2. A reservation incompatible with the object and purpose of this Convention shall not be permitted, nor shall a reservation the effect of which would inhibit the operation of any of the bodies established by this Convention be allowed. A reservation shall be considered incompatible or inhibitive if at least two-thirds of the States Parties to this Convention object to it.

3. Reservations may be withdrawn at any time by notification to this

effect addressed to the Secretary-General. Such notification shall take effect on the date on which it is received.

Article 21

A State Party may denounce this Convention by written notification to the Secretary-General of the United Nations. Denunciation shall take effect one year after the date of receipt of the notification by the Secretary-General.

Article 22

Any dispute between two or more States Parties with respect to the interpretation or application of this Convention, which is not settled by negotiation or by the procedures expressly provided for in this Convention, shall, at the request of any of the parties to the dispute, be referred to the International Court of Justice for decision, unless the disputants agree to another mode of settlement.

Article 23

1. A request for the revision of this Convention may be made at any time by any State Party by means of a notification in writing addressed to the Secretary-General of the United Nations.
2. The General Assembly of the United Nations shall decide upon the steps, if any, to be taken in respect of such a request.

Article 24

The Secretary-General of the United Nations shall inform all States referred to in Article 17, paragraph 1, of this Convention of the following particulars:

(a) Signatures, ratifications and accessions under Articles 17 and 18;
(b) The date of entry into force of this Convention under Article 19;
(c) Communications and declarations received under Articles 14, 20 and 23;
(d) Denunciations under Article 21.

Article 25

1. This Convention, of which the Chinese, English, French, Russian and Spanish texts are equally authentic, shall be deposited in the archives of the United Nations.

2. The Secretary-General of the United Nations shall transmit certified copies of this Convention to all States belonging to any of the categories mentioned in Article 17, paragraph 1, of the Convention.

In faith whereof the undersigned, being duly authorized thereto by their respective Governments, have signed the present Convention, opened for signature at New York, on the seventh day of March, one thousand nine hundred and sixty-six.

ANNEX

The General Assembly,

Recalling the Declaration on the Granting of Independence to Colonial Countries and Peoples contained in its resolution 1514 (XV) of 14 December 1960.

Bearing in mind its resolution 1654 (XVI) of 27 November 1961, which established the Special Committee on the Situation with regard to the Implementation of the Declaration on the Granting of Independence to Colonial Countries and Peoples to examine the application of the Declaration and to carry out its provisions by all means at its disposal,

Bearing in mind also the provisions of Article 15 of the International Convention on the Elimination of All Forms of Racial Discrimination contained in the annex to resolution 2106 A (XX) above,

Recalling that the General Assembly has established other bodies to receive and examine petitions from the peoples of colonial countries,

Convinced that close co-operation between the Committee on the Elimination of Racial Discrimination, established by the International Convention on the Elimination of All Forms of Racial Discrimination, and the bodies of the United Nations charged with receiving and examining petitions from the peoples of colonial countries will facilitate the achievement of the objectives of both the Convention and the Declaration on the Granting of Independence to Colonial Countries and Peoples,

Recognizing that the elimination of racial discrimination in all its forms is vital to the achievement of fundamental human rights and to the assurance of the dignity and worth of the human person, and thus constitutes a pre-emptory obligation under the Charter of the United Nations,

1. *Calls upon* the Secretary-General to make available to the Committee on the Elimination of Racial Discrimination, periodically or at its request, all information in his possession relevant to Article 15 of the International Convention on the Elimination of All Forms of Racial Discrimination;

2. *Requests* the Special Committee on the Situation with regard to the Implementation of the Granting of Independence to Colonial Countries and Peoples, and all other bodies of the United Nations authorized to receive and examine petitions from the peoples of the colonial countries, to transmit to the Committee on the Elimination of Racial Discrimination, periodically or at its request, copies of petitions from those peoples relevant to the Convention, for the comments and recommendations of the said Committee;

3. *Requests* the bodies referred to in paragraph 2 above to include in their annual reports to the General Assembly a summary of the action taken by them under the terms of the present resolution.

V. PROCLAMATION OF TEHRAN, 1968

THE Proclamation was adopted by a United Nations Conference on Human Rights: see the Final Act of the International Conference on Human Rights, Tehran, 22 April–13 May 1968, U.N. Doc. A/CONF. 32/41, Sales No. E.68, XIV 2. The Conference also adopted various resolutions on particular problems, including respect for human rights in occupied territories, and the development of comprehensive legal aid systems.

TEXT

The International Conference on Human Rights,

Having met at Teheran from April 22 to May 13, 1968 to review the progress made in the twenty years since the adoption of the Universal Declaration of Human Rights and to formulate a programme for the future,

Having considered the problems relating to the activities of the United Nations for the promotion and encouragement of respect for human rights and fundamental freedoms,

Bearing in mind the resolutions adopted by the Conference,

Noting that the observance of the International Year for Human Rights takes place at a time when the world is undergoing a process of unprecedented change,

Having regard to the new opportunities made available by the rapid progress of science and technology,

Believing that, in an age when conflict and violence prevail in many parts of the world, the fact of human interdependence and the need for human solidarity are more evident than ever before,

Recognizing that peace is the universal aspiration of mankind and that peace and justice are indispensable to the full realization of human rights and fundamental freedoms,

Solemnly proclaims that :

1. It is imperative that the members of the international community fulfil their solemn obligations to promote and encourage respect for human

rights and fundamental freedoms for all without distinctions of any kind such as race, colour, sex, language, religion, political or other opinions;

2. The Universal Declaration of Human Rights states a common understanding of the peoples of the world concerning the inalienable and inviolable rights of all members of the human family and constitutes an obligation for the members of the international community;

3. The International Covenant on Civil and Political Rights, the International Covenant on Economic, Social and Cultural Rights, the Declaration on the Granting of Independence to Colonial Countries and Peoples, the International Convention on the Elimination of All Forms of Racial Discrimination, as well as other conventions and declarations in the field of human rights adopted under the auspices of the United Nations, the specialized agencies and the regional inter-governmental organizations, have created new standards and obligations to which States should conform;

4. Since the adoption of the Universal Declaration of Human Rights the United Nations has made substantial progress in defining standards for the enjoyment and protection of human rights and fundamental freedoms. During this period many important international instruments were adopted but much remains to be done in regard to the implementation of those rights and freedoms;

5. The primary aim of the United Nations in the sphere of human rights is the achievement by each individual of the maximum freedom and dignity. For the realization of this objective, the laws of every country should grant each individual, irrespective of race, language, religion or political belief, freedom of expression, of information, of conscience and of religion, as well as the right to participate in the political, economic, cultural and social life of his country;

6. States should reaffirm their determination effectively to enforce the principles enshrined in the Charter of the United Nations and in other international instruments that concern human rights and fundamental freedoms;

7. Gross denials of human rights under the repugnant policy of *apartheid* is a matter of the gravest concern to the international community. This policy of *apartheid*, condemned as a crime against humanity, continues seriously to disturb international peace and security. It is therefore imperative for the international community to use every possible means to eradicate this evil. The struggle against *apartheid* is recognized as legitimate;

8. The peoples of the world must be made fully aware of the evils of racial discrimination and must join in combating them. The implementation of this principle of non-discrimination, embodied in the Charter of the United Nations, the Universal Declaration of Human Rights, and other international instruments in the field of human rights, constitutes a most urgent task of mankind, at the international as well as at the national level. All ideologies based on racial superiority and intolerance must be condemned and resisted;

9. Eight years after the General Assembly's Declaration on the Granting of Independence to Colonial Countries and Peoples the problems of colonialism continue to preoccupy the international community. It is a matter of urgency that all Member States should co-operate with the appropriate organs of the United Nations so that effective measures can be taken to ensure that the Declaration is fully implemented;

10. Massive denials of human rights, arising out of aggression or any armed conflict with their tragic consequences, and resulting in untold human misery, engender reactions which could engulf the world in ever growing hostilities. It is the obligation of the international community to co-operate in eradicating such scourges;

11. Gross denials of human rights arising from discrimination on grounds of race, religion, belief or expressions of opinion outrage the conscience of mankind and endanger the foundations of freedom, justice and peace in the world;

12. The widening gap between the economically developed and developing countries impedes the realization of human rights in the international community. The failure of the Development Decade to reach its modest objectives makes it all the more imperative for every nation, according to its capacities, to make the maximum possible effort to close this gap;

13. Since human rights and fundamental freedoms are indivisible, the full realization of civil and political rights without the enjoyment of economic, social and cultural rights, is impossible. The achievement of lasting progress in the implementation of human rights is dependent upon sound and effective national and international policies of economic and social development;

14. The existence of over seven hundred million illiterates throughout the world is an enormous obstacle to all efforts at realizing the aims and purposes of the Charter of the United Nations and the provisions of the Universal Declaration of Human Rights. International action aimed at

9*

eradicating illiteracy from the face of the earth and promoting education at all levels requires urgent attention;

15. The discrimination of which women are still victims in various regions of the world must be eliminated. An inferior status for women is contrary to the Charter of the United Nations as well as the provisions of the Universal Declaration of Human Rights. The full implementation of the Declaration on the Elimination of All Forms of Discrimination Against Women is a necessity for the progress of mankind;

16. The protection of the family and of the child remains the concern of the international community. Parents have a basic human right to determine freely and responsibly the number and the spacing of their children;

17. The aspirations of the younger generation for a better world, in which human rights and fundamental freedoms are fully implemented, must be given the highest encouragement. It is imperative that youth participate in shaping the future of mankind;

18. While recent scientific discoveries and technological advances have opened vast prospects for economic, social and cultural progress, such developments may nevertheless endanger the rights and freedoms of individuals and will require continuing attention;

19. Disarmament would release immense human and material resources now devoted to military purposes. These resources should be used for the promotion of human rights and fundamental freedoms. General and complete disarmament is one of the highest aspirations of all peoples;

Therefore,

The International Conference on Human Rights,

1. *Affirming* its faith in the principles of the Universal Declaration of Human Rights and other international instruments in this field,

2. *Urges* all peoples and governments to dedicate themselves to the principles enshrined in the Universal Declaration of Human Rights and to redouble their efforts to provide for all human beings a life consonant with freedom and dignity and conducive to physical, mental, social and spiritual welfare.

PART FOUR

CONTRIBUTION OF THE INTERNATIONAL LABOUR ORGANIZATION

INTRODUCTION

THE International Labour Organization is one of twelve Specialized Agencies brought into relationship with the United Nations under Articles 57 and 63 of the United Nations Charter. The Organization started its life in 1919, and it has the distinction of being in advance of other international institutions in that its major concern is social justice. The preamble to the Constitution begins: 'Whereas universal and lasting peace can be established only if it is based upon social justice . . .'. In the era of the United Nations there was more emphasis on the attainment of social justice as an aim of international co-operation and action. The Constitution of the I.L.O., with various amendments of 1964 indicated (these are not yet in force), is contained in Brownlie, *Basic Documents in International Law*, 1967, p. 36. The aims of the I.L.O. are set out in the Declaration adopted by the General Conference of the I.L.O. in 1944, printed below.

The I.L.O. has played a prominent and pioneer role in standard-setting in carefully drafted conventions dealing with specific subject matters. This Part includes a selection of the conventions concluded under I.L.O. auspices. The I.L.O., along with other Specialized Agencies, submits periodic reports to the Commission on Human Rights of the Economic and Social Council of the United Nations.

On the work of the I.L.O. see: *The I.L.O. and Human Rights* (Report of the Director-General (Part I) to the International Labour Conference, Fifty-Second Session, 1968; Report Presented by the International Labour Organization to the International Conference on Human Rights, 1968), International Labour Office, Geneva, 1968; C. Wilfred Jenks, *Social Justice in the Law of Nations*, 1970; the same, *The International Protection of Trade Union Freedom*, 1957; the same, *Human Rights and*

International Labour Standards, 1960; McNair, *The Expansion of International Law*, 1962, pp. 29–52; the *International Labour Code*, 1952; Landy, *The Effectiveness of International Supervision: Thirty Years of ILO Experience*, 1966. Further references: *ILO Panorama* (International Labour Office), No. 32 (Sept.–Oct. 1968).

I. DECLARATION CONCERNING THE AIMS AND PURPOSES OF THE INTERNATIONAL LABOUR ORGANIZATION, 1944

TEXT

THE General Conference of the International Labour Organization, meeting in its Twenty-sixth Session in Philadelphia, hereby adopts, this tenth day of May in the year nineteen hundred and forty-four, the present Declaration of the aims and purposes of the International Labour Organization and of the principles which should inspire the policy of its Members.

I

The Conference reaffirms the fundamental principles on which the Organization is based and, in particular, that:

(*a*) labour is not a commodity;

(*b*) freedom of expression and of association are essential to sustained progress;

(*c*) poverty anywhere constitutes a danger to prosperity everywhere;

(*d*) the war against want requires to be carried on with unrelenting vigour within each nation, and by continuous and concerted international effort in which the representatives of workers and employers, enjoying equal status with those of Governments, join with them in free discussion and democratic decision with a view to the promotion of the common welfare.

II

Believing that experience has fully demonstrated the truth of the statement in the Constitution of the International Labour Organization that lasting peace can be established only if it is based on social justice, the Conference affirms that:

(*a*) all human beings, irrespective of race, creed, or sex, have the right to pursue both their material well-being and their spiritual development in conditions of freedom and dignity, of economic security, and equal opportunity;

(b) the attainment of the conditions in which this shall be possible **must** constitute the central aim of national and international policy;

(c) all national and international policies and measures, in particular those of an economic and financial character, should be judged in this light and accepted only in so far as they be held to promote and not to hinder the achievement of this fundamental objective;

(d) it is a responsibility of the International Labour Organization to examine and consider all international economic and financial policies and measures in the light of this fundamental objective;

(e) in discharging the tasks entrusted to it the International Labour Organization, having considered all relevant economic and financial factors, may include in its decisions and recommendations any provisions which it considers appropriate.

III

The Conference recognizes the solemn obligation of the International Labour Organization to further among the nations of the world programmes which will achieve:

(a) full employment and the raising of standards of living;

(b) the employment of workers in the occupations in which they can have the satisfaction of giving the fullest measure of their skill and attainments and make their greatest contribution to the common well-being;

(c) the provision, as a means to the attainment of this end and under adequate guarantees for all concerned, of facilities for training and the transfer of labour, including migration for employment and settlement;

(d) Policies in regard to wages and earnings, hours and other conditions of work calculated to ensure a just share of the fruits of progress to all, and a minimum living wage to all employed and in need of such protection;

(e) the effective recognition of the right of collective bargaining, the co-operation of management and labour in the continuous improvement of productive efficiency, and the collaboration of workers and employers in the preparation and application of social and economic measures;

(f) the extension of social security measures to provide a basic income to all in need of such protection and comprehensive medical care;

(g) adequate protection for the life and health of workers in all occupations;

(h) provision for child welfare and maternity protection;

(i) the provision of adequate nutrition, housing, and facilities for recreation and culture;

(j) the assurance of equality of educational and vocational opportunity.

IV

Confident that the fuller and broader utilization of the world's productive resources necessary for the achievement of the objectives set forth in this Declaration can be secured by effective international and national action, including measures to expand production and consumption, to avoid severe economic fluctuations, to promote the economic and social advancement of the less developed regions of the world, to assure greater stability in world prices of primary products, and to promote a high and steady volume of international trade, the Conference pledges the full co-operation of the International Labour Organization with such international bodies as may be entrusted with a share of the responsibility for this great task and for the promotion of the health, education, and well-being of all peoples.

V

The Conference affirms that the principles set forth in this Declaration are fully applicable to all peoples everywhere and that, while the manner of their application must be determined with due regard to the stage of social and economic development reached by each people, their progressive application to peoples who are still dependent, as well as to those who have already achieved self-government, is a matter of concern to the whole civilized world.

II. CONVENTION CONCERNING FORCED OR COMPULSORY LABOUR, 1930

THE Convention was adopted by the General Conference of the I.L.O. on 10 June 1930, entered into force on 1 May 1932, and has received not less than 105 ratifications. The Convention is aimed at practices in colonial countries and certain independent States at a certain stage of development. Its focus is thus on forced labour as a form of economic exploitation. For the text in English and French: *United Nations Treaty Series*, Vol. 39, p. 55.

The definition of forced labour is not an easy matter. The technical difficulties are discussed by Fawcett, *The Application of the European Convention on Human Rights*, 1969, pp. 43–52. Fawcett comments (p. 48): 'the margin between the planned use of labour and the direction of labour, between free and compulsory employment, can become almost indiscernibly narrow.'

For further reference see Avins, *International and Comparative Law Quarterly*, 16 (1967), p. 29.

TEXT

The General Conference of the International Labour Organization,

> Having been convened at Geneva by the Governing Body of the International Labour Office, and having met in its Fourteenth Session on 10 June 1930, and
>
> Having decided upon the adoption of certain proposals with regard to forced or compulsory labour, which is included in the first item on the agenda of the Session, and
>
> Having determined that these proposals shall take the form of an international Convention,

adopts this twenty-eighth day of June of the year one thousand nine hundred and thirty the following Convention, which may be cited as the Forced Labour Convention, 1930, for ratification by the Members of the International Labour Organization in accordance with the provisions of the Constitution of the International Labour Organization:

Article 1

1. Each Member of the International Labour Organization which ratifies this Convention undertakes to suppress the use of forced or compulsory labour in all its forms within the shortest possible period.

2. With a view to this complete suppression, recourse to forced or compulsory labour may be had, during the transitional period, for public purposes only and as an exceptional measure, subject to the conditions and guarantees hereinafter provided.

3. At the expiration of a period of five years after the coming into force of this Convention, and when the Governing Body of the International Labour Office prepares the report provided for in Article 31 below, the said Governing Body shall consider the possibility of the suppression of forced or compulsory labour in all its forms without a further transitional period and the desirability of placing this question on the agenda of the Conference.

Article 2

1. For the purposes of this Convention the term 'forced or compulsory labour' shall mean all work or service which is exacted from any person under the menace of any penalty and for which the said person has not offered himself voluntarily.

2. Nevertheless, for the purposes of this Convention, the term 'forced or compulsory labour' shall not include—

(*a*) any work or service exacted in virtue of compulsory military service laws for work of a purely military character;

(*b*) any work or service which forms part of the normal civic obligations of the citizens of a fully self-governing country;

(*c*) any work or service exacted from any person as a consequence of a conviction in a court of law, provided that the said work or service is carried out under the supervision and control of a public authority and that the said person is not hired to or placed at the disposal of private individuals, companies or associations;

(*d*) any work or service exacted in cases of emergency, that is to say, in the event of war or of a calamity or threatened calamity, such as fire, flood, famine, earthquake, violent epidemic or epizootic diseases, invasion by animal, insect or vegetable pests, and in general any circumstance that would endanger the existence or the well-being of the whole or part of the population;

(*e*) minor communal services of a kind which, being performed by the members of the community in the direct interest of the said community, can therefore be considered as normal civic obligations incumbent upon the members of the community, provided that the members of the community or their direct representatives shall have the right to be consulted in regard to the need for such services.

Article 3

For the purposes of this Convention the term 'competent authority' shall mean either an authority of the metropolitan country or the highest central authority in the territory concerned.

Article 4

1. The competent authority shall not impose or permit the imposition of forced or compulsory labour for the benefit of private individuals, companies or associations.

2. Where such forced or compulsory labour for the benefit of private individuals, companies or associations exists at the date on which a Member's ratification of this Convention is registered by the Director-General of the International Labour Office, the Member shall completely suppress such forced or compulsory labour from the date on which this Convention comes into force for that Member.

Article 5

1. No concession granted to private individuals, companies or associations shall involve any form of forced or compulsory labour for the production or the collection of products which such private individuals, companies or associations utilize or in which they trade.

2. Where concessions exist containing provisions involving such forced or compulsory labour, such provisions shall be rescinded as soon as possible, in order to comply with Article 1 of this Convention.

Article 6

Officials of the administration, even when they have the duty of encouraging the populations under their charge to engage in some form of labour, shall not put constraint upon the said populations or upon any individual members thereof to work for private individuals, companies or associations.

Article 7

1. Chiefs who do not exercise administrative functions shall not have recourse to forced or compulsory labour.

Chiefs who exercise administrative functions may, with the express permission of the competent authority, have recourse to forced or compulsory labour, subject to the provisions of Article 10 of this Convention.

3. Chiefs who are duly recognized and who do not receive adequate remuneration in other forms may have the enjoyment of personal services, subject to due regulation and provided that all necessary measures are taken to prevent abuses.

Article 8

1. The responsibility for every decision to have recourse to forced or compulsory labour shall rest with the highest civil authority in the territory concerned.

2. Nevertheless, that authority may delegate powers to the highest local authorities to exact forced or compulsory labour which does not involve the removal of the workers from their place of habitual residence. That authority may also delegate, for such periods and subject to such conditions as may be laid down in the regulations provided for in Article 23 of this Convention, powers to the highest local authorities to exact forced or compulsory labour which involves the removal of the workers from their place of habitual residence for the purpose of facilitating the movement of officials of the administration, when on duty, and for the transport of Government stores.

Article 9

Except as otherwise provided for in Article 10 of this Convention, any authority competent to exact forced or compulsory labour shall, before deciding to have recourse to such labour, satisfy itself—

(a) that the work to be done or the service to be rendered is of important direct interest for the community called upon to do the work or render the service;

(b) that the work or service is of present or imminent necessity;

(c) that it has been impossible to obtain voluntary labour for carrying out the work or rendering the service by the offer of rates of wages and conditions of labour not less favourable than those prevailing in the area concerned for similar work or service; and

(d) that the work or service will not lay too heavy a burden upon the present population, having regard to the labour available and its capacity to undertake the work.

Article 10

1. Forced or compulsory labour exacted as a tax and forced or compulsory labour to which recourse is had for the execution of public works by chiefs who exercise administrative functions shall be progressively abolished.

2. Meanwhile, where forced or compulsory labour is exacted as a tax, and where recourse is had to forced or compulsory labour for the execution of public works by chiefs who exercise administrative functions, the authority concerned shall first satisfy itself:

(*a*) that the work to be done or the service to be rendered is of important direct interest for the community called upon to do the work or render the service;

(*b*) that the work or the service is of present or imminent necessity;

(*c*) that the work or service will not lay too heavy a burden upon the present population, having regard to the labour available and its capacity to undertake the work;

(*d*) that the work or service will not entail the removal of the workers from their place of habitual residence;

(*e*) that the execution of the work or the rendering of the service will be directed in accordance with the exigencies of religion, social life and agriculture.

Article 11

1. Only adult able-bodied males who are of an apparent age of not less than 18 and not more than 45 years may be called upon for forced or compulsory labour. Except in respect of the kinds of labour provided for in Article 10 of this Convention, the following limitations and conditions shall apply:

(*a*) whenever possible prior determination by a medical officer appointed by the administration that the persons concerned are not suffering from any infectious or contagious disease and that they are physically fit for the work required and for the conditions under which it is to be carried out;

(*b*) exemption of school teachers and pupils and of officials of the administration in general;

(*c*) the maintenance in each community of the number of adult able-bodied men indispensable for family and social life;

(*d*) respect for conjugal and family ties.

2. For the purposes of sub-paragraph (*c*) of the preceding paragraph, the

regulations provided for in Article 23 of this Convention shall fix the proportion of the resident adult able-bodied males who may be taken at any one time for forced or compulsory labour, provided always that this proportion shall in no case exceed 25 per cent. In fixing this proportion the competent authority shall take account of the density of the population, of its social and physical development, of the seasons, and of the work which must be done by the persons concerned on their own behalf in their locality, and, generally, shall have regard to the economic and social necessities of the normal life of the community concerned.

Article 12

1. The maximum period for which any person may be taken for forced or compulsory labour of all kinds in any one period of twelve months shall not exceed sixty days, including the time spent in going to and from the place of work.

2. Every person from whom forced or compulsory labour is exacted shall be furnished with a certificate indicating the periods of such labour which he has completed.

Article 13

1. The normal working hours of any person from whom forced or compulsory labour is exacted shall be the same as those prevailing in the case of voluntary labour, and the hours worked in excess of the normal working hours shall be remunerated at the rates prevailing in the case of overtime for voluntary labour.

2. A weekly day of rest shall be granted to all persons from whom forced or compulsory labour of any kind is exacted and this day shall coincide as far as possible with the day fixed by tradition or custom in the territories or regions concerned.

Article 14

1. With the exception of the forced or compulsory labour provided for in Article 10 of this Convention, forced or compulsory labour of all kinds shall be remunerated in cash at rates not less than those prevailing for similar kinds of work either in the district in which the labour is employed or in the district from which the labour is recruited, whichever may be the higher.

2. In the case of labour to which recourse is had by chiefs in the exercise of their administrative functions, payment of wages in accordance with

the provisions of the preceding paragraph shall be introduced as soon as possible.

3. The wages shall be paid to each worker individually and not to his tribal chief or to any other authority.

4. For the purpose of payment of wages the days spent in travelling to and from the place of work shall be counted as working days.

5. Nothing in this Article shall prevent ordinary rations being given as a part of wages, such rations to be at least equivalent in value to the money payment they are taken to represent, but deductions from wages shall not be made either for the payment of taxes or for special food, clothing or accommodation supplied to a worker for the purpose of maintaining him in a fit condition to carry on his work under the special conditions of any employment, or for the supply of tools.

Article 15

1. Any laws or regulations relating to workmen's compensation for accidents or sickness arising out of the employment of the worker and any laws or regulations providing compensation for the dependants of deceased or incapacitated workers which are or shall be in force in the territory concerned shall be equally applicable to persons from whom forced or compulsory labour is exacted and to voluntary workers.

2. In any case it shall be an obligation on any authority employing any worker on forced or compulsory labour to ensure the subsistence of any such worker who, by accident or sickness arising out of his employment, is rendered wholly or partially incapable of providing for himself, and to take measures to ensure the maintenance of any persons actually dependent upon such a worker in the event of his incapacity or decease arising out of his employment.

Article 16

1. Except in cases of special necessity, persons from whom forced or compulsory labour is exacted shall not be transferred to districts where the food and climate differ so considerably from those to which they have been accustomed as to endanger their health.

2. In no case shall the transfer of such workers be permitted unless all measures relating to hygiene and accommodation which are necessary to adapt such workers to the conditions and to safeguard their health can be strictly applied.

3. When such transfer cannot be avoided, measures of gradual habitua-

tion to the new conditions of diet and of climate shall be adopted on competent medical advice.

4. In cases where such workers are required to perform regular work to which they are not accustomed, measures shall be taken to ensure their habituation to it, especially as regards progressive training, the hours of work and the provision of rest intervals, and any increase or amelioration of diet which may be necessary.

Article 17

Before permitting recourse to forced or compulsory labour for works of construction or maintenance which entail the workers remaining at the workplaces for considerable periods, the competent authority shall satisfy itself—

(1) that all necessary measures are taken to safeguard the health of the workers and to guarantee the necessary medical care, and, in particular, (*a*) that the workers are medically examined before commencing the work and at fixed intervals during the period of service, (*b*) that there is an adequate medical staff, provided with the dispensaries, infirmaries, hospitals and equipment necessary to meet all requirements, and (*c*) that the sanitary conditions of the workplaces, the supply of drinking water, food, fuel, and cooking utensils, and, where necessary, of housing and clothing, are satisfactory;

(2) that definite arrangements are made to ensure the subsistence of the families of the workers, in particular by facilitating the remittance, by a safe method, of part of the wages to the family, at the request or with the consent of the workers;

(3) that the journeys of the workers to and from the workplaces are made at the expense and under the responsibility to the administration, which shall facilitate such journeys by making the fullest use of all available means of transport;

(4) that, in case of illness or accident causing incapacity to work of a certain duration, the worker is repatriated at the expense of the administration;

(5) that any worker who may wish to remain as a voluntary worker at the end of his period of forced or compulsory labour is permitted to do so without, for a period of two years, losing his right to repatriation free of expense to himself.

Article 18

1. Forced or compulsory labour for the transport of persons or goods, such as the labour of porters or boatmen, shall be abolished within the shortest possible period. Meanwhile the competent authority shall promulgate regulations determining, *inter alia*, (*a*) that such labour shall only be employed for the purpose of facilitating the movement of officials of the administration, when on duty, or for the transport of Government stores, or, in cases of very urgent necessity, the transport of persons other than officials, (*b*) that the workers so employed shall be medically certified to be physically fit, where medical examination is possible, and that where such medical examination is not practicable the person employing such workers shall be held responsible for ensuring that they are physically fit and not suffering from any infectious or contagious disease, (*c*) the maximum load which these workers may carry, (*d*) the maximum distance from their homes to which they may be taken, (*e*) the maximum number of days per month or other period for which they may be taken, including the days spent in returning to their homes, and (*f*) the persons entitled to demand this form of forced or compulsory labour and the extent to which they are entitled to demand it.

2. In fixing the maxima referred to under (*c*), (*d*) and (*e*) in the foregoing paragraph, the competent authority shall have regard to all relevant factors, including the physical development of the population from which the workers are recruited, the nature of the country through which they must travel and the climatic conditions.

3. The competent authority shall further provide that the normal daily journey of such workers shall not exceed a distance corresponding to an average working day of eight hours, it being understood that account shall be taken not only of the weight to be carried and the distance to be covered, but also of the nature of the road, the season and all other relevant factors, and that, where hours of journey in excess of the normal daily journey are exacted, they shall be remunerated at rates higher than the normal rates.

Article 19

1. The competent authority shall only authorise recourse to compulsory cultivation as a method of precaution against famine or a deficiency of food supplies and always under the condition that the food or produce shall remain the property of the individuals or the community producing it.

2. Nothing in this Article shall be construed as abrogating the obligation on members of a community, where production is organized on a communal basis by virtue of law or custom and where the produce or any profit accruing from the sale thereof remain the property of the community, to perform the work demanded by the community by virtue of law or custom.

Article 20

Collective punishment laws under which a community may be punished for crimes committed by any of its members shall not contain provisions for forced or compulsory labour by the community as one of the methods of punishment.

Article 21

Forced or compulsory labour shall not be used for work underground in mines.

Article 22

The annual reports that Members which ratify this Convention agree to make to the International Labour Office, pursuant to the provisions of Article 22 of the Constitution of the International Labour Organization, on the measures they have taken to give effect to the provisions of this Convention, shall contain as full information as possible, in respect of each territory concerned, regarding the extent to which recourse has been had to forced or compulsory labour in that territory, the purposes for which it has been employed, the sickness and death rates, hours of work, methods of payment of wages and rates of wages, and any other relevant information.

Article 23

1. To give effect to the provisions of this Convention the competent authority shall issue complete and precise regulations governing the use of forced or compulsory labour.

2. These regulations shall contain, *inter alia*, rules permitting any person from whom forced or compulsory labour is exacted to forward all complaints relative to the conditions of labour to the authorities and ensuring that such complaints will be examined and taken into consideration.

Article 24

Adequate measures shall in all cases be taken to ensure that the regulations governing the employment of forced or compulsory labour are strictly applied, either by extending the duties of any existing labour inspectorate which has been established for the inspection of voluntary labour to cover the inspection of forced or compulsory labour or in some other appropriate manner. Measures shall also be taken to ensure that the regulations are brought to the knowledge of persons from whom such labour is exacted.

Article 25

The illegal exaction of forced or compulsory labour shall be punishable as a penal offence, and it shall be an obligation on any Member ratifying this Convention to ensure that the penalities imposed by law are really adequate and are strictly enforced.

Article 26

1. Each Member of the International Labour Organization which ratifies this Convention undertakes to apply it to the territories placed under its sovereignty, jurisdiction, protection, suzerainty, tutelage or authority, so far as it has the right to accept obligations affecting matters of internal jurisdiction; provided that, if such Member may desire to take advantage of the provisions of Article 35 of the Constitution of the International Labour Organization, it shall append to its ratification a declaration stating—

(1) the territories to which it intends to apply the provisions of this Convention without modification;
(2) the territories to which it intends to apply the provisions of this Convention with modifications, together with details of the said modifications;
(3) the territories in respect of which it reserves its decision.

2. The aforesaid declaration shall be deemed to be an integral part of the ratification and shall have the force of ratification. It shall be open to any Member, by a subsequent declaration, to cancel in whole or in part the reservations made, in pursuance of the provisions of subparagraphs (2) and (3) of this Article, in the original declaration.

Article 27

The formal ratifications of this Convention under the conditions set forth in the Constitution of the International Labour Organization shall be communicated to the Director-General of the International Labour Office for registration.

Article 28

1. This Convention shall be binding only upon those Members whose ratifications have been registered with the International Labour Office.
2. It shall come into force twelve months after the date on which the ratifications of two Members of the International Labour Organization have been registered with the Director-General.
3. Thereafter, this Convention shall come into force for any Member twelve months after the date on which the ratification has been registered.

Article 29

As soon as the ratifications of two Members of the International Labour Organization have been registered with the International Labour Office, the Director-General of the International Labour Office shall so notify all the Members of the International Labour Organization. He shall likewise notify them of the registration of ratifications which may be communicated subsequently by other Members of the Organization.

Article 30

1. A Member which has ratified this Convention may denounce it after the expiration of ten years from the date on which the Convention first comes into force, by an act communicated to the Director-General of the International Labour Office for registration. Such denunciation shall not take effect until one year after the date on which it is registered with the International Labour Office.
2. Each Member which has ratified this Convention and which does not, within the year following the expiration of the period of ten years mentioned in the preceding paragraph, exercise the right of denunciation provided for in this Article, will be bound for another period of five years and, thereafter, may denounce this Convention at the expiration of each period of five years under the terms provided for in this Article.

Article 31

At the expiration of each period of five years after the coming into force of this Convention, the Governing Body of the International Labour Office shall present to the General Conference a report on the working of this Convention and shall consider the desirability of placing on the agenda of the Conference the question of its revision in whole or in part.

Article 32

1. Should the Conference adopt a new Convention revising this Convention in whole or in part, the ratification by a Member of the new re-

vising Convention shall *ipso jure* involve denunciation of this Convention without any requirement of delay, notwithstanding the provisions of Article 30 above, if and when the new revising Convention shall have come into force.

2. As from the date of the coming into force of the new revising Convention, the present Convention shall cease to be open to ratification by the Members.

3. Nevertheless, this Convention shall remain in force in its actual form and content for those Members which have ratified it but have not ratified the revising Convention.

Article 33

The French and English texts of this Convention shall both be authentic.

III. CONVENTION CONCERNING THE ABOLITION OF FORCED LABOUR, 1957

THIS complements other conventions, including the Slavery Convention, 1926 (above), the Supplementary Convention on Abolition of Slavery, etc., 1956 (above), and the Forced Labour Convention, 1930 (above). It was adopted by the General Conference of the I.L.O. on 25 June 1957, entered into force on 17 January 1959, and has received not less than eighty-eight ratifications. For the text in various languages see: *United Nations Treaty Series*, Vol. 320, p. 291.

The present Convention is concerned especially with forced labour as a means of political coercion.

TEXT

The General Conference of the International Labour Organization,

Having been convened at Geneva by the Governing Body of the International Labour Office, and having met in its Fortieth Session on 5 June 1957,

Having considered the question of forced labour, which is the fourth item on the agenda of the session, and

Having noted the provisions of the Forced Labour Convention, 1930, and

Having noted that the Slavery Convention 1926, provided that all necessary measures shall be taken to prevent compulsory or forced labour from developing into conditions analogous to slavery and that the Supplementary Convention on the Abolition of Slavery, the Slave Trade and Institutions and Practices Similar to Slavery, 1956, provided for the complete abolition of debt bondage and serfdom, and

Having noted that the Protection of Wages Convention, 1949, provided that wages shall be paid regularly and prohibits methods of payment which deprive the worker of a genuine possibility of terminating his employment, and

Having decided upon the adoption of further proposals with regard to the abolition of certain forms of forced or compulsory labour constituting a violation of the rights of man referred to in the Charter of the United

Nations and enunciated by the Universal Declaration of Human Rights, and

Having determined that these proposals shall take the form of an international convention,

Adopts this twenty-fifth day of June of the year one thousand nine hundred and fifty-seven the following convention, which may be cited as the Abolition of Forced Labour Convention, 1957.

Article 1

Each member of the International Labour Organization which ratifies this Convention undertakes to suppress and not to make use of any form of forced or compulsory labour—

- (*a*) As means of political coercion or education or as a punishment for holding or expressing political views or views ideologically opposed to the established political, social or economic system;
- (*b*) As a method of mobilizing and using labour for purposes of economic development;
- (*c*) As a means of labour discipline;
- (*d*) As a punishment for having participated in strikes;
- (*e*) As a means of racial, social, national or religious discrimination.

Article 2

Each member of the International Labour Organization which ratifies this Convention undertakes to take effective measures to secure the immediate and complete abolition of forced or compulsory labour as specified in article 1 of this Convention.

Article 3

The formal ratifications of this Convention shall be communicated to the Director-General of the International Labour Office for registration.

Article 4

This Convention shall be binding only upon those members of the International Labour Organization whose ratifications have been registered with the Director-General.

2. It shall come into force twelve months after the date on which the ratifications of two members have been registered with the Director-General.

3. Thereafter, this Convention shall come into force for any member twelve months after the date on which its ratification has been registered.

Article 5

1. A member which has ratified this Convention may denounce it after the expiration of ten years from the date on which the Convention first comes into force, by an act communicated to the Director-General of the International Labour Office for registration. Such denunciation shall not take effect until one year after the date on which it is registered.

2. Each member which has ratified this Convention and which does not, within the year following the expiration of the period of ten years mentioned in the preceding paragraph, exercise the right of denunciation provided for in this article, will be bound for another period of ten years and, thereafter, may denounce this Convention at the expiration of each period of ten years under the terms provided for in this article.

Article 6

1. The Director-General of the International Labour Office shall notify all Members of the International Labour Organization of the registration of all ratifications and denunciations communicated to him by the members of the Organization.

2. When notifying the members of the Organization of the registration of the second ratification communicated to him, the Director-General shall draw the attention of the members of the Organization to the date upon which the Convention will come into force.

Article 7

The Director-General of the International Labour Office shall communicate to the Secretary-General of the United Nations for registration in accordance with article 102 of the Charter of the United Nations full particulars of all ratifications and acts of denunciation registered by him in accordance with the provisions of the preceding articles.

Article 8

At such times as it may consider necessary the Governing Body of the International Labour Office shall present to the General Conference a report on the working of this Convention and shall examine the desirability of placing on the agenda of the Conference the question of its revision in whole or in part.

Article 9

1. Should the Conference adopt a new convention revising this Conven-

tion in whole or in part, then, unless the new convention otherwise provides—

(*a*) The ratification by a member of the new revising convention shall *ipso jure* involve the immediate denunciation of this Convention, notwithstanding the provisions of article 5 above, if and when the new revising convention shall have come into force;

(*b*) As from the date when the new revising convention comes into force this Convention shall cease to be open to ratification by the members.

2. This Convention shall in any case remain in force in its actual form and content for those members which have ratified it but have not ratified the revising convention.

Article 10

The English and French versions of the text of this Convention are equally authoritative.

IV. FREEDOM OF ASSOCIATION AND PROTECTION OF THE RIGHT TO ORGANIZE CONVENTION, 1948

THIS was adopted by the General Conference of the I.L.O. on 9 July 1948, entered into force on 4 July 1950, and has been ratified by not less than seventy-seven States. For the text in various languages see: *United Nations Treaty Series*, Vol. 68, p. 17.

This Convention and the one which follows (below) protect the major points of trade-union activity and power: freedom to organize and freedom to indulge in collective bargaining. Similar freedom is provided for employers. See also the Right of Association (Agriculture) Convention, 1921; and the Right of Association (Non-Metropolitan Territories) Convention, 1947; *United Nations Treaty Series*, Vol. 171, p. 329; *Yearbook on Human Rights*, 1948, p. 420. It has been pointed out that none of the Conventions recognizes in terms the right to strike.

For further reference see *The I.L.O. and Human Rights*, 1968, pp. 32–41; and the Collective Agreements Recommendation adopted by the I.L.O. General Conference on 29 June 1951, *Yearbook on Human Rights*, 1951, p. 472.

In 1950 the I.L.O. Governing Body decided to establish a Fact-finding and Conciliation Commission on Freedom of Association: see the *Yearbook on Human Rights*, 1949, p. 293. This needs the consent of governments before it can act. However, in the case of a ratified convention the complaints procedure under Article 26 of the Constitution applies.

TEXT

The General Conference of the International Labour Organization,

Having been convened at San Francisco by the Governing Body of the International Labour Office, and having met in its thirty-first session on 17 June 1948;

Having decided to adopt, in the form of a Convention, certain proposals concerning freedom of association and protection of the right to organize, which is the seventh item on the agenda of the session;

Considering that the Preamble to the Constitution of the International Labour Organization declares 'recognition of the principle of freedom of association' to be a means of improving conditions of labour and of establishing peace;

Considering that the Declaration of Philadelphia reaffirms that 'freedom of expression and of association are essential to sustained progress';

Considering that the International Labour Conference, at its thirtieth session, unanimously adopted the principles which should form the basis for international regulation;

Considering that the General Assembly of the United Nations, at its second session, endorsed these principles and requested the International Labour Organization to continue every effort in order that it may be possible to adopt one or several international Conventions;

Adopts this ninth day of July of the year one thousand nine hundred and forty-eight the following Convention, which may be cited as the Freedom of Association and Protection of the Right to Organize Convention, 1948:

PART I

FREEDOM OF ASSOCIATION

Article 1

Each Member of the International Labour Organization for which this Convention is in force undertakes to give effect to the following provisions.

Article 2

Workers and employers, without distinction whatsoever, shall have the right to establish and, subject only to the rules of the organization concerned, to join organizations of their own choosing without previous authorization.

Article 3

1. Workers' and employers' organizations shall have the right to draw up their constitutions and rules, to elect their representatives in full freedom, to organize their administration and activities and to formulate their programmes.

2. The public authorities shall refrain from any interference which would restrict this right or impede the lawful exercise thereof.

Article 4

Workers' and employers' organizations shall not be liable to be dissolved or suspended by administrative authority.

Article 5

Workers' and employers' organizations shall have the right to establish and join federations and confederations and any such organization, federation or confederation shall have the right to affiliate with international organizations of workers and employers.

Article 6

The provisions of articles 2, 3 and 4 hereof apply to federations and confederations of workers' and employers' organizations.

Article 7

The acquisition of legal personality by workers' and employers' organizations, federations and confederations shall not be made subject to conditions of such a character as to restrict the application of the provisions of articles 2, 3 and 4 hereof.

Article 8

1. In exercising the rights provided for in this Convention workers and employers and their respective organizations, like other persons or organized collectivities, shall respect the law of the land.
2. The law of the land shall not be such as to impair, nor shall it be so applied as to impair, the guarantees provided for in this Convention.

Article 9

1. The extent to which the guarantees provided for in this Convention shall apply to the armed forces and the police shall be determined by national laws or regulations.
2. In accordance with the principle set forth in paragraph 8 of article 19 of the Constitution of the International Labour Organization the ratification of this Convention by any Member shall not be deemed to affect any existing law, award, custom or agreement in virtue of which members of the armed forces or the police enjoy any right guaranteed by this Convention.

Article 10

In this Convention the term 'organization' means any organization of workers or of employers for furthering and defending the interests of workers or of employers.

PART II

PROTECTION OF THE RIGHT TO ORGANIZE

Article 11

Each Member of the International Labour Organization for which this Convention is in force undertakes to take all necessary and appropriate measures to ensure that workers and employers may exercise freely the right to organize.

PART III

MISCELLANEOUS PROVISIONS

Article 12

1. In respect of the territories referred to in article 35 of the Constitution of the International Labour Organization as amended by the Constitution of the International Labour Organization Instrument of Amendment, 1946, other than the territories referred to in paragraphs 4 and 5 of the said article as so amended, each Member of the Organization which ratifies this Convention shall communicate to the Director-General of the International Labour Office with or as soon as possible after its ratification a declaration stating:

(*a*) The territories in respect of which it undertakes that the provisions of the Convention shall be applied without modification;

(*b*) The territories in respect of which it undertakes that the provisions of the Convention shall be applied subject to modifications, together with details of the said modifications;

(*c*) The territories in respect of which the Convention is inapplicable and in such cases the grounds on which it is inapplicable;

(*d*) The territories in respect of which it reserves its decision.

2. The undertakings referred to in sub-paragraphs (*a*) and (*b*) of paragraph 1 of this article shall be deemed to be an integral part of the ratification and shall have the force of ratification.

3. Any Member may at any time by a subsequent declaration cancel in whole or in part any reservations made in its original declaration in virtue of sub-paragraph (*b*), (*c*) or (*d*) of paragraph 1 of this article.

4. Any Member may, at any time at which this Convention is subject to

denunciation in accordance with the provisions of article 16, communicate to the Director-General a declaration modifying in any other respect the terms of any former declaration and stating the present position in respect of such territories as it may specify.

Article 13

1. Where the subject matter of this Convention is within the self-governing powers of any non-metropolitan territory, the Member responsible for the international relations of that territory may, in agreement with the Government of the territory, communicate to the Director-General of the International Labour Office a declaration accepting on behalf of the territory the obligations of this Convention.

2. A declaration accepting the obligations of this Convention may be communicated to the Director-General of the International Labour Office:

(a) By two or more Members of the Organization in respect of any territory which is under their joint authority; or

(b) By any international authority responsible for the administration of any territory, in virtue of the Charter of the United Nations or otherwise, in respect of any such territory.

3. Declarations communicated to the Director-General of the International Labour Office in accordance with the preceding paragraphs of this article shall indicate whether the provisions of the Convention will be applied in the territory concerned without modification or subject to modifications; when the declaration indicates that the provisions of the Convention will be applied subject to modifications it shall give details of the said modifications.

4. The Member, Members or international authority concerned may at any time by a subsequent declaration renounce in whole or in part the right to have recourse to any modification indicated in any former declaration.

5. The Member, Members or international authority concerned may, at any time at which this Convention is subject to denunciation in accordance with the provisions of article 16, communicate to the Director-General of the International Labour Office a declaration modifying in any other respect the terms of any former declaration and stating the present position in respect of the application of the Convention.

PART IV

FINAL PROVISIONS

Article 14

The formal ratifications of this Convention shall be communicated to the Director-General of the International Labour Office for registration.

Article 15

1. This Convention shall be binding only upon those Members of the International Labour Organization whose ratifications have been registered with the Director-General.

2. It shall come into force twelve months after the date on which the ratifications of two Members have been registered with the Director-General.

3. Thereafter, this Convention shall come into force for any Member twelve months after the date on which its ratification has been registered.

Article 16

1. A Member which has ratified this Convention may denounce it after the expiration of ten years from the date on which the Convention first comes into force, by an act communicated to the Director-General of the International Labour Office for registration. Such denunciation shall not take effect until one year after the date on which it is registered.

2. Each Member which has ratified this Convention and which does not, within the year following the expiration of the period of ten years mentioned in the preceding paragraph, exercise the right of denunciation provided for in this article, will be bound for another period of ten years and, thereafter, may denounce this Convention at the expiration of each period of ten years under the terms provided for in this article.

Article 17

1. The Director-General of the International Labour Office shall notify all Members of the International Labour Organization of the registration of all ratifications, declarations and denunciations communicated to him by the Members of the Organization.

2. When notifying the Members of the Organization of the registration of the second ratification communicated to him, the Director-General

shall draw the attention of the Members of the Organization to the date upon which the Convention will come into force.

Article 18

The Director-General of the International Labour Office shall communicate to the Secretary-General of the United Nations for registration in accordance with article 102 of the Charter of the United Nations full particulars of all ratifications, declarations and acts of denunciation registered by him in accordance with the provisions of the preceding articles.

Article 19

At the expiration of each period of ten years after the coming into force of this Convention, the Governing Body of the International Labour Office shall present to the General Conference a report on the working of this Convention and shall consider the desirability of placing on the agenda of the Conference the question of its revision in whole or in part.

Article 20

1. Should the Conference adopt a new Convention revising this Convention in whole or in part, then, unless the new Convention otherwise provides,

   (a) The ratification by a Member of the new revising Convention shall *ipso jure* involve the immediate denunciation of this Convention, notwithstanding the provisions of article 16 above, if and when the new revising Convention shall have come into force;

   (b) As from the date when the new revising Convention comes into force this Convention shall cease to be open to ratification by the Members.

2. This Convention shall in any case remain in force in its actual form and content for those Members which have ratified it but have not ratified the revising Convention.

Article 21

The English and French versions of the text of this Convention are equally authoritative.

V. RIGHT TO ORGANIZE AND COLLECTIVE BARGAINING CONVENTION, 1949

THIS was adopted by the General Conference of the I.L.O. on 1 July 1949, entered into force on 18 July 1951, and has been ratified by not less than ninety States. For the text in various languages see *United Nations Treaty Series*, Vol. 96, p. 257. See, further, the note at p. 279 above.

TEXT

[Preamble omitted.]

Article 1

1. Workers shall enjoy adequate protection against acts of anti-union discrimination in respect of their employment.

2. Such protection shall apply more particularly in respect of acts calculated to:

   (*a*) Make the employment of a worker subject to the condition that he shall not join a union or shall relinquish trade union membership;
   (*b*) Cause the dismissal of or otherwise prejudice a worker by reason of union membership or because of participation in union activities outside working hours or, with the consent of the employer, within working hours.

Article 2

1. Workers' and employers' organizations shall enjoy adequate protection against any acts of interference by each other or each others' agents or members in their establishment, functioning or administration.

2. In particular, acts which are designed to promote the establishment of workers' organizations under the domination of employers or employers' organizations, or to support workers' organizations by financial or other means, with the object of placing such organizations under the control of employers or employers' organizations, shall be deemed to constitute acts of interference within the meaning of this article.

Article 3

Machinery appropriate to national conditions shall be established, where necessary, for the purpose of ensuring respect for the right to organize as defined in the preceding articles.

Article 4

Measures appropriate to national conditions shall be taken, where necessary, to encourage and promote the full development and utilization of machinery for voluntary negotiation between employers or employers' organizations and workers' organizations, with a view to the regulation of terms and conditions of employment by means of collective agreements.

Article 5

1. The extent to which the guarantees provided for in this Convention shall apply to the armed forces and the police shall be determined by national laws or regulations.

2. In accordance with the principle set forth in paragraph 8 of article 19 of the Constitution of the International Labour Organization the ratification of this Convention by any Member shall not be deemed to affect any existing law, award, custom or agreement in virtue of which members of the armed forces or the police enjoy any right guaranteed by this Convention.

Article 6

This Convention does not deal with the position of public servants engaged in the administration of the State, nor shall it be construed as prejudicing their rights or status in any way.

Article 7

The formal ratifications of this Convention shall be communicated to the Director-General of the International Labour Office for registration.

Article 8

1. This Convention shall be binding only upon those Members of the International Labour Organization whose ratifications have been registered with the Director-General.

2. It shall come into force twelve months after the date on which the ratifications of two Members have been registered with the Director-General.

10*

3. Thereafter, this Convention shall come into force for any Member twelve months after the date on which its ratification has been registered.

Article 9

1. Declarations communicated to the Director-General of the International Labour Office in accordance with paragraph 2 of article 35 of the Constitution of the International Labour Organization shall indicate:

(a) The territories in respect of which the Member concerned undertakes that the provisions of the Convention shall be applied without modification;

(b) The territories in respect of which it undertakes that the provisions of the Convention shall be applied subject to modifications, together with details of the said modifications;

(c) The territories in respect of which the Convention is inapplicable and in such cases the grounds on which it is inapplicable;

(d) The territories in respect of which it reserves its decision pending further consideration of the position.

2. The undertakings referred to in sub-paragraphs (a) and (b) of paragraph 1 of this article shall be deemed to be an integral part of the ratification and shall have the force of ratification.

3. Any Member may at any time by a subsequent declaration cancel in whole or in part any reservation made in its original declaration in virtue of sub-paragraph (b), (c) or (d) of paragraph 1 of this article.

4. Any Member may, at any time at which the Convention is subject to denunciation in accordance with the provisions of article 11, communicate to the Director-General a declaration modifying in any other respect the terms of any former declaration and stating the present position in respect of such territories as it may specify.

Article 10

1. Declarations communicated to the Director-General of the International Labour Office in accordance with paragraphs 4 or 5 of article 35 of the Constitution of the International Labour Organization shall indicate whether the provisions of the Convention will be applied in the territory concerned without modification or subject to modifications; when the declaration indicates that the provisions of the Convention will be applied subject to modifications, it shall give details of the said modifications.

2. The Member, Members or international authority concerned may at any time by a subsequent declaration renounce in whole or in part the

right to have recourse to any modification indicated in any former declaration.

3. The Member, Members or international authority concerned may, at any time at which this Convention is subject to denunciation in accordance with the provisions of article 11, communicate to the Director-General a declaration modifying in any other respect the terms of any former declaration and stating the present position in respect of the application of the Convention.

Article 11

1. A Member which has ratified this Convention may denounce it after the expiration of ten years from the date on which the Convention first comes into force, by an act communicated to the Director-General of the International Labour Office for registration. Such denunciation shall not take effect until one year after the date on which it is registered.

2. Each Member which has ratified this Convention and which does not, within the year following the expiration of the period of ten years mentioned in the preceding paragraph, exercise the right of denunciation provided for in this article, will be bound for another period of ten years and, thereafter, may denounce this Convention at the expiration of each period of ten years under the terms provided for in this article.

Article 12

1. The Director-General of the International Labour Office shall notify all Members of the International Labour Organization of the registration of all ratifications, declarations, and denunciations communicated to him by the Members of the Organization.

2. When notifying the Members of the Organization of the registration of the second ratification communicated to him, the Director-General shall draw the attention of the Members of the Organization to the date upon which the Convention will come into force.

Article 13

The Director-General of the International Labour Office shall communicate to the Secretary-General of the United Nations for registration in accordance with Article 102 of the Charter of the United Nations full particulars of all ratifications, declarations and acts of denunciations registered by him in accordance with the provisions of the preceding articles.

Article 14

At the expiration of each period of ten years after the coming into force of this Convention, the Governing Body of the International Labour Office shall present to the General Conference a report on the working of this Convention and shall consider the desirability of placing on the agenda of the Conference the question of its revision in whole or in part.

Article 15

1. Should the Conference adopt a new Convention revising this Convention in whole or in part, then, unless the new Convention otherwise provides,

    (*a*) The ratification by a Member of the new revising Convention shall *ipso jure* involve the immediate denunciation of this Convention, notwithstanding the provisions of Article 11 above, if and when the new revising Convention shall have come into force;

    (*b*) As from the date when the new revising Convention comes into force this Convention shall cease to be open to ratification by the Members.

2. This Convention shall in any case remain in force in its actual form and content for those Members which have ratified it but have not ratified the revising Convention.

Article 16

The English and French versions of the text of this Convention are equally authoritative.

VI. EQUAL REMUNERATION CONVENTION, 1951

THE full title is Convention Concerning Equal Remuneration for Men and Women Workers for Work of Equal Value. The Convention was adopted by the General Conference of the I.L.O. on 29 June 1951, entered into force on 23 May 1953, and has been ratified by not less than sixty-nine States. For the text in various languages see *United Nations Treaty Series*, Vol. 165, p. 304. See also the Equal Remuneration Recommendation, 1951, adopted at the same time.

Equality as between the sexes in the matter of wages and salaries has achieved but slow and reluctant recognition, even in the more advanced societies. It would seem that the Socialist countries have gone furthest in recognizing the principle. On the position in the United Kingdom see the Equal Pay Act 1970, a substantial part of which will come into force on 29 December 1975 (see section 9 of the Act).

TEXT

[Preamble omitted.]

Article 1

For the purpose of this Convention:

(*a*) The term 'remuneration' includes the ordinary, basic or minimum wage or salary and any additional emoluments whatsoever payable directly or indirectly whether in cash or in kind, by the employer to the worker and arising out of the worker's employment;

(*b*) The term 'equal remuneration for men and women workers for work of equal value' refers to rates of remuneration established without discrimination based on sex.

Article 2

1. Each Member shall, by means appropriate to the methods in operation for determining rates of remuneration, promote and, in so far as is consistent with such methods, ensure the application to all workers of the principle of equal remuneration for men and women workers for work of equal value.

2. This principle may be applied by means of:

(a) National laws or regulations;
(b) Legally established or recognized machinery for wage determination;
(c) Collective agreements between employers and workers; or
(d) A combination of these various means.

Article 3

1. Where such action will assist in giving effect to the provisions of this Convention measures shall be taken to promote objective appraisal of jobs on the basis of the work to be performed.

2. The methods to be followed in this appraisal may be decided upon by the authorities responsible for the determination of rates of remuneration, or, where such rates are determined by collective agreements, by the parties thereto.

3. Differential rates between workers which correspond, without regard to sex, to differences, as determined by such objective appraisal, in the work to be performed shall not be considered as being contrary to the principle of equal remuneration for men and women workers for work of equal value.

Article 4

Each Member shall co-operate as appropriate with the employers' and workers' organizations concerned for the purpose of giving effect to the provisions of this Convention.

Article 5

The formal ratifications of this Convention shall be communicated to the Director-General of the International Labour Office for registration.

Article 6

1. This Convention shall be binding only upon those Members of the International Labour Organization whose ratifications have been registered with the Director-General.

2. It shall come into force twelve months after the date on which the ratifications of two Members have been registered with the Director-General.

3. Thereafter, this Convention shall come into force for any Member twelve months after the date on which its ratification has been registered.

Article 7

1. Declarations communicated to the Director-General of the International Labour Office in accordance with paragraph 2 of article 35 of the Constitution of the International Labour Organization shall indicate:

(*a*) The territories in respect of which the Member concerned undertakes that the provisions of the Convention shall be applied without modification;

(*b*) The territories in respect of which it undertakes that the provisions of the Convention shall be applied subject to modifications, together with details of the said modifications;

(*c*) The territories in respect of which the Convention is inapplicable and in such cases the grounds on which it is inapplicable;

(*d*) The territories in respect of which it reserves its decisions pending further consideration of the position.

2. The undertakings referred to in sub-paragraphs (*a*) and (*b*) of paragraph 1 of this article shall be deemed to be an integral part of the ratification and shall have the force of ratification.

3. Any Member may at any time by a subsequent declaration cancel in whole or in part any reservation made in its original declaration by virtue of sub-paragraphs (*b*), (*c*) or (*d*) of paragraph 1 of this article.

4. Any Member may, at any time at which the Convention is subject to denunciation in accordance with the provisions of article 9, communicate to the Director-General a declaration modifying in any other respect the terms of any former declaration and stating the present position in respect of such territories as it may specify.

Article 8

1. Declarations communicated to the Director-General of the International Labour Office in accordance with paragraphs 4 or 5 of article 35 of the Constitution of the International Labour Organization shall indicate whether the provisions of the Convention will be applied in the territory concerned without modification or subject to modifications; when the declaration indicates that the provisions of the Convention will be applied subject to modifications, it shall give details of the said modifications.

2. The Member, Members or international authority concerned may at any time by a subsequent declaration renounce in whole or in part the right to have recourse to any modification indicated in any former declaration.

3. The Member, Members or international authority concerned may, at any time at which this Convention is subject to denunciation in accordance with the provisions of article 9, communicate to the Director-General a declaration modifying in any other respect the terms of any former declaration and stating the present position in respect of the application of the Convention.

Article 9

1. A Member which has ratified this Convention may denounce it after the expiration of ten years from the date on which the Convention first comes into force, by an act communicated to the Director-General of the International Labour Office for registration. Such denunciation shall not take effect until one year after the date on which it is registered.

2. Each Member which has ratified this Convention and which does not, within the year following the expiration of the period of ten years mentioned in the preceding paragraph, exercise the right of denunciation provided for in this article, will be bound for another period of ten years and, thereafter, may denounce this Convention at the expiration of each period of ten years under the terms provided for in this article.

Article 10

1. The Director-General of the International Labour Office shall notify all Members of the International Labour Organization of the registration of all ratifications, declarations and denunciations communicated to him by the Members of the Organization.

2. When notifying the Members of the Organization of the registration of the second ratification communicated to him, the Director-General shall draw the attention of the Members of the Organization to the date upon which the Convention will come into force.

Article 11

The Director-General of the International Labour Office shall communicate to the Secretary-General of the United Nations for registration in accordance with Article 102 of the Charter of the United Nations full particulars of all ratifications, declarations and acts of denunciation registered by him in accordance with the provisions of the preceding articles.

Article 12

At such times as it may consider necessary the Governing Body of the International Labour Office shall present to the General Conference a report of the working of this Convention and shall examine the desirability of placing on the agenda of the Conference the question of its revision in whole or in part.

Article 13

1. Should the Conference adopt a new Convention revising this Convention in whole or in part, then, unless the new Convention otherwise provides:

(a) The ratification by a Member of the new revising Convention shall *ipso jure* involve the immediate denunciation of this Convention, notwithstanding the provisions of article 9 above, if and when the new revising Convention shall have come into force;

(b) As from the date when the new revising Convention comes into force this Convention shall cease to be open to ratification by Members.

2. This Convention shall in any case remain in force in its actual form and content for those Members which have ratified it but have not ratified the revising Convention.

Article 14

The English and French versions of the text of this Convention are equally authoritative.

VII. DISCRIMINATION (EMPLOYMENT AND OCCUPATION) CONVENTION, 1958

THE most important aspect of this Convention is its application to racial matters, but it is aimed at other forms of discrimination as well. The Convention was adopted by the General Conference of the I.L.O. on 25 June 1958, entered into force on 15 June 1960, and has been ratified by not less than seventy-two States. For the text in various languages see *United Nations Treaty Series*, Vol. 362, p. 31. The relevant Recommendation of the International Labour Conference is also reproduced below.

TEXT

The General Conference of the International Labour Organization,

Having been convened at Geneva by the Governing Body of the International Labour Office, and having met in its Forty-second Session on 4 June 1958, and

Having decided upon the adoption of certain proposals with regard to discrimination in the field of employment and occupation, which is the fourth item on the agenda of the session, and

Having determined that these proposals shall take the form of an international Convention, and

Considering that the Declaration of Philadelphia affirms that all human beings, irrespective of race, creed or sex, have the right to pursue both their material well-being and their spiritual development in conditions of freedom and dignity, of economic security and equal opportunity, and

Considering further that discrimination constitutes a violation of rights enunciated by the Universal Declaration of Human Rights,

Adopts this twenty-fifth day of June of the year one thousand nine hundred and fifty-eight the following Convention, which may be cited as the Discrimination (Employment and Occupation) Convention, 1958:

Article 1

1. For the purpose of this Convention the term 'discrimination' includes:

(*a*) Any distinction, exclusion or preference made on the basis of race, colour, sex, religion, political opinion, national extraction or social origin, which has the effect of nullifying or impairing equality of opportunity or treatment in employment or occupation;

(*b*) Such other distinction, exclusion or preference which has the effect of nullifying or impairing equality of opportunity or treatment in employment or occupation as may be determined by the Member concerned after consultation with representative employers' and workers' organizations, where such exist, and with other appropriate bodies.

2. Any distinction, exclusion or preference in respect of a particular job based on the inherent requirements thereof shall not be deemed to be discrimination.

3. For the purpose of this Convention the terms 'employment' and 'occupation' include access to vocational training, access to employment and to particular occupations, and terms and conditions of employment.

Article 2

Each Member for which this Convention is in force undertakes to declare and pursue a national policy designed to promote, by methods appropriate to national conditions and practice, equality of opportunity and treatment in respect of employment and occupation, with a view to eliminating any discrimination in respect thereof.

Article 3

Each Member for which this Convention is in force undertakes, by methods appropriate to national conditions and practice—

(*a*) To seek the co-operation of employers' and workers' organizations and other appropriate bodies in promoting the acceptance and observance of this policy;

(*b*) To enact such legislation and to promote such educational programmes as may be calculated to secure the acceptance and observance of the policy;

(*c*) To repeal any statutory provisions and modify any administrative instructions or practices which are inconsistent with the policy;

(*d*) To pursue the policy in respect of employment under the direct control of a national authority;

(*e*) To ensure observance of the policy in activities of vocational guidance, vocational training and placement services under the direction of a national authority;

(*f*) To indicate in its annual reports on the application of the Convention the action taken in pursuance of the policy and the results secured by such action.

Article 4

Any measures affecting an individual who is justifiably suspected of, or engaged in, activities prejudicial to the security of the State shall not be deemed to be discrimination, provided that the individual concerned shall have the right to appeal to a competent body established in accordance with national practice.

Article 5

1. Special measures of protection or assistance provided for in other Conventions or Recommendations adopted by the International Labour Conference shall not be deemed to be discrimination.

2. Any Member may, after consultation with representative employers' and workers' organizations, where such exist, determine that other special measures designed to meet the particular requirements of persons who, for reasons such as sex, age, disablement, family responsibilities or social or cultural status, are generally recognized to require special protection or assistance, shall not be deemed to be discrimination.

Article 6

Each Member which ratifies this Convention undertakes to apply it to non-metropolitan territories in accordance with the provisions of the Constitution of the International Labour Organization.

Article 7

The formal ratifications of this Convention shall be communicated to the Director-General of the International Labour Office for registration.

Article 8

1. This Convention shall be binding only upon those Members of the International Labour Organization whose ratifications have been registered with the Director-General.

2. It shall come into force twelve months after the date on which the ratifications of two Members have been registered with the Director-General.

3. Thereafter, this Convention shall come into force for any Member twelve months after the date on which its ratification has been registered.

Article 9

1. A Member which has ratified this Convention may denounce it after the expiration of ten years from the date on which the Convention first comes into force, by an act communicated to the Director-General of the International Labour Office for registration. Such denunciation shall not take effect until one year after the date on which it is registered.

2. Each Member which has ratified this Convention and which does not, within the year following the expiration of the period of ten years mentioned in the preceding paragraph, exercise the right of denunciation provided for in this article, will be bound for another period of ten years and, thereafter, may denounce this Convention at the expiration of each period of ten years under the terms provided for in this article.

Article 10

1. The Director-General of the International Labour Office shall notify all Members of the International Labour Organization of the registration of all ratifications and denunciations communicated to him by the Members of the Organization.

2. When notifying the Members of the Organization of the registration of the second ratification communicated to him, the Director-General shall draw the attention of the Members of the Organization to the date upon which the Convention will come into force.

Article 11

The Director-General of the International Labour Office shall communicate to the Secretary-General of the United Nations for registration in accordance with Article 102 of the Charter of the United Nations full particulars of all ratifications and acts of denunciation registered by him in accordance with the provisions of the preceding articles.

Article 12

At such times as it may consider necessary the Governing Body of the International Labour Office shall present to the General Conference a report on the working of this Convention and shall examine the desirability of placing on the agenda of the Conference the question of its revision in whole or in part.

Article 13

1. Should the Conference adopt a new Convention revising this Convention in whole or in part, then, unless the new Convention otherwise provides—

(a) The ratification by a Member of the new revising Convention shall *ipso jure* involve the immediate denunciation of this Convention, notwithstanding the provisions of article 9 above, if and when the new revising Convention shall have come into force;

(b) As from the date when the new revising Convention comes into force this Convention shall cease to be open to ratification by the Members.

2. This Convention shall in any case remain in force in its actual form and content for those Members which have ratified it but have not ratified the revising Convention.

Article 14

The English and French versions of the text of this Convention are equally authoritative.

DISCRIMINATION (EMPLOYMENT AND OCCUPATION) RECOMMENDATION, 1958

The General Conference of the International Labour Organization,

Having been convened at Geneva by the Governing Body of the International Labour Office, and having met in its Forty-second Session on 4 June 1958, and

Having decided upon the adoption of certain proposals with regard to discrimination in the field of employment and occupation, which is the fourth item on the agenda of the session, and

Having determined that these proposals shall take the form of a Recommendation supplementing the Discrimination (Employment and Occupation) Convention, 1958,

adopts this twenty-fifth day of June of the Year one thousand nine hundred and fifty-eight the following Recommendation, which may be cited as the Discrimination (Employment and Occupation) Recommendation, 1958;

The Conference recommends that each Member should apply the following provisions:

I. DEFINITIONS

1. (1) For the purpose of this Recommendation the term 'discrimination' includes—

(a) Any distinction, exclusion or preference made on the basis of race, colour, sex, religion, political opinion, national extraction or social origin, which has the effect of nullifying or impairing equality of opportunity or treatment in employment or occupation;

(b) Such other distinction, exclusion or preference which has the effect of nullifying or impairing equality of opportunity or treatment in employment or occupation as may be determined by the Member concerned after consultation with representative employers' and workers' organizations, where such exist, and with other appropriate bodies.

(2) Any distinction, exclusion or preference in respect of a particular job based on the inherent requirements thereof is not deemed to be discrimination.

(3) For the purpose of this Recommendation the terms 'employment' and 'occupation' include access to vocational training, access to employment and to particular occupations, and terms and conditions of employment.

II. Formulation and Application of Policy

2. Each Member should formulate a national policy for the prevention of discrimination in employment and occupation. This policy should be applied by means of legislative measures, collective agreements between representative employers' and workers' organizations or in any other manner consistent with national conditions and practice, and should have regard to the following principles:

(a) The promotion of equality of opportunity and treatment in employment and occupation is a matter of public concern;

(b) All persons should, without discrimination, enjoy equality of opportunity and treatment in respect of—

(i) Access to vocational guidance and placement services;
(ii) Access to training and employment of their own choice on the basis of individual suitability for such training or employment;
(iii) Advancement in accordance with their individual character, experience, ability and diligence;
(iv) Security of tenure of employment;
(v) Remuneration for work of equal value;
(vi) Conditions of work including hours of work, rest periods, annual holidays with pay, occupational safety and occupational

health measures, as well as social security measures and welfare facilities and benefits provided in connexion with employment;

(c) Government agencies should apply non-discriminatory employment policies in all their activities;

(d) Employers should not practise or countenance discrimination in engaging or training any person for employment, in advancing or retaining such person in employment, or in fixing terms and conditions of employment; nor should any person or organization obstruct or interfere, either directly or indirectly, with employers in pursuing this principle;

(e) In collective negotiations and industrial relations the parties should respect the principle of equality of opportunity and treatment in employment and occupation, and should ensure that collective agreements contain no provisions of a discriminatory character in respect of access to, training for, advancement in or retention of employment or in respect of the terms and conditions of employment;

(f) Employers' and workers' organizations should not practise or countenance discrimination in respect of admission, retention of membership or participation in their affairs.

3. Each Member should—

(a) Ensure application of the principles of non-discrimination—

(i) In respect of employment under the direct control of a national authority;

(ii) In the activities of vocational guidance, vocational training and placement services under the direction of a national authority;

(b) Promote their observance, where practicable and necessary, in respect of other employment and other vocational guidance, vocational training and placement services by such methods as—

(i) Encouraging state, provincial or local government departments or agencies and industries and undertakings operated under public ownership or control to ensure the application of the principles;

(ii) Making eligibility for contracts involving the expenditure of public funds dependent on observance of the principles;

(iii) Making eligibility for grants to training establishments and for a licence to operate a private employment agency or a private vocational guidance office dependent on observance of the principles.

4. Appropriate agencies, to be assisted where practicable by advisory committees composed of representatives of employers' and workers' organizations, where such exist, and of other interested bodies, should be established for the purpose of promoting application of the policy in all fields of public and private employment, and in particular—

(*a*) To take all practicable measures to foster public understanding and acceptance of the principles of non-discrimination;

(*b*) To receive, examine and investigate complaints that the policy is not being observed and, if necessary by conciliation, to secure the correction of any practices regarded as in conflict with the policy; and

(*c*) To consider further any complaints which cannot be effectively settled by conciliation and to render opinions or issue decisions concerning the manner in which discriminatory practices revealed should be corrected.

5. Each Member should repeal any statutory provisions and modify any administrative instructions or practices which are inconsistent with the policy.

6. Application of the policy should not adversely affect special measures designed to meet the particular requirements of persons who, for reasons such as sex, age, disablement, family responsibilities or social or cultural status are generally recognized to require special protection or assistance.

7. Any measures affecting an individual who is justifiably suspected of, or engaged in, activities prejudicial to the security of the State should not be deemed to be discrimination, provided that the individual concerned has the right to appeal to a competent body established in accordance with national practice.

8. With respect to immigrant workers of foreign nationality and the members of their families, regard should be had to the provisions of the Migration for Employment Convention (Revised), 1949, relating to equality of treatment and the provisions of the Migration for Employment Recommendation (Revised), 1949, relating to the lifting of restrictions on access to employment.

9. There should be continuing co-operation between the competent authorities, representatives of employers and workers and appropriate bodies to consider what further positive measures may be necessary in the

light of national conditions to put the principles of non-discrimination into effect.

III. Co-ordination of Measures for the Prevention of Discrimination in all Fields

10. The authorities responsible for action against discrimination in employment and occupation should co-operate closely and continuously with the authorities responsible for action against discrimination in other fields in order that measures taken in all fields may be co-ordinated.

VIII. EQUALITY OF TREATMENT
(SOCIAL SECURITY) CONVENTION, 1962

THE Convention concerns one aspect of a particularly sensitive aspect of the principle of equality, namely, equality of treatment for non-nationals. The Convention was adopted by the General Conference of the I.L.O. on 28 June 1962, entered into force on 25 April 1964, and has been ratified by not less than twenty-two States. For the text in various languages see *United Nations Treaty Series*, Vol. 494, p. 271.

See, further, the Social Security (Minimum Standards) Convention, 1952, *United Nations Treaty Series*, Vol. 210, p. 131; and *The I.L.O. and Human Rights*, 1968, pp. 54–5.

TEXT

[Preamble omitted.]

Article 1

In this Convention—

(a) the term 'legislation' includes any social security rules as well as laws and regulations;

(b) the term 'benefits' refers to all benefits, grants and pensions, including any supplements or increments;

(c) the term 'benefits granted under transitional schemes' means either benefits granted to persons who have exceeded a prescribed age at the date when the legislation applicable came into force, or benefits granted as a transitional measure in consideration of events occurring or periods completed outside the present boundaries of the territory of a Member;

(d) the term 'death grant' means any lump sum payable in the event of death;

(e) the term 'residence' means ordinary residence;

(f) the term 'prescribed' means determined by or in virtue of national legislation as defined in subparagraph (a) above;

(g) the term 'refugee' has the meaning assigned to it in Article 1 of the Convention relating to the Status of Refugees of 28 July 1951;

(*h*) the term 'stateless person' has the meaning assigned to it in Article 1 of the Convention relating to the Status of Stateless Persons of 28 September 1954.

Article 2

1. Each Member may accept the obligations of this Convention in respect of any one or more of the following branches of social security for which it has in effective operation legislation covering its own nationals within its own territory:

(*a*) medical care;
(*b*) sickness benefit;
(*c*) maternity benefit;
(*d*) invalidity benefit;
(*e*) old-age benefit;
(*f*) survivors' benefit;
(*g*) employment injury benefit;
(*h*) unemployment benefit; and
(*i*) family benefit.

2. Each Member for which this Convention is in force shall comply with its provisions in respect of the branch or branches of social security for which it has accepted the obligations of the Convention.

3. Each Member shall specify in its ratification in respect of which branch or branches of social security it accepts the obligations of this Convention.

4. Each Member which has ratified this Convention may subsequently notify the Director-General of the International Labour Office that it accepts the obligations of the Convention in respect of one or more branches of social security not already specified in its ratification.

5. The undertakings referred to in paragraph 4 of this Article shall be deemed to be an integral part of the ratification and to have the force of ratification as from the date of notification.

6. For the purpose of the application of this Convention, each Member accepting the obligations thereof in respect of any branch of social security which has legislation providing for benefits of the type indicated in clause (*a*) or (*b*) below shall communicate to the Director-General of the International Labour Office a statement indicating the benefits provided for by its legislation which it considers to be—

(*a*) benefits other than those the grant of which depends either on

direct financial participation by the persons protected or their employer, or on a qualifying period of occupational activity; or
(b) benefits granted under transitional schemes.

7. The communication referred to in paragraph 6 of this Article shall be made at the time of ratification or at the time of notification in accordance with paragraph 4 of this Article; as regards any legislation adopted subsequently, the communication shall be made within three months of the date of the adoption of such legislation.

Article 3

1. Each Member for which this Convention is in force shall grant within its territory to the nationals of any other Member for which the Convention is in force equality of treatment under its legislation with its own nationals, both as regards coverage and as regards the right to benefits, in respect of every branch of social security for which it has accepted the obligations of the Convention.

2. In the case of survivors' benefits, such equality of treatment shall also be granted to the survivors of the nationals of a Member for which the Convention is in force, irrespective of the nationality of such survivors.

3. Nothing in the preceding paragraphs of this Article shall require a Member to apply the provisions of these paragraphs, in respect of the benefits of a specified branch of social security, to the nationals of another Member which has legislation relating to that branch but does not grant equality of treatment in respect thereof to the nationals of the first Member.

Article 4

1. Equality of treatment as regards the grant of benefits shall be accorded without any condition of residence: Provided that equality of treatment in respect of the benefits of a specified branch of social security may be made conditional on residence in the case of nationals of any Member the legislation of which makes the grant of benefits under that branch conditional on residence on its territory.

2. Notwithstanding the provisions of paragraph 1 of this Article, the grant of the benefits referred to in paragraph 6 (a) of Article 2—other than medical care, sickness benefit, employment injury benefit and family benefit—may be made subject to the condition that the beneficiary has resided on the territory of the Member in virtue of the legislation of which

the benefit is due, or, in the case of a survivor, that the deceased had resided there, for a period which shall not exceed—

(a) six months immediately preceding the filing of claim, for grant of maternity benefit and unemployment benefit;

(b) five consecutive years immediately preceding the filing of claim, for grant of invalidity benefit, or immediately preceding death, for grant of survivors' benefit;

(c) ten years after the age of 18, which may include five consecutive years immediately preceding the filing of claim, for grant of old-age benefit.

3. Special provisions may be prescribed in respect of benefits granted under transitional schemes.

4. The measures necessary to prevent the cumulation of benefits shall be determined, as necessary, by special arrangements between the Members concerned.

Article 5

1. In addition to the provisions of Article 4, each Member which has accepted the obligations of this Convention in respect of the branch or branches of social security concerned shall guarantee both to its own nationals and to the nationals of any other Member which has accepted the obligations of the Convention in respect of the branch or branches in question, when they are resident abroad, provision of invalidity benefits, old-age benefits, survivors' benefits and death grants, and employment injury pensions, subject to measures for this purpose being taken, where necessary, in accordance with Article 8.

2. In case of residence abroad, the provision of invalidity, old-age and survivors' benefits of the type referred to in paragraph 6 (a) of Article 2 may be made subject to the participation of the Members concerned in schemes for the maintenance of rights as provided for in Article 7.

3. The provisions of this Article do not apply to benefits granted under transitional schemes.

Article 6

In addition to the provisions of Article 4, each Member which has accepted the obligations of this Convention in respect of family benefit shall guarantee the grant of family allowances both to its own nationals and to the nationals of any other Member which has accepted the obligations of this Convention for that branch, in respect of children who reside on the territory of any such Member, under conditions and within limits to be agreed upon by the Members concerned.

Article 7

1. Members for which this Convention is in force shall, upon terms being agreed between the Members concerned in accordance with Article 8, endeavour to participate in schemes for the maintenance of the acquired rights and rights in course of acquisition under their legislation of the nationals of Members for which the Convention is in force, for all branches of social security in respect of which the Members concerned have accepted the obligations of the Convention.

2. Such schemes shall provide, in particular, for the totalization of periods of insurance, employment or residence and of assimilated periods for the purpose of the acquisition, maintenance or recovery of rights and for the calculation of benefits.

3. The cost of invalidity, old-age and survivors' benefits as so determined shall either be shared among the Members concerned, or be borne by the Member on whose territory the beneficiaries reside, as may be agreed upon by the Members concerned.

Article 8

The Members for which this Convention is in force may give effect to their obligations under the provisions of Articles 5 and 7 by ratification of the Maintenance of Migrants' Pension Rights Conevntion, 1935, by the application of the provisions of that Convention as between particular Members by mutual agreement, or by any multilateral or bilateral agreement giving effect to these obligations.

Article 9

The provisions of this Convention may be derogated from by agreements between Members which do not affect the rights and duties of other Members and which make provision for the maintenance of rights in course of acquisition and of acquired rights under conditions at least as favourable on the whole as those provided for in this Convention.

Article 10

1. The provisions of this Convention apply to refugees and stateless persons without any condition of reciprocity.

2. This Convention does not apply to special schemes for civil servants, special schemes for war victims, or public assistance.

3. This Convention does not require any Member to apply the provisions thereof to persons who, in accordance with the provisions of international instruments, are exempted from its national social security legislation.

Article 11

The Members for which this Convention is in force shall afford each other administrative assistance free of charge with a view to facilitating the application of the Convention and the execution of their respective social security legislation.

Article 12

1. This Convention does not apply to benefits payable prior to the coming into force of the Convention for the Member concerned in respect of the branch of social security under which the benefit is payable.

2. The extent to which the Convention applies to benefits attributable to contingencies occurring before its coming into force for the Member concerned in respect of the branch of social security under which the benefit is payable thereafter shall be determined by multilateral or bilateral agreement or in default thereof by the legislation of the Member concerned.

Article 13

This Convention shall not be regarded as revising any existing Convention.

Article 14

The formal ratifications of this Convention shall be communicated to the Director-General of the International Labour Office for registration.

Article 15

1. This Convention shall be binding only upon those Members of the International Labour Organization whose ratifications have been registered with the Director-General.

2. It shall come into force twelve months after the date on which the ratifications of two Members have been registered with the Director-General.

3. Thereafter, this Convention shall come into force for any Member twelve months after the date on which its ratification has been registered.

Article 16

1. A Member which has ratified this Convention may denounce it after the expiration of ten years from the date on which the Convention first

comes into force, by an act communicated to the Director-General of the International Labour Office for registration. Such denunciation shall not take effect until one year after the date on which it is registered.

2. Each Member which has ratified this Convention and which does not, within the year following the expiration of the period of ten years mentioned in the preceding paragraph, exercise the right of denunciation provided for in this Article, will be bound for another period of ten years and, thereafter, may denounce this Convention at the expiration of each period of ten years under the terms provided for in this Article.

Article 17

1. The Director-General of the International Labour Office shall notify all Members of the International Labour Organization of the registration of all ratifications and denunciations communicated to him by the Members of the Organization.

2. When notifying the Members of the Organization of the registration of the second ratification communicated to him, the Director-General shall draw the attention of the Members of the Organization to the date upon which the Convention will come into force.

Article 18

The Director-General of the International Labour Office shall communicate to the Secretary-General of the United Nations for registration in accordance with article 102 of the Charter of the United Nations full particulars of all ratifications and acts of denunciation registered by him in accordance with the provisions of the preceding Articles.

Article 19

At such times as it may consider necessary the Governing Body of the International Labour Office shall present to the General Conference a report on the working of this Convention and shall examine the desirability of placing on the agenda of the Conference the question of its revision in whole or in part.

Article 20

1. Should the Conference adopt a new Convention revising this Convention in whole or in part, then, unless the new Convention otherwise provides:

(*a*) The ratification by a Member of the new revising Convention shall *ipso jure* involve the immediate denunciation of this Convention, notwithstanding the provisions of Article 16 above, if and when the new revising Convention shall have come into force;

(*b*) As from the date when the new revising Convention comes into force this Convention shall cease to be open to ratification by the Members.

2. This Convention shall in any case remain in force in its actual form and content for those Members which have ratified it but have not ratified the revising Convention.

Article 21

The English and French versions of the text of this Convention are equally authoritative.

IX. SOCIAL POLICY (BASIC AIMS AND STANDARDS) CONVENTION, 1962

THE Convention was adopted by the General Conference of the I.L.O. on 22 June 1962, entered into force on 23 April 1964, and has been ratified by not less than twenty States. For the text in various languages: *United Nations Treaty Series*, Vol. 494, p. 249.

TEXT

The General Conference of the International Labour Organization,

Having been convened at Geneva by the Governing Body of the International Labour Office, and having met in its Forty-sixth Session on 6 June 1962, and

Having decided upon the adoption of certain proposals concerning the revision of the Social Policy (Non-Metropolitan Territories) Convention, 1947, which is the tenth item on the agenda of the Session, primarily with a view to making its continued application and ratification possible for independent States, and

Considering that these proposals must take the form of an international Convention, and

Considering that economic development must serve as a basis for social progress, and

Considering that every effort should be made, on an international, regional or national basis, to secure financial and technical assistance safeguarding the interests of the population, and

Considering that, in appropriate cases, international, regional or national action should be taken with a view to establishing conditions of trade which would encourage production at a high level of efficiency and make possible the maintenance of a reasonable standard of living, and

Considering that all possible steps should be taken by appropriate international, regional and national measures to promote improvement in such fields as public health, housing, nutrition, education, the welfare of children, the status of women, conditions of employment, the remuneration of wage earners and independent producers, the protection of migrant workers, social security, standards of public services and general production, and

Considering that all possible steps should be taken effectively to interest and associate the population in the framing and execution of measures of social progress,

Adopts this twenty-second day of June of the year one thousand nine hundred and sixty-two the following Convention, which may be cited as the Social Policy (Basic Aims and Standards) Convention, 1962:

PART I

GENERAL PRINCIPLES

Article 1

1. All policies shall be primarily directed to the well-being and development of the population and to the promotion of its desire for social progress.

2. All policies of more general application shall be formulated with due regard to their effect upon the well-being of the population.

PART II

IMPROVEMENT OF STANDARDS OF LIVING

Article 2

The improvement of standards of living shall be regarded as the principal objective in the planning of economic development.

Article 3

1. All practicable measures shall be taken in the planning of economic development to harmonize such development with the healthy evolution of the communities concerned.

2. In particular, efforts shall be made to avoid the disruption of family life and of traditional social units, especially by—

   (*a*) close study of the causes and effects of migratory movements and appropriate action where necessary;

(*b*) the promotion of town and village planning in areas where economic needs result in the concentration of population;

(*c*) the prevention and elimination of congestion in urban areas;

(*d*) the improvement of living conditions in rural areas and the establishment of suitable industries in rural areas where adequate manpower is available.

Article 4

The measures to be considered by the competent authorities for the promotion of productive capacity and the improvement of standards of living of agricultural producers shall include—

(*a*) the elimination to the fullest practicable extent of the causes of chronic indebtedness;

(*b*) the control of the alienation of agricultural land to non-agriculturalists so as to ensure that such alienation takes place only when it is in the best interest of the country;

(*c*) the control, by the enforcement of adequate laws or regulations, of the ownership and use of land and resources to ensure that they are used, with due regard to customary rights, in the best interests of the inhabitants of the country;

(*d*) the supervision of tenancy arrangements and of working conditions with a view to securing for tenants and labourers the highest practicable standards of living and an equitable share in any advantages which may result from improvements in productivity or in price levels;

(*e*) the reduction of production and distribution costs by all practicable means and in particular by forming, encouraging and assisting producers' and consumers' co-operatives.

Article 5

1. Measures shall be taken to secure for independent producers and wage earners conditions which will give them scope to improve living standards by their own efforts and will ensure the maintenance of minimum standards of living as ascertained by means of official inquiries into living conditions, conducted after consultation with the representative organizations of employers and workers.

2. In ascertaining the minimum standards of living, account shall be taken of such essential family needs of the workers as food and its nutritive value, housing, clothing, medical care and education.

PART III

Provisions concerning Migrant Workers

Article 6

Where the circumstances under which workers are employed involve their living away from their homes, the terms and conditions of their employment shall take account of their normal family needs.

Article 7

Where the labour resources of one area are used on a temporary basis for the benefit of another area, measures shall be taken to encourage the transfer of part of the workers' wages and savings from the area of labour utilization to the area of labour supply.

Article 8

1. Where the labour resources of a country are used in an area under a different administration, the competent authorities of the countries concerned shall, whenever necessary or desirable, enter into agreements for the purpose of regulating matters of common concern arising in connection with the application of the provisions of this Convention.

2. Such agreements shall provide that the worker shall enjoy protection and advantages not less than those enjoyed by workers resident in the area of labour utilization.

3. Such agreements shall provide for facilities for enabling the worker to transfer part of his wages and savings to his home.

Article 9

Where workers and their families move from low-cost to higher-cost areas, account shall be taken of the increased cost of living resulting from the change.

PART IV

Remuneration of Workers and Related Questions

Article 10

1. The fixing of minimum wages by collective agreements freely negotiated between trade unions which are representative of the workers concerned and employers or employers' organizations shall be encouraged.

2. Where no adequate arrangements exist for the fixing of minimum wages by collective agreement, the necessary arrangements shall be made whereby minimum rates of wages can be fixed in consultation with representatives of the employers and workers, including representatives of their respective organizations, where such exist.

3. The necessary measures shall be taken to ensure that the employers and workers concerned are informed of the minimum wage rates in force and that wages are not paid at less than these rates in cases where they are applicable.

4. A worker to whom minimum rates are applicable and who, since they became applicable, has been paid wages at less than these rates shall be entitled to recover, by judicial or other means authorized by law, the amount by which he has been underpaid, subject to such limitation of time as may be determined by law or regulation.

Article 11

1. The necessary measures shall be taken to ensure the proper payment of all wages earned and employers shall be required to keep registers of wage payments, to issue to workers statements of wage payments and to take other appropriate steps to facilitate the necessary supervision.

2. Wages shall normally be paid in legal tender only.

3. Wages shall normally be paid direct to the individual worker.

4. The substitution of alcohol or other spirituous beverages for all or any part of wages for services performed by the worker shall be prohibited.

5. Payment of wages shall not be made in taverns or stores, except in the case of workers employed therein.

6. Unless there is an established local custom to the contrary, and the competent authority is satisfied that the continuance of this custom is desired by the workers, wages shall be paid regularly at such intervals as will lessen the likelihood of indebtedness among the wage earners.

7. Where food, housing, clothing and other essential supplies and services form part of remuneration, all practicable steps shall be taken by the competent authority to ensure that they are adequate and their cash value properly assessed.

8. All practicable measures shall be taken—

   (a) to inform the workers of their wage rights;
   (b) to prevent any unauthorized deductions from wages; and

(c) to restrict the amounts deductible from wages in respect of supplies and services forming part of remuneration to the proper cash value thereof.

Article 12

1. The maximum amounts and manner of repayment of advances on wages shall be regulated by the competent authority.

2. The competent authority shall limit the amount of advances which may be made to a worker in consideration of his taking up employment; the amount of advances permitted shall be clearly explained to the worker.

3. Any advance in excess of the amount laid down by the competent authority shall be legally irrecoverable and may not be recovered by the withholding of amounts of pay due to the worker at a later date.

Article 13

1. Voluntary forms of thrift shall be encouraged among wage earners and independent producers.

2. All practicable measures shall be taken for the protection of wage earners and independent producers against usury, in particular by action aiming at the reduction of rates of interest on loans, by the control of the operations of money lenders, and by the encouragement of facilities for borrowing money for appropriate purposes through co-operative credit organizations or through institutions which are under the control of the competent authority.

PART V

NON-DISCRIMINATION ON GROUNDS OF RACE, COLOUR, SEX, BELIEF, TRIBAL ASSOCIATION OR TRADE UNION AFFILIATION

Article 14

1. It shall be an aim of policy to abolish all discrimination among workers on grounds of race, colour, sex, belief, tribal association or trade union affiliation in respect of—

(a) labour legislation and agreements which shall afford equitable economic treatment to all those lawfully resident or working in the country;

(b) admission to public or private employment;
(c) conditions of engagement and promotion;
(d) opportunities for vocational training;
(e) conditions of work;
(f) health, safety and welfare measures;
(g) discipline;
(h) participation in the negotiation of collective agreements;
(i) wage rates, which shall be fixed according to the principle of equal pay for work of equal value in the same operation and undertaking.

2. All practicable measures shall be taken to lessen, by raising the rates applicable to the lower-paid workers, any existing differences in wage rates due to discrimination by reason of race, colour, sex, belief, tribal association or trade union affiliation.

3. Workers from one country engaged for employment in another country may be granted in addition to their wages benefits in cash or in kind to meet any reasonable personal or family expenses resulting from employment away from their homes.

4. The foregoing provisions of this Article shall be without prejudice to such measures as the competent authority may think it necessary or desirable to take for the safeguarding of motherhood and for ensuring the health, safety and welfare of women workers.

PART VI

EDUCATION AND TRAINING

Article 15

1. Adequate provision shall be made to the maximum extent possible under local conditions, for the progressive development of broad systems of education, vocational training and apprenticeship, with a view to the effective preparation of children and young persons of both sexes for a useful occupation.

2. National laws or regulations shall prescribe the school-leaving age and the minimum age for and conditions of employment.

3. In order that the child population may be able to profit by existing facilities for education and in order that the extension of such facilities may not be hindered by a demand for child labour, the employment of persons below the school-leaving age during the hours when the schools

are in session shall be prohibited in areas where educational facilities are provided on a scale adequate for the majority of the children of school age.

Article 16

1. In order to secure high productivity through the development of skilled labour, training in new techniques of production shall be provided in suitable cases.

2. Such training shall be organized by or under the supervision of the competent authorities, in consultation with the employers' and workers' organizations of the country from which the trainees come and of the country of training.

PART VII
FINAL PROVISIONS

Article 17

The formal ratifications of this Convention shall be communicated to the Director-General of the International Labour Office for registration.

Article 18

1. This Convention shall be binding only upon those Members of the International Labour Organization whose ratifications have been registered with the Director-General.

2. It shall come into force twelve months after the date on which the ratifications of two Members have been registered with the Director-General.

3. Thereafter, this Convention shall come into force for any Member twelve months after the date on which its ratification has been registered.

Article 19

The coming into force of this Convention shall not involve the *ipso jure* denunciation of the Social Policy (Non-Metropolitan Territories) Convention, 1947, by any Member for which that Convention continues to remain in force, nor shall it close that Convention to further ratification.

Article 20

1. A Member which has ratified this Convention may denounce it after the expiration of ten years from the date on which the Convention first

comes into force, by an act communicated to the Director-General of the International Labour Office for registration. Such denunciation shall not take effect until one year after the date on which it is registered.

2. Each Member which has ratified this Convention and which does not, within the year following the expiration of the period of ten years mentioned in the preceding paragraph, exercise the right of denunciation provided for in this Article, will be bound for another period of ten years and, thereafter, may denounce this Convention at the expiration of each period of ten years under the terms provided for in this Article.

Article 21

1. The Director-General of the International Labour Office shall notify all Members of the International Labour Organization of the registration of all ratifications and denunciations communicated to him by the Members of the Organization.

2. When notifying the Members of the Organization of the registration of the second ratification communicated to him, the Director-General shall draw the attention of the Members of the Organization to the date upon which the Convention will come into force.

Article 22

The Director-General of the International Labour Office shall communicate to the Secretary-General of the United Nations for registration in accordance with article 102 of the Charter of the United Nations full particulars of all ratifications and acts of denunciation registered by him in accordance with the provisions of the preceding Articles.

Article 23

At such times as it may consider necessary the Governing Body of the International Labour Office shall present to the General Conference a report on the working of this Convention and shall consider the desirability of placing on the agenda of the Conference the question of its revision in whole or in part.

Article 24

1. Should the Conference adopt a new Convention revising this Convention in whole or in part, then, unless the new Convention otherwise provides:

    (*a*) the ratification by a Member of the new revising Convention shall *ipso jure* involve the immediate denunciation of this Convention, notwithstanding the provisions of Article 20 above, if and when the new revising Convention shall have come into force;

(b) as from the date when the new revising Convention comes into force this Convention shall cease to be open to ratification by the Members.

2. This Convention shall in any case remain in force in its actual form and content for those Members which have ratified it but have not ratified the revising Convention.

Article 25

The English and French versions of the text of this Convention are equally authoritative.

X. EMPLOYMENT POLICY CONVENTION, 1964

THIS is concerned with economic security and the right to work: see the Universal Declaration of Human Rights, Article 23. The Convention was adopted by the General Conference of the I.L.O. on 9 July 1964, entered into force on 15 July 1966, and has received not less than thirty-one ratifications. For the text in various languages see *United Nations Treaty Series*, Vol. 569, p. 65.

See, further, *The I.L.O. and Human Rights*, International Labour Office, 1968, pp. 76–84.

TEXT

The General Conference of the International Labour Organization,

Having been convened at Geneva by the Governing Body of the International Labour Office, and having met in its Forty-eighth Session on 17 June 1964, and

Considering that the Declaration of Philadelphia recognizes the solemn obligation of the International Labour Organization to further among the nations of the world programmes which will achieve full employment and the raising of standards of living, and that the Preamble to the Constitution of the International Labour Organization provides for the prevention of unemployment and the provision of an adequate living wage, and

Considering further that under the terms of the Declaration of Philadelphia it is the responsibility of the International Labour Organization to examine and consider the bearing of economic and financial policies upon employment policy in the light of the fundamental objective that 'all human beings, irrespective of race, creed or sex, have the right to pursue both their material well-being and their spiritual development in conditions of freedom and dignity, of economic security and equal opportunity', and

Considering that the Universal Declaration of Human Rights provides that 'everyone has the right to work, to free choice of employment, to just and favourable conditions of work and to protection against unemployment', and

Noting the terms of existing international labour Conventions and

Recommendations of direct relevance to employment policy, and in particular of the Employment Service Convention and Recommendation, 1948, the Vocational Guidance Recommendation, 1949, the Vocational Training Recommendation, 1962, and the Discrimination (Employment and Occupation) Convention and Recommendation, 1958, and

Considering that these instruments should be placed in the wider framework of an international programme for economic expansion on the basis of full, productive and freely chosen employment, and

Having decided upon the adoption of certain proposals with regard to employment policy, which are included in the eighth item on the agenda of the session, and

Having determined that these proposals shall take the form of an international Convention,

Adopts this ninth day of July of the year one thousand nine hundred and sixty-four the following Convention, which may be cited as the Employment Policy Convention, 1964:

Article 1

1. With a view to stimulating economic growth and development, raising levels of living, meeting manpower requirements and overcoming unemployment and underemployment, each Member shall declare and pursue, as a major goal, an active policy designed to promote full, productive and freely chosen employment.

2. The said policy shall aim at ensuring that—

   (a) there is work for all who are available for and seeking work;
   (b) such work is as productive as possible;
   (c) there is freedom of choice of employment and the fullest possible opportunity for each worker to qualify for, and to use his skills and endowments in, a job for which he is well suited, irrespective of race, colour, sex, religion, political opinion, national extraction or social origin.

3. The said policy shall take due account of the stage and level of economic development and the mutual relationships between employment objectives and other economic and social objectives, and shall be pursued by methods that are appropriate to national conditions and practices.

Article 2

Each Member shall, by such methods and to such extent as may be appropriate under national conditions—

   (a) decide on and keep under review, within the framework of a co-ordinated economic and social policy, the measures to be adopted for attaining the objectives specified in Article 1;

(b) take such steps as may be needed, including when appropriate the establishment of programmes, for the application of these measures.

Article 3

In the application of this Convention, representatives of the persons affected by the measures to be taken, and in particular representatives of employers and workers, shall be consulted concerning employment policies, with a view to taking fully into account their experience and views and securing their full co-operation in formulating and enlisting support for such policies.

Article 4

The formal ratifications of this Convention shall be communicated to the Director-General of the International Labour Office for registration.

Article 5

1. This Convention shall be binding only upon those Members of the International Labour Organization whose ratifications have been registered with the Director-General.

2. It shall come into force twelve months after the date on which the ratifications of two Members have been registered with the Director-General.

3. Thereafter, this Convention shall come into force for any Member twelve months after the date on which its ratification has been registered.

Article 6

1. A Member which has ratified this Convention may denounce it after the expiration of ten years from the date on which the Convention first comes into force, by an act communicated to the Director-General of the International Labour Office for registration. Such denunciation shall not take effect until one year after the date on which it is registered.

2. Each Member which has ratified this Convention and which does not, within the year following the expiration of the period of ten years mentioned in the preceding paragraph, exercise the right of denunciation provided for in this Article, will be bound for another period of ten years and, thereafter, may denounce this Convention at the expiration of each period of ten years under the terms provided for in this Article.

Article 7

1. The Director-General of the International Labour Office shall notify

all Members of the International Labour Organization of the registration of all ratifications and denunciations communicated to him by the Members of the Organization.

2. When notifying the Members of the Organization of the registration of the second ratification communicated to him, the Director-General shall draw the attention of the Members of the Organization to the date upon which the Convention will come into force.

Article 8

The Director-General of the International Labour Office shall communicate to the Secretary-General of the United Nations for registration in accordance with article 102 of the Charter of the United Nations full particulars of all ratifications and acts of denunciation registered by him in accordance with the provisions of the preceding Articles.

Article 9

At such times as it may consider necessary the Governing Body of the International Labour Office shall present to the General Conference a report on the working of this Convention and shall examine the desirability of placing on the agenda of the Conference the question of its revision in whole or in part.

Article 10

1. Should the Conference adopt a new Convention revising this Convention in whole or in part, then, unless the new Convention otherwise provides—

   (a) the ratification by a Member of the new revising Convention shall *ipso jure* involve the immediate denunciation of this Convention, notwithstanding the provisions of Article 6 above, if and when the new revising Convention shall have come into force;

   (b) as from the date when the new revising Convention comes into force this Convention shall cease to be open to ratification by the Members.

2. This Convention shall in any case remain in force in its actual form and content for those Members which have ratified it but have not ratified the revising Convention.

Article 11

The English and French versions of the text of this Convention are equally authoritative.

PART FIVE

CONTRIBUTION OF THE UNITED NATIONS EDUCATIONAL, SCIENTIFIC, AND CULTURAL ORGANIZATION

UNESCO is a Specialized Agency associated with the United Nations. Several aspects of its work concern human rights; in particular, problems of illiteracy in many countries, and the production and dissemination of studies which combat racial prejudice.

See further *What is UNESCO?*, Unesco Information Manuals—1.

CONVENTION AGAINST DISCRIMINATION
IN EDUCATION, 1960

THE Convention can be compared with the I.L.O. Convention concerning discrimination in respect of employment and occupation, above. The United Nations Sub-Commission on Prevention of Discrimination and Protection of Minorities initiated study of discrimination in education, and in due course it was decided to ask UNESCO to consider the possibility of drafting and adopting a convention on the subject. The General Conference of UNESCO adopted a Convention on 14 December 1960. The Convention entered into force on 22 May 1962 and not less than fifty-three States, including the United Kingdom, have become parties.

For the text in various languages: *United Nations Treaty Series*, Vol. 429, p. 93; *U.K. Treaty Series*, No. 44 (1962), Cmnd. 1760. See also the Protocol instituting a Conciliation and Good Offices Commission to be responsible for seeking the Settlement of any Disputes which may arise between States Parties to the Convention against Discrimination in Education, adopted at Paris, 10 December 1962, *U.K. Treaty Series* No. 23 (1969), Cmnd. 3894. The Protocol has not less than seventeen parties, including the United Kingdom.

TEXT

The General Conference of the United Nations Educational, Scientific and Cultural Organization, meeting in Paris from 14 November to 15 December 1960, at its eleventh session,

Recalling that the Universal Declaration of Human Rights asserts the principle of non-discrimination and proclaims that every person has the right to education,

Considering that discrimination in education is a violation of rights enunciated in that declaration,

Considering that, under the terms of its constitution, the United Nations Educational, Scientific and Cultural Organization has the purpose of instituting collaboration among the nations with a view to furthering for all universal respect for human rights and equality of educational opportunity.

Recognizing that, consequently, the United Nations Educational,

Scientific and Cultural Organization, while respecting the diversity of national educational systems, has the duty not only to proscribe any form of discrimination in education but also to promote equality of opportunity and treatment for all in education,

Having before it proposals concerning the different aspects of discrimination in education, constituting item 17.1.4 of the agenda of the session,

Having decided at its tenth session that this question should be made the subject of an international convention as well as of recommendations to Member States,

Adopts this convention on the fourteenth day of December 1960.

Article 1

1. For the purposes of this convention, the term 'discrimination' includes any distinction, exclusion, limitation or preference which, being based on race, colour, sex, language, religion, political or other opinion, national or social origin, economic condition or birth, has the purpose or effect of nullifying or impairing equality of treatment in education and in particular:

(a) Of depriving any person or group of persons of access to education of any type or at any level;

(b) Of limiting any person or group of persons to education of an inferior standard;

(c) Subject to the provisions of article 2 of this convention, of establishing or maintaining separate educational systems or institutions for persons or groups of persons; or

(d) Of inflicting on any person or group of persons conditions which are incompatible with the dignity of man.

2. For the purposes of this convention, the term 'education' refers to all types and levels of education, and includes access to education, the standard and quality of education, and the conditions under which it is given.

Article 2

When permitted in a State, the following situations shall not be deemed to constitute discrimination, within the meaning of article 1 of this convention:

(a) The establishment or maintenance of separate educational systems or institutions for pupils of the two sexes, if these systems or institutions offer equivalent access to education, provide a teaching staff with qualifications of the same standard as well as school premises and equipment of the same quality, and afford the opportunity to take the same or equivalent courses of study;

(b) The establishment or maintenance, for religious or linguistic reasons, of separate educational systems or institutions offering an education which is in keeping with the wishes of the pupil's parents or legal guardians, if participation in such systems or attendance at such institutions is optional and if the education provided conforms to such standards as may be laid down or approved by the competent authorities, in particular for education of the same level;

(c) The establishment or maintenance of private educational institutions, if the object of the institutions is not to secure the exclusion of any group but to provide educational facilities in addition to those provided by the public authorities, if the institutions are conducted in accordance with that object, and if the education provided conforms with such standards as may be laid down or approved by the competent authorities, in particular for education of the same level.

Article 3

In order to eliminate and prevent discrimination within the meaning of this convention, the States parties thereto undertake:

(a) To abrogate any statutory provisions and any administrative instructions and to discontinue any administrative practices which involve discrimination in education:

(b) To ensure, by legislation where necessary, that there is no discrimination in the admission of pupils to educational institutions;

(c) Not to allow any differences of treatment by the public authorities between nationals, except on the basis of merit or need, in the matter of school fees and the grant of scholarships or other forms of assistance to pupils and necessary permits and facilities for the pursuit of studies in foreign countries;

(d) Not to allow, in any form of assistance granted by the public authorities to educational institutions, any restrictions or preference based solely on the ground that pupils belong to a particular group;

(e) To give foreign nationals resident within their territory the same access to education as that given to their own nationals.

Article 4

The States parties to this convention undertake furthermore to formulate, develop and apply a national policy which, by methods appropriate to the circumstances and to national usage, will tend to promote equality of opportunity and of treatment in the matter of education and in particular:

(*a*) To make primary education free and compulsory; make secondary education in its different forms generally available and accessible to all; make higher education equally accessible to all on the basis of individual capacity; assure compliance by all with the obligation to attend school prescribed by law;

(*b*) To ensure that the standards of education are equivalent in all public educational institutions of the same level, and that the conditions relating to the quality of the education provided are also equivalent;

(*c*) To encourage and intensify by appropriate methods the education of persons who have not received any primary education or who have not completed the entire primary education course and the continuation of their education on the basis of individual capacity;

(*d*) To provide training for the teaching profession without discrimination.

Article 5

1. The States parties to this convention agree that:

(*a*) Education shall be directed to the full development of the human personality and to the strengthening of respect for human rights and fundamental freedoms; it shall promote understanding, tolerance and friendship among all nations, racial or religious groups, and shall further the activities of the United Nations for the maintenance of peace;

(*b*) It is essential to respect the liberty of parents and, where applicable, of legal guardians, firstly to choose for their children institutions other than those maintained by the public authorities but conforming to such minimum education standards as may be laid down or approved by the competent authorities and, secondly, to ensure in a manner consistent with the procedures followed in the State for the application of its legislation, the religious and moral education of the children in conformity with their own convictions; and no person or group of persons should be compelled to receive religious instruction inconsistent with his or their convictions;

(c) It is essential to recognize the right of members of national minorities to carry on their own educational activities, including the maintenance of schools and, depending on the educational policy of each State, the use or the teaching of their own language, provided however:

(i) That this right is not exercised in a manner which prevents the members of these minorities from understanding the culture and language of the community as a whole and from participating in its activities, or which prejudices national sovereignty;

(ii) That the standard of education is not lower than the general standard laid down or approved by the competent authorities; and

(iii) That attendance at such schools is optional.

2. The States parties to this convention undertake to take all necessary measures to ensure the application of the principles enunciated in paragraph 1 of this article.

Article 6

In the application of this convention, the States parties to it undertake to pay the greatest attention to any recommendations hereafter adopted by the General Conference of the United Nations Educational, Scientific and Cultural Organization defining the measures to be taken against the different forms of discrimination in education and for the purpose of ensuring equality of opportunity and treatment in education.

Article 7

The States parties to this convention shall in their periodic reports submitted to the General Conference of the United Nations Educational, Scientific and Cultural Organization on dates and in a manner to be determined by it, give information on the legislative and administrative provisions which they have adopted and other action which they have taken for the application of this convention, including that taken for the formulation and the development of the national policy defined in article 4 as well as the results achieved and the obstacles encountered in the application of that policy.

Article 8

Any dispute which may arise between any two or more States parties to this convention concerning the interpretation or application of this convention, which is not settled by negotiation shall at the request of the parties to the dispute be referred, failing other means of settling the dispute, to the International Court of Justice for decision.

Article 9

Reservations to this convention shall not be permitted.

Article 10

This convention shall not have the effect of diminishing the rights which individuals or groups may enjoy by virtue of agreements concluded between two or more States, where such rights are not contrary to the letter or spirit of this convention.

Article 11

This convention is drawn up in English, French, Russian and Spanish, the four texts being equally authoritative.

Article 12

1. This convention shall be subject to ratification or acceptance by States members of the United Nations Educational, Scientific and Cultural Organization in accordance with their respective constitutional procedures.

2. The instruments of ratification or acceptance shall be deposited with the Director-General of the United Nations Educational, Scientific and Cultural Organization.

Article 13

1. This convention shall be open to accession by all States not members of the United Nations Educational, Scientific and Cultural Organization which are invited to do so by the Executive Board of the Organization.

2. Accession shall be effected by the deposit of an instrument of accession with the Director-General of the United Nations Educational, Scientific and Cultural Organization.

Article 14

This convention shall enter into force three months after the date of the deposit of the third instrument of ratification, acceptance or accession, but only with respect to those States which have deposited their respective instruments on or before that date. It shall enter into force with respect to any other State three months after the deposit of its instrument of ratification, acceptance or accession.

Article 15

The States parties to this convention recognize that the convention is applicable not only to their metropolitan territory but also to all non-self-governing, trust, colonial and other territories for the international relations of which they are responsible; they undertake to consult, if necessary, the governments or other competent authorities of these territories on or before ratification, acceptance or accession with a view to securing the application of the Convention to those territories, and to notify the Director-General of the United Nations Educational, Scientific and Cultural Organization of the territories to which it is accordingly applied, the notification to take effect three months after the date of its receipt.

Article 16

1. Each State party to this convention may denounce the convention on its own behalf or on behalf of any territory for whose international relations it is responsible.

2. The denunciation shall be notified by an instrument in writing, deposited with the Director-General of the United Nations Educational, Scientific and Cultural Organization.

3. The denunciation shall take effect twelve months after the receipt of the instrument of denunciation.

Article 17

The Director-General of the United Nations Educational, Scientific and Cultural Organization shall inform the States Members of the Organization, the States not members of the Organization which are referred to in article 13, as well as the United Nations, of the deposit of all the instruments of ratification, acceptance and accession provided for in articles 12 and 13, and of the notifications and denunciations provided for in articles 15 and 16 respectively.

Article 18

1. This convention may be revised by the General Conference of the United Nations Educational, Scientific and Cultural Organization. Any

such revision shall, however, bind only the States which shall become parties to the revising convention.

2. If the General Conference should adopt a new convention revising this convention in whole or in part, then, unless the new convention otherwise provides, this convention shall cease to be open to ratification, acceptance or accession as from the date on which the new revising convention enters into force.

Article 19

In conformity with Article 102 of the Charter of the United Nations, this convention shall be registered with the Secretariat of the United Nations at the request of the Director-General of the United Nations Educational, Scientific and Cultural Organization.

PART SIX

EUROPEAN INSTITUTIONS AND CONVENTIONS

INTRODUCTION

THE instruments in this Part derive from the work of the Council of Europe, an organization created in 1949 as a sort of social and ideological counterpart to the military aspects of European co-operation represented in the North Atlantic Treaty Organization. The Council of Europe was inspired partly by interest in promotion of European unity, and partly by the political desire for solidarity in the face of the ideology of Communism. After twenty years of life the Council of Europe may be seen as a framework for a good deal of constructive work in specific fields, and not merely or even primarily a vehicle for ideological warfare. The existing membership of the Council of Europe is as follows: (*a*) the original ten signatories of the Statute of the Council of Europe, viz. Belgium, Denmark, France, Ireland, Italy, Luxembourg, the Netherlands, Norway, Sweden, and the United Kingdom; (*b*) eight other States, viz. Greece, Turkey, Iceland, the Federal Republic of Germany, Austria, Cyprus, Switzerland, and Malta. Generally, see *Manual of the Council of Europe* (by 'A Group of Officials of the Secretariat'), London and South Hackensack, N.J., 1970; Robertson, *European Institutions*, 2nd edn., 1966; and *The Law of International Institutions in Europe*, 1961.

I. THE EUROPEAN CONVENTION ON HUMAN RIGHTS AND ITS FIVE PROTOCOLS

THE European Convention was the first essay in giving specific legal content to human rights in an international agreement, and combining this with the establishment of machinery for supervision and enforcement. The provisions have their limitations (see Articles 15, 17, and 26 in particular), and, like most constitutional developments, it has not brought about any dramatic change in the conditions of life of citizens in the States parties to the Convention. Indeed, the direct impact of the Convention might seem to be very limited, since the European Commission of Human Rights in the period from 1953 to the end of 1969 declared only fifty-two applications by individuals admissible out of 3,797 applications considered. However, it is important to understand that the role of the Commission and its associated bodies (the European Court of Human Rights and the Committee of Ministers) is that of review, and not that of an appeal court from the decisions of national tribunals. Their task is to ensure that the standards of the Convention and its Protocols are observed by the administrations of the States concerned. The work of the European Commission and Court has had certain important consequences: valuable material has been provided for the elaboration of the provisions on civil liberties; and anomalies have been exposed in national systems of law, with the result in some cases that the relevant national legislation has been changed for the better. Several individual cases have in fact had the function of providing test cases, and/or have raised issues affecting a whole class of persons; for example, a linguistic minority.

The European Convention was signed in Rome on 4 November 1950 and entered into force on 3 September 1953. Sixteen States have ratified the Convention: Austria, Belgium, Cyprus, Denmark, Greece, Federal Republic of Germany, Iceland, Ireland, Italy, Luxembourg, Malta, Netherlands, Norway, Sweden, Turkey and the United Kingdom. This represents the Council of Europe membership, apart from France and Switzerland. In December 1969 Greece denounced the Convention with effect from June 1970.

Eleven States have recognized the right of individual petition to the European Commission, and accepted the compulsory jurisdiction of the European Court of Human Rights.

The first Protocol to the Convention entered into force on 18 May 1954, and the fourth Protocol on 2 May 1968. The other three Protocols have not yet entered into force. The texts of the Protocols follow that of the principal Convention below.

See generally Robertson, *Human Rights in Europe*, 1963; id., 27 *British Year Book of International Law* (1950), pp. 145–63; id., ibid., vol. 28 (1951), pp. 359–65; Waldock, ibid., vol. 34 (1958), pp. 356–63; Waldock *et al.*, *International and Comparative Law Quarterly*, Suppl. Public. No. 11 (1965); Monconduit, *Commission Européenne des Droits de l'Homme*, 1965; Vasak, *La Convention Européenne des Droits de l'Homme*, 1964; Weil, *The European Convention on Human Rights*, 1963; id., 57 *American Journal of International Law* (1963), pp. 804–27; *Yearbook of the European Convention on Human Rights*, 1958–; Eissen, *Annuaire français de droit international*, 1959, pp. 618–58; Greenberg and Shalit, 63 *Columbia Law Review* (1963), pp. 1384–412; and Fawcett, *The Application of the European Convention on Human Rights*, 1969. Further detail may be found in *European Convention on Human Rights: Collected Texts* (Council of Europe Publication), Strasbourg, October 1969; *Council of Europe Information*, Legal B (70) 67, Sept. 1970 (Note on the Practical Application of the European Convention on Human Rights); Scheuner, in Eide and Schou (eds.), *International Protection of Human Rights*, 1968, p. 193; and McNulty, in the same volume, p. 217.

TEXT

The Governments signatory hereto, being Members of the Council of Europe,

Considering the Universal Declaration of Human Rights proclaimed by the General Assembly of the United Nations on 10 December 1948;

Considering that this Declaration aims at securing the universal and effective recognition and observance of the Rights therein declared;

Considering that the aim of the Council of Europe is the achievement of greater unity between its Members and that one of the methods by which that aim is to be pursued is the maintenance and further realization of Human Rights and Fundamental Freedoms;

Reaffirming their profound belief in those Fundamental Freedoms which are the foundation of justice and peace in the world and are best maintained on the one hand by an effective political democracy and on the other by a common understanding and observance of the Human Rights upon which they depend;

Being resolved, as the Governments of European countries which are likeminded and have a common heritage of political traditions, ideals, freedom and the rule of law to take the first steps for the collective enforcement of certain of the Rights stated in the Universal Declaration;

Have agreed as follows:

Article 1

The High Contracting Parties shall secure to everyone within their juris-diction the rights and freedoms defined in Section 1 of this Convention.

Section I

Article 2

1. Everyone's right to life shall be protected by law. No one shall be deprived of his life intentionally save in the execution of a sentence of a court following his conviction of a crime for which this penalty is pro-vided by law.

2. Deprivation of life shall not be regarded as inflicted in contravention of this Article when it results from the use of force which is no more than absolutely necessary:

   (*a*) in defence of any person from unlawful violence;
   (*b*) in order to effect a lawful arrest or to prevent the escape of a person lawfully detained;
   (*c*) in action lawfully taken for the purpose of quelling a riot or insur-rection.

Article 3

No one shall be subjected to torture or to inhuman or degrading treatment or punishment.

Article 4

1. No one shall be held in slavery or servitude.

2. No one shall be required to perform forced or compulsory labour.

3. For the purpose of this Article the term 'forced or compulsory labour' shall not include:

   (*a*) any work required to be done in the ordinary course of detention imposed according to the provisions of Article 5 of this Convention or during conditional release from such detention;
   (*b*) any service of a military character or, in case of conscientious objectors in countries where they are recognized, service exacted instead of compulsory military service;
   (*c*) any service exacted in case of an emergency or calamity threatening the life or well-being of the community;
   (*d*) any work or service which forms part of normal civic obligations.

Article 5

1. Everyone has the right to liberty and security of person.

No one shall be deprived of his liberty save in the following cases and in accordance with a procedure prescribed by law;

(*a*) the lawful detention of a person after conviction by a competent court;

(*b*) the lawful arrest or detention of a person for non-compliance with the lawful order of a court or in order to secure the fulfilment of any obligation prescribed by law;

(*c*) the lawful arrest or detention of a person effected for the purpose of bringing him before the competent legal authority on reasonable suspicion of having committed an offence or when it is reasonably considered necessary to prevent his committing an offence or fleeing after having done so;

(*d*) the detention of a minor by lawful order for the purpose of educational supervision or his lawful detention for the purpose of bringing him before the competent legal authority;

(*e*) the lawful detention of persons for the prevention of the spreading of infectious diseases, of persons of unsound mind, alcoholics or drug addicts, or vagrants;

(*f*) the lawful arrest or detention of a person to prevent his effecting an unauthorized entry into the country or of a person against whom action is being taken with a view to deportation or extradition.

2. Everyone who is arrested shall be informed promptly, in a language which he understands, of the reasons for his arrest and of any charge against him.

3. Everyone arrested or detained in accordance with the provisions of paragraph 1 (*c*) of this Article shall be brought promptly before a judge or other officer authorized by law to exercise judicial power and shall be entitled to trial within a reasonable time or to release pending trial. Release may be conditioned by guarantees to appear for trial.

4. Everyone who is deprived of his liberty by arrest or detention shall be entitled to take proceedings by which the lawfulness of his detention shall be decided speedily by a court and his release ordered if the detention is not lawful.

5. Everyone who has been the victim of arrest or detention in contravention of the provisions of this Article shall have an enforceable right to compensation.

Article 6

1. In the determination of his civil rights and obligations or of any criminal charge against him, everyone is entitled to a fair and public hearing within a reasonable time by an independent and impartial tribunal established by law. Judgment shall be pronounced publicly but the press and public may be excluded from all or part of the trial in the interest of morals, public order or national security in a democratic society, where the interests of juveniles or the protection of the private life of the parties so require, or to the extent strictly necessary in the opinion of the court in special circumstances where publicity would prejudice the interests of justice.

2. Everyone charged with a criminal offence shall be presumed innocent until proved guilty according to law.

3. Everyone charged with a criminal offence has the following minimum rights:

(*a*) to be informed promptly, in a language which he understands and in detail, of the nature and cause of the accusation against him;

(*b*) to have adequate time and facilities for the preparation of his defence;

(*c*) to defend himself in person or through legal assistance of his own choosing or, if he has not sufficient means to pay for legal assistance, to be given it free when the interests of justice so require;

(*d*) to examine or have examined witnesses against him and to obtain the attendance and examination of witnesses on his behalf under the same conditions as witnesses against him;

(*e*) to have the free assistance of an interpreter if he cannot understand or speak the language used in court.

Article 7

1. No one shall be held guilty of any criminal offence on account of any act or omission which did not constitute a criminal offence under national or international law at the time when it was committed. Nor shall a heavier penalty be imposed than the one that was applicable at the time the criminal offence was committed.

2. This Article shall not prejudice the trial and punishment of any person for any act or omission which, at the time when it was committed, was criminal according to the general principles of law recognized by civilized nations.

Article 8

1. Everyone has the right to respect for his private and family life, his home and his correspondence.

2. There shall be no interference by a public authority with the exercise of this right except such as is in accordance with the law and is necessary in a democratic society in the interests of national security, public safety or the economic well-being of the country, for the prevention of disorder or crime, for the protection of health or morals, or for the protection of the rights and freedoms of others.

Article 9

1. Everyone has the right to freedom of thought, conscience and religion; this right includes freedom to change his religion or belief, and freedom, either alone or in community with others and in public or private, to manifest his religion or belief, in worship, teaching, practice and observance.

2. Freedom to manifest one's religion or beliefs shall be subject only to such limitations as are prescribed by law and are necessary in a democratic society in the interests of public safety, for the protection of public order, health or morals, or for the protection of the rights and freedoms of others.

Article 10

1. Everyone has the right to freedom of expression. This right shall include freedom to hold opinions and to receive and impart information and ideas without interference by public authority and regardless of frontiers. This Article shall not prevent States from requiring the licensing of broadcasting, television or cinema enterprises.

2. The exercise of these freedoms, since it carries with it duties and responsibilities, may be subject to such formalities, conditions, restrictions or penalties as are prescribed by law and are necessary in a democratic society, in the interests of national security, territorial integrity or public safety, for the prevention of disorder or crime, for the protection of health or morals, for the protection of the reputation or rights of others, for preventing the disclosure of information received in confidence, or for maintaining the authority and impartiality of the judiciary.

Article 11

1. Everyone has the right to freedom of peaceful assembly and to freedom of association with others, including the right to form and to join trade unions for the protection of his interests.

2. No restrictions shall be placed on the exercise of these rights other than such as are prescribed by law and are necessary in a democratic society in the interests of national security or public safety, for the prevention of disorder or crime, for the protection of health or morals or for the protection of the rights and freedoms of others. This Article shall not prevent the imposition of lawful restrictions on the exercise of these rights by members of the armed forces, of the police or of the administration of the State.

Article 12

Men and women of marriageable age have the right to marry and to found a family, according to the national laws governing the exercise of this right.

Article 13

Everyone whose rights and freedoms as set forth in this Convention are violated shall have an effective remedy before a national authority notwithstanding that the violation has been committed by persons acting in an official capacity.

Article 14

The enjoyment of the rights and freedoms set forth in this Convention shall be secured without discrimination on any ground such as sex, race, colour, language, religion, political or other opinion, national or social origin, association with a national minority, property, birth or other status.

Article 15

1. In time of war or other public emergency threatening the life of the nation any High Contracting Party may take measures derogating from its obligations under this Convention to the extent strictly required by the exigencies of the situation, provided that such measures are not inconsistent with its other obligations under international law.

2. No derogation from Article 2, except in respect of deaths resulting from lawful acts of war, or from Articles 3, 4 (paragraph 1) and 7 shall be made under this provision.

3. Any High Contracting Party availing itself of this right of derogation shall keep the Secretary-General of the Council of Europe fully informed of the measures which it has taken and the reasons therefor. It shall also inform the Secretary-General of the Council of Europe when such

measures have ceased to operate and the provisions of the Convention are again being fully executed.

Article 16

Nothing in Articles 10, 11, and 14 shall be regarded as preventing the High Contracting Parties from imposing restrictions on the political activity of aliens.

Article 17

Nothing in this Convention may be interpreted as implying for any State, group or person any right to engage in any activity or perform any act aimed at the destruction of any of the rights and freedoms set forth herein or at their limitation to a greater extent than is provided for in the Convention.

Article 18

The restrictions permitted under this Convention to the said rights and freedoms shall not be applied for any purpose other than those for which they have been prescribed.

Section II

Article 19

To ensure the observance of the engagements undertaken by the High Contracting Parties in the present Convention, there shall be set up:

1. A European Commission of Human Rights hereinafter referred to as 'the Commission';

2. A European Court of Human Rights, hereinafter referred to as 'the Court'.

Section III

Article 20

The Commission shall consist of a number of members equal to that of the High Contracting Parties. No two members of the Commission may be nationals of the same State.

Article 21

1. The members of the Commission shall be elected by the Committee of Ministers by an absolute majority of votes, from a list of names drawn

up by the Bureau of the Consultative Assembly; each group of the Representatives of the High Contracting Parties in the Consultative Assembly shall put forward three candidates, of whom two at least shall be its nationals.

2. As far as applicable, the same procedure shall be followed to complete the Commission in the event of other States subsequently becoming Parties to this Convention, and in filling casual vacancies.

Article 22

1. The members of the Commission shall be elected for a period of six years. They may be re-elected. However, of the members elected at the first election, the terms of seven members shall expire at the end of three years.

2. The members whose terms are to expire at the end of the initial period of three years shall be chosen by lot by the Secretary-General of the Council of Europe immediately after the first election has been completed.

3. A member of the Commission elected to replace a member whose term of office has not expired shall hold office for the remainder of his predecessor's term.

4. The members of the Commission shall hold office until replaced. After having been replaced, they shall continue to deal with such cases as they already have under consideration.

Article 23

The members of the Commission shall sit on the Commission in their individual capacity.

Article 24

Any High Contracting Party may refer to the Commission through the Secretary-General of the Council of Europe, any alleged breach of the provisions of the Convention by another High Contracting Party.

Article 25

1. The Commission may receive petitions addressed to the Secretary-General of the Council of Europe from any person, non-governmental organization or group of individuals claiming to be the victim of a violation by one of the High Contracting Parties of the rights set forth in this Convention, provided that the High Contracting Party against which the

complaint has been lodged has declared that it recognizes the competence of the Commission to receive such petitions. Those of the High Contracting Parties who have made such a declaration undertake not to hinder in any way the effective exercise of this right.

2. Such declarations may be made for a specific period.

3. The declarations shall be deposited with the Secretary-General of the Council of Europe who shall transmit copies thereof to the High Contracting Parties and publish them.

4. The Commission shall only exercise the powers provided for in this Article when at least six High Contracting Parties are bound by declarations made in accordance with the preceding paragraphs.

Article 26

The Commission may only deal with the matter after all domestic remedies have been exhausted, according to the generally recognized rules of international law, and within a period of six months from the date on which the final decision was taken.

Article 27

1. The Commission shall not deal with any petition submitted under Article 25 which

(*a*) is anonymous, or
(*b*) is substantially the same as a matter which has already been examined by the Commission or has already been submitted to another procedure of international investigation or settlement and if it contains no relevant new information.

2. The Commission shall consider inadmissible any petition submitted under Article 25 which it considers incompatible with the provisions of the present Convention, manifestly illfounded, or an abuse of the right of petition.

3. The Commission shall reject any petition referred to it which it considers inadmissible under Article 26.

Article 28

In the event of the Commission accepting a petition referred to it:

(*a*) it shall, with a view to ascertaining the facts undertake together with the representatives of the parties an examination of the petition and, if need be, an investigation, for the effective conduct of which the States concerned shall furnish all necessary facilities, after an exchange of views with the Commission:

(b) it shall place itself at the disposal of the parties concerned with a view to securing a friendly settlement of the matter on the basis of respect for Human Rights as defined in this Convention.

Article 29

1. The Commission shall perform the functions set out in Article 28 by means of a Sub-Commission consisting of seven members of the Commission.

2. Each of the parties concerned may appoint as members of this Sub-Commission a person of its choice.

3. The remaining members shall be chosen by lot in accordance with arrangements prescribed in the Rules of Procedure of the Commission.

Article 30

If the Sub-Commission succeeds in effecting a friendly settlement in accordance with Article 28, it shall draw up a Report which shall be sent to the States concerned, to the Committee of Ministers and to the Secretary-General of the Council of Europe for publication. This Report shall be confined to a brief statement of the facts and of the solution reached.

Article 31

1. If a solution is not reached, the Commission shall draw up a Report on the facts and state its opinion as to whether the facts found disclose a breach by the State concerned of its obligations under the Convention. The opinions of all the members of the Commission on this point may be stated in the Report.

2. The Report shall be transmitted to the Committee of Ministers. It shall also be transmitted to the States concerned, who shall not be at liberty to publish it.

3. In transmitting the Report to the Committee of Ministers the Commission may make such proposals as it thinks fit.

Article 32

1. If the question is not referred to the Court in accordance with Article 48 of this Convention within a period of three months from the date of

the transmission of the Report to the Committee of Ministers, the Committee of Ministers shall decide by a majority of two-thirds of the members entitled to sit on the Committee whether there has been a violation of the Convention.

2. In the affirmative case the Committee of Ministers shall prescribe a period during which the Contracting Party concerned must take the measures required by the decision of the Committee of Ministers.

3. If the High Contracting Party concerned has not taken satisfactory measures within the prescribed period, the Committee of Ministers shall decide by the majority provided for in paragraph 1 above what effect shall be given to its original decision and shall publish the Report.

4. The High Contracting Parties undertake to regard as binding on them any decision which the Committee of Ministers may take in application of the preceding paragraphs.

Article 33

The Commission shall meet *in camera*.

Article 34

The Commission shall take its decisions by a majority of the Members present and voting; the Sub-Commission shall take its decisions by a majority of its members.

Article 35

The Commission shall meet as the circumstances require. The meetings shall be convened by the Secretary-General of the Council of Europe.

Article 36

The Commission shall draw up its own rules of procedure.

Article 37

The secretariat of the Commission shall be provided by the Secretary-General of the Council of Europe.

Section IV

Article 38

The European Court of Human Rights shall consist of a number of judges equal to that of the Members of the Council of Europe. No two judges may be nationals of the same State.

Article 39

1. The members of the Court shall be elected by the Consultative Assembly by a majority of the votes cast from a list of persons nominated by the Members of the Council of Europe; each Member shall nominate three candidates, of whom two at least shall be its nationals.

2. As far as applicable, the same procedure shall be followed to complete the Court in the event of the admission of new members of the Council of Europe, and in filling casual vacancies.

3. The candidates shall be of high moral character and must either possess the qualifications required for appointment to high judicial office or be jurisconsults of recognized competence.

Article 40

1. The members of the Court shall be elected for a period of nine years. They may be re-elected. However, of the members elected at the first election the terms of four members shall expire at the end of three years, and the terms of four more members shall expire at the end of six years.

2. The members whose terms are to expire at the end of the initial periods of three and six years shall be chosen by lot by the Secretary-General immediately after the first election has been completed.

3. A member of the Court elected to replace a member whose term of office has not expired shall hold office for the remainder of his predecessor's term.

4. The members of the Court shall hold office until replaced. After having been replaced, they shall continue to deal with such cases as they already have under consideration.

Article 41

The Court shall elect its President and Vice-President for a period of three years. They may be re-elected.

Article 42

The members of the Court shall receive for each day of duty a compensation to be determined by the Committee of Ministers.

Article 43

For the consideration of each case brought before it the Court shall consist of a Chamber composed of seven judges. There shall sit as an *ex officio* member of the Chamber the judge who is a national of any State party concerned, or, if there is none, a person of its choice who shall sit in the capacity of judge; the names of the other judges shall be chosen by lot by the President before the opening of the case.

Article 44

Only the High Contracting Parties and the Commission shall have the right to bring a case before the Court.

Article 45

The jurisdiction of the Court shall extend to all cases concerning the interpretation and application of the present Convention which the High Contracting Parties or the Commission shall refer to it in accordance with Article 48.

Article 46

1. Any of the High Contracting Parties may at any time declare that it recognizes as compulsory *ipso facto* and without special agreement the jurisdiction of the Court in all matters concerning the interpretation and application of the present Convention.

2. The declarations referred to above may be made unconditionally or on condition of reciprocity on the part of several or certain other High Contracting Parties or for a specified period.

3. These declarations shall be deposited with the Secretary-General of the Council of Europe who shall transmit copies thereof to the High Contracting Parties.

Article 47

The Court may only deal with a case after the Commission has acknowledged the failure of efforts for a friendly settlement and within the period of three months provided for in Article 32.

Article 48

The following may bring a case before the Court, provided that the High Contracting Party concerned, if there is only one, or the High Contracting Parties concerned, if there is more than one, are subject to the compulsory jurisdiction of the Court or, failing that, with the consent of the High Contracting Party concerned, if there is only one, or of the High Contracting Parties concerned if there is more than one:

(*a*) the Commission;
(*b*) a High Contracting Party whose national is alleged to be a victim;
12*

(*c*) a High Contracting Party which referred the case to the Commission;

(*d*) a High Contracting Party against which the complaint has been lodged.

Article 49

In the event of dispute as to whether the Court has jurisdiction, the matter shall be settled by the decision of the Court.

Article 50

If the Court finds that a decision or a measure taken by a legal authority or any other authority of a High Contracting Party, is completely or partially in conflict with the obligations arising from the present Convention, and if the internal law of the said Party allows only partial reparation to be made for the consequences of this decision or measure, the decision of the Court shall, if necessary, afford just satisfaction to the injured party.

Article 51

1. Reasons shall be given for the judgment of the Court.
2. If the judgment does not represent in whole or in part the unanimous opinion of the judges, any judge shall be entitled to deliver a separate opinion.

Article 52

The judgment of the Court shall be final.

Article 53

The High Contracting Parties undertake to abide by the decision of the Court in any case to which they are parties.

Article 54

The judgment of the Court shall be transmitted to the Committee of Ministers which shall supervise its execution.

Article 55

The Court shall draw up its own rules and shall determine its own procedure.

Article 56

1. The first election of the members of the Court shall take place after

the declarations by the High Contracting Parties mentioned in Article 46 have reached a total of eight.

2. No case can be brought before the Court before this election.

SECTION V

Article 57

On receipt of a request from the Secretary-General of the Council of Europe any High Contracting Party shall furnish an explanation of the manner in which its internal law ensures the effective implementation of any of the provisions of this Convention.

Article 58

The expenses of the Commission and the Court shall be borne by the Council of Europe.

Article 59

The members of the Commission and of the Court shall be entitled, during the discharge of their functions, to the privileges and immunities provided for in Article 40 of the Statute of the Council of Europe and in the agreements made thereunder.

Article 60

Nothing in this Convention shall be construed as limiting or derogating from any of the human rights and fundamental freedoms which may be ensured under the laws of any High Contracting Party or under any other agreement to which it is a Party.

Article 61

Nothing in this Convention shall prejudice the powers conferred on the Committee of Ministers by the Statute of the Council of Europe.

Article 62

The High Contracting Parties agree that, except by special agreement, they will not avail themselves of treaties, conventions or declarations in force between them for the purpose of submitting, by way of petition, a dispute arising out of the interpretation or application of this Convention to a means of settlement other than those provided for in this Convention.

Article 63

1. Any State may at the time of its ratification or at any time thereafter declare by notification addressed to the Secretary-General of the Council of Europe that the present Convention shall extend to all or any of the territories for whose international relations it is responsible.

2. The Convention shall extend to the territory or territories named in the notification as from the thirtieth day after the receipt of this notification by the Secretary-General of the Council of Europe.

3. The provisions of this Convention shall be applied in such territories with due regard, however, to local requirements.

4. Any State which has made a declaration in accordance with paragraph 1 of this Article may at any time thereafter declare on behalf of one or more of the territories to which the declaration relates that it accepts the competence of the Commission to receive petitions from individuals, non-governmental organizations or groups of individuals in accordance with Article 25 of the present Convention.

Article 64

1. Any State may, when signing this Convention or when depositing its instrument of ratification, make a reservation in respect of any particular provision of the Convention to the extent that any law then in force in its territory is not in conformity with the provision. Reservations of a general character shall not be permitted under this Article.

2. Any reservation made under this Article shall contain a brief statement of the law concerned.

Article 65

1. A High Contracting Party may denounce the present Convention only after the expiry of five years from the date on which it became a Party to it and after six months' notice contained in a notification addressed to the Secretary-General of the Council of Europe, who shall inform the other High Contracting Parties.

2. Such a denunciation shall not have the effect of releasing the High Contracting Party concerned from its obligations under this Convention in respect of any act which, being capable of constituting a violation of such obligations, may have been performed by it before the date at which the denunciation became effective.

3. Any High Contracting Party which shall cease to be a Member of

the Council of Europe shall cease to be a Party to this Convention under the same conditions.

4. The Convention may be denounced in accordance with the provisions of the preceding paragraphs in respect of any territory to which it has been declared to extend under the terms of Article 63.

Article 66

1. This Convention shall be open to the signature of the Members of the Council of Europe. It shall be ratified. Ratifications shall be deposited with the Secretary-General of the Council of Europe.

2. The present Convention shall come into force after the deposit of ten instruments of ratification.

3. As regards any signatory ratifying subsequently, the Convention shall come into force at the date of the deposit of its instrument of ratification.

4. The Secretary-General of the Council of Europe shall notify all the Members of the Council of Europe of the entry into force of the Convention, the names of the High Contracting Parties who have ratified it, and the deposit of all instruments of ratification which may be effected subsequently.

Done at Rome this 4th day of November, 1950, in English and French, both texts being equally authentic, in a single copy which shall remain deposited in the archives of the Council of Europe. The Secretary-General shall transmit certified copies to each of the signatories.

PROTOCOLS

1. *Enforcement of certain Rights and Freedoms not included in Section I of the Convention*

The Governments signatory hereto, being Members of the Council of Europe,

Being resolved to take steps to ensure the collective enforcement of certain rights and freedoms other than those already included in Section I of the Convention for the Protection of Human Rights and Fundamental Freedoms signed at Rome on 4th November, 1950 (hereinafter referred to as 'the Convention'),

Have agreed as follows:

Article 1

Every natural or legal person is entitled to the peaceful enjoyment of his possessions. No one shall be deprived of his possessions except in the public interest and subject to the conditions provided for by law and by the general principles of international law.

The preceding provisions shall not, however, in any way impair the right of a State to enforce such laws as it deems necessary to control the use of property in accordance with the general interest or to secure the payment of taxes or other contributions or penalties.

Article 2

No person shall be denied the right to education. In the exercise of any functions which it assumes in relation to education and to teaching, the State shall respect the right of parents to ensure such education and teaching in conformity with their own religious and philosophical convictions.

Article 3

The High Contracting Parties undertake to hold free elections at reasonable intervals by secret ballot, under conditions which will ensure the free expression of the opinion of the people in the choice of the legislature.

Article 4

Any High Contracting Party may at the time of signature or ratification or at any time thereafter communicate to the Secretary-General of the Council of Europe a declaration stating the extent to which it undertakes that the provisions of the present Protocol shall apply to such of the territories for the international relations of which it is responsible as are named therein.

Any High Contracting Party which has communicated a declaration in virtue of the preceding paragraph may from time to time communicate a further declaration modifying the terms of any former declaration or terminating the application of the provisions of this Protocol in respect of any territory.

A declaration made in accordance with this Article shall be deemed to have been made in accordance with paragraph 1 of Article 63 of the Convention.

Article 5

As between the High Contracting Parties the provisions of Articles 1, 2, 3 and 4 of this Protocol shall be regarded as additional Articles to the Convention and all the provisions of the Convention shall apply accordingly.

Article 6

This Protocol shall be open for signature by the Members of the Council of Europe, who are the signatories of the Convention; it shall be ratified at the same time as or after the ratification of the Convention. It shall enter into force after the deposit of ten instruments of ratification. As regards any signatory ratifying subsequently, the Protocol shall enter into force at the date of the deposit of its instrument of ratification.

The instruments of ratification shall be deposited with the Secretary-General of the Council of Europe, who will notify all Members of the names of those who have ratified.

Done at Paris on the 20th day of March 1952, in English and French, both texts being equally authentic, in a single copy which shall remain deposited in the archives of the Council of Europe. The Secretary-General shall transmit certified copies to each of the signatory Governments.

2. *Conferring upon the European Court of Human Rights Competence to give Advisory Opinions*

The member States of the Council of Europe signatory hereto:

Having regard to the provisions of the Convention for the Protection of Human Rights and Fundamental Freedoms signed at Rome on 4 November 1950 (hereinafter referred to as 'the Convention'), and in particular Article 19 instituting, among other bodies, a European Court of Human Rights (hereinafter referred to as 'the Court');

Considering that it is expedient to confer upon the Court competence to give advisory opinions subject to certain conditions;

Have agreed as follows:

Article 1

1. The Court may, at the request of the Committee of Ministers, give advisory opinions on legal questions concerning the interpretation of the Convention and the Protocols thereto.

2. Such opinions shall not deal with any question relating to the content or scope of the rights or freedoms defined in Section I of the Convention and in the Protocols thereto, or with any other question which the Commission, the Court, or the Committee of Ministers might have to consider in consequence of any such proceedings as could be instituted in accordance with the Convention.

3. Decisions of the Committee of Ministers to request an advisory

opinion of the Court shall require a two-thirds majority vote of the representatives entitled to sit on the Committee.

Article 2

The Court shall decide whether a request for an advisory opinion submitted by the Committee of Ministers is within its consultative competence as defined in Article 1 of this Protocol.

Article 3

1. For the consideration of requests for an advisory opinion, the Court shall sit in plenary session.

2. Reasons shall be given for advisory opinions of the Court.

3. If the advisory opinion does not represent in whole or in part the unanimous opinion of the judges, any judge shall be entitled to deliver a separate opinion.

4. Advisory opinions of the Court shall be communicated to the Committee of Ministers.

Article 4

The powers of the Court under Article 55 of the Convention shall extend to the drawing up of such rules and the determination of such procedure as the Court may think necessary for the purposes of this Protocol.

Article 5

1. This Protocol shall be open to signature by Member States of the Council of Europe, signatories to the Convention, who may become Parties to it by:

   (a) signature without reservation in respect of ratification or acceptance;
   (b) signature with reservation in respect of ratification or acceptance, followed by ratification or acceptance. Instruments of ratification or acceptance shall be deposited with the Secretary-General of the Council of Europe.

2. This Protocol shall enter into force as soon as all the States Parties to the Convention shall have become Parties to the Protocol in accordance with the Provisions of paragraph 1 of this Article.

3. From the date of the entry into force of this Protocol, Articles 1 to 4 shall be considered an integral part of the Convention.

4. The Secretary-General of the Council of Europe shall notify the Member States of the Council of:

(a) any signature without reservation in respect of ratification or acceptance;

(b) any signature with reservation in respect of ratification or acceptance;

(c) the deposit of any instrument of ratification or acceptance;

(d) the date of entry into force of this Protocol in accordance with paragraph 2 of this Article.

In witness whereof the undersigned, being duly authorized thereto, have signed this Protocol.

Done at Strasbourg, this 6th day of May 1963, in English and in French, both texts being equally authoritative, in a single copy which shall remain deposited in the archives of the Council of Europe. The Secretary-General shall transmit certified copies to each of the signatory States.

3. *Amending Articles 29, 30, and 94 of the Convention*

The member States of the Council of Europe, signatories to this Protocol,

Considering that it is advisable to amend certain provisions of the Convention for the Protection of Human Rights and Fundamental Freedoms signed at Rome on 4 November 1960 (hereinafter referred to as 'the Convention') concerning the procedure of the European Commission of Human Rights,

Have agreed as follows:

Article 1

1. Article 29 of the Convention is deleted.

2. The following provision shall be inserted in the Convention:
'Article 29

After it has accepted a petition submitted under Article 25, the Commission may nevertheless decide unanimously to reject the petition if, in the course of its examination, it finds that the existence of one of the grounds for non-acceptance provided for in Article 27 has been established.

In such a case, the decision shall be communicated to the parties.'

Article 2

In Article 30 of the Convention, the word 'Sub-Commission' shall be replaced by the word 'Commission'.

Article 3

1. At the beginning of Article 34 of the Convention, the following shall be inserted:

'Subject to the provisions of Article 29. . . .'

2. At the end of the same Article, the sentence 'the Sub-commission shall take its decisions by a majority of its members' shall be deleted.

Article 4

1. The Protocol shall be open to signature by the member States of the Council of Europe, who may become Parties to it either by:

(*a*) signature without reservation in respect of ratification or acceptance, or

(*b*) signature with reservation in respect of ratification or acceptance, followed by ratification or acceptance. Instruments of ratification or acceptance shall be deposited with the Secretary-General of the Council of Europe.

2. This Protocol shall enter into force as soon as all States Parties to the Convention shall have become Parties to the Protocol, in accordance with the provisions of paragraph 1 of this Article.

3. The Secretary-General of the Council of Europe shall notify the Member States of the Council of:

(*a*) any signature without reservation in respect of ratification or acceptance;

(*b*) any signature with reservation in respect of ratification or acceptance;

(*c*) the deposit of any instrument of ratification or acceptance;

(*d*) the date of entry into force of this Protocol in accordance with paragraph 2 of this Article.

In witness whereof the undersigned, being duly authorized thereto, have signed this Protocol.

Done at Strasbourg, this 6th day of May 1963, in English and in French, both texts being equally authoritative, in a single copy which shall remain deposited in the archives of the Council of Europe. The Secretary-General shall transmit certified copies to each of the signatory States.

4. *Protecting certain Additional Rights*

The Governments signatory hereto, being Members of the Council of Europe.

Being resolved to take steps to ensure the collective enforcement of certain rights and freedoms other than those already included in Section I of the Convention for the Protection of Human Rights and Fundamental Freedoms signed at Rome on 4 November 1950 (hereinafter referred to as 'the Convention') and in Articles 1 to 3 of the First Protocol to the Convention, signed at Paris on 20 March 1952,

Have agreed as follows:

Article 1

No one shall be deprived of his liberty merely on the ground of inability to fulfil a contractual obligation.

Article 2

1. Everyone lawfully within the territory of a State shall, within that territory, have the right to liberty of movement and freedom to choose his residence.

2. Everyone shall be free to leave any country, including his own.

3. No restrictions shall be placed on the exercise of these rights other than such as are in accordance with law and are necessary in a democratic society in the interests of national security or public safety for the maintenance of 'ordre public', for the prevention of crime, for the protection of the rights and freedoms of others.

4. The rights set forth in paragraph 1 may also be subject, in particular areas, to restrictions imposed in accordance with law and justified by the public interest in a democratic society.

Article 3

1. No one shall be expelled, by means either of an individual or of a collective measure, from the territory of the State of which he is a national.

2. No one shall be deprived of the right to enter the territory of the State of which he is a national.

Article 4

Collective expulsion of aliens is prohibited.

Article 5

1. Any High Contracting Party may, at the time of signature or ratifica-

tion of this Protocol, or at any time thereafter, communicate to the Secretary-General of the Council of Europe a declaration stating the extent to which it undertakes that the provisions of this Protocol shall apply to such of the territories for the international relations of which it is responsible as are named therein.

2. Any High Contracting Party which has communicated a declaration in virtue of the preceding paragraph may, from time to time, communicate a further declaration modifying the terms of any former declaration or terminating the application of the provisions of this Protocol in respect of any territory.

3. A declaration made in accordance with this Article shall be deemed to have been made in accordance with paragraph 1 of Article 63 of the Convention.

4. The territory of any State to which this Protocol applies by virtue of ratification or acceptance by that State, and each territory to which this Protocol is applied by virtue of a declaration by that State under this Article, shall be treated as separate territories for the purpose of the references in Articles 2 and 3 to the territory of a State.

Article 6

1. As between the High Contracting Parties the provisions of Articles 1 to 5 of this Protocol shall be regarded as additional articles to the Convention, and all the provisions of the Convention shall apply accordingly.

2. Nevertheless, the right of individual recourse recognized by a declaration made under Article 25 of the Convention, or the acceptance of the compulsory jurisdiction of the Court by a declaration made under Article 46 of the Convention, shall not be effective in relation to this Protocol unless the High Contracting Party concerned has made a statement recognizing such right, or accepting such jurisdiction, in respect of all or any of Articles 1 to 4 of the Protocol.

Article 7

1. This Protocol shall be open for signature by the members of the Council of Europe who are the signatories of the Convention; it shall be ratified at the same time as or after the ratification of the Convention. It shall enter into force after the deposit of five instruments of ratification. As regards any signatory ratifying subsequently, the Protocol shall enter into force at the date of the deposit of its instrument of ratification.

2. The instruments of ratification shall be deposited with the Secretary-General of the Council of Europe, who will notify all members of the names of those who have ratified.

In witness whereof, the undersigned, being duly authorized thereto, have signed this Protocol.

Done at Strasbourg, this 16th day of September 1963, in English and in French, both texts being equally authoritative, in a single copy which shall remain deposited in the archives of the Council of Europe. The Secretary-General shall transmit certified copies to each of the signatory States.

5. *Amending Articles 22 and 40 of the Convention*

The Governments signatory hereto, being Members of the Council of Europe.

Considering that certain inconveniences have arisen in the application of the provisions of Articles 22 and 40 of the Convention for the Protection of Human Rights and Fundamental Freedoms signed at Rome on 4th November 1950 (hereinafter referred to as 'the Convention') relating to the length of the terms of office of the members of the European Commission of Human Rights (hereinafter referred to as 'the Commission') and of the European Court of Human Rights (hereinafter referred to as 'the Court');

Considering that it is desirable to ensure as far as possible an election every three years of one half of the members of the Commission and of one third of the members of the Court;

Considering therefore that it is desirable to amend certain provisions of the Convention,

Have agreed as follows:

Article 1

In Article 22 of the Convention, the following two paragraphs shall be inserted after paragraph (2):

'(3) In order to ensure that, as far as possible, one half of the membership of the Commission shall be renewed every three years, the Committee of Ministers may decide, before proceeding to any subsequent election, that the term or terms of office of one or more members to be elected shall be for a period other than six years but not more than nine and not less than three years.

(4) In cases where more than one term of office is involved and the

Committee of Ministers applies the preceding paragraph, the allocation of the terms of office shall be effected by the drawing of lots by the Secretary-General, immediately after the election.'

Article 2

In Article 22 of the Convention, the former paragraphs (3) and (4) shall become respectively paragraphs (5) and (6).

Article 3

In Article 40 of the Convention, the following two paragraphs shall be inserted after paragraph (2):

'(3) In order to ensure that, as far as possible, one third of the membership of the Court shall be renewed every three years, the Consultative Assembly may decide, before proceeding to any subsequent election, that the term or terms of office of one or more members to be elected shall be for a period other than nine years but not more than twelve and not less than six years.

(4) In cases where more than one term of office is involved and the Consultative Assembly applies the preceding paragraph, the allocation of the terms of office shall be effected by the drawing of lots by the Secretary-General immediately after the election.'

Article 4

In Article 40 of the Convention, the former paragraphs (3) and (4) shall become respectively paragraphs (5) and (6)

Article 5

1. This Protocol shall be open to signature by Members of the Council of Europe, signatories to the Convention, who may become Parties to it by:

   (a) signature without reservation in respect of ratification or acceptance;
   (b) signature with reservation in respect of ratification or acceptance, followed by ratification or acceptance.

Instruments of ratification or acceptance shall be deposited with the Secretary-General of the Council of Europe.

2. This Protocol shall enter into force as soon as all Contracting Parties to the Convention shall have become Parties to the Protocol, in accordance with the provisions of paragraph 1 of this Article.

3. The Secretary-General of the Council of Europe shall notify the Members of the Council of:

(*a*) any signature without reservation in respect of ratification or acceptance;

(*b*) any signature with reservation in respect of ratification or acceptance;

(*c*) the deposit of any instrument of ratification or acceptance;

(*d*) the date of entry into force of this Protocol in accordance with paragraph 2 of this Article.

In witness whereof the undersigned, being duly authorized thereto, have signed this Protocol.

Done at Strasbourg, this 20th day of January 1966, in English and in French, both texts being equally authoritative, in a single copy which shall remain deposited in the archives of the Council of Europe. The Secretary-General shall transmit certified copies to each of the signatory Governments.

II. EUROPEAN SOCIAL CHARTER, 1961

THIS was intended to be complementary to the European Convention on Human Rights. The Charter is concerned to develop and protect social and economic rights, whilst the Convention is concerned with political and civil rights: but this division is by no means exact.

The Charter was signed at Turin on 18 October 1961, and came into force on 26 February 1965: see *Treaty Series*, No. 38 (1965), Cmnd. 2643 (English and French texts, declarations made on ratification). The following States have become parties: Cyprus, Denmark, Federal Republic of Germany, Ireland, Italy, Norway, Sweden, and the United Kingdom. See, further, the European Code of Social Security signed at Strasbourg on 16 April 1964, in force in 1968: *Treaty Series*, No. 10 (1969), Cmnd. 3871 (does not include the Protocol); *European Treaty Series*, No. 48; *European Yearbook*, vol. xii, p. 397.

TEXT

The Government signatory hereto, being Members of the Council of Europe,

Considering that the aim of the Council of Europe is the achievement of greater unity between its Members for the purpose of safeguarding and realizing the ideals and principles which are their common heritage and of facilitating their economic and social progress, in particular by the maintenance and further realization of human rights and fundamental freedoms;

Considering that in the European Convention for the Protection of Human Rights and Fundamental Freedoms signed at Rome on 4th November 1950, and the Protocol thereto signed at Paris on 20th March 1952, the member States of the Council of Europe agreed to secure to their populations the civil and political rights and freedoms therein specified;

Considering that the enjoyment of social rights should be secured without discrimination on grounds of race, colour, sex, religion, political opinion, national extraction or social origin;

Being resolved to make every effort in common to improve the standard of living and to promote the social well-being of both their urban and rural populations by means of appropriate institutions and action,

Have agreed as follows:

PART I

The Contracting Parties accept as the aim of their policy, to be pursued by all appropriate means, both national and international in character, the attainment of conditions in which the following rights and principles may be effectively realized:

(1) Everyone shall have the opportunity to earn his living in an occupation freely entered upon.

(2) All workers have the right to just conditions of work.

(3) All workers have the right to safe and healthy working conditions.

(4) All workers have the right to a fair remuneration sufficient for a decent standard of living for themselves and their families.

(5) All workers and employers have the right to freedom of association in national or international organizations for the protection of their economic and social interests.

(6) All workers and employers have the right to bargain collectively.

(7) Children and young persons have the right to a special protection against the physical and moral hazards to which they are exposed.

(8) Employed women, in case of maternity, and other employed women as appropriate, have the right to a special protection in their work.

(9) Everyone has the right to appropriate facilities for vocational guidance with a view to helping him choose an occupation suited to his personal aptitude and interests.

(10) Everyone has the right to appropriate facilities for vocational training.

(11) Everyone has the right to benefit from any measures enabling him to enjoy the highest possible standard of health attainable.

(12) All workers and their dependents have the right to social security.

(13) Anyone without adequate resources has the right to social and medical assistance.

(14) Everyone has the right to benefit from social welfare services.

(15) Disabled persons have the right to vocational training, rehabilitation and resettlement, whatever the origin and nature of their disability.

(16) The family as a fundamental unit of society has the right to appropriate social, legal and economic protection to ensure its full development.

(17) Mothers and children, irrespective of marital status and family

relations, have the right to appropriate social and economic protection.

(18) The nationals of any one of the Contracting Parties have the right to engage in any gainful occupation in the territory of any one of the others on a footing of equality with the nationals of the latter, subject to restrictions based on cogent economic or social reasons.

(19) Migrant workers who are nationals of a Contracting Party and their families have the right to protection and assistance in the territory of any other Contracting Party.

PART II

The Contracting Parties undertake, as provided for in Part III, to consider themselves bound by the obligations laid down in the following Articles and paragraphs.

The Right to Work
Article 1

With a view to ensuring the effective exercise of the right to work, the Contracting Parties undertake:

(1) to accept as one of their primary aims and responsibilities the achievement and maintenance of as high and stable a level of employment as possible, with a view to the attainment of full employment;

(2) to protect effectively the right of the worker to earn his living in an occupation freely entered upon;

(3) to establish or maintain free employment services for all workers;

(4) to provide or promote appropriate vocational guidance, training and rehabilitation.

The Right to Just Conditions of Work
Article 2

With a view to ensuring the effective exercise of the right to just conditions of work, the Contracting Parties undertake:

(1) to provide for reasonable daily and weekly working hours, the working week to be progressively reduced to the extent that the increase of productivity and other relevant factors permit;

(2) to provide for public holidays with pay;

(3) to provide for a minimum of two weeks annual holiday with pay;

(4) to provide for additional paid holidays or reduced working hours for

workers engaged in dangerous or unhealthy occupations as prescribed;

(5) to ensure a weekly rest period which shall, as far as possible, coincide with the day recognized by tradition or custom in the country or region concerned as a day of rest.

The Right to Safe and Healthy Working Conditions
Article 3

With a view to ensuring the effective exercise of the right to safe and healthy working conditions, the Contracting Parties undertake:

(1) to issue safety and health regulations;
(2) to provide for the enforcement of such regulations by measures of supervision;
(3) to consult, as appropriate, employers' and workers' organizations on measures intended to improve industrial safety and health.

The Right to a Fair Remuneration
Article 4

With a view to ensuring the effective exercise of the right to a fair remuneration, the Contracting Parties undertake:

(1) to recognize the right of workers to a remuneration such as will give them and their families a decent standard of living;
(2) to recognize the right of workers to an increased rate of remuneration for overtime work, subject to exceptions in particular cases;
(3) to recognize the right of men and women workers to equal pay for work of equal value;
(4) to recognize the right of all workers to a reasonable period of notice for termination of employment;
(5) to permit deductions from wages only under conditions and to the extent prescribed by national laws or regulations or fixed by collective agreements or arbitration awards.

The exercise of these rights shall be achieved by freely concluded collective agreements, by statutory wage-fixing machinery, or by other means appropriate to national conditions.

The Right to Organize
Article 5

With a view to ensuring or promoting the freedom of workers and employers to form local, national or international organizations for the protection of their economic and social interests and to join those organizations, the Contracting Parties undertake that national law shall not be such as to impair, nor shall it be so applied as to impair, this freedom. The extent to which the guarantees provided for in this Article shall apply to the police shall be determined by national laws or regulations. The principle governing the application to the members of the armed forces of these guarantees and the extent to which they shall apply to persons in this category shall equally be determined by national laws or regulations.

The Right to Bargain Collectively

Article 6

With a view to ensuring the effective exercise of the right to bargain collectively, the Contracting Parties undertake:

(1) to promote joint consultation between workers and employers;

(2) to promote, where necessary and appropriate, machinery for voluntary negotiations between employers or employers' organizations and workers' organizations, with a view to the regulation of terms and conditions of employment by means of collective agreements;

(3) to promote the establishment and use of appropriate machinery for conciliation and voluntary arbitration for the settlement of labour disputes;

and recognize:

(4) the right of workers and employers to collective action in cases of conflicts of interest, including the right to strike, subject to obligations that might arise out of collective agreements previously entered into.

The Right of Children and Young Persons to Protection

Article 7

With a view to ensuring the effective exercise of the right of children and young persons to protection, the Contracting Parties undertake:

(1) to provide that the minimum age of admission to employment shall be 15 years, subject to exceptions for children employed in prescribed light work without harm to their health, morals or education;

(2) to provide that a higher minimum age of admission to employment

shall be fixed with respect to prescribed occupations regarded as dangerous or unhealthy;

(3) to provide that persons who are still subject to compulsory education shall not be employed in such work as would deprive them of the full benefit of their education;

(4) to provide that the working hours of persons under 16 years of age shall be limited in accordance with the needs of their development, and particularly with their need for vocational training;

(5) to recognize the right of young workers and apprentices to a fair wage or other appropriate allowances;

(6) to provide that the time spent by young persons in vocational training during the normal working hours with the consent of the employer shall be treated as forming part of the working day;

(7) to provide that employed persons of under 18 years of age shall be entitled to not less than three weeks' annual holiday with pay;

(8) to provide that persons under 18 years of age shall not be employed in night work with the exception of certain occupations provided for by national laws or regulations;

(9) to provide that persons under 18 years of age employed in occupations prescribed by national laws or regulations shall be subject to regular medical control;

(10) to ensure special protection against physical and moral dangers to which children and young persons are exposed, and particularly against those resulting directly or indirectly from their work.

The Right of Employed Women to Protection

Article 8

With a view to ensuring the effective exercise of the right of employed women to protection, the Contracting Parties undertake:

(1) to provide either by paid leave, by adequate social security benefits or by benefits from public funds for women to take leave before and after childbirth up to a total of at least 12 weeks;

(2) to consider it as unlawful for an employer to give a woman notice of dismissal during her absence on maternity leave or to give her notice of dismissal at such a time that the notice would expire during such absence;

(3) to provide that mothers who are nursing their infants shall be entitled to sufficient time off for this purpose;

(4) (*a*) to regulate the employment of women workers on night work in industrial employment;

(b) to prohibit the employment of women workers in underground mining, and, as appropriate, on all other work which is unsuitable for them by reason of its dangerous, unhealthy, or arduous nature.

The Right to Vocational Guidance

Article 9

With a view to ensuring the effective exercise of the right to vocational guidance, the Contracting Parties undertake to provide or promote, as necessary, a service which will assist all persons, including the handicapped, to solve problems related to occupational choice and progress, with due regard to the individual's characteristics and their relation to occupational opportunity: this assistance should be available free of charge, both to young persons, including school children, and to adults.

The Right to Vocational Training

Article 10

With a view to ensuring the effective exercise of the right to vocational training, the Contracting Parties undertake:

(1) to provide or promote, as necessary, the technical and vocational training of all persons, including the handicapped, in consultation with employers' and workers' organizations, and to grant facilities for access to higher technical and university education, based solely on individual aptitude;

(2) to provide or promote a system of apprenticeship and other systematic arrangements for training young boys and girls in their various employments;

(3) to provide or promote, as necessary:

   (a) adequate and readily available training facilities for adult workers;

   (b) special facilities for the re-training of adult workers needed as a result of technological development or new trends in employment;

(4) to encourage the full utilization of the facilities provided by appropriate measures such as:

   (a) reducing or abolishing any fees or charges;

   (b) granting financial assistance in appropriate cases;

   (c) including in the normal working hours time spent on supplementary training taken by the worker, at the request of his employer, during employment;

(d) ensuring, through adequate supervision, in consultation with the employers' and workers' organizations, the efficiency of apprenticeship and other training arrangements for young workers, and the adequate protection of young workers generally.

The Right to Protection of Health

Article 11

With a view to ensuring the effective exercise of the right to protection of health, the Contracting Parties undertake, either directly or in co-operation with public or private organizations, to take appropriate measures designed *inter alia*:

(1) to remove as far as possible the cases of ill-health;

(2) to provide advisory and educational facilities for the promotion of health and the encouragement of individual responsibility in matters of health;

(3) to prevent as far as possible epidemic, endemic and other diseases.

The Right to Social Security

Article 12

With a view to ensuring the effective exercise of the right to social security, the Contracting Parties undertake:

(1) to establish or maintain a system of social security;

(2) to maintain the social security system at a satisfactory level at least equal to that required for ratification of International Labour Convention (No. 102) Concerning Minimum Standards of Social Security;

(3) to endeavour to raise progressively the system of social security to a higher level;

(4) to take steps, by the conclusion of appropriate bilateral and multi-lateral agreements, or by other means, and subject to the conditions laid down in such agreements, in order to ensure:

(a) equal treatment with their own nationals of the nationals of other Contracting Parties in respect of social security rights,

including the retention of benefits arising out of social security
legislation, whatever movements the persons protected may
undertake between the territories of the Contracting Parties;

(b) the granting, maintenance and resumption of social security
rights by such means as the accumulation of insurance or
employment periods completed under the legislation of each of
the Contracting Parties.

The Right to Social and Medical Assistance

Article 13

With a view to ensuring the effective exercise of the right to social and
medical assistance, the Contracting Parties undertake:

(1) to ensure that any person who is without adequate resources and
who is unable to secure such resources either by his own efforts or
from other sources, in particular by benefits under a social security
scheme, be granted adequate assistance, and, in case of sickness, the
care necessitated by his condition;

(2) to ensure that persons receiving such assistance shall not, for that
reason, suffer from a diminution of their political or social rights;

(3) to provide that everyone may receive by appropriate public or
private services such advice and personal help as may be required
to prevent, to remove, or to alleviate personal or family want;

(4) to apply the provisions referred to in paragraphs 1, 2 and 3 of this
Article on an equal footing with their nationals to nationals of other
Contracting Parties lawfully within their territories, in accordance
with their obligations under the European Convention on Social
and Medical Assistance, signed at Paris on 11th December 1953.[1]

The Right to Benefit from Social Welfare Services

Article 14

With a view to ensuring the effective exercise of the right to benefit from
social welfare services, the Contracting Parties undertake:

(1) to promote or provide services which, by using methods of social
work, would contribute to the welfare and development of both
individuals and groups in the community, and to their adjustment
to the social environment;

[1] 'Treaty Series No. 42 (1955)', Cmnd. 9512.

(2) to encourage the participation of individuals and voluntary or other organizations in the establishment and maintenance of such services.

The Right of Physically or Mentally Disabled Persons to Vocational Training, Rehabilitation and Social Resettlement

Article 15

With a view to ensuring the effective exercise of the right of the physically or mentally disabled to vocational training, rehabilitation and resettlement, the Contracting Parties undertake:

(1) to take adequate measures for the provision of training facilities, including, where necessary, specialized institutions, public or private;

(2) to take adequate measures for the placing of disabled persons in employment, such as specialized placing services, facilities for sheltered employment and measures to encourage employers to admit disabled persons to employment.

The Right of the Family to Social, Legal and Economic Protection

Article 16

With a view to ensuring the necessary conditions for the full development of the family, which is a fundamental unit of society, the Contracting Parties undertake to promote the economic, legal and social protection of family life by such means as social and family benefits, fiscal arrangements, provision of family housing, benefits for the newly married, and other appropriate means.

The Right of Mothers and Children to Social and Economic Protection

Article 17

With a view to ensuring the effective exercise of the right of mothers and children to social and economic protection, the Contracting Parties will take all appropriate and necessary measures to that end, including the establishment or maintenance of appropriate institutions or services.

The Right to Engage in a Gainful Occupation in the Territory of Other Contracting Parties

Article 18

With a view to ensuring the effective exercise of the right to engage in a

13 + B.D.H.R.

gainful occupation in the territory of any other Contracting Party, the Contracting Parties undertake:

(1) to apply existing regulations in a spirit of liberality;
(2) to simplify existing formalities and to reduce or abolish chancery dues and other charges payable by foreign workers or their employers;
(3) to liberalize, individually or collectively, regulations governing the employment of foreign workers;

and recognize:

(4) the right of their nationals to leave the country to engage in a gainful occupation in the territories of the other Contracting Parties.

The Right of Migrant Workers and their Families to Protection and Assistance

Article 19

With a view to ensuring the effective exercise of the right of migrant workers and their families to protection and assistance in the territory of any other Contracting Party, the Contracting Parties undertake:

(1) to maintain or to satisfy themselves that there are maintained adequate and free services to assist such workers, particularly in obtaining accurate information, and to take all appropriate steps, so far as national laws and regulations permit, against misleading propaganda relating to emigration and immigration;
(2) to adopt appropriate measures within their own jurisdiction to facilitate the departure, journey and reception of such workers and their families, and to provide, within their own jurisdiction, appropriate services for health, medical attention and good hygienic conditions during the journey;
(3) to promote co-operation, as appropriate, between social services, public and private, in emigration and immigration countries;
(4) to secure for such workers lawfully within their territories, insofar as such matters are regulated by law or regulations or are subject to the control of administrative authorities, treatment not less favourable than that of their own nationals in respect of the following matters:
   (*a*) remuneration and other employment and working conditions;
   (*b*) membership of trade unions and enjoyment of the benefits of collective bargaining;
   (*c*) accommodation;

(5) to secure for such workers lawfully within their territories treatment not less favourable than that of their own nationals with regard to employment taxes, dues or contributions payable in respect of employed persons;

(6) to facilitate as far as possible the reunion of the family of a foreign worker permitted to establish himself in the territory;

(7) to secure for such workers lawfully within their territories treatment not less favourable than that of their own nationals in respect of legal proceedings relating to matters referred to in this Article;

(8) to secure that such workers lawfully residing within their territories are not expelled unless they endanger national security or offend against public interest or morality;

(9) to permit, within legal limits, the transfer of such parts of the earnings and savings of such workers as they may desire;

(10) to extend the protection and assistance provided for in this Article to self-employed migrants insofar as such measures apply.

PART III

Undertakings

Article 20

1. Each of the Contracting Parties undertakes:

(a) to consider Part I of this Charter as a declaration of the aims which it will pursue by all appropriate means, as stated in the introductory paragraph of that Part;

(b) to consider itself bound by at least five of the following Articles of Part II of this Charter: Articles 1, 5, 6, 12, 13, 16 and 19;

(c) in addition to the Articles selected by it in accordance with the preceding sub-paragraph, to consider itself bound by such a number of Articles or numbered paragraphs of Part II of the Charter as it may select, provided that the total number of Articles or numbered paragraphs by which it is bound is not less than 10 Articles or 45 numbered paragraphs.

2. The Articles or paragraphs selected in accordance with sub-paragraphs (b) and (c) of paragraph 1 of this Article shall be notified to the Secretary-General of the Council of Europe at the time when the instrument of ratification or approval of the Contracting Party concerned is deposited.

3. Any Contracting Party may, at a later date, declare by notification to the Secretary-General that it considers itself bound by any Articles or

any numbered paragraphs of Part II of the Charter which it has not already accepted under the terms of paragraph 1 of this Article. Such undertakings subsequently given shall be deemed to be an integral part of the ratification or approval, and shall have the same effect as from the thirtieth day after the date of the notification.

4. The Secretary-General shall communicate to all the signatory Governments and to the Director-General of the International Labour Office any notification which he shall have received pursuant to this Part of the Charter.

5. Each Contracting Party shall maintain a system of labour inspection appropriate to national conditions.

PART IV

Reports concerning Accepted Provisions
Article 21

The Contracting Parties shall send to the Secretary-General of the Council of Europe a report at two-yearly intervals, in a form to be determined by the Committee of Ministers, concerning the application of such provisions of Part II of the Charter as they have accepted.

Reports concerning Provisions which are not accepted
Article 22

The Contracting Parties shall send to the Secretary-General, at appropriate intervals as requested by the Committee of Ministers, reports relating to the provisions of Part II of the Charter which they did not accept at the time of their ratification or approval or in a subsequent notification. The Committee of Ministers shall determine from time to time in respect of which provisions such reports shall be requested and the form of the reports to be provided.

Communication of Copies
Article 23

1. Each Contracting Party shall communicate copies of its reports referred to in Articles 21 and 22 to such of its national organizations as are members of the international organizations of employers and trade unions to be invited under Article 27, paragraph 2, to be represented at meetings of the Sub-committee of the Governmental Social Committee.

2. The Contracting Parties shall forward to the Secretary-General any comments on the said reports received from these national organizations, if so requested by them.

Examination of the Reports

Article 24

The reports sent to the Secretary-General in accordance with Articles 21 and 22 shall be examined by a Committee of Experts, who shall have also before them any comments forwarded to the Secretary-General in accordance with paragraph 2 of Article 23.

Committee of Experts

Article 25

1. The Committee of Experts shall consist of not more than seven members appointed by the Committee of Ministers from a list of independent experts of the highest integrity and of recognized competence in international social questions, nominated by the Contracting Parties.

2. The members of the Committee shall be appointed for a period of six years. They may be reappointed. However, of the members first appointed, the terms of office of two members shall expire at the end of four years.

3. The members whose terms of office are to expire at the end of the initial period of four years shall be chosen by lot by the Committee of Ministers immediately after the first appointment has been made.

4. A member of the Committee of Experts appointed to replace a member whose term of office has not expired shall hold office for the remainder of his predecessor's term.

Participation of the International Labour Organization

Article 26

The International Labour Organization shall be invited to nominate a representative to participate in a consultative capacity in the deliberations of the Committee of Experts.

Sub-Committee of the Governmental Social Committee

Article 27

1. The reports of the Contracting Parties and the conclusions of the Committee of Experts shall be submitted for examination to a Sub-

committee of the Governmental Social Committee of the Council of Europe.

2. The Sub-committee shall be composed of one representative of each of the Contracting Parties. It shall invite no more than two international organizations of employers and no more than two international trade union organizations as it may designate to be represented as observers in a consultative capacity at its meetings. Moreover, it may consult no more than two representatives of international non-governmental organizations having consultative status with the Council of Europe, in respect of questions with which the organizations are particularly qualified to deal, such as social welfare, and the economic and social protection of the family.

3. The Sub-committee shall present to the Committee of Ministers a report containing its conclusions and append the report of the Committee of Experts.

Consultative Assembly

Article 28

The Secretary-General of the Council of Europe shall transmit to the Consultative Assembly the conclusions of the Committee of Experts. The Consultative Assembly shall communicate its views on these Conclusions to the Committee of Ministers.

Committee of Ministers

Article 29

By a majority of two-thirds of the members entitled to sit on the Committee, the Committee of Ministers may, on the basis of the report of the Sub-committee, and after consultation with the Consultative Assembly, make to each Contracting Party any necessary recommendations.

PART V

Derogations in time of War or Public Emergency

Article 30

1. In time of war or other public emergency threatening the life of the nation any Contracting Party may take measures derogating from its obligations under this Charter to the extent strictly required by the exigencies of the situation, provided that such measures are not inconsistent with its other obligations under international law.

2. Any Contracting Party which has availed itself of this right of derogation shall, within a reasonable lapse of time, keep the Secretary-General of the Council of Europe fully informed of the measures taken and of the reasons therefor. It shall likewise inform the Secretary-General when such measures have ceased to operate and the provisions of the Charter which it has accepted are again being fully executed.

3. The Secretary-General shall in turn inform other Contracting Parties and the Director-General of the International Labour Office of all communications received in accordance with paragraph 2 of this Article.

Restrictions
Article 31

1. The rights and principles set forth in Part I when effectively realized, and their effective exercise as provided for in Part II, shall not be subject to any restrictions or limitations not specified in those Parts, except such as are prescribed by law and are necessary in a democratic society for the protection of the rights and freedoms of others or for the protection of public interest, national security, public health, or morals.

2. The restrictions permitted under this Charter to the rights and obligations set forth herein shall not be applied for any purpose other than that for which they have been prescribed.

Relations between the Charter and Domestic Law or International Agreements
Article 32

The provisions of this Charter shall not prejudice the provisions of domestic law or of any bilateral or multilateral treaties, conventions or agreements which are already in force, or may come into force, under which more favourable treatment would be accorded to the persons protected.

Implementation by Collective Agreements
Article 33

1. In member States where the provisions of paragraphs 1, 2, 3, 4 and 5 of Article 2, paragraphs 4, 6 and 7 of Article 7 and paragraphs 1, 2, 3, and 4 of Article 10 of Part II of this Charter are matters normally left to agreements between employers or employers' organizations and workers' organizations, or are normally carried out otherwise than by law, the undertakings of those paragraphs may be given and compliance with

them shall be treated as effective if their provisions are applied through such agreements or other means to the great majority of the workers concerned.

2. In member States where these provisions are normally the subject of legislation, the undertakings concerned may likewise be given, and compliance with them shall be regarded as effective if the provisions are applied by law to the great majority of the workers concerned.

Territorial Application

Article 34

1. This Charter shall apply to the metropolitan territory of each Contracting Party. Each signatory Government may, at the time of signature or of the deposit of its instrument of ratification or approval, specify, by declaration addressed to the Secretary-General of the Council of Europe, the territory which shall be considered to be its metropolitan territory for this purpose.

2. Any Contracting Party may, at the time of ratification or approval of this Charter or at any time thereafter, declare by notification addressed to the Secretary-General of the Council of Europe, that the Charter shall extend in whole or in part to a non-metropolitan territory or territories specified in the said declaration for whose international relations it is responsible or for which it assumes international responsibility. It shall specify in the declaration the Articles or paragraphs of Part II of the Charter which it accepts as binding in respect of the territories named in the declaration.

3. The Charter shall extend to the territory or territories named in the aforesaid declaration as from the thirtieth day after the date on which the Secretary-General shall have received notification of such declaration.

4. Any Contracting Party may declare at a later date by notification addressed to the Secretary-General of the Council of Europe, that, in respect of one or more of the territories to which the Charter has been extended in accordance with paragraph 2 of this Article, it accepts as binding any Articles or any numbered paragraphs which it has not already accepted in respect of that territory or territories. Such undertakings subsequently given shall be deemed to be an integral part of the original declaration in respect of the territory concerned, and shall have the same effect as from the thirtieth day after the date of the notification.

5. The Secretary-General shall communicate to the other signatory

Governments and to the Director-General of the International Labour Office any notification transmitted to him in accordance with this Article.

Signature, Ratification and Entry into Force
Article 35

1. This Charter shall be open for signature by the Members of the Council of Europe. It shall be ratified or approved. Instruments of ratification or approval shall be deposited with the Secretary-General of the Council of Europe.

2. This Charter shall come into force as from the thirtieth day after the date of deposit of the fifth instrument of ratification or approval.[1]

3. In respect of any signatory Government ratifying subsequently, the Charter shall come into force as from the thirtieth day after the date of deposit of its instrument of ratification or approval.

4. The Secretary-General shall notify all the Members of the Council of Europe and the Director-General of the International Labour Office, of the entry into force of the Charter, the names of the Contracting Parties which have ratified or approved it and the subsequent deposit of any instruments of ratification or approval.

Amendments
Article 36

Any Member of the Council of Europe may propose amendments to this Charter in a communication addressed to the Secretary-General of the Council of Europe. The Secretary-General shall transmit to the other Members of the Council of Europe any amendments so proposed, which shall then be considered by the Committee of Ministers and submitted to the Consultative Assembly for opinion. Any amendments approved by the Committee of Ministers shall enter into force as from the thirtieth day after all the Contracting Parties have informed the Secretary-General of their acceptance. The Secretary-General shall notify all the Members of the Council of Europe and the Director-General of the International Labour Office of the entry into force of such amendments.

Denunciation
Article 37

1. Any Contracting Party may denounce this Charter only at the end of

---

[1] The Charter entered into force on 26 February, 1965.

13*

a period of five years from the date on which the Charter entered into force for it, or at the end of any successive period of two years, and, in each case, after giving six months notice to the Secretary-General of the Council of Europe, who shall inform the other Parties and the Director-General of the International Labour Office accordingly. Such denunciation shall not affect the validity of the Charter in respect of the other Contracting Parties provided that at all times there are not less than five such Contracting Parties.

2. Any Contracting Party may, in accordance with the provisions set out in the preceding paragraph, denounce any Article or paragraph of Part II of the Charter accepted by it provided that the number of Articles or paragraphs by which this Contracting Party is bound shall never be less than 10 in the former case and 45 in the latter and that this number of Articles or paragraphs shall continue to include the Articles selected by the Contracting Party among those to which special reference is made in Article 20, paragraph 1, sub-paragraph (b).

3. Any Contracting Party may denounce the present Charter or any of the Articles or paragraphs of Part II of the Charter, under the conditions specified in paragraph 1 of this Article in respect of any territory to which the said Charter is applicable by virtue of a declaration made in accordance with paragraph 2 of Article 34.

Appendix

Article 38

The Appendix to this Charter shall form an integral part of it.

In witness whereof, the undersigned, being duly authorized thereto, have signed this Charter.

Done at Turin, this 18th day of October 1961, in English and French, both texts being equally authoritative, in a single copy which shall be deposited within the archives of the Council of Europe. The Secretary-General shall transmit certified copies to each of the Signatories.

APPENDIX TO THE SOCIAL CHARTER
SCOPE OF THE SOCIAL CHARTER IN TERMS OF PERSONS PROTECTED:

1. Without prejudice to Article 12, paragraph 4 and Article 13, paragraph 4, the persons covered by Articles 1 to 17 include foreigners only insofar as they are nationals of other Contracting Parties lawfully resident or working regularly within the territory of the Contracting Party con-

cerned, subject to the understanding that these Articles are to be interpreted in the light of the provisions of Articles 18 and 19.

This interpretation would not prejudice the extension of similar facilities to other persons by any of the Contracting Parties.

2. Each Contracting Party will grant to refugeees as defined in the Convention relating to the Status of Refugees, signed at Geneva on 28th July, 1951,[1] and lawfully staying in its territory, treatment as favourable as possible, and in any case not less favourable than under the obligations accepted by the Contracting Party under the said Convention and under any other existing international instruments applicable to those refugees.

PART I		*PART II*
Paragraph 18	and	*Article 18, paragraph 1*

It is understood that these provisions are not concerned with the question of entry into the territories of the Contracting Parties and do not prejudice the provisions of the European Convention on Establishment, signed at Paris on 13th December, 1955.[2]

PART II

Article 1, paragraph 2

This provision shall not be interpreted as prohibiting or authorizing any union security clause or practice.

Article 4, paragraph 4

This provision shall be so understood as not to prohibit immediate dismissal for any serious offence.

Article 4, paragraph 5

It is understood that a Contracting Party may give the undertaking required in this paragraph if the great majority of workers are not permitted to suffer deductions from wages either by law or through collective agreements or arbitration awards, the exceptions being those persons not so covered.

Article 6, paragraph 4

It is understood that each Contracting Party may, insofar as it is concerned, regulate the exercise of the right to strike by law, provided that

---

[1] Above, p 135.
[2] 'Miscellaneous No. 1 (1957)', Cmnd. 41.

any further restriction that this might place on the right can be justified under the terms of Article 31.

Article 7, paragraph 8

It is understood that a Contracting Party may give the undertaking required in this paragraph if it fulfils the spirit of the undertaking by providing by law that the great majority of persons under 18 years of age shall not be employed in night work.

Article 12, paragraph 4

The words 'and subject to the conditions laid down in such agreements' in the introduction to this paragraph are taken to imply *inter alia* that with regard to benefits which are available independently of any insurance contribution a Contracting Party may require the completion of a prescribed period of residence before granting such benefits to nationals of other Contracting Parties.

Article 13, paragraph 4

Governments not Parties to the European Convention on Social and Medical Assistance may ratify the Social Charter in respect of this paragraph provided that they grant to nationals of other Contracting Parties a treatment which is in conformity with the provisions of the said Convention.

Article 19, paragraph 6

For the purpose of this provision, the term 'family of a foreign worker' is understood to mean at least his wife and dependent children under the age of 21 years.

PART III

It is understood that the Charter contains legal obligations of an international character, the application of which is submitted solely to the supervision provided for in Part IV thereof.

Article 20, paragraph 1

It is understood that the 'numbered paragraphs' may include Articles consisting of only one paragraph.

PART V

Article 30

The term 'in time of war or other public emergency' shall be so understood as to cover also the *threat* of war.

PART SEVEN

LATIN AMERICAN DEVELOPMENTS

INTRODUCTION

LATIN America provides a store of contradictions in the field of human rights. Legal and political sophistication belongs to some of the Latin American socially élite groups, and the outcome of this sophistication is a desire to adopt legal instruments such as the American Convention on Human Rights (below, p. 399), which is broadly similar to the European Convention (above, p. 339). At the same time social conditions in nearly all of Latin America entail inequalities and deprivation on such a scale that recourse to guarantees of the classical Western political and civil rights is manifestly inadequate. Moreover, in the absence of general social and economic development, the position relating to civil and political rights is itself precarious. The successful use of international machinery to improve standards of government must normally depend upon the existence of a certain, reasonably uniform, level of development in the States concerned.

The position in Latin America has special features. The whole question of human rights is bound up with the status of aliens and their property: powerful foreign corporations will wish to rely on human rights standards to preserve an economic *status quo* favourable to their interests. More significant is the relation of human rights to the regional security system represented by the Organization of American States. There is abundant evidence that the concept of human rights in Latin America has been employed as a weapon against revolutionary regimes, particularly Cuba. Regimes which threaten the system of private property and foreign private investment are likely to be denounced by the O.A.S. organs as 'threats to regional security' and as inimical to human rights, whilst military regimes which accept the economic *status quo* will remain free from condemnation. The paradox is thus the likely use of machinery for the protection of human rights to justify intervention in the name of the regional organ, the O.A.S., with the purpose of conserving a system which tolerates appalling social injustice. Even so, formal adherence by governments to agreements containing guarantees of human rights will help politicians striving to improve social conditions, and will improve the possibility of reporting abuses.

For general reference see *The Inter-American System*, Inter-American Institute of International Legal Studies, 1966; Schreiber, *The Inter-American Commission on Human Rights*, 1970; Cabranes, *Michigan Law Review*, 65 (1967), 1147–82; Cabranes, *American Journal of International Law*, 62 (1968), 889–908; Vasak, *La Commission interaméricaine des droits de l'homme*, 1968.

I. AMERICAN DECLARATION OF THE RIGHTS AND DUTIES OF MAN, 1948

THE Declaration is to be found in the Final Act of the Ninth International Conference of American States, Bogotá, Colombia, held in 1948. It was based on a revision of a draft first prepared in 1946 by the Inter-American Juridical Committee. The Declaration was not intended to be binding, and its status was that of a recommendation of the Conference.

TEXT

Whereas:

The American peoples have acknowledged the dignity of the individual, and their national constitutions recognize that juridical and political institutions, which regulate life in human society, have as their principal aim the protection of the essential rights of man and the creation of circumstances that will permit him to achieve spiritual and material progress and attain happiness;

The American States have on repeated occasions recognized that the essential rights of man are not derived from the fact that he is a national of a certain state, but are based upon attributes of his human personality;

The international protection of the rights of man should be the principal guide of an evolving American law;

The affirmation of essential human rights by the American States together with the guarantees given by the internal régimes of the states establish the initial system of protection considered by the American States as being suited to the present social and juridical conditions, not without a recognition on their part that they should increasingly strengthen that system in the international field as conditions become more favourable,

The Ninth International Conference of American States

Agrees

To adopt the following

AMERICAN DECLARATION OF THE RIGHTS AND DUTIES OF MAN

PREAMBLE

All men are born free and equal, in dignity and in rights, and, being endowed by nature with reason and conscience, they should conduct themselves as brothers one to another.

The fulfillment of duty by each individual is a prerequisite to the rights of all. Rights and duties are interrelated in every social and political activity of man. While rights exalt individual liberty, duties express the dignity of that liberty.

Duties of a juridical nature presuppose others of a moral nature which support them in principle and constitute their basis.

Inasmuch as spiritual development is the supreme end of human existence and the highest expression thereof, it is the duty of man to serve that end with all his strength and resources.

Since culture is the highest social and historical expression of that spiritual development, it is the duty of man to preserve, practice and foster culture by every means within his power.

And, since moral conduct constitutes the noblest flowering of culture, it is the duty of every man always to hold it in high respect.

CHAPTER ONE. RIGHTS

Article I

Every human being has the right to life, liberty and the security of his person.

Article II

All persons are equal before the law and have the rights and duties established in this Declaration, without distinction as to race, sex, language, creed or any other factor.

Article III

Every person has the right freely to profess a religious faith, and to manifest and practice it both in public and in private.

Article IV

Every person has the right to freedom of investigation, of opinion, and of the expression and dissemination of ideas, by any medium whatsoever.

Article V

Every person has the right to the protection of the law against abusive attacks upon his honor, his reputation, and his private and family life.

Article VI

Every person has the right to establish a family, the basic element of society, and to receive protection therefor.

Article VII

All women, during pregnancy and the nursing period, and all children have the right to special protection, care and aid.

Article VIII

Every person has the right to fix his residence within the territory of the state of which he is a national, to move about freely within such territory, and not to leave it except by his own will.

Article IX

Every person has the right to the inviolability of his home.

Article X

Every person has the right to the inviolability and transmission of his correspondence.

Article XI

Every person has the right to the preservation of his health through sanitary and social measures relating to food, clothing, housing and medical care, to the extent permitted by public and community resources.

Article XII

Every person has the right to an education, which should be based on the principles of liberty, morality and human solidarity.

Likewise every person has the right to an education that will prepare him to attain a decent life, to raise his standard of living, and to be a useful member of society.

The right to an education includes the right to equality of opportunity in every case, in accordance with natural talents, merit and the desire to utilize the resources that the state or the community is in a position to provide.

Every person has the right to receive, free, at least a primary education.

Article XIII

Every person has the right to take part in the cultural life of the community, to enjoy the arts, and to participate in the benefits that result from intellectual progress, especially scientific discoveries.

He likewise has the right to the protection of his moral and material interests as regards his inventions or any literary, scientific or artistic works of which he is the author.

Article XIV

Every person has the right to work, under proper conditions, and to follow his vocation freely, in so far as existing conditions of employment permit.

Every person who works has the right to receive such remuneration as will, in proportion to his capacity and skill, assure him a standard of living suitable for himself and for his family.

Article XV

Every person has the right to leisure time, to wholesome recreation, and to the opportunity for advantageous use of his free time to his spiritual, cultural and physical benefit.

Article XVI

Every person has the right to social security which will protect him from the consequences of unemployment, old age, and any disabilities arising from causes beyond his control that make it physically or mentally impossible for him to earn a living.

Article XVII

Every person has the right to be recognized everywhere as a person having rights and obligations, and to enjoy the basic civil rights.

Article XVIII

Every person may resort to the courts to ensure respect for his legal rights. There should likewise be available to him a simple, brief procedure whereby the courts will protect him from acts of authority that, to his prejudice, violate any fundamental constitutional rights.

Article XIX

Every person has the right to the nationality to which he is entitled by law and to change it, if he so wishes, for the nationality of any other country that is willing to grant it to him.

Article XX

Every person having legal capacity is entitled to participate in the government of his country, directly or through his representatives, and to take part in popular elections, which shall be by secret ballot, and shall be honest, periodic and free.

Article XXI

Every person has the right to assemble peaceably with others in a formal public meeting or an informal gathering, in connection with matters of common interest of any nature.

Article XXII

Every person has the right to associate with others to promote, exercise and protect his legitimate interests of a political, economic, religious, social, cultural, professional, labor union or other nature.

Article XXIII

Every person has a right to own such private property as meets the essential needs of decent living and helps to maintain the dignity of the individual and of the home.

Article XXIV

Every person has the right to submit respectful petitions to any competent authority, for reasons of either general or private interest, and the right to obtain a prompt decision thereon.

Article XXV

No person may be deprived of his liberty except in the cases and according to the procedures established by pre-existing law.

No person may be deprived of liberty for nonfulfillment of obligations of a purely civil character.

Every individual who has been deprived of his liberty has the right to have the legality of his detention ascertained without delay by a court, and the right to be tried without undue delay, or otherwise, to be released. He also has the right to humane treatment during the time he is in custody.

Article XXVI

Every accused person is presumed to be innocent until proved guilty.

Every person accused of an offense has the right to be given an impartial and public hearing, and to be tried by courts previously established in accordance with pre-existing laws, and not to receive cruel, infamous or unusual punishment.

Article XXVII

Every person has the right, in case of pursuit not resulting from ordinary crimes, to seek and receive asylum in foreign territory, in accordance with the laws of each country and with international agreements.

Article XXVIII

The rights of man are limited by the rights of others, by the security of all, and by the just demands of the general welfare and the advancement of democracy.

CHAPTER TWO. DUTIES

Article XXIX

It is the duty of the individual so to conduct himself in relation to others that each and every one may fully form and develop his personality.

Article XXX

It is the duty of every person to aid, support, educate and protect his minor children, and it is the duty of children to honor their parents always and to aid, support and protect them when they need it.

Article XXXI

It is the duty of every person to acquire at least an elementary education.

Article XXXII

It is the duty of every person to vote in the popular elections of the country of which he is a national, when he is legally capable of doing so.

Article XXXIII

It is the duty of every person to obey the law and other legitimate commands of the authorities of his country and those of the country in which he may be.

Article XXXIV

It is the duty of every able-bodied person to render whatever civil and military service his country may require for its defense and preservation, and, in case of public disaster, to render such services as may be in his power.

It is likewise his duty to hold any public office to which he may be elected by popular vote in the state of which he is a national.

Article XXXV

It is the duty of every person to cooperate with the state and the community with respect to social security and welfare, in accordance with his ability and with existing circumstances.

Article XXXVI

It is the duty of every person to pay the taxes established by law for the support of public services.

Article XXXVII

It is the duty of every person to work, as far as his capacity and possibilities permit, in order to obtain the means of livelihood or to benefit his community.

Article XXXVIII

It is the duty of every person to refrain from taking part in political activities that, according to law, are reserved exclusively to the citizens of the state in which he is an alien.

II. DECLARATION OF PUNTA DEL ESTE, 1961

THE appearance of the Castro regime in Cuba created the fear that Socialist policies would find support elsewhere in Latin America. In 1961 the American Republics attempted to create a regional programme of social and economic development which would meet the competition of Socialist programmes. The Charter of Punta del Este established the Alliance for Progress. The document which follows is the accompanying 'Declaration to the Peoples of America', which is of considerable significance, in that it accepts the relation between liberty and economic and social security. In this respect it presents a contrast to the Declaration of 1948 set out above. The implementation of the Alliance for Progress has not been successful.

TEXT

DECLARATION TO THE PEOPLES OF AMERICA

Assembled in Punta del Este, inspired by the principles consecrated in the Charter of the Organization of American States, in Operation Pan America and in the Act of Bogotá, the representatives of the American Republics hereby agree to establish an Alliance for Progress: a vast effort to bring a better life to all the peoples of the Continent.

This Alliance is established on the basic principle that free men working through the institution of representative democracy can best satisfy man's aspirations, including those for work, home and land, health and schools. No system can guarantee true progress unless it affirms the dignity of the individual which is the foundation of our civilization.

Therefore the countries signing this declaration in the exercise of their sovereignty have agreed to work toward the following goals during the coming years:

To improve and strengthen democratic institutions through application of the principle of self-determination by the people.

To accelerate economic and social development, thus rapidly bringing about a substantial and steady increase in the average income in order to narrow the gap between the standard of living in Latin American countries and that enjoyed in the industrialized countries.

To carry out urban and rural housing programs to provide decent homes for all our people.

To encourage, in accordance with the characteristics of each country, programs of comprehensive agrarian reform, leading to the effective transformation, where required, of unjust structures and systems of land tenure and use; with a view to replacing latifundia and dwarf holdings by an equitable system of property so that, supplemented by timely and adequate credit, technical assistance and improved marketing arrangements, the land will become for the man who works it the basis of his economic stability, the foundation of his increasing welfare, and the guarantee of his freedom and dignity.

To assure fair wages and satisfactory working conditions to all our workers; to establish effective systems of labor-management relations and procedures for consultation and cooperation among government authorities, employers' associations, and trade unions in the interests of social and economic development.

To wipe out illiteracy; to extend, as quickly as possible, the benefits of primary education to all Latin Americans; and to provide broader facilities, on a vast scale, for secondary and technical training and for higher education.

To press forward with programs of health and sanitation in order to prevent sickness, combat contagious disease, and strengthen our human potential.

To reform tax laws, demanding more from those who have most, to punish tax evasion severely, and to redistribute the national income in order to benefit those who are most in need, while, at the same time, promoting savings and investment and reinvestment of capital.

To maintain monetary and fiscal policies which, while avoiding the disastrous effects of inflation or deflation, will protect the purchasing power of the many, guarantee the greatest possible price stability, and form an adequate basis for economic development.

To stimulate private enterprise in order to encourage the development of Latin American countries at a rate which will help them to provide jobs for their growing populations, to eliminate unemployment, and to take their place among the modern industrialized nations of the world.

To find a quick and lasting solution to the grave problem created by excessive price fluctuations in the basic exports of Latin American countries on which their prosperity so heavily depends.

To accelerate the integration of Latin America so as to stimulate the economic and social development of the Continent. This process has already begun through the General Treaty of Economic Integration of Central America and, in other countries, through the Latin American Free Trade Association.

This declaration expresses the conviction of the nations of Latin America that these profound economic, social, and cultural changes can come about only through the self-help efforts of each country. Nonetheless, in order to achieve the goals which have been established with the necessary speed, domestic efforts must be reinforced by essential contributions of external assistance.

The United States, for its part, pledges its efforts to supply financial and technical cooperation in order to achieve the aims of the Alliance for Progress. To this end, the United States will provide a major part of the minimum of twenty billion dollars, principally in public funds, which Latin America will require over the next ten years from all external sources in order to supplement its own efforts.

The United States will provide from public funds, as an immediate contribution to the economic and social progress of Latin America, more than one billion dollars during the twelve months which began on March 13, 1961, when the Alliance for Progress was announced.

The United States intends to furnish development loans on a long-term basis, where appropriate running up to fifty years and in general at very low or zero rates of interest.

For their part, the countries of Latin America agree to devote a steadily increasing share of their own resources to economic and social development, and to make the reforms necessary to assure that all share fully in the fruits of the Alliance for Progress.

Further, as a contribution to the Alliance for Progress, each of the countries of Latin America will formulate a comprehensive and well-conceived national program for the development of its own economy.

Independent and highly qualified experts will be made available to Latin American countries in order to assist in formulating and examining national development plans.

Conscious of the overriding importance of this declaration, the signatory countries declare that the inter-American community is now beginning a new era when it will supplement its institutional, legal, cultural and social accomplishments with immediate and concrete actions to secure a better life, under freedom and democracy, for the present and future generations.

III. AMERICAN CONVENTION ON
HUMAN RIGHTS, 1969

THE Bogotá Conference of 1948 had expressed a tentative interest in a proposal that an Inter-American Court be created to guarantee the basic rights of man, but no further development occurred until the Fifth Meeting of Consultation of Ministers of Foreign Afiairs at Santiago, Chile, in 1959. The meeting resolved that the Inter-American Council of Jurists should prepare a draft Convention on Human Rights and that a convention should also be prepared on the creation of an Inter-American Court for the Protection of Human Rights.

The same meeting decided that an Inter-American Commission on Human Rights should be organized. The Commission came into being in 1960 as 'an autonomous entity of the Organization of American States, the function of which is to promote respect for human rights'. For the text of the statute see *The Inter-American System*, Inter-American Institute of International Legal Studies, 1966, p. 372. On the performance of the Commission see the same work, pp. 43–56; Schreiber, *The Inter-American Commission on Human Rights*, 1970; and Cabranes, *Michigan Law Review*, 65 (1967), p. 1147 and pp. 1164–73.

The culmination of Latin American interest in human rights was the Inter-American Specialized Conference on Human Rights held at San José, Costa Rica, 7–22 November 1969. The American Convention on Human Rights was signed on 22 November 1969 by the following States: Chile, Colombia, Costa Rica, El Salvador, Ecuador, Guatemala, Honduras, Nicaragua, Panama, Paraguay, Uruguay, and Venezuela. The Convention provides for a Commission and a Court, and bears a general resemblance to the European Convention, above. However, there are significant differences; for example, in the powers of the Commission, which are both broad and vague in the American Convention.

The text appeared in O.A.S. Official Records OEA/Ser. K/XVI/I.I, Document 65, Rev. 1, Corr. 2, 7 January 1970.

TEXT

PREAMBLE

The American states signatory to the present Convention,

Reaffirming their intention to consolidate in this hemisphere, within the framework of democratic institutions, a system of personal liberty and social justice based on respect for the essential rights of man;

Recognizing that the essential rights of man are not derived from one's being a national of a certain state, but are based upon attributes of the human personality, and that they therefore justify international protection in the form of a convention reinforcing or complementing the protection provided by the domestic law of the American states;

Considering that these principles have been set forth in the Charter of the Organization of American States, in the American Declaration of the Rights and Duties of Man, and in the Universal Declaration of Human Rights, and that they have been reaffirmed and refined in other international instruments, worldwide as well as regional in scope;

Reiterating that, in accordance with the Universal Declaration of Human Rights, the ideal of free men enjoying freedom from fear and want can be achieved only if conditions are created whereby everyone may enjoy his economic, social, and cultural rights, as well as his civil and political rights; and

Considering that the Third Special Inter-American Conference (Buenos Aires, 1967) approved the incorporation into the Charter of the Organization itself of broader standards with respect to economic, social, and educational rights and resolved that an inter-American convention on human rights should determine the structure, competence, and procedure of the organs responsible for these matters,

Have agreed upon the following:

PART I

STATE OBLIGATIONS AND RIGHTS PROTECTED

CHAPTER I. GENERAL OBLIGATIONS

Obligation to Respect Rights

Article 1

1. The States Parties to this Convention undertake to respect the rights and freedoms recognized herein and to ensure to all persons subject to their jurisdiction the free and full exercise of those rights and freedoms, without any discrimination for reasons of race, color, sex, language, religion, political or other opinion, national or social origin, economic status, birth, or any other social condition.

2. For the purposes of this Convention, 'person' means every human being.

Domestic Legal Effects

Article 2

Where the exercise of any of the rights or freedoms referred to in Article 1 is not already ensured by legislative or other provisions, the States Parties undertake to adopt, in accordance with their constitutional processes and the provisions of this Convention, such legislative or other measures as may be necessary to give effect to those rights or freedoms.

CHAPTER II. CIVIL AND POLITICAL RIGHTS

Right to Juridical Personality

Article 3

Every person has the right to recognition as a person before the law.

Right to Life

Article 4

1. Every person has the right to have his life respected. This right shall be protected by law, and, in general, from the moment of conception. No one shall be arbitrarily deprived of his life.

2. In countries that have not abolished the death penality, it may be imposed only for the most serious crimes and pursuant to a final judgment rendered by a competent court and in accordance with a law establishing such punishment, enacted prior to the commission of the crime. The application of such punishment shall not be extended to crimes to which it does not presently apply.

3. The death penalty shall not be reestablished in states that have abolished it.

4. In no case shall capital punishment be inflicted for political offenses or related common crimes.

5. Capital punishment shall not be imposed upon persons who, at the time the crime was committed, were under 18 years of age or over 70 years of age; nor shall it be applied to pregnant women.

6. Every person condemned to death shall have the right to apply for amnesty, pardon, or commutation of sentence, which may be granted in all cases. Capital punishment shall not be imposed while such a petition is pending decision by the competent authority.

Right to Humane Treatment

Article 5

1. Every person has the right to have his physical, mental, and moral integrity respected.

2. No one shall be subjected to torture or to cruel, inhuman, or degrading punishment or treatment. All persons deprived of their liberty shall be treated with respect for the inherent dignity of the human person.

3. Punishment shall not be extended to any person other than the criminal.

4. Accused persons shall, save in exceptional circumstances, be segregated from convicted persons, and shall be subject to separate treatment appropriate to their status as unconvicted persons.

5. Minors while subject to criminal proceedings shall be separated from adults and brought before specialized tribunals, as speedily as possible, so that they may be treated in accordance with their status as minors.

6. Punishments consisting of deprivation of liberty shall have as an essential aim the reform and social readaptation of the prisoners.

Freedom from Slavery

Article 6

1. No one shall be subject to slavery or to involuntary servitude, which are prohibited in all their forms, as are the slave trade and traffic in women.

2. No one shall be required to perform forced or compulsory labor. This provision shall not be interpreted to mean that, in those countries in which the penalty established for certain crimes is deprivation of liberty at forced labor, the carrying out of such a sentence imposed by a competent court is prohibited. Forced labor shall not adversely affect the dignity or the physical or intellectual capacity of the prisoner.

3. For the purposes of this article the following do not constitute forced or compulsory labor:

(*a*) work or service normally required of a person imprisoned in execution of a sentence or formal decision passed by the competent judicial authority. Such work or service shall be carried out under the supervision and control of public authorities, and any persons performing such work or service shall not be placed at the disposal of any private party, company, or juridical person;

(*b*) military service and, in countries in which conscientious objectors are recognized, national service that the law may provide for in lieu of military service;

(c) service exacted in time of danger or calamity that threatens the existence or the well-being of the community; or

(d) work or service that forms part of normal civic obligations.

Right to Personal Liberty

Article 7

1. Every person has the right to personal liberty and security.

2. No one shall be deprived of his physical liberty except for the reasons and under the conditions established beforehand by the constitution of the State Party concerned or by a law established pursuant thereto.

3. No one shall be subject to arbitrary arrest or imprisonment.

4. Anyone who is detained shall be informed of the reasons for his detention and shall be promptly notified of the charge or charges against him.

5. Any person detained shall be brought promptly before a judge or other officer authorized by law to exercise judicial power and shall be entitled to trial within a reasonable time or to be released without prejudice to the continuation of the proceedings. His release may be subject to guarantees to assure his appearance for trial.

6. Anyone who is deprived of his liberty shall be entitled to recourse to a competent court, in order that the court may decide without delay on the lawfulness of his arrest or detention and order his release if the arrest or detention is unlawful. In States Parties whose laws provide that anyone who believes himself to be threatened with deprivation of his liberty is entitled to recourse to a competent court in order that it may decide on the lawfulness of such threat, this remedy may not be restricted or abolished. The interested party or another person in his behalf is entitled to seek these remedies.

7. No one shall be detained for debt. This principle shall not limit the orders of a competent judicial authority issued for nonfulfillment of duties of support.

Right to a Fair Trial

Article 8

1. Every person has the right to a hearing, with due guarantees and within a reasonable time, by a competent, independent, and impartial tribunal, previously established by law, in the substantiation of any accusation of

a criminal nature made against him or for the determination of his rights and obligations of a civil, labor, fiscal, or any other nature.

2. Every person accused of a criminal offense has the right to be presumed innocent so long as his guilt has not been proven according to law. During the proceedings, every person is entitled, with full equality, to the following minimum guarantees:

(a) the right of the accused to be assisted without charge by a translator or interpreter, if he does not understand or does not speak the language of the tribunal or court;

(b) prior notification in detail to the accused of the charges against him;

(c) adequate time and means for the preparation of his defense;

(d) the right of the accused to defend himself personally or to be assisted by legal counsel of his own choosing, and to communicate freely and privately with his counsel;

(e) the inalienable right to be assisted by counsel provided by the state, paid or not as the domestic law provides, if the accused does not defend himself personally or engage his own counsel within the time period established by law;

(f) the right of the defense to examine witnesses present in the court and to obtain the appearance, as witnesses, of experts or other persons who may throw light on the facts;

(g) the right not to be compelled to be a witness against himself or to plead guilty; and

(h) the right to appeal the judgment to a higher court.

3. A confession of guilt by the accused shall be valid only if it is made without coercion of any kind.

4. An accused person acquitted by a nonappealable judgment shall not be subjected to a new trial for the same cause.

5. Criminal proceedings shall be public, except insofar as may be necessary to protect the interests of justice.

Freedom from Ex Post Facto Laws

Article 9

No one shall be convicted of any act or omission that did not constitute a criminal offense, under the applicable law, at the time it was committed. A heavier penalty shall not be imposed than the one that was applicable at the time the criminal offense was committed. If subsequent to the commission of the offense the law provides for the imposition of a lighter punishment, the guilty person shall benefit therefrom.

Right to Compensation

Article 10

Every person has the right to be compensated in accordance with the law in the event he has been sentenced by a final judgment through a miscarriage of justice.

Right to Privacy

Article 11

1. Everyone has the right to have his honor respected and his dignity recognized.

2. No one may be the object of arbitrary or abusive interference with his private life, his family, his home, or his correspondence, or of unlawful attacks on his honor or reputation.

3. Everyone has the right to the protection of the law against such interference or attacks.

Freedom of Conscience and Religion

Article 12

1. Everyone has the right to freedom of conscience and of religion. This includes freedom to maintain or to change one's religion or beliefs, and freedom to profess or disseminate one's religion or beliefs either individually or together with others, in public or in private.

2. No one shall be subject to restrictions that might impair his freedom to maintain or to change his religion or beliefs.

3. Freedom to manifest one's religion and beliefs may be subject only to the limitations prescribed by law that are necessary to protect public safety, order, health, or morals, or the rights or freedoms of others.

4. Parents or guardians, as the case may be, have the right to provide for the religious and moral education of their children or wards that is in accord with their own convictions.

Freedom of Thought and Expression

Article 13

1. Everyone shall have the right to freedom of thought and expression. This right shall include freedom to seek, receive, and impart information

and ideas of all kinds, regardless of frontiers, either orally, in writing, in print, in the form of art, or through any other medium of one's choice.

2. The exercise of the right provided for in the foregoing paragraph shall not be subject to prior censorship but shall be subject to subsequent imposition of liability, which shall be expressly established by law to the extent necessary in order to ensure:

(a) respect for the rights or reputations of others; or
(b) the protection of national security, public order, or public health or morals.

3. The right of expression may not be restricted by indirect methods or means, such as the abuse of government or private controls over newsprint, radio broadcasting frequencies, or equipment used in the dissemination of information, or by any other means tending to impede the communication and circulation of ideas and opinions.

4. Notwithstanding the provisions of paragraph 2 above, public entertainments may be subject by law to prior censorship for the sole purpose of regulating access to them for the moral protection of childhood and adolescence.

5. Any propaganda for war and any advocacy of national, racial, or religious hatred that constitute incitements to lawless violence or to any other similar illegal action against any person or group of persons on any grounds including those of race, color, religion, language, or national origin shall be considered as offenses punishable by law.

Right of Reply

Article 14

1. Anyone injured by inaccurate or offensive statements or ideas disseminated to the public in general by a legally regulated medium of communication has the right to reply or make a correction using the same communications outlet, under such conditions as the law may establish.

2. The correction or reply shall not in any case remit other legal liabilities that may have been incurred.

3. For the effective protection of honor and reputation, every publisher, and every newspaper, motion picture, radio, and television company, shall have a person responsible, who is not protected by immunities or special privileges.

Right of Assembly

Article 15

The right of peaceful assembly, without arms, is recognized. No restrictions may be placed on the exercise of this right other than those imposed in conformity with the law and necessary in a democratic society in the interest of national security, public safety or public order, or to protect public health or morals or the rights or freedoms of others.

Freedom of Association

Article 16

1. Everyone has the right to associate freely for ideological, religious, political, economic, labor, social, cultural, sports, or other purposes.

2. The exercise of this right shall be subject only to such restrictions established by law as may be necessary in a democratic society, in the interest of national security, public safety or public order, or to protect public health or morals or the rights and freedoms of others.

3. The provisions of this article do not bar the imposition of legal restrictions, including even deprivation of the exercise of the right of association, on members of the armed forces and the police.

Rights of the Family

Article 17

1. The family is the natural and fundamental group unit of society and is entitled to protection by society and the state.

2. The right of men and women of marriageable age to marry and to raise a family shall be recognized, if they meet the conditions required by domestic laws, insofar as such conditions do not affect the principle of nondiscrimination established in this Convention.

3. No marriage shall be entered into without the free and full consent of the intending spouses.

4. The States Parties shall take appropriate steps to ensure the equality of rights and the adequate balancing of responsibilities of the spouses as to marriage, during marriage, and in the event of its dissolution. In case of dissolution, provision shall be made for the necessary protection of any children solely on the basis of their own best interests.

5. The law shall recognize equal rights for children born out of wedlock and those born in wedlock.

Right to a Name
Article 18

Every person has the right to a given name and to the surnames of his parents or that of one of them. The law shall regulate the manner in which this right shall be ensured for all, by the use of assumed names if necessary.

Rights of the Child
Article 19

Every minor child has the right to the measures of protection required by his condition as a minor on the part of his family, society, and the state.

Right to Nationality
Article 20

1. Every person has the right to a nationality.

2. Every person has the right to the nationality of the state in whose territory he was born if he does not have the right to any other nationality.

3. No one shall be arbitrarily deprived of his nationality or of the right to change it.

Right to Property
Article 21

1. Everyone has the right to the use and enjoyment of his property. The law may subordinate such use and enjoyment to the interest of society.

2. No one shall be deprived of his property except upon payment of just compensation, for reasons of public utility or social interest, and in the cases and according to the forms established by law.

3. Usury and any other form of exploitation of man by man shall be prohibited by law.

Freedom of Movement and Residence
Article 22

1. Every person lawfully in the territory of a State Party has the right to move about in it and to reside in it subject to the provisions of the law.

2 . Every person has the right to leave any country freely, including his own.

3. Th e exercise of the foregoing rights may be restricted only pursuant

to a law to the extent necessary in a democratic society to prevent crime or to protect national security, public safety, public order, public morals, public health, or the rights or freedoms of others.

4. The exercise of the rights recognized in paragraph 1 may also be restricted by law in designated zones for reasons of public interest.

5. No one can be expelled from the territory of the state of which he is a national or be deprived of the right to enter it.

6. An alien lawfully in the territory of a State Party to this Convention may be expelled from it only pursuant to a decision reached in accordance with law.

7. Every person has the right to seek and be granted asylum in a foreign territory, in accordance with the legislation of the state and international conventions, in the event he is being pursued for political offenses or related common crimes.

8. In no case may an alien be deported or returned to a country, regardless of whether or not it is his country of origin, if in that country his right to life or personal freedom is in danger of being violated because of his race, nationality, religion, social status, or political opinions.

9. The collective expulsion of aliens is prohibited.

Right to Participate in Government

Article 23

1. Every citizen shall enjoy the following rights and opportunities:

  (*a*) to take part in the conduct of public affairs, directly or through freely chosen representatives;
  (*b*) to vote and to be elected in genuine periodic elections, which shall be by universal and equal suffrage and by secret ballot that guarantees the free expression of the will of the voters; and
  (*c*) to have access, under general conditions of equality, to the public service of his country.

2. The law may regulate the exercise of the rights and opportunities referred to in the preceding paragraph only on the basis of age, nationality, residence, language, education, civil and mental capacity, or sentencing by a competent court in criminal proceedings.

Right to Equal Protection

Article 24

All persons are equal before the law. Consequently, they are entitled, without discrimination, to equal protection of the law.

Right to Judicial Protection

Article 25

1. Everyone has the right to simple and prompt recourse, or any other effective recourse, to a competent court or tribunal for protection against acts that violate his fundamental rights recognized by the constitution or laws of the state concerned or by this Convention, even though such violation may have been committed by persons acting in the course of their official duties.

2. The States Parties undertake:

(*a*) to ensure that any person claiming such remedy shall have his rights determined by the competent authority provided for by the legal system of the state;
(*b*) to develop the possibilities of judicial remedy; and
(*c*) to ensure that the competent authorities shall enforce such remedies when granted.

CHAPTER III. ECONOMIC, SOCIAL, AND CULTURAL RIGHTS

Progressive Development

Article 26

The States Parties undertake to adopt measures, both internally and through international cooperation, especially those of an economic and technical nature, with a view to achieving progressively, by legislation or other appropriate means, the full realization of the rights implicit in the economic, social, educational, scientific, and cultural standards set forth in the Charter of the Organization of American States as amended by the Protocol of Buenos Aires.

Chapter IV. Suspension of Guarantees, Interpretation, and Application

Suspension of Guarantees

Article 27

1. In time of war, public danger, or other emergency that threatens the independence or security of a State Party, it may take measures derogating from its obligations under the present Convention to the extent and for the period of time strictly required by the exigencies of the situation, provided that such measures are not inconsistent with its other obligations under international law and do not involve discrimination on the ground of race, color, sex, language, religion, or social origin.

2. The foregoing provision does not authorize any suspension of the following articles: Article 3 (Right to Juridical Personality), Article 4 (Right to Life), Article 5 (Right to Humane Treatment), Article 6 (Freedom from Slavery), Article 9 (Freedom from Ex Post Facto Laws), Article 12 (Freedom of Conscience and Religion), Article 17 (Rights of the Family), Article 18 (Right to a Name), Article 19 (Rights of the Child), Article 20 (Right to Nationality), and Article 23 (Right to Participate in Government), or of the judicial guarantees essential for the protection of such rights.

3. Any State Party availing itself of the right of suspension shall immediately inform the other States Parties, through the Secretary General of the Organization of American States, of the provisions the application of which it has suspended, the reasons that gave rise to the suspension, and the date set for the termination of such suspension.

Federal Clause

Article 28

1. Where a State Party is constituted as a federal state, the national government of such State Party shall implement all the provisions of the Convention over whose subject matter it exercises legislative and judicial jurisdiction.

2. With respect to the provisions over whose subject matter the constituent units of the federal state have jurisdiction, the national government shall immediately take suitable measures, in accordance with its constitution and its laws, to the end that the competent authorities of the constituent units may adopt appropriate provisions for the fulfillment of this Convention.

3. Whenever two or more States Parties agree to form a federation or other type of association they shall take care that the resulting federal or other compact contains the provisions necessary for continuing and rendering effective the standards of this Convention in the new state that is organized.

Restrictions Regarding Interpretation

Article 29

No provision of this Convention shall be interpreted as:

(*a*) permitting any State Party, group, or person to suppress the enjoyment or exercise of the rights and freedoms recognized in this Convention or to restrict them to a greater extent than is provided for herein;

(*b*) restricting the enjoyment or exercise of any right or freedom recognized by virtue of the laws of any State Party or by virtue of another convention to which one of the said states is a party;

(*c*) precluding other rights or guarantees that are inherent in the human personality or derived from representative democracy as a form of government; or

(*d*) excluding or limiting the effect that the American Declaration of the Rights and Duties of Man and other international acts of the same nature may have.

Scope of Restrictions

Article 30

The restrictions that, pursuant to this Convention, may be placed on the enjoyment or excrise of the rights or freedoms recognized herein may not be applied except in accordance with the laws enacted for reasons of general interest and in accordance with the purpose for which such restrictions have been established.

Recognition of Other Rights

Article 31

Other rights and freedoms recognized in accordance with the procedures established in Articles 76 and 77 may be included in the system of protection of this Convention.

CHAPTER V. PERSONAL RESPONSIBILITIES

Relationship between Duties and Rights

Article 32

1. Every person has responsibilities to his family, his community, and mankind.

2. The rights of each person are limited by the rights of others, by the security of all, and by the just demands of the general welfare, in a democratic society.

PART II

MEANS OF PROTECTION

CHAPTER VI. COMPETENT ORGANS

Article 33

The following organs shall have competence with respect to matters relating to the fulfillment of the commitments made by the States Parties to this Convention:

  (*a*) the Inter-American Commission on Human Rights, referred to as 'The Commission'; and
  (*b*) the Inter-American Court of Human Rights, referred to as 'The Court.'

CHAPTER VII. INTER-AMERICAN COMMISSION ON HUMAN RIGHTS

SECTION I. ORGANIZATION

Article 34

The Inter-American Commission on Human Rights shall be composed of seven members, who shall be persons of high moral character and recognized competence in the field of human rights.

Article 35

The Commission shall represent all the member countries of the Organization of American States.

Article 36

1. The members of the Commission shall be elected in a personal

capacity by the General Assembly of the Organization from a list of candidates proposed by the governments of the member states.

2. Each of those governments may propose up to three candidates, who may be nationals of the states proposing them or of any other member state of the Organization of American States. When a slate of three is proposed, at least one of the candidates shall be a national of a state other than the one proposing the slate.

Article 37

1. The members of the Commission shall be elected for a term of four years and may be reelected only once, but the terms of three of the members chosen in the first election shall expire at the end of two years. Immediately following that election the General Assembly shall determine the names of those three members by lot.

2. No two nationals of the same state may be members of the Commission.

Article 38

Vacancies that may occur on the Commission for reasons other than the normal expiration of a term shall be filled by the Permanent Council of the Organization in accordance with the provisions of the Statute of the Commission.

Article 39

The Commission shall prepare its Statute, which it shall submit to the General Assembly for approval. It shall establish its own Regulations.

Article 40

Secretariat services for the Commission shall be furnished by the appropriate specialized unit of the General Secretariat of the Organization. This unit shall be provided with the resources required to accomplish the tasks assigned to it by the Commission.

SECTION 2. FUNCTIONS

Article 41

The main functions of the Commission shall be to promote respect for and defense of human rights. In the exercise of its mandate, it shall have the following functions and powers:

(a) to develop an awareness of human rights among the peoples of America;

(*b*) to make recommendations to the governments of the member states, when it considers such action advisable, for the adoption of progressive measures in favor of human rights within the framework of their domestic law and constitutional provisions as well as appropriate measures to further the observance of those rights;

(*c*) to prepare such studies or reports as it considers advisable in the performance of its duties;

(*d*) to request the governments of the member states to supply it with information on the measures adopted by them in matters of human rights;

(*e*) to respond, through the General Secretariat of the Organization of American States, to inquiries made by the member states on matters related to human rights and, within the limits of its possibilities, to provide those states with the advisory services they request;

(*f*) to take action on petitions and other communications pursuant to its authority, under the provisions of Articles 44 through 51 of this Convention; and

(*g*) to submit an annual report to the General Assembly of the Organization of American States.

Article 42

The States Parties shall transmit to the Commission a copy of each of the reports and studies that they submit annually to the Executive Committees of the Inter-American Economic and Social Council and the Inter-American Council for Education, Science, and Culture, in their respective fields, so that the Commission may watch over the promotion of the rights implict in the economic, social, educational, scientific, and cultural standards set forth in the Charter of the Organization of American States as amended by the Protocol of Buenos Aires.

Article 43

The States Parties undertake to provide the Commission with such information as it may request of them as to the manner in which their domestic law ensures the effective application of any provisions of this Convention.

SECTION 3. COMPETENCE

Article 44

Any person or group of persons, or any nongovernmental entity legally recognized in one or more member states of the Organization, may lodge

14*

petitions with the Commission containing denunciations or complaints of violation of this Convention by a State Party.

Article 45

1. Any State Party may, when it deposits its instrument of ratification of or adherence to this Convention, or at any later time, declare that it recognizes the competence of the Commission to receive and examine communications in which a State Party alleges that another State Party has committed a violation of a human right set forth in this Convention.

2. Communications presented by virtue of this article may be admitted and examined only if they are presented by a State Party that has made a declaration recognizing the aforementioned competence of the Commission. The Commission shall not admit any communication against a State Party that has not made such a declaration.

3. A declaration concerning recognition of competence may be made to be valid for an indefinite time, for a specified period, or for a specific case.

4. Declarations shall be deposited with the General Secretariat of the Organization of American States, which shall transmit copies thereof to the member states of that Organization.

Article 46

1. Admission by the Commission of a petition or communication lodged in accordance with Articles 44 or 45 shall be subject to the following requirements:

   (a) that the remedies under domestic law have been pursued and exhausted in accordance with generally recognized principles of international law;
   (b) that the petition or communication is lodged within a period of six months from the date on which the party alleging violation of his rights was notified of the final judgment;
   (c) that the subject of the petition or communication is not pending before another international procedure for settlement; and
   (d) that, in the case of Article 44, the petition contains the name, nationality, profession, domicile, and signature of the person or persons or of the legal representative of the entity lodging the petition.

2. The provisions of paragraphs 1 (a) and 1 (b) of this article shall not be applicable when:

(*a*) the domestic legislation of the state concerned does not afford due process of law for the protection of the right or rights that have allegedly been violated;

(*b*) the party alleging violation of his rights has been denied access to the remedies under domestic law or has been prevented from exhausting them; or

(*c*) there has been unwarranted delay in rendering a final judgment under the aforementioned remedies.

Article 47

The Commission shall consider inadmissible any petition or communication submitted under Articles 44 or 45 if:

(*a*) any of the requirements indicated in Article 46 has not been met;

(*b*) the petition or communication does not state facts that tend to establish a violation of the rights guaranteed by this Convention;

(*c*) the statements of the petitioner or of the state indicate that the petition or communication is manifestly groundless or obviously out of order; or

(*d*) the petition or communication is substantially the same as one previously studied by the Commission or by another international organization.

SECTION 4. PROCEDURE

Article 48

1. When the Commission receives a petition or communication alleging violation of any of the rights protected by this Convention, it shall proceed as follows:

(*a*) If it considers the petition or communication admissible, it shall request information from the government of the state indicated as being responsible for the alleged violations and shall furnish that government a transcript of the pertinent portions of the petition or communication. This information shall be submitted within a reasonable period to be determined by the Commission in accordance with the circumstances of each case.

(*b*) After the information has been received, or after the period established has elapsed and the information has not been received, the Commission shall ascertain whether the grounds for the petition or communication still exist. If they do not, the Commission shall order the record to be closed.

(*c*) The Commission may also declare the petition or communication inadmissible or out of order on the basis of information or evidence subsequently received.

(*d*) If the record has not been closed, the Commission shall, with the knowledge of the parties, examine the matter set forth in the petition or communication in order to verify the facts. If necessary and advisable, the Commission shall carry out an investigation, for the effective conduct of which it shall request, and the states concerned shall furnish to it, all necessary facilities.

(*e*) The Commission may request the states concerned to furnish any pertinent information and, if so requested, shall hear oral statements or receive written statements from the parties concerned.

(*f*) The Commission shall place itself at the disposal of the parties concerned with a view to reaching a friendly settlement of the matter on the basis of respect for the human rights recognized in this Convention.

2. However, in serious and urgent cases, only the presentation of a petition or communication that fufills all the formal requirements of admissibility shall be necessary in order for the Commission to conduct an investigation with the prior consent of the state in whose territory a violation has allegedly been committed.

Article 49

If a friendly settlement has been reached in accordance with paragraph 1 (*f*) of Article 48, the Commission shall draw up a report, which shall be transmitted to the petitioner and to the States Parties to this Convention, and shall then be communicated to the Secretary General of the Organization of American States for publication. This report shall contain a brief statement of the facts and of the solution reached. If any party in the case so requests, the fullest possible information shall be provided to it.

Article 50

1. If a settlement is not reached, the Commission shall, within the time limit established by its Statute, draw up a report setting forth the facts and stating its conclusions. If the report, in whole or in part, does not represent the unanimous agreement of the members of the Commission, any member may attach to it a separate opinion. The written and oral statements made by the parties in accordance with paragraph 1 (*e*) of Article 48 shall also be attached to the report.

2. The report shall be transmitted to the states concerned, which shall not be at liberty to publish it.

3. In transmitting the report, the Committee may make such proposals and recommendations as it sees fit.

Article 51

1. If, within a period of three months from the date of the transmittal of the report of the Commission to the states concerned, the matter has not either been settled or submitted by the Commission or by the state concerned to the Court and its jurisdiction accepted, the Commission may, by the vote of an absolute majority of its members, set forth its opinion and conclusions concerning the question submitted for its consideration.

2. Where appropriate, the Commission shall make pertinent recommendations and shall prescribe a period within which the state is to take the measures that are incumbent upon it to remedy the situation examined.

3. When the prescribed period has expired, the Commission shall decide by the vote of an absolute majority of its members whether the state has taken adequate measures and whether to publish its report.

CHAPTER VIII. INTER-AMERICAN COURT OF HUMAN RIGHTS

SECTION I. ORGANIZATION

Article 52

1. The Court shall consist of seven judges, nationals of the member states of the Organization, elected in an individual capacity from among jurists of the highest moral authority and of recognized competence in the field of human rights, who possess the qualifications required for the exercise of the highest judicial functions in conformity with the law of the state of which they are nationals or of the state that proposes them as candidates.

2. No two judges may be nationals of the same state.

Article 53

1. The judges of the Court shall be elected by secret ballot by an absolute majority vote of the States Parties to the Convention in the General Assembly of the Organization, from a panel of candidates proposed by those states.

2. Each of the States Parties may propose up to three candidates, nationals of the state that proposes them or of any other member state of the Organization of American States. When a slate of three is proposed, at least one of the candidates shall be a national of a state other than the one proposing the slate.

Article 54

1. The judges of the Court shall be elected for a term of six years and may be reelected only once. The term of three of the judges chosen in the first election shall expire at the end of three years. Immediately after the election, the names of the three judges shall be determined by lot in the General Assembly.

2. A judge elected to replace a judge whose term has not expired shall complete the term of the latter.

3. The judges shall continue in office until the expiration of their term. However, they shall continue to serve with regard to cases that they have begun to hear and that are still pending, for which purposes they shall not be replaced by the newly elected judges.

Article 55

1. If a judge is a national of any of the States Parties to a case submitted to the Court, he shall retain his right to hear that case.

2. If one of the judges called upon to hear a case should be a national of one the States Parties to the case, any other State Party in the case may appoint a person of its choice to serve on the Court as an *ad hoc* judge.

3. If among the judges called upon to hear a case none is a national of any of the States Parties to the case, each of the latter may appoint an *ad hoc* judge.

4. An *ad hoc* judge shall possess the qualifications indicated in Article 52.

5. If several States Parties to the Convention should have the same interest in a case, they shall be considered as a single party for purposes of the above provisions. In case of doubt, the Court shall decide.

Article 56

Five judges shall constitute a quorum for the transaction of business by the Court.

Article 57

The Commission shall appear in all cases before the Court.

Article 58

1. The Court shall have its seat at the place determined by the States Parties to the Convention in the General Assembly of the Organization; however, it may convene in the territory of any member state of the Organization of American States when a majority of the Court consider it desirable, and with the prior consent of the state concerned.

The seat of the Court may be changed by the States Parties to the Convention in the General Assembly by a two thirds vote.

2. The Court shall appoint its own Secretary.

3. The Secretary shall have his office at the place where the Court has its seat and shall attend the meetings that the Court may hold away from its seat.

Article 59

The Court shall establish its Secretariat, which shall function under the direction of the Secretary of the Court, in accordance with the administrative standards of the General Secretariat of the Organization in all respects not incompatible with the independence of the Court. The staff of the Court's Secretariat shall be appointed by the Secretary General of the Organization, in consultation with the Secretary of the Court.

Article 60

The Court shall draw up its Statute, which it shall submit to the General Assembly for approval. It shall adopt its own Rules of Procedure.

SECTION 2. JURISDICTION AND FUNCTIONS

Article 61

1. Only the States Parties and the Commission shall have the right to submit a case to the Court.

2. In order for the Court to hear a case, it is necessary that the procedures set forth in Articles 48 to 50 shall have been completed.

Article 62

1. A State Party may, upon depositing its instrument of ratification or adherence to this Convention, or at any subsequent time, declare that it recognizes as binding, *ipso facto*, and not requiring special agreement, the jurisdiction of the Court on all matters relating to the interpretation or application of this Convention.

2. Such declaration may be made unconditionally, on the condition of reciprocity, for a specified period, or for specific cases. It shall be presented to the Secretary General of the Organization, who shall transmit copies thereof to the other member states of the Organization and to the Secretary of the Court.

3. The jurisdiction of the Court shall comprise all cases concerning the interpretation and application of the provisions of this Convention that are submitted to it, provided that the States Parties to the case recognize or have recognized such jurisdiction, whether by special declaration pursuant to the preceding paragraphs, or by a special agreement.

Article 63

1. If the Court finds that there has been a violation of a right or freedom protected by this Convention, the Court shall rule that the injured party be ensured the enjoyment of his right or freedom that was violated. It shall also rule, if appropriate, that the consequences of the measure or situation that constituted the breach of such right or freedom be remedied and that fair compensation be paid to the injured party.

2. In cases of extreme gravity and urgency, and when necessary to avoid irreparable damage to persons, the Court shall adopt such provisional measures as it deems pertinent in matters it has under consideration. With respect to a case not yet submitted to the Court, it may act at the request of the Commission.

Article 64

1. The member states of the Organization may consult the Court regarding the interpretation of this Convention or of other treaties concerning the protection of human rights in the American states. Within their spheres of competence, the organs listed in Chapter X of the Charter of the Organization of American States, as amended by the Protocol of Buenos Aires, may in like manner consult the Court.

2. The Court, at the request of a member state of the Organization, may provide that state with opinions regarding the compatibility of any of its domestic laws with the aforesaid international instruments.

Article 65

To each regular session of the General Assembly of the Organization of American States the Court shall submit, for the Assembly's consideration, a report on its work during the previous year. It shall specify, in particular, the cases in which a state has not complied with its judgments, making any pertinent recommendations.

SECTION 3. PROCEDURE

Article 66

1. Reasons shall be given for the judgment of the Court.

2. If the judgment does not represent in whole or in part the unanimous opinion of the judges, any judge shall be entitled to have his dissenting or separate opinion attached to the judgment.

Article 67

The judgment of the Court shall be final and not subject to appeal. In case of disagreement as to the meaning or scope of the judgment, the Court shall interpret it at the request of any of the parties, provided the request is made within ninety days from the date of notification of the judgment.

Article 68

1. The States Parties to the Convention undertake to comply with the judgment of the Court in any case to which they are parties.

2. That part of a judgment that stipulates compensatory damages may be executed in the country concerned in accordance with domestic procedure governing the execution of judgments against the state.

Article 69

The parties to the case shall be notified of the judgment of the Court and it shall be transmitted to the States Parties to the Convention.

CHAPTER IX. COMMON PROVISIONS

Article 70

1. The judges of the Court and the members of the Commission shall enjoy, from the moment of their election and throughout their term of office, the immunities extended to diplomatic agents in accordance with international law. During the exercise of their official function they shall, in addition, enjoy the diplomatic privileges necessary for the performance of their duties.

2. At no time shall the judges of the Court or the members of the Commission be held liable for any decisions or opinions issued in the exercise of their functions.

Article 71

The position of judge of the Court or member of the Commission is incompatible with any other activity that might affect the independence or impartiality of such judge or member, as determined in the respective statutes.

Article 72

The judges of the Court and the members of the Commission shall receive emoluments and travel allowances in the form and under the conditions set forth in their statutes, with due regard for the importance and independence of their office. Such emoluments and travel allowances shall be determined in the budget of the Organization of American States, which shall also include the expenses of the Court and its Secretariat. To this end, the Court shall draw up its own budget and submit it for approval to the General Assembly through the General Secretariat. The latter may not introduce any changes in it.

Article 73

The General Assembly may, only at the request of the Commission or the Court, as the case may be, determine sanctions to be applied against members of the Commission or judges of the Court when there are justifiable grounds for such action as set forth in the respective statutes. A vote of a two-thirds majority of the member states of the Organization shall be required for a decision in the case of members of the Commission and, in the case of judges of the Court, a two-thirds majority vote of the States Parties to the Convention shall also be required.

PART III

GENERAL AND TRANSITORY PROVISIONS

CHAPTER X. SIGNATURE, RATIFICATION, RESERVATIONS, AMENDMENTS, PROTOCOLS, AND DENUNCIATION

Article 74

1. This Convention shall be open for signature and ratification by or adherence of any member state of the Organization of American States.

2. Ratification of or adherence to this Convention shall be made by the deposit of an instrument of ratification or adherence with the General Secretariat of the Organization of American States. As soon as eleven

states have deposited their instruments of ratification or adherence, the Convention shall enter into force. With respect to any state that ratifies or adheres thereafter, the Convention shall enter into force on the date of the deposit of its instrument of ratification or adherence.

3. The Secretary General shall inform all member states of the Organization of the entry into force of the Convention.

Article 75

This Convention shall be subject to reservations only in conformity with the provisions of the Vienna Convention on the Law of Treaties signed on May 23, 1969.

Article 76

1. Proposals to amend this Convention may be submitted to the General Assembly for the action it deems appropriate by any State Party directly, and by the Commission or the Court through the Secretary General.

2. Amendments shall enter into force for the states ratifying them on the date when two thirds of the States Parties to this Convention have deposited their respective instruments of ratification. With respect to the other States Parties, amendments shall enter into force on the dates on which they deposit their respective instruments of ratification.

Article 77

1. In accordance with Article 31, any State Party and the Commission may submit proposed protocols to this Convention for consideration by the States Parties at the General Assembly with a view to gradually including other rights and freedoms within its system of protection.

2. Each Protocol shall determine the manner of its entry into force and shall be applied only among the States Parties to it.

Article 78

1. The States Parties may denounce this Convention at the expiration of a five-year period starting from the date of its entry into force and by means of notice given one year in advance. Notice of the denunciation shall be addressed to the Secretary General of the Organization, who shall inform the other States Parties.

2. Such a denunciation shall not have the effect of releasing the State Party concerned from the obligations contained in this Convention with

respect to any act that may constitute a violation of those obligations and that has been taken by that state prior to the effective date of denunciation.

CHAPTER XI. TRANSITORY PROVISIONS

SECTION 1. INTER-AMERICAN COMMISSION ON HUMAN RIGHTS

Article 79

Upon the entry into force of this Convention, the Secretary General shall, in writing, request each member state of the Organization to present, within ninety days, its candidates for membership on the Inter-American Commission on Human Rights. The Secretary General shall prepare a list in alphabetical order of the candidates presented, and transmit it to the member states of the Organization at least thirty days prior to the next session of the General Assembly.

Article 80

The members of the Commission shall be elected by secret ballot of the General Assembly from the list of candidates referred to in Article 79. The candidates who obtain the largest number of votes and an absolute majority of the votes of the representatives of the member states shall be declared elected. Should it become necessary to have several ballots in order to elect all the members of the Commission, the candidates who receive the smallest number of votes shall be eliminated successively, in the manner determined by the General Assembly.

SECTION 2. INTER-AMERICAN COURT OF HUMAN RIGHTS

Article 81

Upon the entry into force of this Convention, the Secretary General shall, in writing, request each State Party to present, within ninety days, its candidates for membership on the Inter-American Court of Human Rights. The Secretary General shall prepare a list in alphabetical order of the candidates presented and transmit it to the States Parties at least thirty days prior to the next session of the General Assembly.

Article 82

The judges of the Court shall be elected from the list of candidates referred to in Article 81, by secret ballot of the States Parties to the Convention in the General Assembly. The candidates who obtain the largest number of votes and an absolute majority of the votes of the representatives of the States Parties shall be declared elected. Should it become necessary to have several ballots in order to elect all the judges of the Court, the candidates who receive the smallest number of votes shall be eliminated successively, in the manner determined by the States Parties.

[Statements and reservations, etc., omitted.]

PART EIGHT

DEVELOPMENTS IN AFRICA AND ASIA

THERE is little to report in terms of formal agreements between States. The States concerned are within the United Nations system, with the exception of China, North and South Korea, and North and South Vietnam. The documents which are set out in this Part are declarations of policy, and are useful in indicating the special concerns of Afro-Asian States in general, although the documents set out are directly concerned with the African continent. See further, the Charter of the Organization of African Unity, in Brownlie, *Basic Documents in International Law*, p. 59.

I. FIRST CONFERENCE OF INDEPENDENT AFRICAN STATES, 1958

THIS Conference was held at Accra, 15–22 April 1958. The Declaration and certain of the resolutions of the Conference are reproduced below.

TEXT

DECLARATION

We, the African States assembled here in Accra, in this our first Conference, conscious of our responsibilities to humanity and especially to the peoples of Africa, and desiring to assert our African personality on the side of peace, hereby proclaim and solemnly reaffirm our unswerving loyalty to the Charter of the United Nations, the Universal Declaration of Human Rights and the Declaration of the Asian-African Conference held at Bandung.

We further assert and proclaim the unity among ourselves and our solidarity with the dependent peoples of Africa as well as our friendship with all nations. We resolve to preserve the unity of purpose and action in international affairs which we have forged among ourselves in this historic Conference; to safeguard our hard-won independence, sovereignty and territorial integrity; and to preserve among ourselves the fundamental unity of outlook on foreign policy so that a distinctive African Personality will play its part in co-operation with other peace-loving nations to further the cause of peace.

We pledge ourselves to apply all our endeavours to avoid being committed to any action which might entangle our countries to the detriment of our interests and freedom; to recognize the right of the African peoples to independence and self-determination and to take appropriate steps to hasten the realization of this right; to affirm the right of the Algerian people to independence and self-determination and to exert all possible effort to hasten the realization of their independence; to uproot forever the evil of racial discrimination in all its forms wherever it may be found; to persuade the Great Powers to discontinue the production and testing of nuclear and thermo-nuclear weapons; and to reduce conventional weapons.

Furthermore, mindful of the urgent need to raise the living standards of our peoples by developing to the fullest possible advantage the great and varied resources of our lands, We hereby pledge ourselves to co-ordinate our economic planning through a joint economic effort and study the economic potentialities, the technical possibilities and related problems existing in our respective States; to promote co-ordinated industrial planning either through our own individual efforts and/or through co-operation with Specialized Agencies of the United Nations; to take measures to increase trade among our countries by improving communications between our respective countries; and to encourage the investment of foreign capital and skills provided they do not compromise the independence, sovereignty and territorial integrity of our States.

Desirous of mobilizing the human resources of our respective countries in furtherance of our social and cultural aspirations, We will endeavour to promote and facilitate the exchange of teachers, professors, students, exhibitions, educational, cultural and scientific material which will improve cultural relations between the African States and inculcate greater knowledge amongst us through such efforts as joint youth festivals, sporting events, etc.; We will encourage and strengthen studies of African culture, history and geography in the institutions of learning in the African States; and We will take all measures in our respective countries to ensure that such studies are correctly orientated.

We have charged our Permanent Representatives at the United Nations to be the permanent machinery for co-ordinating all matters of common concern to our States; for examining and making recommendations on concrete practical steps for implementing our decisions; and for preparing the grounds for future Conferences.

Faithful to the obligations and responsibilities which history has thrown upon us as the vanguard of the complete emancipation of Africa, we do hereby affirm our dedication to the causes which we have proclaimed.

RESOLUTIONS

1. Exchange of Views on Foreign Policy

The Conference of Independent African States,

Having made the widest exchange of views on all aspects of foreign policy,

Having achieved a unanimity on fundamental aims and principles,

Desiring to pursue a common foreign policy with a view to safeguarding the hard-won independence, sovereignty and territorial integrity of the Participating States,

Deploring the division of the greater part of the world into two antagonistic blocs,

1. Affirms the following fundamental principles:

A. Unswerving loyalty to and support of the Charter of the United Nations and respect for decisions of the United Nations;

B. Adherence to the principles enunciated at the Bandung Conference, namely:

   (i) Respect for the fundamental human rights and for the purposes and principles of the Charter of the United Nations.

   (ii) Respect for the sovereignty and territorial integrity of all nations.

   (iii) Recognition of the equality of all races and of the equality of all nations, large and small. . . .

2. THE FUTURE OF THE DEPENDENT TERRITORIES IN AFRICA

The Conference of Independent African States,

Recognizing that the existence of colonialism in any shape or form is a threat to the security and independence of the African States and to world peace,

Considering that the problems and the future of dependent territories in Africa are not the exclusive concern of the Colonial Powers but the responsibility of all members of the United Nations and in particular of the Independent African States,

Condemning categorically all colonial systems still enforced in our Continent and which impose arbitrary rule and repression on the people of Africa,

Convinced that a definite date should be set for the attainment of independence by each of the Colonial Territories in accordance with the will of the people of the territories and the provisions of the Charter of the United Nations,

1. Calls upon the Administering Powers to respect the Charter of the United Nations in this regard, and to take rapid steps to implement the provisions of the Charter and the political aspirations of the people, namely self-determination and independence, according to the will of the people;

2. Calls upon the Administering Powers to refrain from repression and arbitrary rule in these territories and to respect all human rights as pro-

vided for in the Charter of the United Nations and the Universal Declaration of Human Rights;

3. Calls upon the Administering Powers to bring to an end immediately every form of discrimination in these territories;

4. Recommends that all Participating Governments should give all possible assistance to the dependent peoples in their struggle to achieve self-determination and independence;

5. Recommends that the Independent African States assembled here should offer facilities for training and educating peoples of the dependent territories;

6. Decides that the 15th April of every year be celebrated as Africa Freedom Day.

4. RACISM

The Conference of Independent African States,

Considering that the practice of racial discrimination and segregation is evil and inhuman,

Deeply convinced that racialism is a negation of the basic principles of human rights and dignity to the extent where it is becoming an element of such explosiveness which is spreading its poisonous influence more and more widely in some parts of Africa that it may well engulf our Continent in violence and bloodshed,

Noting with abhorrence the recent statement made by the head of the South African Government on his re-election to the effect that he will pursue a more relentless policy of discrimination and persecution of the coloured people in South Africa,

1. Condemns the practice of racial discrimination and segregation in all its aspects all over the world, especially in the Union of South Africa, in the Central African Federation, Kenya and in other parts of Africa;

2. Appeals to the religious bodies and spiritual leaders of the world to support all efforts directed towards the eradication of racialism and segregation;

3. Calls upon all members of the United Nations and all peoples of the world to associate themselves with the Resolutions passed by the United Nations and the Bandung Conference condemning this inhuman practice;

4. Calls upon all members of the United Nations to intensify their efforts to combat and eradicate this degrading form of injustice;

5. Recommends that all Participating Governments should take vigorous measures to eradicate where they arise vestiges of racial discrimination in their respective countries.

II. SECOND CONFERENCE OF INDEPENDENT AFRICAN STATES, 1960

THE Conference was held at Addis Ababa, 15–24 June 1960. Certain of its resolutions are reproduced below.

TEXT

9. ERADICATION OF COLONIAL RULE FROM AFRICA

The Conference of the Independent African States meeting in Addis Ababa,

Recalling the declaration of Bandung and the resolutions of Accra and Monrovia proclaiming that colonialism in all its manifestations constitutes an evil which should speedily be brought to an end;

Reaffirming that the subjugation of peoples to alien domination and exploitation constitutes a denial of fundamental rights which is contrary to the Charter of the United Nations and the Universal Declaration of Human Rights, and is an impediment to the promotion of World Peace and Co-operation;

Considering that Africa is the only Continent where a large proportion of the inhabitants still live under colonial domination with all its privations and indignities;

Considering further that the present awakening of the people of Africa and the independence movements can no longer be contained, without the risk of seriously compromising relations between the diverse nations;

Believing that the restoration of natural rights and human dignity to the Africans, in those parts of Africa, at present under foreign subjugation, as well as the peaceful enjoyment of the hard-won freedom by the peoples of the Independent African States, could only be achieved through the complete eradication of colonial rule from our Continent;

Recalling the courageous stand taken by the freedom fighters in Africa, and saluting the memory of those who sacrificed their lives in defending the liberty of their respective countries;

Conscious of the responsibility of the Independent African States towards those peoples fighting for independence and also of the active solidarity which should be shown towards all African freedom fighters;

Taking into consideration the petitions presented by the representatives of the nationalist movements in the non-independent countries of Africa (Angola, Kenya, Uganda, Northern and Southern Rhodesia, Ruanda-Urundi, the Union of South Africa and South-West Africa);

1. Urges the Colonial Powers to fix dates in conformity with the will of the people for the immediate attainment of Independence by all non-independent countries and to communicate those dates to the people concerned;

2. Resolves that the Independent African States continue to exert concerted action to achieve through all possible peaceful means the complete eradication of colonial rule from Africa;

3. Condemns the practice of colonial Powers of enlisting Africans, against their own will, in foreign armed forces to suppress the liberation movements in Africa;

4. Appeals to the conscience of all Africans to resist enlistment in such foreign armed forces;

5. Appeals further to leaders, political parties and other organizations of non-independent countries, at this historical phase of their struggle, to unite in a national front to achieve speedy liberation of their countries;

6. Decides to establish a special fund to aid Freedom Fighters in Africa (Africa Freedom Fund);

7. Decides that such a fund be administered by an organ to be established by the Conference in accordance with rules and regulations to be adopted by the Conference;

8. Agrees that the Independent African State contribute to the Africa Freedom Fund on the basis of equitable shares to be agreed upon by the Conference;

9. Recommends to extend assistance and to accord facilities to genuine African political refugees;

10. Decides to offer, if so desired, its good offices to assist in settling differences among leaders and political parties of non-independent countries through its permanent machinery;

11. Appeals to the colonial Powers to refrain from suppressing national liberation movements, to release immediately all political prisoners, detainees and persons under restrictive orders.

10. ERADICATION OF COLONIAL RULE FROM AFRICA:
MEANS TO PREVENT NEW FORMS OF
COLONIALISM IN AFRICA

The Conference of the Independent African States meeting in Addis Ababa,

Welcoming the recent attainment of independence by several countries of Africa;

Reaffirming its faith in the total liberation and emancipation of Africa in the shortest possible time;

Considering the difficulties with which the emerging nations of Africa may be confronted in the political, economic and social fields;

Noting that new forms of colonialism could be introduced into these territories, under the guise of economic, financial and technical assistance;

Considering that some of the non-independent countries may, out of necessity and under pressure, enter into agreements and pacts with foreign Powers which would restrict in advance their total independence and hinder their future freedom of action;

1. Calls upon all colonial Powers to refrain from any action which might compromise the sovereignty and independence of the emerging States;

2. Declares that assistance to the emerging States should be without political conditions;

3. Urges the leaders of the emerging States to consider seriously this question before committing themselves to action which might prejudice the future of their countries;

4. Recommends that independent African States should consider the possibility of introducing a system whereby economic and technical aid can be provided by them collectively;

5. Urges the leaders of non-independent countries to resist any attempt at Balkanization which is detrimental to the ultimate goal of African unity;

6. Recommends that the Independent African States be wary of colonial penetration through economic means and that they institute effective control over the working machineries of foreign companies operating in their territories.

12. POLICY OF APARTHEID AND RACIAL DISCRIMINATION IN AFRICA

The Conference of Independent African States meeting in Addis Ababa,

Having learned with indignation of the death of many African political leaders in the prisons of the Union of South Africa, thus adding to the already long list of victims of the shameful policy of racial discrimination;

Recalling resolution No. 1375 (XIV), adopted by the United Nations General Assembly, condemning the policy of apartheid and racial discrimination practised by the Government of the Union of South Africa;

Recalling further the Security Council's Resolution of April 1, 1960, recognizing the existence of a situation in South Africa which, if continued, might endanger international peace and security;

Reaffirming the declaration of Bandung and the resolutions adopted at Accra and Monrovia regarding this shameful policy;

Noting that, despite world opinion and the resolutions adopted by the United Nations, the Government of the Union of South Africa still persists in its evil policy of apartheid and racial discrimination;

1. Desires to pay homage to all victims of the shameful policy of apartheid and racial discrimination;

2. Decides to assist the victims of racial discrimination and furnish them with all the means necessary to attain their political objectives of liberty and democracy;

3. Calls upon Member States to sever diplomatic relations or refrain from establishing diplomatic relations, as the case may be, to close African ports to all vessels flying the South African flag, to enact legislation prohibiting their ships from entering South African ports, to boycott all South African goods, to refuse landing and passage facilities to all aircraft belonging to the Government and companies registered under the laws of the Union of South Africa and to prohibit all South African aircraft from flying over the air-space of the Independent African States;

4. Invites the Arab States to approach all petroleum companies with a view to preventing Arab oil from being sold to the Union of South Africa and recommends that the African States refuse any concession to any company which continues to sell petroleum to the Union of South Africa;

5. Invites the Independent African States which are members of the British Commonwealth to take all possible steps to secure the exclusion of the Union of South Africa from the British Commonwealth;

6. Recommends that appropriate measures be taken by the United Nations in accordance with Article 41 of the Charter;

7. Appeals to world public opinion to persevere in the effort to put an end to the terrible situation caused by apartheid and racial discrimination;

8. Decides to instruct the Informal Permanent Machinery to take all steps necessary to secure that effect shall be given to the above recommendations and to furnish full information on cases of racial discrimination in the Union of South Africa, so that the outside world may be correctly informed about such practices.

III. LAGOS CONFERENCE ON THE
RULE OF LAW, 1961

THE International Commission of Jurists is a non-governmental organization, supported largely by funds from American sources. Its interest in the Rule of Law in Africa and Asia dates from the post-colonial phase. The Lagos Conference was sponsored by the I.C.J., and produced some detailed conclusions on special aspects of the Rule of Law. For the Act of Athens and the Declaration of Delhi see *The International Commission of Jurists: Basic Facts*, Geneva, 1962, pp. 17, 18.

TEXT

RESOLUTION OF THE CONFERENCE:
THE LAW OF LAGOS

The African Conference on the Rule of Law, consisting of 194 judges, practising lawyers and teachers of law from twenty-three African nations as well as nine countries of other continents,

Assembled in Lagos, Nigeria, in January 1961 under the aegis of the International Commission of Jurists,

Having discussed freely and frankly the Rule of Law with particular reference to Africa, and

Having reached conclusions regarding Human Rights in relation to Government security, Human Rights in relation to aspects of criminal and administrative law, and the responsibility of the Judiciary and of the Bar for the protection of the rights of the individual in society,

Now solemnly:

Recognizes that the Rule of Law is a dynamic concept which should be employed to safeguard and advance the will of the people and the political rights of the individual and to establish social, economic, educational and cultural conditions under which the individual may achieve his dignity and realize his legitimate aspirations in all countries, whether dependent or independent,

Reaffirms the Act of Athens and the Declaration of Delhi with special reference to Africa and

Declares

1. That the principles embodied in the *Conclusions* of this Conference which are annexed hereto should apply to any society, whether free or otherwise, but that the Rule of Law cannot be fully realized unless legislative bodies have been established in accordance with the will of the people who have adopted their Constitution freely;

2. That in order to maintain adequately the Rule of Law all Governments should adhere to the principle of democratic representation in their Legislatures;

3. That fundamental human rights, especially the right to personal liberty, should be written and entrenched in the Constitutions of all countries and that such personal liberty should not in peacetime be restricted without trial in a Court of Law;

4. That in order to give full effect to the Universal Declaration of Human Rights of 1948, this Conference invites the African Governments to study the possibility of adopting an African Convention of Human Rights in such a manner that the *Conclusions* of this Conference will be safeguarded by the creation of a court of appropriate jurisdiction and that recourse thereto be made available for all persons under the jurisdiction of the signatory States;

5. That in order to promote the principles and the practical application of the Rule of Law, the judges, practising lawyers and teachers of law in African countries should take steps to establish branches of the International Commission of Jurists.

This Resolution shall be known as the Law of Lagos.
Done at Lagos this 7th day of January, 1961.

CONCLUSIONS

COMMITTEE I

HUMAN RIGHTS AND GOVERNMENT SECURITY—THE LEGISLATIVE, EXECUTIVE AND JUDICIARY

I

1. The exigencies of modern society necessitate the practice of the Legislature delegating to the Executive the power to make rules having the force of legislation.

2. The power of the Executive to make rules or regulations having legislative effect should derive from the express mandate of the Legislature; these rules and regulations should be subject to approval by that

body. The object and scope of such executive power should be clearly defined.

3. The Judiciary should be given the jurisdiction to determine in every case upon application whether the circumstances have arisen or the conditions have been fulfilled under which such power is to be or has been exercised.

4. Every constitution should provide that, except during a period of emergency, legislation should as far as possible be delegated only in respect of matters of economic and social character and that the exercise of such powers should not infringe upon fundamental human rights.

5. The proclamation of a state of emergency is a matter of most serious concern as it directly affects and may infringe upon human rights. It is the sense of the Conference that the dangers of survival of the nation such as arise from a sudden military challenge may call for urgent and drastic measures by the Executive which by the nature of things are susceptible only to *a posteriori* legislative ratification and judicial review. In any other case, however, it is the Parliament duly convened for the purpose that should declare whether or not the state of emergency exists. Wherever it is impossible or inexpedient to summon Parliament for this purpose, for example during Parliamentary recess, the Executive should be competent to declare a state of emergency, but in such a case Parliament should meet as soon as possible thereafter.

6. The Conference is of the opinion that real danger exists when, to quote the words of the General Rapporteur, 'The citizenry, whether by legislative or executive action, or abuse of the judicial process, are made to live as if in a perpetual state of emergency.'

7. The Conference feels that in all cases of the exercise of emergency powers, any person who is aggrieved by the violation of his rights should have access to the courts for determination whether the power has been lawfully exercised.

II

The Conference, having considered the relative rights and obligations of legislative, executive and judicial institutions and their functions as affecting human rights and government security with particular reference to the observance of the Rule of Law in both independent and dependent countries in Africa and elsewhere; and having taken cognizance of allegations that discriminatory legislation based on race, colour or creed exists to the detriment of fundamental human rights of large sections of the population,

Requests the International Commission of Jurists to investigate, examine, consider and report on the legal conditions in Africa and elsewhere with particular regard to the existence of the Rule of Law and the observation of fundamental human rights.

COMMITTEE II

HUMAN RIGHTS AND ASPECTS OF CRIMINAL AND ADMINISTRATIVE LAW

The Rule of Law is of universal validity and application as it embraces those institutions and principles of justice which are considered minimal to the assurance of human rights and the dignity of man.

Further as a preamble to these *Conclusions* it is decided to adopt the following text from the *Conclusions* of the Second Committee of the International Congress of Jurists, New Delhi, India, 1959:

'The Rule of Law depends not only on the provision of adequate safeguards against abuse of power by the Executive, but also on the existence of effective government capable of maintaining law and order and of ensuring adequate social and economic conditions of life for the society.

'The following propositions relating to the Executive and the Rule of Law are accordingly formulated on the basis of certain conditions which are either satisfied, or in the case of newly independent countries still struggling with difficult economic and social problems are in process of being satisfied. These conditions require the existence of an Executive invested with sufficient power and resources to discharge its functions with efficiency and integrity. They require the existence of a Legislature elected by democratic process and not subject, either in the manner of its election or otherwise, to manipulation by the Executive. They require the existence of an independent Judiciary which will discharge its duties fearlessly. They finally call for the earnest endeavour of government to achieve such social and economic conditions within a society as will ensure a reasonable standard of economic security, social welfare and education for the mass of the people.'

1. Taking full cognizance of and incorporating herein by reference Clause III 3 (*a*) of the *Conclusions* of the First Committee of the above-mentioned International Congress of Jurists in New Delhi [1] it is recognized

---

[1] 'The Legislative must . . . not discriminate in its laws in respect of individuals, classes of persons, or minority groups on the ground of race, religion, sex or other such reasons not affording a proper basis for making a distinction between human beings, classes, or minorities.'

and agreed that legislation authorizing administrative action by the Executive should not be discriminatory with respect to race, creed, sex or other such reasons and any such discriminatory provisions contained in legislation are considered contrary to the Rule of Law.

2. While recognizing that inquiry into the merits of the propriety of an individual administrative act by the Executive may in many cases not be appropriate for the ordinary courts, it is agreed that there should be available to the person aggrieved a right of access to:

(a) a hierarchy of administrative courts of independent jurisdiction; or

(b) where these do not exist, to an administrative tribunal subject to the overriding authority of the ordinary courts.

3. The minimum requirements for such administrative action and subsequent judicial review as recommended in paragraph 2 above are as follows:

(a) that the full reasons for the action of the Executive be made known to the person aggrieved; and

(b) that the aggrieved person shall be given a fair hearing; and

(c) that the grounds given by the Executive for its action shall not be regarded as conclusive but shall be objectively considered by the court.

4. It is desirable that, whenever reasonable in the prevailing circumstances, the action of the Executive shall be suspended while under review by the courts.

5. (i) No person of sound mind shall be deprived of his liberty except upon a charge of a specific criminal offence; further, except during a public emergency, preventive detention without trial is held to be contrary to the Rule of Law.

(ii) During a period of public emergency, legislation often authorizes preventive detention of an individual if the Executive finds that public security so requires. Such legislation should provide the individual with safeguards against continuing arbitrary confinement by requiring a prompt administrative hearing and decision upon the need and justification for detention with a right to judicial review. It should be required that any declaration of public emergency by the Executive be reported to and subject to ratification by the Legislature. Moreover, both the declaration of public emergency and any consequent detention of individuals should be effective only for a specified and limited period of time (not exceeding six months).

(iii) Extension of the period of public emergency should be effected by the Legislature only after careful and deliberate consideration of the necessity therefor. Finally, during any period of public emergency the Executive should only take such measures as are reasonably justifiable for the purpose of dealing with the situation which exists during that period.

6. The courts and magistrates shall permit an accused person to be or to remain free pending trial except in the following cases which are deemed proper grounds for refusing bail:

(a) in the case of a very grave offence;

(b) if the accused is likely to interfere with witnesses or impede the course of justice;

(c) if the accused is likely to commit the same or other offences;

(d) if the accused may fail to appear for trial.

7. The power to grant bail is a judicial function which shall not be subject to control by the Executive. Although a court should hear and consider the views and representations of the Executive, the fact that investigation of the case is being continued is not a sufficient ground for refusing bail. Bail should be commensurate with the economic means of the accused, and, whether by appeal or independent application, a higher court should have the power to release provisionally an accused person who has been denied bail by the lower court.

8. After conviction and pending review, the trial or appellate court should have discretionary power to admit the convicted person to bail subject to the grounds set forth in paragraph 6 above.

9. It is recommended that greater use be made of the summons requiring appearance in court to answer a criminal charge in place of arrest and the consequent necessity for bail and provisional release.

COMMITTEE III

THE RESPONSIBILITY OF THE JUDICIARY AND OF THE BAR FOR THE PROTECTION OF THE RIGHTS OF THE INDIVIDUAL IN SOCIETY

The Conference reaffirms the *Conclusions* reached by the Fourth Committee of the International Congress of Jurists, New Delhi, India, 1959, which are appended hereto; and having regard to the particular problems of emerging States, wishes to emphasize certain points in particular, and to add others.

1. In a free society practising the Rule of Law, it is essential that the

absolute independence of the Judiciary be guaranteed. Members of the legal profession in any country have, over and above their ordinary duties as citizens, a special duty to seek ways and means of securing in their own country the maximum degree of independence for the Judiciary.

2. It is recognized that in different countries there are different ways of appointing, promoting and removing judges by means of action taken by the Executive and Legislative powers. It is not recommended that these powers should be abrogated where they have been universally accepted over a long period as working well—provided that they conform to the principles expressed in Clauses II, III, IV and V of the Report of the Fourth Committee at New Delhi.

3. In respect of any country in which the methods of appointing, promoting and removing judges are not yet fully settled, or do not ensure the independence of the Judiciary, it is recommended:

(a) that these powers should not be put into the hands of the Executive or the Legislative, but should be entrusted exclusively to an independent organ such as the Judicial Service Commission of Nigeria or the *Conseil supérieur de la magistrature* in the African French-speaking countries;

(b) that in any country in which the independence of the Judiciary is not already fully secured in accordance with these principles, they should be implemented immediately in respect of all judges, especially those having criminal jurisdiction.

4. It is recommended that all customary, traditional or local law should be administered by the ordinary courts of the land, and emphasized that for so long as that law is administered by special courts, all the principles enunciated here and at New Delhi, for safeguarding the Rule of Law, apply to those courts.

5. The practice, whereby in certain territories judicial powers, especially in criminal matters, are exercised by persons who have no adequate legal training or experience, or who as administrative officers are subject to the control of the Executive is one which falls short of the Rule of Law.

6. (a) To maintain the respect for the Rule of Law it is necessary that the legal profession should be free from any interference;

(b) In countries where an organized Bar exists, the lawyers themselves should have the right to control the admission to the profession and the discipline of the members according to rules established by law;

(c) In countries where an organized Bar does not exist, the power to discipline lawyers should be exercised by the Judiciary in consultation with senior practising lawyers and never by the Executive.

7. The Conference, reaffirms Clause X of the *Conclusions* of the Fourth Committee at New Delhi, and recommends that all steps should be taken to ensure equal access to law for both rich and poor, especially by a provision for and an organization of a system of Legal Aid in both criminal and civil matters.

8. The Conference expressly reaffirms the principle that retroactive legislation especially in criminal matters is inconsistent with the Rule of Law.

APPENDIX

REPORT OF COMMITTEE IV INTERNATIONAL CONGRESS OF JURISTS, NEW DELHI, 1959

THE JUDICIARY AND THE LEGAL PROFESSION UNDER THE RULE OF LAW

Clause I

An independent Judiciary is an indispensable requisite of a free society under the Rule of Law. Such independence implies freedom from interference by the Executive or Legislative with the exercise of the judicial function, but does not mean that the judge is entitled to act in an arbitrary manner. His duty is to interpret the law and the fundamental principles and assumptions that underlie it. It is implicit in the concept of independence set out in the present paragraph that provision should be made for the adequate remuneration of the Judiciary and that a judge's right to the remuneration settled for his office should not during his term of office be altered to his disadvantage.

Clause II

There are in different countries varying ways in which the Judiciary are appointed, re-appointed (where re-appointment arises) and promoted, involving the Legislative, Executive, the Judiciary itself, in some countries the representatives of the practising legal profession, or a combination of two or more of these bodies. The selection of judges by election and particularly by re-election, as in some countries, presents special risks to the independence of the Judiciary which are more likely to be avoided only where tradition has circumscribed by prior agreement the list of candidates and has limited political controversy. There are also potential dangers in exclusive appointment by the Legislative, Executive, or Judiciary, and where there is on the whole general satisfaction with calibre and independence of judges it will be found that either in law or in

15*

practice there is some degree of co-operation (or at least consultation) between the Judiciary and the authority actually making the appointment.

Clause III

The principle of irremovability of the Judiciary, and their security of tenure until death or until a retiring age fixed by statute is reached, is an important safeguard of the Rule of Law. Although it is not impossible for a judge appointed for a fixed term to assert his independence, particularly if he is seeking re-appointment, he is subject to greater difficulties and pressure than a judge who enjoys security of tenure for his working life.

Clause IV

The reconciliation of the principle of irremovability of the Judiciary with the possibility of removal in exceptional circumstances necessitates that the grounds for removal should be before a body of judicial character assuring at least the same safeguards to the judge as would be accorded to an accused person in a criminal trial.

Clause V

The considerations set out in the preceding paragraph should apply to: (1) the ordinary civil and criminal Courts; (2) administrative Courts or constitutional Courts, not being subordinate to the ordinary Courts. The members of administrative tribunals, whether professional lawyers or laymen, as well as laymen exercising other judicial functions (juries, assessors, Justices of the Peace, etc.) should only be appointed and removable in accordance with the spirit of these considerations, in so far as they are applicable to their particular positions. All such persons have in any event the same duty of independence in the performance of their judicial function.

Clause VI

It must be recognized that the Legislative has responsibility for fixing the general framework and laying down the principles of organization of judicial business and that, subject to the limitations on delegations of legislative power which have been dealt with elsewhere, it may delegate part of this responsibility to the Executive. However, the exercise of such responsibility by the Legislative including any delegation to the Executive should not be employed as an indirect method of violating the independence of the Judiciary in the exercise of its judicial functions.

Clause VII

It is essential to the maintenance of the Rule of Law that there should be an organized legal profession free to manage its own affairs. But it is recognized that there may be general supervision by the Courts and that there may be regulations governing the admission to and pursuit of the legal profession.

Clause VIII

Subject to his professional obligation to accept assignments in appropriate circumstances, the lawyer should be free to accept any case which is offered to him.

Clause IX

While there is some difference of emphasis between various countries as to the extent to which a lawyer may be under a duty to accept a case it is conceived that:

1. Wherever a man's life, liberty, property or reputation are at stake he should be free to obtain legal advice and representation; if this principle is to become effective, it follows that lawyers must be prepared frequently to defend persons associated with unpopular causes and minority views with which they themselves may be entirely out of sympathy;

2. Once a lawyer has accepted a brief he should not relinquish it to the detriment of his client without good and sufficient cause;

3. It is the duty of a lawyer which he should be able to discharge without fear of consequences to press upon the Court any argument of law or of fact which he may think proper for the due presentation of the case by him.

Clause X

Equal access to law for the rich and poor alike is essential to the maintenance of the Rule of Law. It is, therefore, essential to provide adequate legal advice and representation to all those, threatened as to their life, liberty, property or reputation who are not able to pay for it. This may be carried out in different ways and is on the whole at present more comprehensively observed in regard to criminal as opposed to civil cases. It is necessary, however, to assert the full implications of the principle, in particular in so far as 'adequate' means legal advice or representation by lawyers of the requisite standing and experience. This is a question which cannot be altogether dissociated from the question of adequate remuneration for the services rendered. The primary obligation rests on the legal profession to sponsor and use its best effort to ensure that adequate legal advice and representation are provided. An obligation also rests upon the State and the community to assist the legal profession in carrying out this responsibility.

IV. RESOLUTIONS OF THE FIRST ASSEMBLY OF THE HEADS OF STATE AND GOVERNMENT OF THE ORGANIZATION OF AFRICAN UNITY, 1964

THE text of the Charter of the Organization of African Unity may be found in Brownlie, *Basic Documents in International Law*, p. 59; and Legum, *Pan-Africanism*, rev. edn., 1965, p. 281. The First Assembly of the Heads of State and Government of the O.A.U. met in Cairo in July 1964. Certain of the resolutions adopted are set out below.

TEXT
RACIAL DISCRIMINATION IN THE USA

Recalling United Nations General Assembly Resolution 1904 (XVIII) of 20 November 1963 containing a Declaration on the elimination of all forms of racial discrimination;

Recalling other resolutions of the General Assembly of the United Nations and of its Specialized Agencies on the elimination of all forms of racial discrimination;

Taking into account resolution CIAS/PLEN. 2 Res. 26–5 of the Summit Conference of Independent African States held at Addis Ababa in May 1963 condemning racial discrimination in all its forms in Africa and in all parts of the world;

Considering that a hundred years have passed since the Emancipation Proclamation was signed in the United States of America;

Noting with satisfaction the recent enactment of the Civil Rights Act designed to secure for American Negroes their basic human rights;

Deeply disturbed, however, by continuing manifestations of racial bigotry and racial oppression against Negro citizens of the United States of America;

Reaffirms that the existence of discriminatory practices is a matter of deep concern to Member States of the Organization of African Unity;

Urges the Government authorities in the United States of America to intensify their efforts to ensure the total elimination of all forms of discrimination based on race, colour, or ethnic origin.

REPORT OF THE COMMITTEE OF LIBERATION

Recalling Resolution No. CIAS/Plen/Rev/2(A) adopted by the Assembly of Heads of State and Government in Addis Ababa on 25 May 1963 and Resolution 15 (II) of the Second Session of the Council of Ministers held in Lagos, Nigeria;

Having examined the report of the Committee for the Liberation Movement of Africa;

Noting with satisfaction the work so far accomplished by the Co-ordination Committee;

Noting that some progress has been made by some nationalist liberation movements with the assistance of the Co-ordination Committee to establish common action fronts with a view to strengthening the effectiveness of their actions;

Regretting the continued existence of multiple rival movements in the territories under foreign domination in spite of efforts of the Committee;

Considering that certain Member States have not yet paid their voluntary contribution for 1963 to the Special Fund;

Reaffirming the will of Member States to continue by all means the intensification of the struggle for the independence of the territories under foreign domination;

1. Maintains the Liberation Committee as presently composed;

2. Decides the budget of the Special Fund to be £800,000 for the budget year 1964 which shall be collected from Member States in accordance with Article XXIII of the Charter of the Organization of African Unity;

3. Requests each Member State to pay its obligatory contribution in accordance with operative paragraph 2 above to the Special Liberation Fund in Dar-es-Salaam;

4. Requests the Administrative Secretary-General to exercise supervisory powers over the Committee Secretariat.

APARTHEID AND RACIAL DISCRIMINATION

Recalling the previous resolutions of the Council of Ministers on apartheid and racial discrimination and in particular the resolution adopted by the Summit Conference held in Addis Ababa in May 1963;

Reaffirming resolution CM/Res.13 (II);

Having examined the reports of the Administrative Provisional Secretary-General of the Organization of African Unity, the Resolutions of the International Conference on Economic Sanctions against South Africa which was held in London, in April 1964, the report of the Delegation of Foreign Ministers of Liberia, Tunisia, Madagascar and Sierra Leone appointed by the Conference of Heads of State and Government at Addis Ababa in May 1963, and the report of the African Group at the United Nations;

Noting with grave concern the consistent refusal of the South African Government to give consideration to appeals made by every sector of world opinion and their non-compliance with the resolutions of the United Nations Security Council and the General Assembly;

Noting further that the attitude of certain states towards the Government of South Africa and their continued close relations with that Government only encourages it to persist in its policies of apartheid and its contempt for the United Nations;

Convinced of the desirability of stepping up as a matter of urgency the action of the African States in regard to the application of sanctions against the South African Government;

Expressing its deep concern for the trials conducted according to the arbitrary and inhuman laws of the Government of South Africa against the opponents of policies of apartheid and for the recent convictions and sentences passed on African nationalists, particularly Nelson Mandela and Walter Sisulu;

1. Calls for the release of Nelson Mandela, Walter Sisulu, Mangalisso Sobukue and all other Nationalists imprisoned or detained under the arbitrary laws of South Africa;

2. Extends the mandate of the four Foreign Ministers of Liberia, Madagascar, Sierra Leone and Tunisia to continue their action before the Security Council;

3. Appeals to all oil producing countries to cease, as a matter of urgency, their supply of oil and petroleum products to South Africa;

4. Calls on all African States to implement forthwith the decision taken in Addis Ababa in May 1963 to boycott South African goods and to cease the supply of mineral and other raw materials and the importation of South African goods;

5. Requests the co-operation of all countries and in particular that of the Major Trading Partners in the boycott of South Africa;

6. Establishes a body within the OAU General Secretariat, entrusted, among others, with the following functions:

(*a*) to plan co-ordination among the Member States and to ensure the strictest implementation of the resolutions of the Organization of African Unity;

(*b*) to harmonize co-operation with friendly States with a view to implementing an effective boycott of South Africa;

(*c*) to collect and disseminate information about States, foreign financial, economic and commercial institutions which trade with the Government of South Africa;

(*d*) to promote, in co-operation with other international bodies, the campaign for international economic sanctions against South Africa by all appropriate means, in particular countering the propaganda and pressures of the South African Government.

PART NINE

THE CONCEPT OF EQUALITY

INTRODUCTION

THE substance of this Part consists of a passage from the Dissenting Judgment of Judge Tanaka, the Japanese member of the International Court of Justice, in the *South-West Africa Cases* (Second Phase), 1966. In that case the Court (by the casting vote of the President) failed to deal with the merits of the submissions of the applicant States (Ethiopia and Liberia) that South Africa had violated her international obligations. However, half of the members of the Court, including Judge Tanaka, were prepared to deal with the issues of substance raised by the applications.

The passage reproduced is from the *Reports of Judgments, Advisory Opinions and Orders* of the International Court of Justice, 1966, at pp. 284–316. It contains what is probably the best exposition of the concept of equality in the existing literature. Its importance derives from two sources: first, the lack of sound analysis of the concept in the literature at large; and second, the prominence of the principle of equality, or the standard of non-discrimination in legislation and other instruments concerning human rights.

For further reference see the *Advisory Opinion on Minority Schools in Albania*, 1935; *Judgments, Orders and Advisory Opinions of the Permanent Court of International Justice*, Series A/B, No. 64; the U.S. Supreme Court in *Brown* v. *Board of Education*, 347 U.S. 483 (1954); and the European Court of Human Rights in the *Case relating to certain aspects of the laws on the use of languages in education in Belgium* (the *Belgian Linguistics* case), Judgment of 23 July 1968, Publications of the European Court of Human Rights, Series A, 1968.

DISSENTING OPINION OF JUDGE TANAKA, SOUTH WEST AFRICA CASES (SECOND PHASE), 1966

TEXT

Now we shall examine Nos. 3 and 4 of the Applicants' final submissions. Submission No. 3 reads as follows:

'Respondent, by laws and regulations, and official methods and measures, which are set out in the pleadings herein, has practised apartheid, i.e., has distinguished as to race, colour, national or tribal origin in establishing the rights and duties of the inhabitants of the Territory; that such practice is in violation of its obligations as stated in Article 2 of the Mandate and Article 22 of the Covenant of the League of Nations; and that Respondent has the duty forthwith to cease the practice of apartheid in the Territory;' (Applicants' final submissions, C.R. 65/35, p. 69).

At the same time, Applicants have presented another submission (Submission No. 4) which states as follows:

'Respondent, by virtue of economic, political, social and educational policies applied within the Territory, by means of laws and regulations, and official methods and measures, which are set out in the pleadings herein, has, in the light of applicable international standards or international legal norm, or both, failed to promote to the utmost the material and moral well-being and social progress of the inhabitants of the Territory; that its failure to do so is in violation of its obligations as stated in Article 2 of the Mandate and Article 22 of the Covenant; and that Respondent has the duty forthwith to cease its violations as aforesaid and to take all practicable action to fulfil its duties under such Articles;' (Applicants' final submissions, 19 May 1965, C.R. 65/35, pp. 69–70).

The President, Sir Percy Spender, for the purpose of clarification, addressed a question to the Applicants in relation to Submissions 3 and

4 in the Memorials at page 197, which are not fundamentally different from the above-mentioned Final Submissions Nos. 3 and 4. He asked what was the distinction between one (i.e., Submission No. 3) and the other (i.e., Submission No. 4). (C.R. 65/23, 28 April 1965, p. 31.)

The response of the Applicants on this point was that the distinction between the two Submissions 3 and 4 was verbal only (19 May 1965, C.R. 65/35, p. 71). This response, being made after the amendment of the Applicants' submissions, may be considered as applicable to the amended Submissions Nos. 3 and 4.

It should be pointed out that the main difference between the original and the Final Submissions Nos. 3 and 4 is that a phrase, namely: 'in the light of applicable international standards or international legal norm, or both' is inserted between 'has' and 'failed to promote to the utmost . . .' which seems to make clear the substantive identity existing between these two submissions.

Now we shall analyse each of these submissions, which occupy the central issue of the whole of the Applicants' submissions and upon which the greater part of the arguments of the Parties has been focused. This issue is without doubt the question concerning the policy of apartheid which the Respondent as Mandatory is alleged to have practised.

First, we shall deal with the concept of apartheid. The Applicants, in defining apartheid, said: 'Respondent . . . has distinguished as to race, colour, national or tribal origin in establishing the rights and duties of the inhabitants of the Territory.'

It may be said that, as between the Parties, no divergence of opinion on the concept of apartheid itself exists, notwithstanding that the Respondent prefers to use other terminology, such as 'separate development', instead of 'apartheid'. Anyhow, it seems that there has been no argument concerning the concept of apartheid itself. Furthermore, we can also recognize that the Respondent has never denied its practice of apartheid; but it wants to establish the legality and reasonableness of this policy under the mandates system and its compatibility with the obligations of the Respondent as Mandatory, as well as its necessity to perform these obligations.

Submission No. 3 contends that such practice (i.e., the practice of apartheid) is in violation of its obligations as stated in Article 2 of the Mandate and Article 22 of the Covenant. However, the Applicants' contention is not clear as to whether the violation, by the practice of apartheid, of the Respondent's obligation is conceived from the viewpoint of politics or law. If we consider Submission No. 3, only on the basis of its literal interpretation, it may be considered to be from the viewpoint of politics; this means that the policy of apartheid is not in conformity with the objectives of the Mandate, namely the promotion of well-being and social progress of the inhabitants without regard to any conceivable legal norm or standards. If the Applicants maintain this position, the issue would be a matter of discretion and the case, so far as this point is concerned, would not be justiciable, as the Respondent has contended.

Now the Applicants do not allege the violation of obligations by the Respondent independently of any legal norm or standards. Since the Applicants amended Submission No. 4 in the Memorials and inserted a phrase 'in the light of applicable international standards or international legal norm', the violation of the obligations as stated in Article 2 of the Mandate and Article 22 of the Covenant (Submission No. 3) which is identical with the failure to promote to the utmost the material and moral well-being and social progress of the inhabitants of the Territory (Submission No. 4) has come to possess a special meaning; namely of a juridical character. Applicants' cause is no longer based directly on a violation of the well-being and progress by the practice of apartheid, but on the alleged violation of certain international standards or international legal norm and not directly on the obligation to promote the well-being and social progress of the inhabitants. There is no doubt that, if such standards and norm exist, their observance in itself may constitute a part of Respondent's general obligations to promote the well-being and social progress.

From what is said above, the relationship between the Applicants' Submissions Nos. 3 and 4 may be understood as follows. The two submissions deal with the same subject-matter, namely the illegal character of the policy and practice of apartheid. However, the contents of each submission are not quite the same, consequently the distinction between the two submissions is not verbal only, as Applicants stated in answer to the question of the President; each seems to be supplementary to the other.

Briefly, the Applicants' Submissions Nos. 3 and 4, as newly formulated, rest upon a norm and/or standard. This norm or standard has been added by the Applicants to Submission No. 4. The existence of this norm or standard to be applied to the Mandate relationships, according to the Applicants' allegation, constitutes a legal limitation of the Respondent's discretionary power and makes the practice of apartheid illegal, and accordingly a violation of the obligations incumbent on the Mandatory.

What the Applicants mean by apartheid is as follows:

'Under apartheid, the status, rights, duties, opportunities and burdens of the population are determined and allotted arbitrarily on the basis of race, color and tribe, in a pattern which ignores the needs and capacities of the groups and individuals affected, and subordinates the interests and rights of the great majority of the people to the preferences of a minority. . . . It deals with apartheid in practice, as it actually is and as it actually has been in the life of the people of the Territory. . . .' (Memorials, p. 108.)

The Applicants contend the existence of a norm or standards which prohibit the practice of apartheid. These norm or standards are nothing other than those of non-discrimination or non-separation.

The Respondent denies the existence of a norm or standard to prohibit the practice of apartheid and tries to justify this practice from the discretionary nature of the Mandatory's power. The Respondent emphasizes that the practice of apartheid is only impermissible when it is carried out in bad faith.

From the viewpoint of the Applicants, the existence, and objective validity, of a norm of non-discrimination make the question of the intention or motivation irrelevant for the purposes of determining whether there has been a violation of this norm. The principle that a legal precept, as opposed to a moral one, in so far as it is not specifically provided otherwise, shall be applied objectively, independently of motivation on the part of those concerned and independently of other individual circumstances, may be applicable to the Respondent's defence of *bona fides*.

Here we are concerned with the existence of a legal norm or standards regarding non-discrimination. It is a question which is concerned with the sources of international law, and, at the same time, with the mandate law. Furthermore, the question is intimately related to the essence and nature of fundamental human rights, the promotion and encouragement of respect for which constitute one of the purposes of the United Nations (Article 1, paragraph 3, Charter of the United Nations), in which the principle of equality before the law occupies the most important part —a principle, from the Applicants' view, antithetical to the policy of apartheid.

What is meant by 'international norm or standards' can be understood as being related to the principle of equality before the law.

The question is whether a legal norm on equality before the law exists in the international sphere and whether it has a binding power upon the Respondent's conduct in carrying out its obligations as Mandatory. The question is whether the principle of equality before the law can find its place among the sources of international law which are referred to in Article 38, paragraph 1.

Now we shall examine one by one the sources of international law enumerated by the above-mentioned provision.

First we consider the international conventions (or treaties). Here we are not concerned with 'special' or 'particular' law-making bilateral treaties, but only with law-making multilateral treaties such as the Charter of the United Nations, the Constitution of the International Labour Organization, the Genocide Convention, which have special significance as legislative methods. However, even such law-making treaties bind only signatory States and they do not bind States which are not parties to them.

The question is whether the Charter of the United Nations contains a legal norm of equality before the law and the principle of non-discrimination on account of religion, race, colour, sex, language, political creed, etc. The achievement of international co-operation in 'promoting and encouraging respect for human rights and for fundamental freedoms for all without distinction as to race, sex, language, or religion' constitutes one of the purposes of the United Nations (Article 1, paragraph 3). Next, the General Assembly shall initiate studies and make recommendations for the purpose of: ' . . .(b) . . . and assisting in the realization of human rights and fundamental freedoms without distinction as to race, sex, language, or religion' (Article 13, paragraph 1 (b)). 'Universal respect for, and observance of, human rights and fundamental freedoms for all without distinction as to race, sex, language, or religion' is one of the items which shall be promoted by the United Nations in the field of international economic and social co-operation (Articles 55 (c), 56). In this field, the Economic and Social Council may make recommendations for the purpose of promoting respect for, and observance of, human rights and fundamental freedoms for all (Article 62, paragraph 2, Charter). Finally, 'to encourage respect for human rights and for fundamental freedoms for all without distinction as to race, sex, language or religion' is indicated as one of the basic objectives of the trusteeship system (Article 76 (c)).

The repeated references in the Charter to the fundamental rights and freedoms—at least four times—presents itself as one of its differences from the Covenant of the League of Nations, in which the existence of intimate relationships between peace and respect for human rights were not so keenly felt as in the Charter of the United Nations. However, the Charter did not go so far as to give the definition to the fundamental rights and freedoms, nor to provide any machinery of implementation for the protection and guarantee of these rights and freedoms. The 'Universal Declaration of Human Rights and Fundamental Freedoms' of 1948 which wanted to formulate each right and freedom and give them concrete content, is no more than a declaration adopted by the General Assembly and not a treaty binding on the member States. The goal of the codification on the matter of human rights and freedoms has until now not been reached save in very limited degree, namely with the European Convention for the Protection of Human Rights and Fundamental Freedoms of 1953, the validity of which is only regional and not universal and with a few special conventions, such as 'genocide' and political rights of women, the application of which is limited to their respective matters.

In view of these situations, can the Applicants contend, as an interpretation of the Charter, that the existence of a legal norm on equality before the law, which prescribes non-discrimination on account of religions, race, colour, etc., accordingly forbids the practice of apartheid? Is what the Charter requires limited only 'to achieve international co-operation . . . in promoting and encouraging respect for human rights and for fundamental freedoms . . .' and other matters referred to above?

Under these circumstances it seems difficult to recognize that the Charter expressly imposes on member States any legal obligation with respect to the fundamental human rights and freedoms. On the other hand, we cannot ignore the enormous importance which the Charter attaches to the realization of fundamental human rights and freedoms. Article 56 states: 'All Members pledge themselves to take joint and separate action in co-operation with the Organization for the achievement of the purposes set forth in Article 55.' (Article 55 enumerates the purposes of international economic and social co-operation, in which 'universal respect for, and observance of, human rights and fundamental freedoms' is included.) Well, those who pledge themselves to take action in co-operation with the United Nations in respect of the promotion of universal respect for, and observance of, human rights and fundamental freedoms, cannot violate, without contradiction, these rights and freedoms. How can one, on the one hand, preach respect for human rights to others and, on the other hand, disclaim for oneself the obligation to respect them? From the provisions of the Charter referring to the human rights and fundamental freedoms it can be inferred that the legal obligation to respect human rights and fundamental freedoms is imposed on member States.

Judge Spiropoulos confirmed the binding character of the human rights provisions of the Charter:

'As the obligation to respect human rights was placed upon Member States by the Charter, it followed that any violation of human rights was a violation of the provision of the Charter.' (*G.A.*, *O.R.*, *3rd Session, 6th Committee*, 138th Meeting, 7 December 1948, p. 765.)

Judge Jessup also attributed the same character to the human rights provisions:

'Since this book is written *de lege ferenda*, the attempt is made throughout to distinguish between the existing law and the future goals of the law. It is already the law, at least for Members of the United Nations, that respect for human dignity and fundamental human rights is obligatory. The duty is imposed by the Charter.' (Philip C. Jessup, *Modern Law of Nations*, 1948, p. 91.)

Without doubt, under the present circumstances, the international protection of human rights and fundamental freedoms is very imperfect. The work of codification in this field of law has advanced little from the viewpoint of defining each human right and freedom, as well as the machinery for their realization. But there is little doubt of the existence of human rights and freedoms; if not, respect for these is logically inconceivable; the Charter presupposes the existence of human rights and freedoms which shall be respected; the existence of such rights and freedoms is unthinkable without corresponding obligations of persons concerned and a legal norm underlying them. Furthermore, there is no doubt that these obligations are not only moral ones, and that they also have a legal character by the very nature of the subject-matter.

Therefore, the legislative imperfections in the definition of human rights and freedoms and the lack of mechanism for implementation, do not constitute a reason for denying their existence and the need for their legal protection.

Furthermore, it must be pointed out that the Charter provisions, as indicated above, repeatedly emphasize the principle of equality before the law by saying, 'without distinction as to race, sex, language or religion'.

Under the hypothesis that in the United Nations Charter there exists a legal norm or standards of non-discrimination, are the Applicants, referring to this norm, entitled to have recourse to the International Court of Justice according to Article 7, paragraph 2, of the Mandate? The Respondent contends that such an alleged norm does not constitute a part of the mandate agreement, and therefore the question on this norm falls outside the dispute, which, by the compromissory clause, is placed under the jurisdiction of the International Court of Justice. The Applicants' contention would amount to the introduction of a new element into the mandate agreement which is alien to this instrument.

It is evident that, as the Respondent contends, the mandate agreement does not stipulate equality before the law clause, and that this clause does not formally constitute a part of the mandate instrument. Nevertheless, the equality principle, as an integral part of the Charter of the United Nations or as an independent source of general international law, can be directly applied to the matter of the Mandate either as constituting a kind of law of the Mandate *in sensu lato* or, at least in respect of standards, as a principle of interpretation of the mandate agreement. Accordingly, the dispute concerning the legality of apartheid comes within the field of the interpretation and application of the provisions of the Mandate stipulated in Article 7, paragraph 2, of the Mandate.

This conclusion is justified only on the presupposition that the Respondent is bound by the Charter of the United Nations not only as a member State but also as a Mandatory. The Charter, being of the nature of special international law, or the law of the organized international community, must be applied to all matters which come within the purposes and competence of the United Nations and with which member States are concerned, including the matter of the Mandate. Logic requires that, so long as we recognize the unity of personality, the same principle must govern both the conduct of a member State in the United Nations itself and also its conduct as a mandatory, particularly in the matter of the protection and guarantee of human rights and freedoms.

Concerning the Applicants' contention attributing to the norm of non-discrimination or non-separation the character of customary international law, the following points must be noted.

The Applicants enumerate resolutions and declarations of international organs which condemn racial discrimination, segregation, separation and apartheid, and contend that the said resolutions and declarations were adopted by an overwhelming majority, and therefore have binding power in regard to an opposing State, namely the Respondent. Concerning the question whether the consent of all States is required for the creation of a customary international law or not, we consider that the answer must be in the negative for the reason that Article 38, paragraph 1 (*b*), of the Statute does not exclude the possibility of a few dissidents for the purpose of the creation of a customary international law and that the contrary view of a particular State or States would result in the permission of obstruction by veto, which could not have been expected by the legislator who drafted the said Article.

An important question involved in the Applicants' contention is whether resolutions and declarations of international organs can be recognized as a factor in the custom-generating process in the interpretation of Article 38, paragraph 1 (*b*), that is to say, as 'evidence of a general practice'.

According to traditional international law, a general practice is the result of the repetition of individual acts of States constituting consensus in regard to a certain content of a rule of law. Such repetition of acts is an historical process extending over a long period of time. The process of the formation of a customary law in this case may be described as individualistic. On the contrary, this process is going to change in adapting itself to changes in the way of international life. The appearance of organizations such as the League of Nations and the United Nations, with their agencies and affiliated institutions, replacing an important part of the traditional individualistic method of international negotiation by the method of 'parliamentary diplomacy' (Judgment on the *South West Africa* cases, *I.C.J. Reports 1962*, p. 346), is bound to influence the mode of generation of customary international law. A State, instead of pronouncing its view to a few States directly concerned, has the opportunity, through the medium of an organization, to declare its position to all members of the organization and to know immediately their reaction on the same matter. In former days, practice, repetition and *opinio juris sive necessitatis*, which are the ingredients of customary law might be combined together in a very long and slow process extending over centuries. In the contemporary age of highly developed techniques of communication and information, the formation of a custom through the medium of international organizations is greatly facilitated and accelerated; the establishment of such a custom would require no more than one generation or even far less than that. This is one of the examples of the transformation of law inevitably produced by change in the social substratum.

Of course, we cannot admit that individual resolutions, declarations, judgments, decisions, etc., have binding force upon the members of the organization. What is required for customary international law is the repetition of the same practice; accordingly, in this case resolutions, declarations, etc., on the same matter in the same, or diverse, organizations must take place repeatedly.

Parallel with such repetition, each resolution, declaration, etc., being considered as the manifestation of the collective will of individual participant States, the will of the international community can certainly be formulated more quickly and more accurately as compared with the traditional method of the normative process. This collective, cumulative and organic process of custom-generation can be characterized as the middle way between legislation by convention and the traditional process of custom making, and can be seen to have an important role from the viewpoint of the development of international law.

In short, the accumulation of authoritative pronouncements such as resolutions, declarations, decisions, etc., concerning the interpretation of the Charter by the competent organs of the international community can be characterized as evidence of the international custom referred to in Article 38, paragraph 1 (*b*).

In the present case the Applicants assert the existence of the international norm and standards of non-discrimination and non-separation and refer to this source of international law. They enumerate resolutions of the General Assembly which repeatedly and strongly deny the apartheid policy of racial discrimination as an interpretation of the Charter (General Assembly resolution 1178 (XII) of 26 November 1957; resolution 1248 (XIII) of 30 October 1958; resolution 1375 (XIV) of 17 November 1959; resolution 1598 (XV) of 13 April 1961; and resolutions of the Security Council (with regard to apartheid as practised in the Republic of South Africa); resolution of 7 August 1953 which declares the inconsistency of the policy of the South African Government with the principles contained in the Charter of the United Nations and with its obligations as a member State of the United Nations; resolution of 4 December 1963 which declares '. . . the policies of apartheid and racial discrimination . . . are abhorrent to the conscience of mankind . . .'. The Applicants cite also the report of the Committee on South West Africa for 1956).

Moreover, the 11 trust territories agreements, each of them containing a provision concerning the norm of official non-discrimination or non-separation on the basis of membership in a group or race, may be considered as contributions to the development of the universal acceptance of the norm of non-discrimination, in addition to the meaning which each provision possesses in each trusteeship agreement, by virtue of Article 38, paragraph 1 (*a*), of the Statute.

Furthermore, the Universal Declaration of Human Rights adopted by the General Assembly in 1948, although not binding in itself, constitutes evidence of the interpretation and application of the relevant Charter provisions. The same may be said of the Draft Declaration on Rights and Duties of States adopted by the International Law Commission in 1949, the Draft Covenant on civil and political rights, the Draft Covenant on Economic, Social and Cultural Rights, the Declaration on the Elimination of all Forms of Racial Discrimination adopted by the General Assembly of the United Nations on 20 November 1963 and of regional treaties and declarations, particularly the European Convention for the Protection of Human Rights and Fundamental Freedoms signed on 3 September 1953, the Charter of the Organization of American States signed on 30 April 1948, the American Declaration of the Rights and Duties of Man, 1948, the Draft Declaration of International Rights and Duties, 1945.

From what has been said above, we consider that the norm of non-discrimination or non-separation on the basis of race has become a rule of customary international law as is contended by the Applicants, and as a result, the Respondent's obligations as Mandatory are governed by this legal norm in its capacity as a member of the United Nations either directly or at least by way of interpretation of Article 2, paragraph 2.

One of the contentions concerning the application of the said legal norm is that, if such a legal norm exists for judging the Respondent's obligations under Article 2, paragraph 2, of the Mandate, it would be the one in existence at the time the Mandate was entrusted to the Respondent. This is evidently a question of inter-temporal law.

The Respondent's position is that of denying the application of a new law to a matter which arose under an old law, namely the negation of retroactivity of a new customary law. The Applicant's argument is based on 'the relevance of the evolving practice and views of States, growth of experience and increasing knowledge in political and social science to the determination of obligations bearing on the nature and purpose of the Mandate in general, and Article 2, paragraph 2'; briefly, it rests on the assertion of the concept of the 'continuous, dynamic and ascending growth' of the obligation of the Mandatory.

Our view on this question is substantially not very different from that of the Applicants. The reason why we recognize the retroactive application of a new customary law to a matter which started more than 40 years ago is as follows.

The matter in question is in reality not that of an old law and a new law, that is to say, it is not a question which arises out of an amendment of a law and which should be decided on the basis of the principle of the protection of *droit acquis* and therefore of non-retroactivity. In the present case, the protection of the acquired rights of the Respondent is not the issue, but its obligations, because the main purposes of the mandate system are ethical and humanitarian. The Respondent has no right to behave in an inhuman way today as well as during these 40 years. Therefore, the recognition of the generation of a new customary international law on the matter of non-discrimination is not to be regarded as detrimental to the Mandatory, but as an authentic interpretation of the already existing provisions of Article 2, paragraph 2, of the Mandate and the Covenant. It is nothing other than a simple clarification of what was not so clear 40 years ago. What ought to have been clear 40 years ago has been revealed by the creation of a new customary law which plays the role of authentic interpretation the effect of which is retroactive.

Briefly, the method of the generation of customary international law is in the stage of transformation from being an individualistic process to being a collectivistic process. This phenomenon can be said to be the adaptation of the traditional creative process of international law to the reality of the growth of the organized international community. It can be characterized, considered from the sociological viewpoint, as a transition from traditional custom-making to international legislation by treaty.

Following the reference to Article 38, paragraph 1 (*b*), of the Statute, the Applicants base their contention on the legal norm alternatively on Article 38, paragraph 1 (*c*), of the Statute, namely 'the general principles of law recognized by civilized nations'.

Applicants refer to this source of international law both as an independent ground for the justification of the norm of non-discrimination and as a supplement and reinforcement of the other arguments advanced by them to demonstrate their theory.

The question is whether the legal norm of non-discrimination or non-separation denying the practice of apartheid can be recognized as a principle enunciated in the said provision.

The wording of this provision is very broad and vague; the meaning is not clear. Multiple interpretations ranging from the most strict to the most liberal are possible. To decide this question we must clarify the meaning of 'general principles of law'. To restrict the meaning to private law principles or principles of procedural law seems from the viewpoint of literal interpretation untenable. So far as the 'general principles of law' are not qualified, the 'law' must be understood to embrace all branches of law, including municipal law, public law, constitutional and administrative law, private law, commercial law, substantive and procedural law, etc. Nevertheless, analogies drawn from these laws should not be made mechanically, that is to say, to borrow the expression of Lord McNair, 'by means of importing private law institutions "lock, stock and barrel" ready-made and fully equipped with a set of rules'. (*I.C.J. Reports 1950*, p. 148.)

What international law can with advantage borrow from these sources must be from the viewpoint of underlying or guiding 'principles'. These principles, therefore, must not be limited to statutory provisions and institutions of national laws: they must be extended to the fundamental concepts of each branch of law as well as to law in general so far as these can be considered as 'recognized by civilized nations.'

Accordingly, the general principles of law in the sense of Article 38, paragraph 1 (*c*), are not limited to certain basic principles of law such as the limitation of State sovereignty, third-party judgment, limitation of the right of self-defence, *pacta sunt servanda*, respect for acquired rights, liability for unlawful harm to one's neighbour, the principle of good faith, etc. The word 'general' may be understood to possess the same meaning as in the case of the '*general* theory of law', 'théorie *générale* de droit', 'die *Allgemeine* Rechtslehre', namely common to all branches of law. But the principles themselves are very extensive and can be interpreted to include not only the general theory of law, but the general theories of each branch of municipal law, so far as recognized by civilized nations. They may be conceived, furthermore, as including not only legal principles but the fundamental legal concepts of which the legal norms are composed such as person, right, duty, property, juristic act, contract, tort, succession, etc.

In short, they may include what can be considered as 'juridical truth' (Bin Cheng, *General Principles of Law as Applied by International Courts and Tribunals*, 1953, p. 24).

The question is whether a legal norm of non-discrimination and non-separation has come into existence in international society, as the Applicants contend. It is beyond all doubt that the presence of laws against racial discrimination and segregation in the municipal systems of virtually every State can be established by comparative law studies. The recognition of this norm by civilized nations can be ascertained. If the condition of 'general principles' is fulfilled, namely if we can say that the general principles include the norm concerning the protection of human rights by adopting the wide interpretation of the provision of Article 38, paragraph 1 (c), the norm will find its place among the sources of international law.

In this context we have to consider the relationship between a norm of a human rights nature and international law. Originally, general principles are considered to be certain private law principles found by the comparative law method and applicable by way of analogy to matters of an international character. These principles are of a nature common to all nations, that is of the character of *jus gentium*. These principles, which originally belong to private law and have the character of *jus gentium*, can be incorporated in international law so as to be applied to matters of an international nature by way of analogy, as we see in the case of the application of some rules of contract law to the interpretation of treaties. In the case of the international protection of human rights, on the contrary, what is involved is not the application by analogy of a principle or a norm of private law to a matter of international character, but the recognition of the juridical validity of a similar legal fact without any distinction as between the municipal and the international legal sphere.

In short, human rights which require protection are the same; they are not the product of a particular juridical system in the hierarchy of the legal order, but the same human rights must be recognized, respected and protected everywhere man goes. The uniformity of national laws on the protection of human rights is not derived, as in the cases of the law of contracts and commercial and maritime transactions, from considerations of expediency by the legislative organs or from the creative power of the custom of a community, but it already exists in spite of its more-or-less vague form. This is of nature *jus naturale* in roman law.

The unified national laws of the character of *jus gentium* and of the law of human rights, which is of the character of *jus naturale* in roman law, both constituting a part of the law of the world community which may be designated as World Law, Common Law of Mankind (Jenks), Transnational Law (Jessup), etc., at the same time constitute a part of international law through the medium of Article 38, paragraph 1 (c). But there is a difference between these two cases. In the former, the general principles are presented as common elements among diverse national laws; in the latter, only one and the same law exists and this is valid through all kinds of human societies in relationships of hierarchy and co-ordination.

This distinction between the two categories of law of an international character is important in deciding the scope and extent of Article 38, paragraph 1 (c). The Respondent contends that the suggested application by the Applicants of a principle recognized by civilized nations is not a correct analogy and application as contemplated by Article 38, paragraph 1 (c). The Respondent contends that the alleged norm of non-differentiation as between individuals within a State on the basis of membership of a race, class or group could not be transferred by way of analogy to the international relationship, otherwise it would mean that all nations are to be treated equally despite the difference of race, colour, etc.—a conclusion which is absurd. (C.R. 65/47, p. 7.) If we limit the application of Article 38, paragraph 1 (c), to a strict analogical extension of certain principles of municipal law, we must recognize that the contention of the Respondent is well-founded. The said provision, however, does not limit its application to cases of analogy with municipal, or private law which has certainly been a most important instance of the application of this provision. We must include the international protection of human rights in the application of this provision. It must not be regarded as a case of analogy. In reality, there is only one human right which is valid in the international sphere as well as in the domestic sphere.

The question here is not of an 'international', that is to say, inter-State nature, but it is concerned with the question of the international validity of human rights, that is to say, the question whether a State is obliged to protect human rights in the international sphere as it is obliged in the domestic sphere.

The principle of the protection of human rights is derived from the concept of man as a *person* and his relationship with society which cannot be separated from universal human nature. The existence of human rights does not depend on the will of a State; neither internally on its law or any other legislative measure, nor internationally on treaty or custom, in which the express or tacit will of a State constitutes the essential element.

A State or States are not capable of creating human rights by law or by convention; they can only confirm their existence and give them protection. The role of the State is no more than declaratory. It is exactly the same as the International Court of Justice ruling concerning the *Reservations to the Genocide Convention* case (*I.C.J. Reports 1951*, p. 23):

'The solution of these problems must be found in the special characteristics of the Genocide Convention. . . . The origins of the Convention show that it was the intention of the United Nations to condemn and punish genocide as "a crime under international law" involving a denial of the right of existence of entire human groups, a denial which shocks the conscience of mankind and results in great losses to humanity, and which is contrary to moral law and to the spirit and aims of the United Nations (resolution 96 (1) of the General Assembly, December 11th, 1946). The first consequence arising from this conception is that the principles underlying the Convention are principles which are recognized by civilized nations as binding on States, *even without any conventional obligation*. A second consequence is the universal character both of the condemnation of genocide and of the co-operation required "in order to liberate mankind from such an odious scourge" (Preamble to the Convention).' (Italics added.)

Human rights have always existed with the human being. They existed independently of, and before, the State. Alien and even stateless persons must not be deprived of them. Belonging to diverse kinds of communities and societies—ranging from family, club, corporation, to State and international community, the human rights of man must be protected everywhere in this social hierarchy, just as copyright is protected domestically and internationally. There must be no legal vacuum in the protection of human rights. Who can believe, as a reasonable man, that the existence of human rights depends upon the internal or international legislative measures, etc., of the State and that accordingly they can be validly abolished or modified by the will of the State?

If a law exists independently of the will of the State and, accordingly, cannot be abolished or modified even by its constitution, because it is deeply rooted in the conscience of mankind and of any reasonable man, it may be called 'natural law' in contrast to 'positive law'.

Provisions of the constitutions of some countries characterize fundamental human rights and freedoms as 'inalienable', 'sacred', 'eternal', 'inviolate', etc. Therefore, the guarantee of fundamental human rights and freedoms possesses a super-constitutional significance.

If we can introduce in the international field a category of law, namely *jus cogens*, recently examined by the International Law Commission, a kind of imperative law which constitutes the contrast to the *jus dispositivum*, capable of being changed by way of agreement between States, surely the law concerning the protection of human rights may be considered to belong to the *jus cogens*.

As an interpretation of Article 38, paragraph 1 (*c*), we consider that the concept of human rights and of their protection is included in the general principles mentioned in that Article.

Such an interpretation would necessarily be open to the criticism of falling into the error of natural law dogma. But it is undeniable that in Article 38, paragraph 1 (*c*), some natural law elements are inherent. It extends the concept of the source of international law beyond the limit of legal positivism according to which, the States being bound only by their own will, international law is nothing but the law of the consent and auto-limitation of the State. But this viewpoint, we believe, was clearly overruled by Article 38, paragraph 1 (*c*), by the fact that this provision does not require the consent of States as a condition of the recognition of the general principles. States which do not recognize this principle or even deny its validity are nevertheless subject to its rule. From this kind of source international law could have the foundation of its validity extended beyond the will of States, that is to say, into the sphere of natural law and assume an aspect of its supra-national and supra-positive character.

The above-mentioned character of Article 38, paragraph 1 (*c*), of the Statute is proved by the process of the drafting of this article by the Committee of Jurists. The original proposal made by Baron Descamps referred to '*la conscience juridique des peuples civilisés*', a concept which clearly indicated an idea originating in natural law. This proposal met with the opposition of the positivist members of the Committee, represented by Mr. Root. The final draft, namely Article 38, paragraph 1 (*c*), is the product of a compromise between two schools, naturalist and positivist, and therefore the fact that the natural law idea became incorporated therein is not difficult to discover (see particularly Jean Spiropoulos, *Die Allgemeine Rechtsgrundsätze im Völkerrecht*, 1928, pp. 60 ff.; Bin Cheng, *op. cit.*, pp. 24–26).

Furthermore, an important role which can be played by Article 38, paragraph 1 (*c*), in filling in gaps in the positive sources in order to avoid *nonliquet* decisions, can only be derived from the natural law character of this provision. Professor Brierly puts it, 'its inclusion is important as a rejection of the positivistic doctrine, according to which international law consists solely of rules to which States have given their consent' (J. L. Brierly, *The Law of Nations*, 6th ed., p. 63). Mr. Rosenne comments on the general principles of law as follows:

> 'Having independent existence, their validity as legal norms does not derive from the consent of the parties as such. . . . The Statute places this element on a footing of formal equality with two positivist elements of custom and treaty, and thus is positivist recognitions of the Grotian concept of the co-existence implying no subjugation of positive law and so-called natural law of nations in the Grotian sense.' (Shabtai Rosenne, *The International Court of Justice*, 1965, Vol. II, p. 610.)

Now the question is whether the alleged norm of non-discrimination and non-separation as a kind of protection of human rights can be considered as recognized by civilized nations and included in the general principles of law.

First the recognition of a principle by civilized nations, as indicated above, does not mean recognition by *all* civilized nations, nor does it mean recognition by an official act such as a legislative act; therefore the recognition is of a very elastic nature. The principle of equality before the law, however, is stipulated in the list of human rights recognized by the municipal system of virtually every State no matter whether the form of government be republican or monarchical and in spite of any differences in the degree of precision of the relevant provisions. This principle has become an integral part of the constitutions of most of the civilized countries in the world. Common-law countries must be included. (According to *Constitutions of Nations*, 2nd edn., by Amos J. Peaslee, 1956, Vol. I, p. 7, about 73 per cent. of the national constitutions contain clauses respecting equality.)

The manifestation of the recognition of this principle does not need to be limited to the act of legislation as indicated above; it may include the attitude of delegations of member States in cases of participation in resolutions, declarations, etc., against racial discrimination adopted by the organs of the League of Nations, the United Nations and other organizations which, as we have seen above, constitute an important element in the generation of customary international law.

From what we have seen above, the alleged norm of non-discrimination and non-separation, being based on the United Nations Charter, particularly Articles 55 (*c*), 56, and on numerous resolutions and declarations of the General Assembly and other organs of the United Nations, and owing to its nature as a general principle, can be regarded as a source of international law according to the provisions of Article 38, paragraph 1 (a)–(c). In this case three kinds of sources are cumulatively functioning to defend the above-mentioned norm: (1) international convention, (2) international custom and (3) the general principles of law.

Practically the justification of any one of these is enough, but theoretically there may be a difference in the degree of importance among the three. From a positivistic, voluntaristic viewpoint, first the convention, and next the custom, is considered important, and general principles occupy merely a supplementary position. On the contrary, if we take the supra-national objective viewpoint, the general principles would come first and the two others would follow them. If we accept the fact that convention and custom are generally the manifestation and concretization of already existing general principles, we are inclined to attribute to this third source of international law the primary position vis-á-vis the other two.

To sum up, the principle of the protection of human rights has received recognition as a legal norm under three main sources of international law, namely (1) international conventions, (2) international custom and (3) the general principles of law. Now, the principle of equality before the law or equal protection by the law presents itself as a kind of human rights norm. Therefore, what has been said on human rights in general can be applied to the principle of equality. (Cf. Wilfred Jenks, *The Common Law of Mankind*, 1958, p. 121. The author recognizes the principle of respect for human rights including equality before the law as a general principle of law.)

Here we must consider the principle of equality in relationship to the Mandate. The contention of the Applicants is based on this principle as condemning the practice of apartheid. The Applicants contend not only that this practice is in violation of the obligations of the Respondent imposed upon it by Article 2 of the Mandate and Article 22 of the Covenant (Submission No. 3), but that the Respondent, by virtue of economic, political, social and educational policies has, in the light of applicable international standards or international legal norms, or both, failed to promote to the utmost the material and moral well-being and social progress of the inhabitants of the Territory. What the Applicants seek to establish seems to be that the Respondent's practice of apartheid constitutes a violation of international standards and/or an international legal norm, namely the principle of equality and, as a result, a violation of the obligations to promote to the utmost, etc. If the violation of this principle exists, this will be necessarily followed by failure to promote the well-being, etc. The question is whether the principle of equality is applicable to the relationships of the Mandate or not. The Respondent denies that the Mandate includes in its content the principle of equality as to race, colour, etc.

Regarding this point, we would refer to our above-mentioned view concerning the Respondent's contention that the alleged norm of non-discrimination of the Charter does not constitute a part of the mandate agreement, and therefore the question of this norm falls outside the dispute under Article 7, paragraph 2, of the Mandate.

We consider that the principle of equality, although it is not expressly mentioned in the mandate instrument constitutes, by its nature, an integral part of the mandates system and therefore is embodied in the Mandate. From the natural-law character of this principle its inclusion in the Mandate must be justified.

It appears to be a paradox that the inhabitants of the mandated territories are internationally more protected than citizens of States by the application of Article 7, paragraph 2, but this interpretation falls outside the scope of the present proceedings.

Next, we shall consider the content of the principle of equality which must be applied to the question of apartheid.

IV

As we have seen above, the objectives of the mandates system, being the material and moral well-being and social progress of the inhabitants of the territory, are in themselves of a political nature. Their achievement must be measured by the criteria of politics and the method of their realization belongs to the matter of the discretion conferred upon the Mandatory by Article 2, paragraph 1, of the Mandate, and Article 22 of the Covenant of the League.

The discretionary power of the Mandatory, however, is not unlimited. Besides the general rules which prohibit the Mandatory from abusing its power and *mala fides* in performing its obligations, and besides the individual provisions of the Mandate and the Covenant, the Mandatory is subject to the Charter of the United Nations as a member State, the customary international law, general principles of law, and other sources of international law enunciated in Article 38, paragraph 1. According to the contention of the Applicants, the norm and/or standards which prohibit the practice of apartheid, are either immediately or by way of interpretation of the Mandate binding upon the discretionary power of the Mandatory. The Respondent denies the existence of such norm and/or standards.

The divergence of views between the Parties is summarized in the following formula: whether or not the policy of racial discrimination or separate development is *per se* incompatible with the well-being and social progress of the inhabitants, or in other terms, whether the policy of apartheid is illegal and constitutes a breach of the Mandate, or depends upon the motive (*bona fides* or *mala fides*), the result or effect. From the Respondent's standpoint apartheid is not *per se* prohibited but only a special kind of discrimination which leads to oppression is prohibited.

This divergence of fundamental standpoints between the Parties is reflected in their attitudes as to what extent their contentions depend on the evidence. Contrary to the Applicants' attitude in denying the necessity of calling witnesses and experts and of an inspection *in loco*, the Respondent abundantly utilized numerous witnesses and experts and requested the Court to visit South West Africa, South Africa and other parts of Africa to make an inspection *in loco*.

First, we shall examine the content of the norm and standards of which violation by the Respondent is alleged by the Applicants.

The Applicants contend, as set forth in the Memorials (p. 108) that the Respondent's violation of its obligations under the said paragraph 2 of Article 2 of the Mandate consists in a 'systematic course of positive action which inhibits the well-being, prevents the social progress and thwarts the development of the overwhelming majority' of the inhabitants of the Territory. In pursuit of such course of action, and as a pervasive feature thereof, the Respondent has, by governmental action, installed and maintained the policy of apartheid, or separate development. What is meant by apartheid is as follows:

'Under *apartheid*, the status, rights, duties, opportunities and burdens of the population are determined and allotted arbitrarily on the basis of race, color and tribe, in a pattern which ignores the needs and capacities of the groups and individuals affected, and subordinates the interests and rights of the great majority of the people to the preferences of a minority.' (Memorials, p. 108.)

Such policy, the Applicants contend, 'runs counter to modern conceptions of human rights, dignities and freedom, irrespective of race, colour or creed', which conclusion is denied by the Respondent.

The alleged legal norms of non-discrimination or non-separation by which, by way of interpretation of Article 2, paragraph 2, of the Mandate, apartheid becomes illegal, are defined by the Applicants as follows:

'In the following analysis of the relevant legal norms, the terms "non-discrimination" or "non-separation" are used in their prevalent and customary sense: stated negatively, the terms refer to the absence of governmental policies or actions which allot status, rights, duties, privileges or burdens on the basis of membership in a group, class or race rather than on the basis of individual merit, capacity or potential: stated affirmatively, the terms refer to governmental policies and actions the objective of which is to protect equality of opportunity and equal protection of the laws to individual persons as such.' (Reply, p. 274.)

What the Applicants want to establish, are the legal norms of 'non-discrimination' or 'non-separation' which are of a *per se*, non-qualified absolute nature, namely that the decision of observance or otherwise of the norm does not depend upon the motive, result, effect, etc. Therefore from the standpoint of the Applicants, the violation of the norm of non-discrimination is established if there exists a simple fact of discrimination without regard to the intent of oppression on the part of the Mandatory.

On the other hand, the Respondent does not recognize the existence of the norm of non-discrimination of an absolute character and seeks to prove the necessity of group differentiation in the administration of a multi-racial, multi-national, or multi-lingual community. The pleadings and verbatim records are extremely rich in examples of different treatment of diverse population groups in multi-cultural societies in the world. Many examples of different treatment quoted by the Respondent and testified to by the witnesses and experts appear to belong to the system of protection of minority groups in multi-cultural communities and cover not only the field of public law but also of private law.

The doctrine of different treatment of diverse population groups constitutes a fundamental political principle by which the Respondent administers not only the Republic of South Africa, but the neighbouring Territory of South West Africa. The geographical, historical, ethnological, economic and cultural differences and varieties between several population groups, according to the contention of the Respondent, have necessitated the adoption of the policy of apartheid or 'separate development'. This policy is said to be required for the purpose of the promotion of the well-being and social progress of the inhabitants of the Territory. The Respondent insists that each population group developing its own characteristics and individuality, to attain self-determination, separate development should be the best way to realize the well-being and social progress of the inhabitants. The other alternative, namely the mixed integral society in the sense of Western democracy would necessarily lead to competition, friction, struggle, chaos, bloodshed, and dictatorship as examples may be found in some other African countries. Therefore, the most appropriate method of administration of the Territory is the principle of indirect rule maintaining and utilizing the merits of tribalism.

Briefly, it seems that the idea underlying the policy of apartheid or separate development is the racial philosophy which is not entirely identical with ideological Nazism but attributes great importance to the racial or ethnological factors in the fields of politics, law, economy and culture. Next, the method of apartheid is of sociological and, therefore, strong deterministic tendency, as we can guess from the fact that at the oral proceedings the standpoint of the Respondent was energetically sustained by many witnesses—experts who were sociologists and ethnologists.

Contrary to the standpoint of the Applicants who condemn the policy of apartheid or separate development of the Respondent as illegal, the latter conceives this policy as something neutral. The Respondent says that it can be utilized as a tool to attain a particular end, good or bad, as a knife can serve a surgeon as well as a murderer.

Before we decide this question, general consideration of the content of the principle of equality before the law is required. Although the existence of this principle is universally recognized as we have seen above, its precise content is not very clear.

This principle has been recognized as one of the fundamental principles of modern democracy and government based on the rule of law. Judge Lauterpacht puts it:

'The claim to equality before the law is in a substantial sense the most fundamental of the rights of man. It occupies the first place in most written constitutions. It is the starting point of all other liberties. (Sir Hersch Lauterpacht, *An International Bill of the Rights of Man*, 1945, p. 115.)

Historically, this principle was derived from the Christian idea of the
16*

equality of all men before God. All mankind are children of God, and, consequently, brothers and sisters, notwithstanding their natural and social differences, namely man and woman, husband and wife, master and slave, etc. The idea of equality of man is derived from the fact that human beings 'by the common possession of reason' distinguish themselves 'from other living beings'. (Lauterpacht, *op. cit.*, p. 116.) This idea existed already in the Stoic philosophy, and was developed by the scholastic philosophers and treated by natural law scholars and encyclopedists of the seventeenth and eighteenth centuries. It received legislative formulation, however, at the end of the eighteenth century first by the Bills of Rights of some American states, next by the Declaration of the French Revolution, and then in the course of the nineteenth century the equality clause, as we have seen above, became one of the common elements of the constitutions of modern European and other countries.

Examining the principle of equality before the law, we consider that it is philosophically related to the concepts of freedom and justice. The freedom of individual persons, being one of the fundamental ideas of law, is not unlimited and must be restricted by the principle of equality allotting to each individual a sphere of freedom which is due to him. In other words the freedom can exist only under the premise of the equality principle.

In what way is each individual allotted his sphere of freedom by the principle of equality? What is the content of this principle? The principle is that what is equal is to be treated equally and what is different is to be treated differently, namely proportionately to the factual difference. This is what was indicated by Aristotle as *justitia commutativa* and *justitia distributiva*.

The most fundamental point in the equality principle is that all human beings as persons have an equal value in themselves, that they are the aim itself and not means for others, and that, therefore, slavery is denied. The idea of equality of men as persons and equal treatment as such is of a metaphysical nature. It underlies all modern, democratic and humanitarian law systems as a principle of natural law. This idea, however, does not exclude the different treatment of persons from the consideration of the differences of factual circumstances such as sex, age, language, religion, economic condition, education, etc. To treat different matters equally in a mechanical way would be as unjust as to treat equal matters differently.

We know that law serves the concrete requirements of individual human beings and societies. If individuals differ one from another and societies also, their needs will be different, and accordingly, the content of law may not be identical. Hence is derived the relativity of law to individual circumstances.

The historical development of law tells us that, parallel to the trend of generalization the tendency of individualization or differentiation is remarkable as may be exemplified by the appearance of a system of commercial law separate from the general private law in civil law countries, creation of labour law. The acquisition of independent status by commercial and labour law can be conceived as the conferment of a kind of privilege or special treatment to a merchant or labour class. In the field of criminal law the recent tendency of criminal legislative policy is directed towards the individualization of the penalty.

We can say accordingly that the principle of equality before the law does not mean the absolute equality, namely equal treatment of men without regard to individual, concrete circumstances, but it means the relative equality, namely the principle to treat equally what are equal and unequally what are unequal.

The question is, in what case equal treatment or different treatment should exist. If we attach importance to the fact that no man is strictly equal to another and he may have some particularities, the principle of equal treatment could be easily evaded by referring to any factual and legal differences and the existence of this principle would be virtually denied. A different treatment comes into question only when and to the extent that it corresponds to the nature of the difference. To treat unequal matters differently according to their inequality is not only permitted but required. The issue is whether the difference exists. Accordingly, not every different treatment can be justified by the existence of differences, but only such as corresponds to the differences themselves, namely that which is called for by the idea of justice—'the principle to treat equal equally and unequal according to its inequality, constitutes an essential content of the idea of justice' (Goetz Hueck, *Der Grundsatz der Gleichmässigen Behandlung in Privatrecht*, 1958, p. 106) [*translation*].

Briefly, a different treatment is permitted when it can be justified by the criterion of justice. One may replace justice by the concept of reasonableness generally referred to by the Anglo-American school of law.

Justice or reasonableness as a criterion for the different treatment logically excludes arbitrariness. The arbitrariness which is prohibited, means the purely objective fact and not the subjective condition of those concerned. Accordingly, the arbitrariness can be asserted without regard to his motive or purpose.

There is no doubt that the principle of equality is binding upon administrative organs. The discretionary power exercised on considerations of expediency by the administrative organs is restricted by the norm of equality and the infringement of this norm makes an administrative measure illegal. The judicial power also is subjected to this principle. Then, what about the legislative power? Under the constitutions which express this principle in a form such as 'all citizens are equal before the law', there may be doubt whether or not the legislators also are bound by the principle of equality. From the nature of this principle the answer must be in the affirmative. The legislators cannot be permitted to exercise their power arbitrarily and unreasonably. They are bound not only in exercising the ordinary legislative power but also the power to establish the constitution. The reason therefor is that the principle of equality being in the nature of natural law and therefore of a supra-constitutional character, is placed at the summit of hierarchy of the system of law, and that all positive laws including the constitution shall be in conformity with this principle.

The Respondent for the purpose of justifying its policy of apartheid or separate development quotes many examples of different treatment such as minorities treaties, public conveniences (between man and woman), etc. Nobody would object to the different treatment in these cases as a violation of the norm of non-discrimination or non-separation on the hypothesis that such a norm exists. The Applicants contend for the unqualified application of the norm of non-discrimination or non-separation, but even from their point of view it would be impossible to assert that the above-mentioned cases of different treatment constitute a violation of the norm of non-discrimination.

Then, what is the criterion to distinguish a permissible discrimination from an impermissible one?

In the case of the minorities treaties the norm of non-discrimination as a reverse side of the notion of equality before the law prohibits a State to exclude members of a minority group from participating in rights, interests and opportunities which a majority population group can enjoy. On the other hand, a minority group shall be guaranteed the exercise of their own religious and education activities. This guarantee is conferred on members of a minority group, for the purpose of protection of their interests and not from the motive of discrimination itself. By reason of protection of the minority this protection cannot be imposed upon members of minority groups, and consequently they have the choice to accept it or not.

In any event, in case of a minority, members belonging to this group, enjoying the citizenship on equal terms with members of majority groups, have conferred on them the possibility of cultivating their own religious, educational or linguistic values as a recognition of their fundamental human rights and freedoms.

The spirit of the minorities treaties, therefore, is not negative and prohibitive, but positive and permissive.

Whether the spirit of the policy of apartheid or separate development is common with that of minorities treaties to which the Respondent repeatedly refers, whether the different treatment between man and woman concerning the public conveniences can be referred to for the purpose of justifying the policy of apartheid or not, that is the question.

In the case of apartheid, we cannot deny the existence of reasonableness in some matters that diverse ethnic groups should be treated in certain aspects differently from one another. As we have seen above, differentiation in law and politics is one of the most remarkable tendencies of the modern political society. This tendency is in itself derived from the concept of justice, therefore it cannot be judged as wrong. It is an adaptation of the idea of justice to social realities which, as its structure, is going to be more complicated and multiplicate from the viewpoint of economic, occupational, cultural and other elements.

Therefore, different treatment requires reasonableness to justify it as is stated above. The reason may be the protection of some fundamental human rights and freedoms as we have seen in the case of minorities treaties, or of some other nature such as incapacity of minors to conclude contracts, physical differences between man and woman.

In the case of the protection of minorities, what is protected is not the religious or linguistic group as a whole but the individuals belonging to this group, the former being nothing but a name and not a group. In the case of different treatment of minors or between man and woman, it is clear that minors, disabled persons or men or women in a country do not constitute respectively a group. But whether a racial or ethnic group can be treated in the same way as categories such as minors, disabled persons, men and women, is doubtful. Our conclusion on this point is negative. The reasons therefor are that the scientific and clear-cut definition of race is not established; that what man considers as a matter of common-sense as criteria to distinguish one race from the other, are the appearance, particularly physical characteristics such as colour, hair, etc., which do not constitute in themselves relevant factors as the basis for different political or legal treatment; and that, if there exists the necessity to treat one race differently from another, this necessity is not derived from the physical characteristics or other racial qualifications but other factors, namely religious, linguistic, educational, social, etc., which in themselves are not related to race or colour.

Briefly, in these cases it is possible that the different treatment in certain aspects is reasonably required by the differences of religion, language, education, custom, etc., not by reason of race or colour. Therefore, the Respondent tries in some cases to justify the different treatment of population groups by the concept of cultural population groups. The different treatment would be justified if there really existed the need for it by reason of cultural differences. The different treatment, however, should be condemned if cultural reasons are referred to for the purpose of dissimulating the underlying racial intention.

In any case, as we have seen above, all human beings are equal before the law and have equal opportunities without regard to religion, race, language, sex, social groups, etc. As persons they have the dignity to be treated as such. This is the principle of equality which constitutes one of the fundamental human rights and freedoms which are universal to all mankind. On the other hand, human beings, being endowed with individuality, living in different surroundings and circumstances are not all alike, and they need in some aspects politically, legally and socially different treatment. Hence the above-mentioned examples of different treatment are derived. Equal treatment is a prinicple but its mechanical application ignoring all concrete factors engenders injustice. Accordingly, it requires different treatment, taken into consideration, of concrete circumstances of individual cases. The different treatment is permissible and required by the considerations of justice; it does not mean a disregard of justice.

Equality being a principle and different treatment an exception, those who refer to the different treatment must prove its *raison d'être* and its reasonableness.

The Applicants' norm of non-discrimination or non-separation, being conceived as of a *per se* nature, would appear not to permit any exception. The policy of apartheid or separate development which allots status, rights, duties, privileges or burdens on the basis of membership in a group, class or race rather than on the basis of individual merit, capacity or potential is illegal whether the motive be *bona fide* or *mala fide*, oppressive or benevolent; whether its effect or result be good or bad for the inhabitants. From this viewpoint all protective measures taken in the case of minorities treaties and other matters would be included in the illegal discrimination—a conclusion which might not be expected from the Applicants. These measures, according to the Applicants, would have nothing to do with the question of discrimination. The protection the minorities treaties intended to afford to the inhabitants is concerned with life, liberty and free exercise of religion. On the contrary, the Respondent argues the existence of the same reason in the policy of apartheid—the reason of protective measures in the case of minorities treaties.

We must recognize, on the one hand, the legality of different treatment so far as justice or reasonableness exists in it. On the other hand, we cannot recognize all measures of different treatment as legal, which have been and will be performed in the name of apartheid or separate development. The Respondent tries to prove by the pleadings and the testimony of the witnesses and experts the existence of a trend of differentiation in accordance with different religious, racial, linguistic groups. From the viewpoint of the Applicants, the abundant examples quoted by the Respondent and the testimony of witnesses and experts cannot serve as the justification of the policy of apartheid, because they belong to an entirely different plane from that of apartheid and because they are of a nature quite heterogeneous to the policy of apartheid, which is based on a particular racial philosophy and group sociology.

The important question is whether there exists, from the point of view of the requirements of justice, any necessity for establishing an exception to the principle of equality, and the Respondent must prove this necessity, namely the reasonableness of different treatment.

On the aspect of 'reasonableness' two considerations arise. The one is the consideration whether or not the individual necessity exists to establish an exception to the general principle of equality before the law and equal opportunity. In this sense the necessity may be conceived as of the same nature as in the case of minorities treaties of which the objectives are protective and beneficial. The other is the consideration whether the different treatment does or does not harm the sense of dignity of individual persons.

For instance, if we consider education, on which the Parties argued extensively, we cannot deny the value of vernacular as the medium of instruction and the result thereof would be separate schooling as between children of diverse population groups, particularly between the Whites and the Natives. In this case separate education and schooling may be recognized as reasonable. This is justified by the nature of the matter in question. But even in such a case, by reason of the matter which is related to a delicate racial and ethnic problem, the manner of dealing with this matter should be extremely careful. But, so far as the public use of such facilities as hotels, buses, etc., justification of discriminatory and separate treatment by racial groups cannot be found in the same way as separation between smokers and non-smokers in a train.

We cannot condemn all measures derived from the Respondent's policy of apartheid or separate development, particularly as proposed by the Odendaal Commission, on the ground that they are motivated by the racial concept, and therefore devoid of the reasonableness. There may be some measures which are of the same character as we see in the protection measures in the case of the minorities treaties and others. We cannot approve, however, all measures constituting a kind of different treatment of apartheid policy as reasonable.

One of the characteristics of the policy of apartheid is marked by its restrictive tendency on the basis of racial distinction. The policy includes on the one hand protective measures for the benefit of the Natives as we see in the institutions of reserves and homelands connected with restrictions on land rights; however, on the other hand, several kinds of restrictions of rights and freedoms are alleged to exist regarding those Natives who live and work in the southern sector, namely the White area outside the reserves. These restrictions, if they exist, in many cases presenting themselves as violation of respective human rights and freedoms at the same time, would constitute violation of the principle of equality before the law (particularly concerning the discrimination between the Natives and the Whites).

Here we are not required to give answers exhaustively in respect of the Applicants' allegations of violation by the Respondent of the Mandate concerning the legislation (*largo sensu*) applicable in the Territory. The items enumerated by the Applicants in the Memorials (pp. 118–166) are not included in their submissions. We are not obliged to pronounce our views thereon. By way of illustration we shall examine a few points. What is required from us is a decision on the question of whether the Respondent's policy of apartheid constitutes a violation of Article 2, paragraph 2, of the Mandate or not.

For the purpose of illustration we shall consider freedom of choice of occupations (cf. Memorials, pp. 121, 122 and 136).

In the field of civil service, participation by 'Natives' in the general administration appears, in practice, to be confined to the lowest and least-skilled categories, such as messengers and cleaners. This practice of 'job-reservation' for Natives is exemplified by allusion to the territorial budget, which classifies jobs as between 'European' and 'Natives'.

In the mining industry the Natives are excluded from certain occupations, such as those of prospector for precious and base minerals, dealer in unwrought precious metals, manager, assistant manager, sectional or underground manager, etc., in mines owned by persons of 'European' descent, officer in the Police Force. Concerning these occupations, 'ceilings' are put on the promotion of the Natives. The role of the 'Native' is confined to that of unskilled labourer.

In the fishing industry, the enterprises are essentially 'European' owned and operated. The role of the 'Native' is substantially confined to unskilled labour (Memorials, p. 119).

As regards railways and harbours, all graded posts in the Railway and Harbours Administration are reserved to 'Europeans', subject to temporary exceptions. The official policy appears to be that 'non-Europeans' should not be allowed to occupy graded posts.

The question is whether these restrictions are reasonable or not, whether there is a necessity to establish exceptions to the general application of the principle of equality or non-discrimination or not.

The matter of 'ceilings' was dealt with minutely and at length in the oral proceedings by the Parties. The Respondent's defence against the condemnation of arbitrariness, injustice and unreasonableness on the part of the Applicants may be summarized in two points: the one is the reason of social security and the other is the principle of balance or reciprocity.

The Respondent contends that the Whites in general do not desire to serve under the authority of the Natives in the hierarchy of industrial or bureaucratic systems. If this fact be ignored and the Natives occupy leading positions in which they would be able to supervise Whites friction between the two groups necessarily would occur and the social peace would be disturbed. This argument of the Respondent seems to be based on a pessimistic view of the possibility of harmonious coexistence of diverse racial and ethnic elements in an integrated society.

It is not deniable that there may exist certain causes of friction, conflict and animosity between diverse racial and ethnic groups which produce obstacles to their coexistence and co-operation in a friendly political community. We may recognize this as one aspect of reality of human nature and social life. It is, however, no less true that mankind aspires and strives towards the ideal of the achievement of a harmonious society composed of racially heterogeneous elements overcoming difficulties which may result from the primitive instinctive sentiment of racial prejudice and antagonism. Such sentiment must be overcome and not approved. In modern, democratic societies we have to expect this result mainly from the progress of humanitarian education. But the mission of politics and law cannot be said to be less important in minimizing racial prejudice and antagonism and avoiding collapse and tragedy. The State is obliged to educate the people by means of legislative and administrative measures for the same purpose.

To take into consideration the psychological effect upon the Whites who would be subjected to the supervision of the Natives if a ceiling did not exist, that is nothing else but the justification or official recognition of racial prejudice or sentiment of racial superiority on the part of the White population which does harm to the dignity of man.

Furthermore, individuals who could have advanced by their personal merits if there existed no ceiling are unduly deprived of their opportunity for promotion.

It is contended by the Respondent that those who are excluded from the jobs proportionate to their capacity and ability in the White areas, can find the same jobs in their own homelands where no restriction exists in regard to them. But even if they can find jobs in their homelands the conditions may not be substantially the same and, accordingly, in most cases, they may not be inclined to go back to the northern sector, their homelands, and they cannot be forced to do so.

The Respondent probably being aware of the unreasonableness in such hard cases, tries to explain it as a necessary sacrifice which should be paid by individuals for the maintenance of social security. But it is unjust to require a sacrifice for the sake of social security when this sacrifice is of such importance as humiliation of the dignity of the personality.

The establishment of ceilings in regard to certain jobs violates human rights of the Natives in two respects: one is violation of the principle of equality before the law and equal opportunity; the other is violation of the right of free choice of employment.

The Respondent furthermore advocates the establishment of ceilings by the principle of reciprocity or balance between two legal situations, namely one existing in the White areas where certain rights and freedoms of the Natives are restricted and the other situation existing in the Native areas where the corresponding rights and freedoms of the Whites are restricted. The Respondent seeks to prove by this logic that in such circumstances the principle of equality of the Whites and the Natives is observed. Unequal treatment unfavourable to one population group in area A, however, cannot be justified by similar treatment of the other population group in area B. Each unequal treatment constitutes an independent illegal conduct; the one cannot be counter-balanced by the other, as set-off is not permitted between two obligations resulting from illegal acts.

Besides, from the viewpoint of group interest, those of the Natives living in the White area outside the reserves are, owing to the number of the Native population, far bigger than those of the Whites living in the Native areas, the idea of counter-balance is quantitatively unjust.

It is also maintained, in respect of the restrictive policy as regards study to become an engineer by a non-White person, that the under-lying purpose of this policy is to prevent the frustration on the part of the individual which he might experience when he could not find White assistants willing to serve under him. The sentiment of frustration on the part of non-White individuals, however, should not be rightly referred to as a reason for establishing a restriction on the educational opportunity of non-Whites, firstly because the question is that the frustration is caused by the racial prejudice on the part of the Whites which in itself must be eliminated and secondly because a more important matter is to open to the non-Whites the future possibility of social promotion. Therefore, the reason of the frustration of non-Whites cannot be justified.

Finally, we wish to make the following conclusive and supplementary remarks on the matter of the Applicants' Submissions Nos. 3 and 4.

1. The principle of equality before the law requires that what are equal are to be treated equally and what are different are to be treated differently. The question arises: what is equal and what is different.

2. All human beings, notwithstanding the differences in their appearance and other minor points, are equal in their dignity as persons. Accordingly, from the point of view of human rights and fundamental freedoms, they must be treated equally.

3. The principle of equality does not mean absolute equality, but recognizes relative equality, namely different treatment proportionate

to concrete individual circumstances. Different treatment must not be given arbitrarily; it requires reasonableness, or must be in conformity with justice, as in the treatment of minorities, different treatment of the sexes regarding public conveniences, etc. In these cases, the differentiation is aimed at the protection of those concerned, and it is not detrimental and therefore not against their will.

4. Discrimination according to the criterion of 'race, colour, national or tribal origin' in establishing the rights and duties of the inhabitants of the territory is not considered reasonable and just. Race, colour, etc., do not constitute in themselves factors which can influence the rights and duties of the inhabitants as in the case of sex, age, language, religion, etc. If differentiation be required, it would be derived from the difference of language, religion, custom, etc., not from the racial difference itself. In the policy of apartheid the necessary logical and material link between difference itself and different treatment, which can justify such treatment in the case of sex, minorities, etc., does not exist.

We cannot imagine in what case the distinction between Natives and Whites, namely racial distinction apart from linguistic, cultural or other differences, may necessarily have an influence on the establishment of the rights and duties of the inhabitants of the territory.

5. Consequently, the practice of apartheid is fundamentally unreasonable and unjust. The unreasonableness and injustice do not depend upon the intention or motive of the Mandatory, namely its *mala fides*. Distinction on a racial basis is in itself contrary to the principle of equality which is of the character of natural law, and accordingly illegal.

The above-mentioned contention of the Respondent that the policy of apartheid has a neutral character, as a tool to attain a particular end, is not right. If the policy of apartheid is a means, the axiom that the end cannot justify the means can be applied to this policy.

6. As to the alleged violation by the Respondent of the obligations incumbent upon it under Article 2, paragraph 2, of the Mandate, the policy of apartheid, including in itself elements not consistent with the principle of equality before the law, constitutes a violation of the said Article, because the observance of the principle of equality before the law must be considered as a necessary condition of the promotion of the material and moral well-being and the social progress of the inhabitants of the territory.

7. As indicated above, so far as the interpretation of Article 2, para-

graph 2, of the Mandate is concerned, only questions of a legal nature belong to the matter upon which the Court is competent. Diverse activities which the Respondent as Mandatory carries out as a matter of discretion, to achieve the promotion of the material and moral well-being and the social progress of the inhabitants, fall outside the scope of judicial examination as matters of a political and administrative nature.

Accordingly, questions of whether the ultimate goal of the mandates system should be independence or annexation, and in the first alternative whether a unitary or federal system in regard to the local administration is preferable, whether or in what degree the principle of indirect rule or respect for tribal custom may or must be introduced—such questions, which have been very extensively argued in the written proceedings as well as in the oral proceedings, have, despite their substantial connection with the policy of apartheid, no relevance to a decision on the question of apartheid, from the legal viewpoint.

These questions are of a purely political or administrative character, the study and examination of which might have belonged or may belong to competent organs of the League or the United Nations.

8. The Court cannot examine and pronounce the legality or illegality of the policy of apartheid as a whole; it can decide that there exist some elements in the apartheid policy which are not in conformity with the principle of equality before the law or international standard or international norm of non-discrimination and non-separation. The Court can declare if it is requested to examine the laws, proclamations, ordinances and other governmental measures enacted to implement the policy of apartheid in the light of the principle of equality. For the purpose of the present cases, the foregoing consideration of a few points as illustrations may be sufficient to establish the Respondent's violation of the principle of equality, and accordingly its obligations incumbent upon it by Article 2, paragraph 2, of the Mandate and Article 22 of the Covenant.

9. Measures complained of by the Applicants appear in themselves to be violations of some of the human rights and fundamental freedoms such as rights concerning the security of the person, rights of residence, freedom of movement, etc., but such measures, being applied to the 'Natives' only and the 'Whites' being excluded therefrom, these violations, if they exist, may constitute, at the same time, violations of the principle of equality and non-discrimination also.

In short, we interpret the Applicants' Submissions Nos. 3 and 4 in such a way that their complaints include the violation by the Respondent of two kinds of human rights, namely individual human rights and rights to equal protection of the law. There is no doubt that the Respondent as Mandatory is obliged to protect all human rights and fundamental freedoms including rights to equal protection of the law as a necessary prerequisite of the material and moral well-being and the social progress of the inhabitants of the Territory. By this reason, what has been explained above about the principle of equality in connection with Article 38, paragraph 1 (*c*), is applicable to human rights and fundamental freedoms in general.

10. From the procedural viewpoint, two matters must be considered. The one is concerned with the effect of the Applicants' amendment of the Submissions Nos. 3 and 4 (Memorials, 15 April 1961, pp. 197–199) by the submissions of 19 May 1965 (C.R. 65/35). Since the amendment of the submissions is allowed until the stage of oral proceedings, and the amendment was made within the scope of the claim set forth in the Applications, there is no reason to deny its effectiveness. Furthermore, we wish to mention that the Respondent raised no objection during the course of the oral proceedings regarding the amendment.

The other is concerned with the question of choice by the Court of the reasons underlying its decisions.

Concerning this question, we consider that, although the Court is bound by the submissions of the Parties, it is entirely free to choose the reasons for its decisions. The Parties may present and develop their own argument as to the interpretation of the provisions of the Mandate, the Covenant, the Charter, etc., but the Court, so far as legal questions are concerned, quite unfettered by what has been put forward by the Parties, can exercise its power of interpretation in approving or rejecting the submissions of the Parties.

For the foregoing reasons, the Applicants' Submissions Nos. 3 and 4 are well-founded.

PART TEN

TRADE AND DEVELOPMENT

INTRODUCTION

THIS Part is intended to present the issues relating to the economic foundations of human rights. Economic inequalities between States are severe and are a chronic feature of international relations. The formal rules and standards concerning the Rule of Law and human rights have little meaning or possibility of effective application in societies in which a substantial proportion of the population are subject to unemployment, malnutrition, starvation, and illiteracy. The present structure of international 'trade and development' is not producing a stable and adequate growth in the underdeveloped countries; on the contrary, growth rates in these countries over the last two decades have been smaller than those of the industrial countries. This, together with the fact of a considerably faster growth of population in underdeveloped countries, has resulted in a progressive widening of the large gap between the average incomes of the inhabitants of the rich industrial and the poor underdeveloped countries. See, further, U.N. General Assembly resolutions 2158 (XXI), on Permanent Sovereignty over Natural Resources, adopted on 25 November 1966, and 2542 (XXIV), Declaration on Social Progress and Development, adopted on 11 December 1969, especially Articles 7, 17, 23, 24, and 25.

I. SOME ECONOMIC FOUNDATIONS OF HUMAN RIGHTS: A STUDY PREPARED BY JOSÉ FIGUERES

THIS paper was published as an official document, U.N. Doc. A/CONF. 32/L.2 (8 February 1968) of the International Conference on Human Rights, held at Tehran in 1968 under the auspices of the United Nations. The author is a specialist in economics, and former President of Costa Rica.

TEXT

INTRODUCTION

1. The Secretary-General of the United Nations, in his statement to the Economic and Social Council at its forty-third session in 1967, declared that *faith in the dignity of man*, and in the equal rights of men and women, is the basic reason for the Organization to promote social progress and better standards of living for all (A/6703, introduction).

2. His statement affirms that *economic and social development* is an indispensable means to the full realization of human rights in the modern world.

3. This theme has been steadily and progressively elaborated by the United Nations and its organs during the twenty-two years of the Organization's growth.

4. There have been numerous pronouncements. The Universal Declaration of Human Rights, article 22, states that everyone is entitled to the realization of the economic, social and cultural rights indispensable for the full development of his personality. This requires national and international efforts in accordance with the resources of each State.

5. Article 23 of the Declaration recognizes the right of everyone to work, to free choice of employment, to just and favourable conditions of work, to protection against unemployment and to equal pay for equal work.

6. Also affirmed is the right of everyone who works to a remuneration ensuring for his family an existence consistent with human dignity. His

income being supplemented, if necessary, by other means of social protection.

7. Another right proclaimed by the Declaration, article 25, is that of everyone to an adequate standard of health and well-being for himself and his family.

8. Of particular interest for the purposes of this study is article 28 of the Declaration, which states that everyone is entitled to a *social and international order* in which the rights and freedoms of the Declaration can be fully realized.

9. The Declaration on Permanent Sovereignty over Natural Resources contained in General Assembly resolution 1803 (XVII) of 14 December 1962 (article 1), provides that the rights of peoples and nations to permanent sovereignty over their natural resources must be exercised in their own interest.

10. It further states (article 2) that the exploration, development and disposition of such resources, as well as the foreign capital required for these purposes, should conform to the rules that the nations consider to be necessary for the authorization, restriction or prohibition of such activities.

11. It stipulates (article 6) that international co-operation for development, whether public or private investments, exchange of goods or services, technical assistance or exchange of scientific information shall be so conducted as to further the independent national life and the sovereignty of the developing nations.

12. The International Covenant on Economic, Social and Cultural Rights (a binding legal instrument adopted in 1966 by the General Assembly) not only contains the basic economic and social rights first enunciated in the Universal Declaration, but also in some cases strengthens and supplements them.

13. One right, however, which was omitted in the Declaration but is now included in the Covenant (article 1) states that all peoples are entitled to self-determination and may therefore freely determine their political status and the pursuit of their economic, social and cultural development. In no case may a people be deprived of its means of subsistence.

14. Article 2 (i) imposes another important obligation. Each State Party shall take steps, individually and internationally, to the maximum of its available resources, to achieve progressively the full realization of the rights recognized in the Covenant. This shall be done by all appropriate means, including particularly the adoption of legislative measures.

15. Article 11 (1) of the International Covenant on Economic, Social and Cultural Rights, after recognizing the right of everyone to an ade-

quate standard of living for himself and his family, goes beyond the Universal Declaration and adds that everyone has the right to the continuous improvement of living conditions.

16. Of interest to the present study is also article 11 (2) of the Covenant. It provides that the States Parties, recognizing the fundamental right of everyone to be free from hunger, commit themselves to undertake the measures and programmes that may be needed to improve methods of production, conservation and distribution of *food*.

17. Among other things, agrarian systems shall be developed or reformed so as to achieve the highest utilization of natural and human resources.

18. Also, an efficient distribution of the world food supplies should be ensured, taking into account the problems of both food importing and food exporting nations.

19. Worth noting for this study is also article 23, which stipulates that international action for the purposes of the Covenant includes such methods as conventions, agreements, recommendations, international assistance, regional meetings and technical consultations organized in conjunction with the Governments concerned.

20. The preceding paragraphs illustrate the unceasing efforts of the United Nations to ensure for everyone the fullest measure of human dignity. These efforts include setting goals and standards in the economic and social spheres, and prescribing means and methods for their attainment.

21. This paper is written by one who fully shares the objectives of the United Nations, and is guided by them in his study. It is intended to serve a dual purpose, broadly speaking: (*a*) it seeks to identify the obstacles to the full enjoyment of human rights encountered in the economic and social struggles by the peoples of the less developed world; (*b*) it attempts to suggest some measures that should be taken if economic and social factors are to stop denying to those peoples their full range of human rights.

22. The nature of the subject may help explain why the body of this study contains some of the features of an essay in economics. Indeed, it may be described as a study in 'The Economic Foundations of Human Rights'.

I. ENUNCIATIONS

23. We live at a time when human rights have been beautifully enunciated in numerous documents, subscribed to by many nations. These enunciations, in themselves, are no small accomplishment.

24. Ethical codes have always preceded ethical conduct. A certain time is needed for education and adaptation. Even afterwards, perfection is never attained.

25. The Universal Declaration of Human Rights and the Covenants are now in the period of education and adaptation. Actual life in many nations is still far behind the principles. Men tend to be impatient about the apparent slow progress, because they forget that the lives of nations, of institutions, of mankind, are longer than the lives of individuals.

26. The Latin American Republics organized themselves under democratic principles when they won their independence during the first quarter of the nineteenth century.

27. For a hundred and fifty years these societies have been in the process of education and adaptation.

28. Later the principles were vigorously reiterated in the Charter of the Organization of American States, and in the documents of several subsequent conferences. Whatever the remaining shortcomings, these countries are now relatively advanced towards democratic life. It would be inconceivable to adopt today a non-democratic credo, except by force.

29. If it had not been for the enunciation of principles that were difficult to fulfil, the progress that has been made by these nations would not exist, and probably the vices of dictatorship would be officially sanctioned today.

30. I do not mean that it will take a hundred and fifty years for the Declaration of Human Rights to be implemented throughout the world. All processes move faster in our time. I do mean, however, that we should not be discouraged by differences between principle and fact.

II. Sovereignty

31. The new nations that have emerged since the Second World War, are still in a state of mind inclined to eradicate the remnants of colonialism and to consolidate political independence or sovereignty. There is a tendency to believe that national sovereignty automatically brings personal liberties. This is not so, as Latin America has well learned through its history.

32. It takes some time to understand that independence, however costly, should really be a means to an end. The end should be the full comprehension and enjoyment of human rights by all the people.

33. Another temporary disillusion that the emerging countries find is that independence, by itself, does not bring about economic development and social well-being.

34. Some socialists of the nineteenth century thought that general welfare was only a matter of equitable distribution of existing wealth and income, not realizing how small wealth and income were. Some of the revolutionary heroes of independence in our time, and their followers, seem to have underestimated the difficulties of development. Abundance for all the people does not come automatically with sovereignty.

35. Human rights, in their economic and social aspects, can only be achieved by a combination of high production and fair distribution. In theory at least, you could even have a society juridically so constituted that everybody enjoys civil rights and everybody is poor.

36. In actual practice, however, aspirations are so high in all modern countries that you cannot maintain political stability in the unrest provoked by the lack of fulfilment of human wants.

III. Economic Rights

37. The two Covenants of the United Nations correctly equate economic and social rights with civil and political rights.

38. The dignity of man is not respected, by himself or by others, when he is not allowed to earn a decent living. By the same token, in the international field a nation is not sufficiently respected, whatever her political independence, while her work and her trade with other nations do not allow her fully to support all her citizens.

39. The provision of an adequate standard of living for all members of society requires a high degree of economic development.

40. Before the Industrial Revolution such abundance of goods and services would have been unthinkable. It was tacitly agreed, except by some reformers, that the work of the community could only produce the welfare of a privileged minority. Today, for the first time in human history, some countries are producing enough for practically all their citizens.

41. The poorer nations, which still constitute the majority of mankind, want to do likewise. They want to develop.

42. It is of common interest to all peoples, and to the harmony of the human family, that these retarded nations should develop. The economic and social rights cannot be universally fulfilled until the necessary amount of goods and services are produced by all nations.

IV. Internal Obstacles

43. In their development efforts, poor countries encounter two sets of difficulties: internal and international. The internal obstacles to development are, among others, the following:

44. Lack of capital, which is a consequence of insufficient savings, and in turn, of low income; deficient technology; improper land tenure and tax systems; rapid population growth; poor general education; bad health, largely caused by malnutrition.

45. It would be hard to tell which of these internal deficiencies is more serious. They all cause one another in a series of vicious circles. Some people mention political instability first. I wonder if political instability is not also the effect of the other deficiencies.

V. International Obstacles

46. The international causes of under-development are less generally recognized. Small nations cannot develop without an intense trade with the advanced countries, (a) because their people want to consume the products of foreign industry or agriculture; (b) because industrialization requires capital goods produced in the developed countries; and (c) because indispensable services such as communications and transportation are largely the property of the rich countries.

47. The poor countries have to pay for all three—consumer goods, capital goods, services—with their natural resources, such as minerals, and with their agricultural labour turned into a few commodities like coffee, tea, cocoa, bananas and sugar.

48. There is a close association between human rights and the objectives of the United Nations Conference on Trade and Development, established in New York and Geneva in 1964. The Conference was convened for the purpose of studying trade between the rich and poor countries, and to try to find means of correcting the trends that are widening the gap between the two groups.

49. Trade between rich and poor nations *could* be an instrument of uniform world development. If economic and social rights were universally effective, one hour of human work spent in one country would be traded for one hour spent in another. This rule, still a distant goal, would give most retarded countries sufficient foreign income for their development.

VI. Productivity

50. There are activities in which the product of one hour of work depends largely on the amount of capital investment behind the worker. Also, on the amount of applied technology. A trained driver with a power shovel moves a hundred times more earth than a labourer with a hand shovel.

51. When a poor nation can export products in which investment and technology increase production per man-hour of work, it should be the common interest of both traders, the buying and the selling countries, to make such capital and such knowledge available.

52. The field for improvement of productivity through larger investment is more restricted in agriculture than in industry. Little more could be done to improve the advanced methods already applied in some areas to the production of coffee, tea, cocoa, bananas. Yet, when the coffee farmer buys a truck from an industrial country, he exchanges hours of work at the rate of ten or twenty to one.

53. Internally, in an advanced society, there are activities where productivity per man-hour has increased greatly, like the steel industry. There are other activities where there has been no increased productivity, like the work of the barber, or, for that matter, the teacher or the musician. Logically, the compensation has increased more or less uniformly for the steel worker and for the barber, thus relating wages to the productivity of the whole economy, and not of a particular activity. The barber who serves the steel worker, indirectly produces steel also. This is in accord with the aspirations of the economic and social rights.

54. In an integrated mankind, the same principles should apply internationally. Fantastic as it may sound in our time, there is no moral reason why the Colombian labourer who supplies the Detroit worker who makes his truck, with his morning cup of coffee, should earn less (sometimes twenty times less) than his northern colleague. The fair rule would be 'equal pay for equal effort'.

VII. Slave Labour

55. The advanced societies of today abhor even the remnants of slave labour. Minimum wage legislation prevents the economically strong employer from hiring cheap labour, when labour is weak. No low wages for foreign workers are allowed. The United States, with a legal minimum wage of $1.50 an hour, could import millions and millions of labourers for one third that legal wage. Such bargain is prevented not only by the power of the trade unions, but also by the moral sense of the nation, expressed in its legislation. It would be contrary to the economic and social rights of man.

56. Yet, the toil of countless workers at cheap wages is imported to the rich countries in the form of raw materials or primary products, particularly agricultural products. 'Free trade' is allowed between private

importers who bargain from the strength of a rich economy, and private exporters who are part of the weakness of a poor economy.

57. Private exporters in poor countries are not responsible for the well-being of their people. Their interest is to have a margin between what they pay to local producers and workers, and the price they get from foreign importers. They continue to do a good business, at any level of prices and wages, unintentionally retarding economic development and social improvement.

58. This shows the need of more study for reasonable regulations of international trade, at least in the relation between rich and poor nations.

59. Such trade might to some extent be entrusted to public institutions with a social responsibility. Or it could be regulated by such means as the International Wheat Agreement which, in times of surplus, has protected the farming communities against undeliberate exploitation in international trade.

60. The goal might be: when two or more countries trade intensely, supplying each other with needed goods and services, their joint economies should provide uniformly adequate standards of living for all their people.

VIII. Surpluses

61. Surpluses of certain commodities are one of the paradoxes of our time, when two thirds of mankind suffer from scarcities of nearly everything.

62. In the rich countries, agricultural surpluses are the result of market stabilization programmes, without which the development of the rural areas would have been impossible. Large though this problem is sometimes thought to be, it is really small by comparison to the problem of export surpluses in poor countries.

63. For the less developed nations, the prices of a few exports, easily depressed by overproduction, are a question of development or stagnation. And stagnation produces social and political unrest, with all the chain reaction of ill effects.

64. The anomaly is that even at the present (1967) depressed prices, the tendency continues to over-production in coffee and other tropical products. As the economic situation in the producing countries deteriorates, the prices of other crops diminish and the temptation increases to produce more coffee.

65. Furthermore, the tendency to consume imported articles is growing constantly, spurred by the variety of desirable gadgets from the industrial

countries, by advertising and by instalment payment sales. All this has negative effects on developing societies.

66. Neither the balance of payments nor the economy as a whole can afford to have too many people rapidly improving their standard of living at the same time. Colour television in one family deprives several families of the bare essentials of life. This is one of the effects of trade between rich and poor nations.

IX. Diversification

67. The other effect of overstimulated consumption for commercial aims in the poor countries is a tendency to further over-produce coffee, cocoa, tea, as the only possible means of payment for increasing imports. This depresses prices even more, and the vicious circle goes on.

68. It is easy to recommend crop diversification and industrialization. Yet substitute crops for coffee, for example, are extremely difficult to find. Latitude, altitude, the rain system, soil, the local culture of whole societies that have grown together with coffee culture, all these factors present great obstacles to change. There are some flat areas of Brazil where coffee can be changed for something else at a bearable cost. Over one billion trees have been uprooted there. But on the hills of Colombia, the five Central American countries and others, nobody has found even a half-economical way of substituting crops.

69. Industrialization is going on everywhere at the slow pace permitted by the low prices of exports. It will be a long uphill effort.

X. Wages and Taxation

70. The 'natural' way to prevent disastrous over-production is, of course, to allow prices to drop. The people who starve will not produce any more coffee.

71. Until recently, this was the only prescription given by some influential groups in the developed countries. One early exception was the International Sugar Agreement, when low prices could hurt the foreign investments in Cuba, or the sugar-beet producers of California or Florida.

72. The first important step to protect the poor economies from free trade exploitation was the International Coffee Agreement of 1962. The difficulties it has encountered, both in the producing and consuming countries, are a measure of the complexity of the problem. In spite of all, the Agreement has saved the numerous coffee countries from an even more serious recession than they are suffering today.

73. In the process of world development, we may expect more trade agreements to come for important commodities. Cocoa is now being negotiated. It would help the cause of economic and social rights, if certain rules were adopted in these agreements:

I. A 'development price' should be established for each important commodity. Perhaps it is too early in human progress to speak of a 'just price'. A just price would be one that would provide equal compensation for equal effort, anywhere in the world. So far this is not realistic.

A development price is a more modest aspiration. It could be defined as a level of compensation that would provide for (a) a certain legal minimum wage for salaried workers in all areas producing the specific commodity, (b) a certain rate of taxation in the country of origin for development purposes, and (c) a reasonable rate of capitalization for the farmer.

I know from experience that a development price is not difficult to determine for each commodity.

II. The developed, importing nations, should not pay less than the development price for those amounts of the commodity that they normally consume. This could be accomplished by the import quota system, as in sugar in the United States and other countries, or by import duties returnable to the producing country, as it is done with Puerto Rican rum in the continental United States.

III. In addition to the effects of the quota system, over-production should be fought by (a) wages, and (b) taxation.

All commodity agreements should include clauses that make it compulsory for the producing countries to enact and to make effective a uniform minimum wage in all areas producing the same article. This would prevent undue competition from the less socially advanced countries, with its depressing effects on prices. It would also increase the cost of production for the individual farmers, with a consequent effect of diminishing surpluses.

The agreement should include a minimum rate of taxation on the commodity in all producing countries. This would be a source of development revenues. Also, by reducing the income left to the farmers, it would discourage over-production.

Allowing prices to drop as a means of avoiding surpluses, diminishes the national income of the developing countries, and makes world problems more complex. Increasing the farmers' costs by wages and taxes has the same effect on surpluses, at the same time maintaining a higher national income.

XI. More Difficulties

74. Difficult as the commodity price inequities are to remedy, there are other forms of unintended international exploitation which may be even harder to stop.

75. Private foreign investments, even if they were available in the amounts necessary for a relatively rapid development, could create problems for both the investing and the receiving countries. If a large proportion of important decisions affecting the economy of a country are made abroad, they are bound to create frictions, even if only because of psychological reasons.

76. Foreign enterprises would be a greater help to world development, and a normal business for investors, if their ownership and their technology were eventually and gradually transferred to the host countries under honest, mutually agreed terms.

77. In mixed economy nations, some utilities and natural monopolies could be transferred to local public institutions, and some manufacturing facilities to private companies, of local or mixed capital.

78. There are already successful examples of such transactions. An oil refinery, a telephone network, can be paid for in ten or twenty years (interest and profit to the investors included) by a small surcharge on the gallon or on the call. The capital so withdrawn by the first owners can be profitably re-used for other ventures, simultaneously doing business and helping world development.

79. It is an excess of permanent ownership from abroad that should be avoided, or at least it should not be abused.

XII. Communications

80. International communications and transportation pose another problem for the developing countries. Both services are indispensable, and both constitute a heavy drain on foreign exchange.

81. Each developed country likes to own as much as possible of the airlines, the shipping companies, the cable and electronic facilities that serve the world. This is due both to commercial and to strategic reasons.

82. Many developing countries have made the effort, perhaps out of proportion to their possibilities, to have their own 'flag airline', or to own a few steamships. As the size and price of aircraft go up, more local companies are turning out to be too small.

83. International ownership of communications and transportation

facilities should be encouraged. The Governments of developed countries, which usually subsidize their own companies, could take a broader view and facilitate the proportional ownership of the poor countries, as a step towards an equitable distribution of the world income, and as a psychological satisfaction to smaller nations.

XIII. Hard Selling

84. Commercial advertising and instalment selling of consumer goods in the poor countries, make the difficulties of development more acute.

85. In the last half century, a country of the size and the political system of the Soviet Union was able to consume internally what it could produce internally.

86. More recently, a short effort was made by a small country, South Korea, at the beginning of General Clark's régime. Foreign 'luxuries' were publicly burnt at the market place. This came close to Plato's ideal location for his modern city: away from the sea, banning outside traders, free from debilitating foreign ideas.

87. Obviously this is not the trend of our world. Our problem is to reconcile the development effort, the need to capitalize, the need to save foreign exchange to pay for capital goods, with the inordinate consumption of non-essential articles from the developed nations, encouraged by advertising and sales promotions.

88. All consumption is now considered an economic virtue, especially since the Great Depression of the thirties, as a popularization of what people conceive as Keynes' remedy for all ills. The ancient virtue of thrift, which made possible the development of Europe and the United States, has been practically discarded from the moral code.

89. In applying the policies of developed countries, where high consumption is needed to match high production, to the under-developed countries where production is low, we are using Peter's medicine to prevent John's illness.

90. I refer, of course, to high consumption of non-indispensable foreign goods and services, which weakens the balance of payments, lessens the acquisition of capital goods, and retards development.

91. Particularly in a democracy, it is difficult to limit advertising and instalment buying of foreign goods. In spite of high customs duties and exchange restrictions, the balance of payments of poor countries continues to be one of the main obstacles to development. This is one of the most difficult disadvantages of trade with the rich nations.

XIV. Technology

92. Technology, strangely enough, sometimes poses another obstacle to the retarded countries. Constant technological progress in the developed world brings about rapid obsolescence, which is too costly for the poor nations. Ever more sophisticated machines and gadgets strengthen the demand for foreign exchange, without a corresponding increase in the means of payment.

93. Synthetic products that substitute natural products are another source of worry. At this moment the threat of chemical fibres to abacá, sisal and jute is very serious for many countries in Asia, Africa and Latin America.

94. Research on synthetics is carried on by the large chemical firms which, as private business, are not responsible for world development. In the long run their new products represent progress. But the world is still divided between developed and under-developed nations.

95. For many areas of the world, natural fibres are the only export product, the only means of paying for capital goods, and therefore for development. By custom and by nature, these areas are difficult to cultivate with other crops. And they have the land and the labour to supply any expansion of world demand.

96. Those of us who are in the firing line of the development struggle cannot help but wonder why the admirable chemical companies do not devote their resources instead to find new uses for natural fibres. There must be an interesting field for research in fibre disintegration. This would be a contribution, and not a hindrance, to the fight on poverty in the large sisal, jute and abacá areas of the world.

97. With technological progress unrelated to any plan or orientation of the world economy, companies in the advanced countries are increasing the need for aid and for more taxes.

98. There is even talk of synthetic coffee. If this succeeds, who is going to feed fourteen Latin American nations and an equal number of African countries?

XV. Aid

99. There are two possible ways of meeting the various disadvantages of international trade to the development of the weak economies. One is to study case by case (commodity prices, different kinds of foreign investments, international services, artificially stimulated consumption, advancing technology, etc.) and find the best possible remedy for each.

Another is simply to adopt an over-all compensating policy by that modern invention, foreign aid.

100. Probably the solution will be a combination of both measures, as transitory mechanisms until a world economic balance is attained. On the one side commodity agreements establishing development prices, with clauses concerning wages and taxes. On the other hand direct pecuniary compensation to the developing countries, in amounts that should be much larger than at present, preferably handled by international agencies from contributions of all developed countries, large and small.

101. Commodity agreements will probably become unnecessary in the future, after the poor countries develop to a certain level, because then industrialization and higher wages and salaries will make cheap production of primary articles impossible.

102. Foreign aid, of course, is a temporary measure. As more countries develop, they should also become contributors to the international funds.

XVI. Food Bank

103. So far I have been dealing with economic and social rights in areas that are partly the concern of UNCTAD. I will now make a reference to a specific contemporary problem on which FAO has shown deep interest: the world food shortage.

104. It is my paradoxical observation that the farmers of the world (of a hungry world) live under the spectre of abundance.

105. The danger of falling food prices under any local or seasonal abundance is such, that many producers are detained by fear of losses. Especially farmers of a certain size who use bank financing for their crops.

106. The risks of nature are bad enough for the farmer: rain or drought, bumper harvests or crop failures. The risks of the market, however, should be run by society.

107. A World Food Bank should be created. Let each agricultural area have surplus buying agencies at guaranteed prices. Establish strategic reserves in the major ports of the world. Be prepared to absorb bumper crops at one end and crop failures at another.

108. Many of the practical difficulties in this plan, such as quality control and proper preservation, have already been met by the internal agricultural programmes of several nations.

109. Experience shows that when the market is guaranteed, the farmer himself goes after technical assistance, to increase production or to reduce costs. On the other hand, in the absence of a guaranteed market, it takes a great educational effort to diffuse better methods, seeds, etc.

110. We might say that the farmers of the world have a right to proper compensation for their work, and the peoples of the world have a right to be fed. A means to fulfil such rights would be a World Food Bank.

111. The World Food Bank could be an instrument of both, FAO and UNCTAD, performing two similar functions with physical reserves: (*a*) encourage and regulate the world's food supplies; (*b*) stabilize the market for important commodities that constitute the means of international payment for under-developed countries.

112. The Bank would be a sister institution of the International Monetary Fund and the World Bank. Belatedly this would implement John Maynard Keynes' ideas at the Bretton Woods Conference in 1944.

XVII. More Aid

113. Let me return to foreign aid, as a means of compensating for the weak bargaining position of poor countries, and as an expression of world solidarity.

114. This is the wrong time (1967) to speak about the amounts of aid that would be needed for a satisfactory rate of world development. The largest contributing country, the United States, is presently reducing its participation.

115. In 1964, UNCTAD recommended 1 per cent of the national income of developed countries to go to foreign aid. In 1966 it was found that the amount given had acually diminished, instead of approaching the goal of 1 per cent. In the meantime, independent scholars have suggested that the total needs are about 2 per cent of the income of the developed world.

116. This would mean, for the United States alone, about 17 billion dollars a year, instead of the two and one-half to three billion which the Congress is debating now. For all advanced nations together, East and West, 2 per cent might [amount][1] to an outlay of about 40 billion dollars a year in aid to the whole under-developed world.

XVIII. Aid Per Head

117. There are different ways of estimating not only what should be given in aid, in the absence of proper trade regulations, but also what could be effectively used.

118. In 1955, in my speech at the First Conference of Western Hemispheric Presidents held in Panama, I suggested that the Latin American continent could use in the first years of an intensive development

[1] Editorial insertion.

programme roughly US $10.00 per inhabitant. Today, in 1967, I doubt if Latin America could do much with less than twenty or twenty-five United States dollars per person.

119. The difference is to be found in the drop of export prices. Twelve yearly crops of coffee and cocoa have been sold at two-thirds of what may be considered as a development price. The backlog of needs has accumulated, in spite of the programmes and financial help of the Alliance for Progress. Without the Alliance, present problems of all kinds would be a great deal worse.

120. Of course, if prices had been fairer there would have been more general consumption, and even some waste, in the small privileged circles that can afford waste. But undoubtedly, capital formation would have gone on at a reasonable rate, as it did during the early fifties when export prices were better.

121. Now it seems that an outside injection of capital of say US $20.00 per inhabitant, as an average for the first few years of an intensive programme, would be needed and could be effectively used in Latin America. With a population of 200 million, this amounts to four billion dollars a year. Current development aid to the whole continent, coming almost exlusively from the United States, is between one half and one billion a year.

XIX. Aid in Kind

122. If, and when, foreign aid is ever given in the necessary amounts to establish a sound economic world order in a few decades, probably a large proportion of it will have to be given in kind, not in money.

123. So far the developing countries have seriously objected not only to political 'strings attached', but also to policies that would force them to buy the products of the respective aid-giving nation. I do not see why such objection should continue if intensive programmes were undertaken with all the needed aid.

124. In our time, even the strong economies are suffering from balance of payments deficits. This is attributed to defects in the world monetary system. Probably the phenomenon has deeper sources. It may be related to international trade, because the strong economies are simultaneously stimulating and preventing a healthy growth of the weak economies and markets.

125. Of course troops on foreign soil tend to create a deficit at one end and inflation at the other. There may be other causes, and probably other evils, that also cannot be stopped easily.

126. If foreign aid were given in the necessary amounts in money and not in kind, the effects on the balance of payments of the aid-giving countries would be detrimental.

127. On the other hand, if a large part of the aid is given in kind, or, if the recipient nations make most of their purchases in the respective giving country, surpluses in industrial capacity could be utilized, at a low cost to the over-all economy of the developed countries.

128. Overhead costs are currently covered by present production and sales. Any addition in volume, within the capacity of the industrial system, requires relatively small outlays.

129. Aid in kind would present some difficulties to the larger retarded countries, where certain industries like tractor-building are already established. With a certain degree of flexibility in all policies, such obstacles can be surmounted.

130. Besides, if foreign aid is handled by international agencies, goods representing surpluses of industrial capacity could go to a common pool, and would be distributed according to circumstances.

131. Thus the members of the family of nations would be applying the old motto: 'From each according to his possibilities; to each according to his needs'.

XX. War Expenses

132. What are the probabilities of an all-out effort of development of the retarded world if, in the absence of well-regulated trade, this would require an aid contribution by all developed nations, large and small, of 2 per cent of their income.

133. I am more familiar with the political situation in the United States than in other countries. And, of course, I understand that, as of today, such contribution is politically impossible, even if it is considered to be economically possible and desirable.

134. For our present purpose, we may consider that the national product of the United States is supporting three main kinds of expenditures: (a) the current standard of living; (b) war expenses; and (c) development, both international and internal. Let us not forget internal development: pollution, traffic jams, riot areas, etc.

135. In order to increase one of the three expenditures appreciably, one or the other two must be curtailed. So far it is development that has been sacrificed, because it is politically the weakest. For internal reasons it is difficult to reduce the standard of living or even its rate of growth.

And for international reasons it is considered risky to reduce the war expenses.

136. No matter how trite or how unrealistic the suggestion may be, it is the war expenses that should diminish. Now that military forces are largely concentrated in two super-Powers, it ought to be less difficult than in previous centuries to establish civilized relations among the peoples of the world. The military expenses of some poor countries are, if one may use a strong word, preposterous.

137. The arithmetic involved is child's play. If we were to reduce present war expenses by one half, we would still have enough funds to maintain order, and to continue the exploration of space, the atom, the bottom of the sea and the heart of our earth.

138. Not counting the large sums appropriated for war emergencies, the permanent military budgets of the nations of the world now reach a combined total of about US $140 billion.

139. If we are allowed to dream about a better humanity; if, as some anthropologists think, mankind is heading toward integration and not to extinction; if we could cut war expenses by half, the more developed countries, without sacrificing their standard of living or their rate of growth, could devote the funds thus released to development, part internal and part international.

140. And if all nations did the same, as they should, perhaps in less than half a century our planet would be embellished by the blossoming of the Great Human Society.

XXI. CONCLUSION

141. I have read the documents that tell the story of the accomplishments of the United Nations in the field of human rights.

142. While a long road lies ahead in this field of man's progress, those achievements, that some persons might be tempted to regard as modest, plus the undoubtable greatness and permanency of the Declaration and the Covenants, make the last two decades of initiation in human rights the best spent period in the history of mankind.

143. Much that I have said in this paper belongs to the realm of enunciations. More ideas, more time, more education, more adaptation will be needed. Yet, the rate of progress is an accelerating movement.

144. According to these views, the fulfilment of human rights *requires* economic and social development.

145. Development requires not only corrections to the internal causes

of poverty in the retarded nations, but also a full revision of all economic relations with the advanced countries.

146. Since several of these relations are difficult to change, an over-all compensation may have to be given for a time, in the form of increased foreign aid.

147. The increase in foreign aid may be dependent on the reduction of war expenses. This is no surprise. Human rights and world peace dwell side by side in the hearts of men. The United Nations is endeavouring to achieve both.

148. Peace will help development. Development will engender peace. They are both causes and effects. They strengthen each other. Their common goal is the reign of human rights.

II. TOWARDS A NEW TRADE POLICY FOR DEVELOPMENT: REPORT BY THE SECRETARY-GENERAL OF THE UNITED NATIONS CONFERENCE ON TRADE AND DEVELOPMENT, 1964

THIS Report was prepared by Raul Prebisch, Secretary-General of UNCTAD, and published as a U.N. Document, E/CONF. 46/3 (U.N., Sales No. 64, II.B.4). The excerpts which follow are from pp. 6–10 and 27–31. Reference should also be made to Gunnar Myrdal, *Economic Theory and Under-Developed Regions*, 1957 (published in University Paperbacks, 1963), especially Chapters I and II.

TEXT

The potential of modern technology is so enormous that the developing countries should not have to wait as long as the present industrially advanced countries had to wait to develop their technologies step by step and use them for the eradication of poverty and its inherent evils. Indeed, they cannot wait as long, because the acceleration of their development is an absolute necessity that brooks no delay. The pressure exerted by the masses for real improvements in their levels of living has never been as strong as it is now, and in the years to come it will become a growing source of internal and world-wide tension if it is not met by a vigorous policy of economic and social development in which international co-operation must play a decisive role.

The obstacles which the economic and social structures of the peripheral countries place in the way of development policy are well known. It is quite clear that important decisions must be taken to bring about structural changes, as has been indicated in previous reports of the United Nations and its specialized agencies. Suffice it to state here that, without such structural changes, and without a determined political effort to promote development and remove the internal obstacles from its path, measures of international co-operation, however good in themselves, will be very limited in their effect.

2. THE OLD ORDER

The imposing code of rules and principles, drawn up at Havana and partially embodied in the General Agreement on Tariffs and Trade (GATT), does not reflect a positive conception of economic policy in the sense of a rational and deliberate design for influencing economic forces so as to change their spontaneous course of evolution and attain clear objectives. On the contrary, it seems to be inspired by a conception of policy which implies that the expansion of trade to the mutual advantage of all merely requires the removal of the obstacles which impede the free play of these forces in the world economy. These rules and principles are also based on an abstract notion of economic homogeneity which conceals the great structural differences between industrial centres and peripheral countries with all their important implications. Hence, GATT has not served the developing countries as it has the developed ones. In short, GATT has not helped to create the new order which must meet the needs of development, nor has it been able to fulfil the impossible task of restoring the old order.

In the context of the nineteenth century and the initial decades of the twentieth, as we see it, there was no place for this idea of rationally influencing and so modifying the course of events. The course of events had merely to be followed and anything that obstructed it eliminated. Development in the periphery was a spontaneous phenomenon of limited scope and social depth; it came about under the dynamic influence of a unique combination of external factors which have since ceased to exist.

The situation can be presented simply in the following terms. During the last quarter of the nineteenth century, the United Kingdom, as the world's leading dynamic centre, accounted for 36 per cent of world exports of manufactures and 27 per cent of the imports of primary commodities. Since the historical accident of the industrial revolution happened in the United Kingdom before it did in other parts of the world, that country, with its limited resources and given its level of technology at the time, had to grow outwards and there emerged the classic pattern of exchanging manufactured goods for primary commodities. Imports of primary goods and other commodities by the United Kingdom grew apace, as did their share in the national income: the over-all import coefficient rose from approximately 18 per cent in 1850 to the very high figure of almost 36 per cent in 1880–84, as a result of free trade. This phenomenon influenced the rest of Europe, although not to the same extent, and its effects on the development of countries on the periphery of the world economy were striking.

Actually the process was the opposite of that which has gradually come into existence since the end of the First World War and especially since the great depression: the substitution of imports of food and raw materials for domestic production and not *vice versa*.

There was another factor which encouraged the growth of consumption and primary commodity imports: these imports were not yet subject to the adverse effects of technological progress as they would be in later years. Per capita income was still able to sustain an active demand for foodstuffs, synthetic production of raw materials had not yet begun on a larger scale, and European farmers still clung to their traditional methods.

3. THE GREAT DEPRESSION AND WORLD TRADE

It is sufficient to mention these facts to emphasize the radical change which was ushered in during the First World War as a result of political and economic factors and which grew in scope and intensity as a result of the world depression of the 1930's.

The United States displaced the United Kingdom as the leading dynamic centre. This was more than a mere change of hegemony; it had a far-reaching influence on the rest of the world. The enormous natural resources of the vast territory of the United States and the resolutely protectionist policy it pursued from the start of its development were apparent in the steady decline of its import coefficient. In 1929, on the eve of the world depression, this coefficient was barely 5 per cent of total income and the restrictive measures resulting from the depression reduced it still further. In 1939, at the beginning of the Second World War, it had fallen to 3.2 per cent.

The effects of these developments on the rest of the world were of enormous importance. With the advent of the great depression, the order that dated back to the nineteenth century, and which the First World War had seriously shaken, now disintegrated. The trends towards agricultural self-sufficiency were encouraged to an extraordinary degree in the industrial countries, which were striving to cut their imports in order to cope with the violent contraction in their exports. Bilateralism and discrimination emerged as means of mitigating the intensity of this phenomenon. This movement spread throughout the world and forced many developing countries to adopt even more drastic restrictive measures, since the value of primary exports was declining more sharply than that of industrial goods.

The precipitous fall in the import coefficient of the United States, the leading dynamic centre, and the slow recovery in the level of its activity, compelled the other countries of the world to lower their import coefficients too by all kinds of restrictive expedients. Under the most-favoured-nation clause, the restrictions ought to have been applied to all countries alike, but the discrimination fostered by bilateralism allowed them to be directed mainly against the United States, as a means of remedying the acute dollar shortage.

This problem recurred after the Second World War. As in the 1930's, recourse was then had to bilateralism but this phase was very short-lived. Western Europe decided to attack its difficulties boldly, not just by adopting negative and defensive attitudes but by positive action of enormous scope: the modernization of its economy, which boosted its export capacity, and the policy of integration, which promoted its reciprocal trade to the particular detriment of imports paid for in dollars. While this attitude contributed to over-all equilibrium, it had a serious effect on some developing countries. So it was that the European Economic Community (EEC) and the European Free Trade Association (EFTA) came into existence.

Thus ended the long period of structural imbalance vis-à-vis the United States, which not only unreservedly welcomed the formation of the Community but also offered it its firm support.

In their turn, eight socialist countries[1] formed their own grouping, the Council for Mutual Economic Assistance (CMEA), in order to integrate certain important activities, plan them jointly, and import greater fluidity to the reciprocal trade of the participating countries.

A new order is thus emerging among the more advanced industrialized States and the next few years will reveal its ultimate significance more clearly: it remains to be seen whether this new order will be one in which vast regions withdraw into their shells and isolate themselves with a minimum of trade between them, or whether it will be one in which they take advantage of a closer economic link involving new forms of the international division of labour.

Hence the vital significance of the massive cut in tariffs proposed by the late President Kennedy for the next round of GATT negotiations. The success of these negotiations among the advanced countries which conduct their trade relations mainly by means of tariffs will thus have a considerable influence on the future development of the world economy.

[1] For the sake of brevity, the term 'socialist countries' in this report refers to the countries designated as 'countries with centrally planned economies' in United Nations publications.

The EEC authorities have repeatedly affirmed the outward-looking character of their economic policy, a position which coincides with that of the United States. There has been a gradual relaxation of that country's traditional protectionism and it is to be hoped that this new policy can now enter upon a very broad phase.

The socialist States of CMEA have also repeatedly expressed their support of the principle of the international division of labour. The success of the Kennedy round and the improvement in the international political atmosphere could considerably facilitate the adoption of formulae which would enable the socialist countries to play an active part in world trade by removing the obstacles which obstruct their participation. This refers not only to relations between them and other industrially advanced countries, irrespective of the differences in their economic and social systems, but also to relations with the developing countries, in view of the interdependence of world trade.

4. THE DISINTEGRATION OF THE OLD PATTERN AND THE DEVELOPING COUNTRIES

All this is highly important for the developing countries, but it is far from enough, as will be seen later. What was happening in those countries after the great depression, while such significant changes were taking place in the industrial countries?

The break-down of the old pattern of trade created new problems for the developing countries. The persistent trend towards external imbalance began, first, as a result of the contraction of their exports during the great depression and, later as a result of their slow rate of growth. From the outset, a number of countries tried to counteract this imbalance by means of import substitution, i.e., by inward-looking industrialization, without foreign markets, and later, after the Second World War, by continuing this policy without interruption and by drawing on the international financial resources made available to them.

The external imbalance was thus covered, but in a precarious manner in the countries which at that time were pushing ahead with their industrialization. As time went on, the consequences of this system became increasingly apparent. Industrialization encounters growing difficulties in the countries where it is pursued furthest. These difficulties arise from the smallness of national markets and also from the following peculiar fact. The further substitution proceeds in respect of some imports, the more other imports grow because of the heavier demand for capital goods and, subsequently, because of the effects of higher income.

In addition to this pressure, the adverse effects of the decline in the terms of trade in recent years have weakened the effectiveness of financial contributions from international sources.

Furthermore, these contributions entail a heavy burden of servicing which is mounting rapidly, mainly owing to the amount of amortization in respect of relatively short-term credits. Thus servicing competes with an active demand for imports for the relatively scanty supply of foreign exchange earned by exports.

This phenomenon has no historical parallel. The old pattern of international trade, as it existed in the nineteenth century, was characterized, as has already been pointed out, by a strong and steady growth in exports, which provided the means for servicing debts. Any difficulties which arose were due not to structural defects, as now, but rather to financial misbehaviour or short-term cyclical contractions. In addition to all this, there is the mounting burden of external payments for maritime freight and insurance. The developing countries own only 6 per cent of the world maritime tonnage and this creates a series of problems. Moreover, while the system of shipping conferences may be explained by the very nature of sea transport, it involves combines that restrict competition and affects the developing countries as regards both the cost of services and the impact of this cost on various products depending on their degree of processing. The desire to extend import substitution policy to these services is therefore very understandable, but the information so far available in support of this policy is very meagre. All this necessitates further inquiry, and it is to be hoped that the information needed for the purpose will be forthcoming.

This is a characteristic picture of many of the developing countries, especially those where industrialization has made most headway. None of the others, however, is, over the short or long term, immune to the persistent tendency towards imbalance, except in certain exceptional cases; and what is now happening in the more industrialized developing countries foreshadows what will happen in the others unless a conscious and deliberate effort is made to influence the course of economic events and to apply the enlightened policy which those events have made imperative.

Chapter IV. Gatt and the Developing Countries

1. The Achievements of GATT

GATT has important achievements to its credit. Following the inter-war period of chaos, it introduced a new concept of a rule of law in world trade. One may criticize the particular character of some of the law that has been applied. But this should not be allowed to obscure the fact that the decision of Governments that world trade should be subject to this law was in itself of vital importance in this field.

In the past, increases in trade restrictions by particular countries have frequently led to a spiral of retaliation in which all have lost and none have gained. The application of a rule of law in world trade has already helped to limit excesses of this type and could do much more if the law itself were made more responsive to contemporary needs.

A second virtue of GATT is its machinery for complaint and consultation. Each member country has an opportunity to bring forward instances in which it feels that it has suffered injury at the hands of another member, and can claim the redress authorized or adequate compensation, although it must be admitted that this procedure has often not been effective in practice.

GATT also provides a forum in which countries can discuss the impact of one another's trade policies, with a view to reaching a satisfactory accommodation.

Within this framework of rules and consultative machinery, GATT has brought about considerable reductions in the tariffs and other restrictions on world trade that were established during the difficult period following the great depression.

It is true, however, that these reductions have been of benefit mainly to the industrial countries and that the developing countries generally have obtained very little direct benefit from this process. But in so far as the reduction of tariffs and restrictions may have created a more favourable basis for growth in the industrial countries, some indirect benefit will have accrued to the developing countries in the form of a higher demand for their exports than would otherwise have occurred.

Finally, since the publication of the report, *Trends in International Trade*, in October 1958, GATT has been making a serious effort to conduct its activities in a way that would take more adequate account of the unsatisfactory position of developing countries in world trade. Still, it must be admitted that the positive results of these efforts, after more than five years, have been somewhat disappointing. But the problem itself has been recognized, and this recognition led to the consideration of a Programme of Action by a GATT Meeting of Ministers in May 1963, and subsequently to efforts to implement that Programme. The matter now rests with Governments: if this Programme of Action could be fully carried out by all countries concerned, a very important step forward would have been taken. The resolutions relating to the Kennedy round were also adopted at this Meeting of Ministers. The principle of not demanding full reciprocity from the developing countries was accepted, among others, during these negotiations on tariffs and other barriers to trade. In addition, the achievement of satisfactory conditions of access to world markets for agricultural products was set as an objective.

The GATT Tariff Conference of 1960/61 resulted in very limited benefits for the less developed countries; it is to be hoped that the Kennedy round will produce a more favourable balance in view of its significance as crucial evidence of the practical benefits which GATT can offer to the developing countries.

Furthermore, it is acknowledged that GATT has a very efficient secretariat, a fact that is borne out by its studies and the careful prepartion of its negotiations; and it has also shown its ability to adapt itself to the changing realities of the times.

The above comments on GATT should be approached within a broad perspective. We can now see clearly things which were still confused and vague in the Havana days. The absolute necessity of industralization for the peripheral countries had not been recognized or realized nor had the need to intensify this process as advanced techniques permeated into agriculture. Another thing which was not properly understood was the persistent trend towards external imbalance, which was attributed more to the inflationary policy of Governments than to the nature of the growth phenomenon. In addition, the developing countries were still very far from stating their position and defining their aspirations and attitudes. The end of the colonial era was only just in sight. And social tensions in the developing countries were not then so conspicuous or so pressing as they now are. We can now see all this clearly and there is an increasingly strong feeling that a very great effort will have to be made to alleviate and eliminate those tensions, which have such a great impact on world peace.

This effort could no longer take the form of a few rules and principles specifying what must be avoided; it is essential also to determine what must be done and to formulate a policy which meets this need for positive action.

Why has GATT not been as efficacious for the developing countries as for the industrial countries? There are two main reasons. First, the Havana Charter, as has already been said, is based on the classic concept that the free play of international economic forces by itself leads to the optimum expansion of trade and the most efficient utilization of the world's productive resources; rules and principles are therefore established to guarantee this free play. Secondly, the rules and principles in question have not always been strictly complied with and, even though they seem to have been observed in the letter in certain instances, the spirit underlying them has not been respected.

2. The Structural Differences and their Consequences

The free play concept is admissible in relations between countries that are structurally similar, but not between those whose structures are altogether different as are those of the industrially advanced and the developing countries. These structural differences show themselves in various ways which were outlined in the preceding section.

The structural origin of the deterioration in the terms of trade has already been indicated and there is no need to revert to the subject here. It will be recalled that the Havana Charter mentions this phenomenon at one point. Elsewhere, however, in the articles relating to commodity agreements, the predominant idea that ultimately emerges is that basic market trends should not be impeded.

We have also commented on the disparities in international demand, which also derive from structural differences. This is a fundamental point which does not seem to have been given the importance it deserves in the Havana Charter. Thus, in seeking to lower or eliminate tariffs and restrictions with a view to promoting trade, neither the Charter nor the Agreement draws any distinction between developed and developing countries. And since there is an initial assumption of homogeneity, such reductions have to be equivalent everywhere. This is the principle of conventional reciprocity that prevailed until recently. The fact that these disparities place primary and industrial exporting countries in diametrically opposite positions has not been taken into consideration. Hence the importance of the fact that the need to depart from the idea of conventional reciprocity was recognized in the Kennedy round.

The former group of countries, given the relatively slow growth of their primary exports, cannot cope with the intensive demand for industrial imports unless they alter the composition of the imports in question, replacing some of them by domestic production so as to be able to increase others. In the absence of an export trade in manufactured goods, the only alternative left open to the developing countries is to grow at the slow tempo set by their primary exports, or to encourage these substitution activities by means of protectionism so as to develop more rapidly and prevent or correct the external imbalance as they develop.

If protectionism is kept within certain bounds, i.e., if it is applied only to the extent necessary to counteract the disparity in demand, there is no reason why it should have a depressive effect on the dynamics of world trade; on the contrary, it should have a purely balancing influence. Within these limits, not only is industrialization compatible with the development of primary production and exports, but an optimum relation between the two, conducive to intensive economic development, is conceivable. Of course, if a developing country weakens its primary export position by measures which act as disincentives and its place is not filled by other exporting countries, these depressive effects on international trade will be inevitable. But such effects, however we may look at them, are not inherent in the industrialization of the peripheral countries.

On the other hand, protectionism in respect of primary production in the countries exporting manufactured goods does exert a depressive influence, since the disparity in demand, instead of being levelled out, is accentuated, to the obvious detriment of world trade and the growth of the developing countries. In this form, protectionism helps in these centres to slow down still further the growth of the developing countries' primary exports, and hence the expansion of imports of the manufactures needed for their development. In other words, protectionism in respect of primary production in the industrial countries has definitely unfavourable repercussions on international trade and compels the peripheral countries to adopt further import substitution measures so they can continue their development; thus it makes this development even more difficult by curtailing their opportunities for an advantageous international division of labour. The Havana Charter fails to recognize this lack of symmetry and its practical implications for trade policy.

Given the prevailing conception, the objective pursued when that Charter was drawn up could be summed up in the following simple terms. The restrictions and tariffs which had been doing so much to disintegrate the world economy had to be gradually removed and the free play of international economic forces thus restored. The reduction and elimination of restrictions and tariffs would also cover the primary commodities imported by the industrial countries, and, in return, the countries exporting these primary commodities would have to lower their import tariffs on manufactured goods.

Herein lies the concept of the symmetry of a situation that was far from symmetrical: if the peripheral countries wished to reap the benefits of a liberal tariff policy for primary imports in the industrial centres, they likewise had to make equivalent concessions in their own tariffs. This is the serious drawback of such a conception of trade policy: the failure to take into account the fact that those equivalent concessions would intensify the trend towards trade imbalance inherent in the disparity of international demand, instead of helping to correct it.

Great strides have been made of late towards recognizing that these rules of reciprocity in trade negotiations must be changed because of the economic inequality between countries. A clear distinction must be made, however, between this conventional reciprocity and real reciprocity.

This is a very important point which must be borne in mind. The request for reciprocity in negotiations between countries which have not structural disparity in their demand is logical. Indeed, it is essential for the stability of the world economy that any expansion of exports which a given country achieves on the basis of concessions from the others should be accompanied by concessions granted to the latter, so that its imports from them can increase.

In the case of trade between the developing and the industrial countries, the situation is different. Since the former tend to import more than they export—owing to the international disparity in demand—concessions granted by the industrial countries tend to rectify this disparity and are soon reflected in an expansion of their exports to the developing countries. In other words, the developing economies, given their great potential demand for imports, can import more than they would otherwise have been able to do had those concessions not been granted. Thus there is a real or implicit reciprocity, independent of the play of conventional concessions. And this is what must be recognized in international trade policy.

This distinction is inherent at the transitional stage through which the developing countries are passing. The disparity in world demand does not have to be a permanent phenomenon. As the structure of production gradually changes with industrialization and industrial exports, this disparity will tend to disappear. Indeed, as such exports, both to advanced and to other developing countries, make headway, the disparity can be levelled out gradually. When this happens—and only then—will the bases have been laid for conventional reciprocity between the industrialized countries and countries that are pressing on along the road of industrialization. But this is a long process for most of the developing countries.

III. RICHER AND POORER:
THE WIDENING INCOME GAP

THE gap between the incomes and the standard of living of the poorer developing and the much richer developed countries has been widening continuously over the last two decades. It can be seen from Table 1 that average production per head of population (*per capita* production) in developing countries increased at an annual rate of 2 to 2·7 per cent

TABLE 1
Growth of real gross product of developing countries by region, and of developed countries, 1950–65

	Annual compound growth rates (percentage)		
	1950–55	1955–60	1960–65
Developing countries[1]	4·7	4·5	4·6
Per capita	2·7	1·9	2·0
Asia	4·2	3·8	4·3
Per capita	2·2	1·5	1·8
Latin America	5·0	5·0	4·9
Per capita	2·9	1·3	2·0
Developed market economy countries	4·7	3·3	5·0
Per capita	3·4	2·0	3·7
Socialist countries of Eastern Europe and Asia[2]	9·8	8·2	6·7
Per capita	8·2	6·6	5·4

Source: United Nations, UNCTAD document TD/B/C.3/34, page 3.

[1] In addition to Asia and Latin America, this series includes the following African and Middle Eastern countries: Algeria, Congo (Kinshasa), Ghana, Kenya, Malawi, Morocco, Nigeria, Southern Rhodesia, Sudan, Tanzania (Tanganyika only), Tunisia, Uganda, United Arab Republic, Zambia; and Iraq, Israel, Lebanon, Syria.

[2] Gross material product.

TABLE 2

Growth rates of total product, population and per capita product per annum of developing countries, by regions, in 1960–65, 1966 and 1967

(Percentages)

Regions	1960–65			1966			1967			1960–67		
	GDP	Popu-lation	Per/Cap. GDP	GDP	Popu-lation	Per/Cap. GDP	GDP	Popu-lation	Per/Cap. GDP	GDP	Popu-lation	Per/Cap. GDP
Europe	7·6	1·4	6·1	8·5	1·5	6·9	3·4	1·5	1·9	7·1	1·4	5·6
Africa	3·3	2·3	1·1	1·8	2·4	−0·6	—	2·4	—	3·1	2·3	0·9
North of Sahara	2·4	2·5	−0·1	0·4	2·7	−2·2	—	2·7	—	2·2	2·6	−0·3
South of Sahara	3·9	2·3	1·6	2·6	2·3	0·3	—	2·4	—	3·7	2·3	1·4
Latin America	4·7	2·9	1·7	4·5	2·9	1·6	4·4	3·0	1·4	4·7	2·9	1·7
North and Central	5·8	3·2	2·5	7·2	3·2	3·9	5·9	3·3	2·5	6·0	3·2	2·7
South	4·2	2·7	1·5	3·1	2·8	0·3	3·8	2·8	1·0	4·0	2·7	1·3
Asia	4·9	2·5	2·3	4·6	2·6	1·9	7·5	2·5	4·9	5·2	2·5	2·6
Middle East	7·6	2·7	4·8	5·5	2·7	2·7	6·8	3·1	3·6	7·2	2·8	4·4
South	3·5	2·4	1·1	2·6	2·5	0·1	8·5	2·4	6·0	4·1	2·4	1·6
Far East	5·8	2·7	2·9	7·0	2·7	4·2	6·3	2·6	3·6	5·9	2·7	3·1
Total developing countries[1]	5·0	2·5	2·4	4·7	2·5	2·1	5·5	2·5	3·0	5·0	2·5	2·4

Source: Development Assistance, 1968 Review, OECD (1968), Table VI–I, page 117.

[1] Using 1960 weights.

between 1950 and 1965, whereas in the developed countries the rate of growth was about 3·5 per cent throughout most of that period. The Table also shows that the gap was widening at a faster rate in the first five years of the 1960s (at 3·7% minus 2%=1·7% per annum) than ten years earlier in 1950–55, when it amounted to less than 1 per cent per year (i.e. 3·4% minus 2·7%=0·7%).

Statistically, this development can be explained by the facts that total production has increased at a lower rate and population has grown faster in developing countries than in developed countries. Table 2 compares the rates of growth of production and population in Europe with the rates in developing countries. It can be seen that between 1960 and 1967 gross domestic product (GDP) rose at an annual rate of over 7 per cent in Europe as compared with 5 per cent in developing countries. During the same period population rose at 1·4 per cent per annum in Europe and at 2·5 per cent in developing countries. The result was an annual rate of growth in *per capita* GDP of 5·6 per cent in Europe compared with 2·4 per cent in developing countries.

The figures of growth in *per capita* income in developing countries are derived from changes in total income and population in each country; they are not intended to suggest that all inhabitants of the countries concerned have enjoyed an equal rate of increase in their income. It is necessary to examine changes in the distribution of income to ascertain the benefits derived by the different sections of the community from a given over-all growth in income. The data on income distribution in developing countries are rather imperfect, but such information as can be gathered indicates that the primary beneficiaries of the growth of income have been the richer classes of the community. This would suggest that the growing gap between the incomes of the developing and developed countries is accompanied by a parallel and increasing divergence between the incomes of the richer and poorer sections of the population within many developing countries.

INDEX